Library Science Text Series

Introduction
to
United States Public Documents

Joe Morehead

INTRODUCTION TO

United States Public Documents

Third Edition

Libraries Unlimited, Inc.   1983
Littleton, Colorado

LIBRARIES UNLIMITED, INC.
P.O. Box 263
Littleton, Colorado 80160

Library of Congress Cataloging in Publication Data

Morehead, Joe, 1931-
    Introduction to United States public documents.

    (Library science text series)
    Includes bibliographical references and index.
    1. United States--Government publications.
2. United States. Government Printing Office.
I. Title. II. Series.
Z1223.Z7M67   1983   015.73   82-22866
ISBN 0-87287-359-5
ISBN 0-87287-362-5 (pbk.)

for B and A, again

Table of Contents

List of Illustrations

Figure

Preface to the Third Edition

The purpose of this text is to set forth an introductory account of the basic sources of information that comprise the bibliographic structure of federal government publications. Like the previous editions, the work serves as a reference source for institutions that acquire public documents, as a text for library school students, as a resource for professional librarians and their clientele, and as a guide for researchers who must access the vast amount of information produced by or for the federal establishment. The emphasis remains a contemporary one; the reader is encouraged to consult other historical or specialized studies for more detailed information.

This edition has been extensively revised and updated to include the many changes that have occurred in the production and distribution of government information. New or expanded material includes the continual growth and evolution of the *Monthly Catalog of United States Government Publications*, the significant changes in the format and distribution of the Congressional Serial Set, a detailed account of the legislative process including private legislation, the 1980 census, and the proliferation of online databases and microform collections covering federal documentation. The basic reference and bibliographic sources discussed in the chapters represent selective categories rather than an exhaustive recital of individual titles and series. Because this work is an introduction to the field, I have attempted to do no more than present the contours of government sources and their salient characteristics, and the cited materials are exemplary rather than definitive.

The narrative begins with an introductory overview of issues, problems, and themes associated with public policy and the information transfer process. Chapters 2 through 4 describe the administrative machinery and general bibliographic systems by which both government and libraries execute the delivery and sharing of public information. Chapter 5 presents an account of the subventionary activities of agencies like the National Technical Information

Service and Educational Resources Information Center. Chapter 6 discusses some of the prominent guides, indexes, and checklists which provide access to government publications. The remaining chapters examine the types of products and services generated by or in support of the activities of the five acknowledged arms of the federal establishment—the constitutionally created legislative, executive, and judicial branches, the independent agencies with regulatory powers, and the advisory committees and commissions. Appendix A provides a summary of online databases containing government information, and Appendix B is a list of acronyms and abbreviations used in the text. Rounding out the work are separate title/series and subject/name indexes.

Whereas the last decade was in large measure distinguished by a positive response on the part of government to the needs of users, the present decade has given rise to a political climate which is potentially inimical to a munificent vision of public access. Librarians and information science personnel should not underestimate their role in defense of the principle that government information belongs to the people. The rewards of working with government publications are based upon this commitment as well as knowledge of the bibliographic apparatus by which access is achieved.

No one can gain mastery of United States public documents by perusing a text; skills that the librarian earns require the day-to-day experience that comes only with professional service. For regardless of the benefits that present and future technologies confer upon the bibliographic enterprise, the public will continue to rely, perhaps more than ever, upon professional expertise to retrieve information from the vast and variegated body of government materials. It is my hope that this prologue to the working situation will better acquaint the reader with some of these diverse and unfailingly interesting sources of information.

Joe Morehead
School of Library and Information Science
The University at Albany

Acknowledgments

Several individuals have been of considerable assistance to me in the preparation of this work. My thanks to graduate students Timothy L. Wheeler and Karling C. Abernathy, who verified and updated many of the titles and series discussed in the text. I am also grateful to LeRoy C. Schwarzkopf, distinguished librarian and editor of *Documents to the People*, whose knowledge and wisdom over the years have been a source of inspiration. I appreciate, too, the expertise of the editors and staff at Libraries Unlimited, who capably managed the transformation of manuscript to printed work.

A special measure of gratitude goes to Tae Moon Lee, Government Documents Librarian at the SUNY at Albany Library, whose research abilities have contributed greatly to this effort. His knowledge and professional skills have made my task significantly less difficult. Responsibility for the book's shortcomings is solely that of the author.

1

Public Documents: An Overview

The chapters that follow these introductory remarks focus upon the bibliographic structure and reference value of basic categories of federal government materials. Implicit in this account, however, are issues, principles, and problems that underlie the production, dissemination, control, and use of the products and services generated by or for the federal establishment. Some of these issues are philosophical in nature and mirror the shifting political ideologies of the body politic; others involve perennial problems of terminology, public-private sector coordination and cooperation, and user needs; still others entail difficult decisions of organization and management associated with the structure and forms of government information.

Often these thematic considerations admit of no satisfactory resolution. They reflect current public policy which changes with the winds of political fortune or arise when new information technologies demand a reassessment of current practices. Documents librarians have a dual task, that of mastering the bibliographic systems which comprise the basic structure of government information while diligently responding to the themes, issues, and politics inherent in this enterprise. The principles that animate the efforts of the Government Documents Round Table of the American Library Association are worthy testimony to this dual obligation.

DEFINITIONS

The quest for appropriate definitions of basic terms remains difficult if not intractable. The official definition at 44 U.S.C. 1901 is unsatisfactory: "Government publication, as used in this chapter [Depository Library Program], means informational matter which is published as an individual document at Government expense, or as required by law." An attempt to encompass the public documents of all governmental entities was proffered by a committee of the Government Documents Round Table in 1977. It defined a "government publication/document" as "any publication in book, serial, or non-book form published by or for a government agency, e.g., the publications of Federal, State, Local, and Foreign governments and of intergovernmental organizations to which governments belong and appoint representatives, such as the United Nations, Organization of American States, and the Erie Basin Commission."[1] In a bill introduced in 1979, later amended as part of the abortive Title 44 revision debacle (see Chapter 2), the term "public document" was defined as "a document, publication, form, machine-readable data file, microform, audio or visual presentation, or similar matter, reproduced for public use, wholly or partially at Government expense, by printing or other means but such term does not include any such matter which, as determined by the issuing Government entity—(A) is required for official administrative or operational purposes only and is without public interest or educational value or (B) is classified or designated under statute or executive order as requiring a specific degree of protection against unauthorized disclosure for reasons of national defense or foreign policy."[2] While the latter avoids the simplistic brevity of 44 U.S.C. 1901, it takes us through a bewildering maze of terms and exemptions.

An advisory committee to the Joint Committee on Printing sought to distinguish between *government information* and *government publications.* The former includes "anything compiled/generated/maintained by a governmental entity, including published material or unpublished records, electronically recorded files, films, documents, working papers, memoranda, and similar materials, whether or not it is made available to the public under title 44 of the U.S. Code, the Freedom of Information Act, through the Federal Privacy Act, the Sunshine Act, or any other law or by administrative discretion." The committee defined a government publication as "any portion of government information produced by a governmental entity which is made available to the public through printing, electronic transfer, or any other form of reproduction at government expense and which is offered for public sale/rental or for free distribution."[3]

There have been other attempts to define a public document within the context of government information. Perhaps no wholly satisfactory definition can ever be devised. Working definitions will always need to be refined and redefined as a consequence of political, social, and technological forces. Nevertheless, the task must be addressed continually. Far from being a mere exercise in academic punctilio, a proper definition of a public document bears substantially on the practical implications of collection development, classification, organization, bibliographic control, and access. Generally, the community of documents librarians prefers an expansive definition exempting as little as possible, while government generally favors a more restrictive definition.

THE SIZE AND STRUCTURE OF GOVERNMENT

The federal colossus dwarfs all other private or public entities. It numbers close to 5 million uniformed and civilian employees, or one of every twenty workers in the United States. Despite the Reagan administration's efforts to sell federal land to private developers, the government's landholdings total over 700 million acres, "nearly equal in size to all the U.S. east of the Mississippi River, plus Arkansas, Louisiana and Texas." In addition, it owns or leases almost 500,000 buildings. The value of its nonmilitary equipment is estimated at about $50 billion. And under fiscal 1982 budget projections, the federal establishment spends at the rate of over $75 million *every hour.*[4]

Figures of this magnitude impact upon several areas of the discipline of documents librarianship. Many agencies and congressional committees have overlapping mandates, thus generating duplication of information. Moreover, the dynamics of change have a profound effect upon the proper assignment of government materials, for even if a government publication has been adequately defined as such, its provenance must be accurately ascertained. Changes in the organization of agencies require changes in the classification of documents, an activity which James Bennett Childs called "the constant and never-changing need to determine when and by what act the agencies were and are being established, and which are currently instrumentalities of the federal government."[5] Government reorganization often plays havoc with the appropriate control of materials, and this activity must be monitored closely by librarians. It is the author's conviction that knowledge of the structure, organization, and hierarchical relationships among government entities markedly improves the ability of documents librarians to serve their clientele.

RETRENCHMENT AS PUBLIC POLICY

On April 20, 1981, a presidential ukase announced a moratorium on new periodicals, pamphlets, and audiovisual products. "The Federal Government is spending too much money on public relations, publicity, and advertising. Much of this waste consists of unnecessary and expensive films, magazines, and pamphlets." The directive went on to say that "While we have a duty to keep the citizens of this country accurately and fully informed about Government programs and activities, we should not use this as a licence to produce films, pamphlets, and magazines that do not truly serve the public interest."[6] Following this statement, a salvo of bulletins and memoranda from the Office of Management and Budget directed executive agencies to conduct a comprehensive review of all existing periodicals, pamphlets, and audiovisual products, and those planned for future fiscal years to identify and eliminate those titles not allegedly in the public interest.

At first blush, this "war on waste" seemed to be an expression of common sense and good management. There are a large number of publications, usually of the pamphlet variety, that comprise what may be called the *didactic* literature of government — *The Pocket Guide to Babysitting*, *Aunt Sammy's Radio Recipes*, *Shade Tree Pruning*, etc. In this area it is indeed difficult if not impossible to separate utility from public relations, content from propaganda. The self-aggrandizing publishing activities of agencies were criticized by former Senator Abraham Ribicoff, who said, "Individual agencies which cannot describe in detail their publications policies and programs — their size, their cost, their justification for existing — are similarly incapable of deciding which publications are useful, which are propagandistic and which serve no official purpose other than to seek to glorify their Federal agency."[7] In a little over a year after the moratorium, the administration estimated that some 2,000 publications had been eliminated; OMB then lifted the ban but continued to monitor costs and content.

But in its zeal to cut the cost of government, the Reagan administration has carried this putative war on waste to ominous lengths. Useful periodicals like the *Statistical Reporter* (PrEx 2.11; item 855-C) and *Housing and Urban Development Trends* (HH 1.14; item 581-E-10) have been eliminated. Important statistical surveys and programs of the Census Bureau and the Bureau of Labor Statistics have been reduced, postponed, or abandoned; for example, the administration asked Congress "to cancel the 1982 Census of Agriculture, and to change the frequency from every five years to every ten years."[8] There has been a dramatic "slippage of information from paper to microfiche and from microfiche to computer-tape only"[9] that affects libraries with inadequate equipment and funding in accessing such information in that format. Budget cuts at the National Archives have severely curtailed the ability of scholars to perform research, a situation that the distinguished historian Barbara Tuchman likened to "the burning of the Library at Alexandria in the third century, B.C."[10]

The executive branch is not the only villain in this piece. A feckless Congress has mandated the Government Printing Office to accelerate the conversion of publications to a microformat without considering user convenience and in some cases resulting in an abrogation of GPO's pledge to allow librarians a choice of format. Retrenchment policies are always accompanied by statements that invoke the buzz words of the 1980s: severe budget constraints, diminished resources, reducing costs, etc. What began as a program to eliminate trivial and duplicative films, periodicals, and pamphlets has been transformed into a systematic assault on access to public information.

BIBLIOGRAPHIC CONTROL

On March 1, 1883, the Joint Committee on Printing entrusted Benjamin Perley Poore with the task of compiling a complete list of all federal government publications. Fourteen helpers were assigned to Poore, none of whom possessed any experience while "some proved to be so entirely incompetent that no use could be made of what they did." Poore compared the direction of his task to that of "Christopher Columbus when he steered westward on his voyage of discovery, confident that a new world existed, but having no knowledge of its distance or the direction in which it lay." Perhaps Poore may be forgiven this stunning metaphor; when he was charged with this duty, "no one could estimate how many publications were to be cataloged, where they were to be found, how long it would take to perform the work, or what would be the probable cost." But Poore and his ragtag group of assistants persevered; and the result, known as *Poore's Catalogue*, comprised 63,063 entries covering the period 1774-1881 (see Chapter 6). Readers are surprised to learn that Poore's efforts represent the *first* comprehensive, official, federal bibliographic enterprise.[11]

In 1978 a survey of seventy-four federal departments and agencies was conducted by the Congressional Research Service of the Library of Congress at the request of the Senate Committee on Governmental Affairs. The main purpose of the study was to determine the agencies' management of public affairs and public information programs through the issuing of government publications, but the findings provided data of interest beyond that purpose.

Based on the responses of the agencies queried, approximately 102,000 government publications were issued in an eighteen-month period from January 1977 to June 1978. But during this same period, the *Monthly Catalog of United States Government Publications* recorded about 66,000 titles. This means that about 36,000 publications failed to reach the desk of the catalogers at the Government Printing Office's Library Division, a violation of 44 U.S.C. 1710.

One startling fact emerged from the survey: Most agencies keep no central file on publications and have no ability to determine accurately and promptly the extent of their publishing activities. The figure of 102,000 itself was but an estimate; as the survey noted, "it is imperative to remember that this number cannot be verified and is probably not comprehensive." Although we may surmise that some of those 36,000 publications not listed in the *Monthly Catalog* found their way into some libraries, nevertheless the bibliographic shortfall is significant.[12]

Advances in information technology have brought us a far more sophisticated bibliographic capability than that enjoyed by Poore and his nineteenth-century colleagues. Yet all our skills are helpless in the face of careless agency practices. Agency accountability and compliance with Title 44 are an absolute precondition of effective bibliographic control. Those who work with documents find this lack of agency accountability pandemic at all levels of government. It is the weakest link in that chain of information transfer from producer to user, an absence of management control which no computer seems able to overcome.

ACCESS TO GOVERNMENT INFORMATION

The fundamental theme underlying any account of government publications as sources of information is *public access*. A federal advisory body defined public access as "any proper method by which the general public may examine, reproduce, or otherwise obtain access to information produced by a governmental entity," and this definition "encompasses any information (printed, microform, and electronic) of the government (executive, judicial and legislative) made available to the public."[13]

The critical part of this definition is the last phrase. What kinds of information are to be "made available to the public"? We know that governments are obliged to publish and disseminate numerous accounts of their activities and deliberations as symbolic evidence of their claim to legitimacy. We also know that certain information is not publicly available: classified defense or other national security data; individual census or tax forms, the disclosure of which would constitute an unwarranted invasion of privacy; internal working documents; proprietary information about businesses; and the like. That is to say, public access is an abridged right. As one federal official noted, it is analogous to the constitutional right to free speech. "You cannot yell 'fire' in a crowded theatre."[14]

It is appropriate that the debate over the proper balance between the government's duty to withhold information and public access is continual. The federal Freedom of Information Act (5 U.S.C. 552), as amended, places the burden of proof upon the government (custodian) to justify secrecy rather than the individual (seeker) to obtain access. The Privacy Act (5 U.S.C. 552a note) is intended to assist individuals in obtaining information about themselves. A House committee characterized the essential difference between the two measures: "the Privacy Act requires the disclosure of records containing personal information to the individual who is the subject of the record but restricts the disclosure of those records to others, whereas the [Freedom of Information Act] requires that all types of information be released to anyone making a request provided that, among other things, it does not violate the privacy of any individual." Both laws complement each other and derive from the premise that government secrecy is "the incubator for corruption."[15]

But to the right to know and the right to privacy must be added another principle—in Bernard M. Fry's words, "the right to be informed." This right, "if not implemented in an efficient and effective manner, diminishes the citizen's knowledge of his governments' programs and policies and their pervading influence on his everyday life." Indeed, while information that must be requested under the Freedom of Information and Privacy acts is important, "an even more important and positive need is to assure that the large volume of significant government documents published daily by the GPO and other Federal agencies is promptly and adequately disseminated and becomes effectively accessible to the using public."[16]

The means of disseminating government information, however, are influenced by political ideology. What is the role of the private sector in this enterprise? Should the cost of federal information be borne by society as a whole through general taxation, or should it be sold to users or user groups? These and related issues are reflected implicitly or addressed explicitly in the chapters that follow.

INFORMATION TECHNOLOGY AND PUBLIC ACCESS

The technologies of the computer and micropublishing harnessed to the service of information requirements pervade the chapters of this text and are summarized in Appendix A. In this endeavor the private sector has assumed a leadership role. Commercial publishing of government information in a microformat is all but ubiquitous today and was an entrenched industry long before the Government Printing Office established its micropublishing program. For computerized information systems, commercial organizations provide the only access to online databases. Outstanding products like LEGIS (see Chapter 7) are not available to libraries. Thus commercial online services, based on an hourly connect-time rate and in some cases telecommunications costs for network access, lie beyond the financial capabilities of many libraries. And since public funds are currently (and increasingly) being used to produce electronic data files rather than to produce the same information in traditional print or on microfiche, more government information is, ironically, becoming less available to users. Moreover, the General Counsel to the Government Printing Office issued an opinion to the effect that current provisions of Chapter 19 of Title 44 do *not* oblige the Government Printing Office to provide access to computer databases belonging to federal entities. The Government Documents Round Table is aware of this predicament and has urged the Joint Committee on Printing to review Title 44 and amend it if necessary.[17]

A study published by Charles R. McClure in 1981 indicated that "depository librarians are involved in little online searching of government document data bases, have limited access to online terminals, have received little training in the use of online data bases, and acquire virtually no microformatted government publications online." This is unfortunate because the "marriage of online data base searching with micrographics" affords documents librarians greater access to a wider range of government information as well as more effective ordering and accounting procedures.[18] It is in this deplorable situation that we find reflected the philosophical issues discussed above – the definition of government information as it applies to the depository library program, the role of the public and private sectors in selling and distributing public information, the right to be informed. If federal agencies continue to provide critical data, such as statistical series, in computer tape format only, then present deposit and distribution legislation or regulations must be amended to satisfy user requirements.

FEDERAL/STATE COOPERATION

Existing cooperative arrangements among depository and non-depository libraries for the sharing of government information have proved feasible and popular (see Chapter 4). Another cooperative venture was launched in 1981, when the Depository Library Council asked the Public Printer to "investigate the feasibility of requiring each State to prepare a plan to coordinate the Federal Documents Depository Program within each State." On a voluntary basis many states have responded enthusiastically to this concept, and a former Superintendent of Documents viewed the effort as a "qualitative leap which soon will provide greater access to documents to more Americans at less cost."[19] Whether "state plan" initiatives will achieve these desiderata remains to be seen, but the effort has encouraged an examination of resources and coordination among regional depository institutions, selective depository libraries, and other libraries within the several states to articulate mutually beneficial policies.

One must be somewhat skeptical of "bootstrap" efforts like this in which the federal government is not a dues-paying participant. Over the years the Congress has appropriated no monies to assist regional depository libraries in carrying out their considerable responsibilities mandated by 44 U.S.C. 1912 and administrative directives. The budget to administer the depository library program was under $15 million for fiscal year 1982. With total federal spending at the rate of over $75 million an hour, it does not require a doctorate in mathematics to comprehend the minuscule sum expended for this nation's major instrument for the provision of public access to government information. The words "diminished resources," that shibboleth of the current decade, find their quintessential paradigm in the appropriations for the depository library enterprise.

Public access to information remains as fundamental to our freedom today as it was to the fourth president of the United States. James Madison, in a letter to W. T. Berry in 1822, proclaimed:

A popular government, without popular information, or the means of acquiring it, is but a prologue to a farce or a tragedy; or, perhaps both. Knowledge will forever govern ignorance; and a people who mean to be their own governors, must arm themselves with the power which knowledge gives.[20]

SUMMARY

Documents librarianship is a service profession; accordingly, user needs transcend all other issues. Government information must be reasonably easy to obtain physically; that is, by means of a nearby depository or non-depository library, from one's representative or senator, or in other ways — within a reasonable amount of time. Government information must be reasonably easy to locate bibliographically. This principle involves a psychological dimension. Studies have shown that seekers of information will give up if the search for verification and location consumes too much time and effort. Government information must be reasonably inexpensive or free — at least free to use in a library. We must never forget that it is the public who pays our elected and appointed officials to generate this information. Finally, government information must be reasonably accurate; vitiated data are inimical to informed decision making.

The first three principles comprise all facts and issues subsumed in the following chapters. They involve good faith among government, the library community, and users. Stated in other terms, the relationship between public policy and access to information may be perceived as a triadic association, an often unholy trinity consisting of supplier, custodian, and user. As supplier, the federal government is concerned primarily with economics. If a method of distribution is found to be cost effective, then it will be visited upon libraries regardless of countervailing considerations. As custodian, the library community must guard against the tendency to devise policies that contribute to internal operational convenience at the expense of the convenience of its customers. And what of this last group, the maligned users? All they want is an agreeable confluence of those factors which permit the satisfaction of their needs: access to the bibliographic records, availability of textual materials in complaisant forms, and discerning professional service.

If the goals of supplier and custodian were more nearly *pro bono publico*, fewer user complaints and indignities would be reported. In this uncertain decade, with its emphasis on recision and retrenchment, greater efforts must be assayed to achieve a quality relationship between government and librarian for the lasting benefit of that user they both profess to serve.

REFERENCES

1. DttP 5: 187 (September 1977).

2. DttP 7: 192 (September 1979). This definition was embodied in section 101 (3) of H.R. 4572, the Public Printing Reorganization Act of 1979, a measure that did not even survive the marking-up process.

3. U.S. Congress, Joint Committee on Printing, Ad Hoc Advisory Committee on Review of Title 44, *Federal Government Printing and Publishing: Policy Issues* (Washington: Government Printing Office, 1979), pp. 30-31. (Y 4.P93/1:P93/6).

4. *U.S. News & World Report*, February 16, 1981, pp. 54-55.

5. James Bennett Childs, "Bibliographic Control of Federal, State and Local Documents," *Library Trends* 15: 6 (July 1966).

6. *Weekly Compilation of Presidential Documents*, April 24, 1981, p. 447.

7. *Congressional Record* (daily edition), May 7, 1979, p. S5459.

8. DttP 10: 27 (January 1982).

9. DttP 10: 145 (July 1982).

10. *The Washington Post*, March 3, 1982, pp. D1, D4.

11. Preface to Poore's *A Descriptive Catalogue of the Government Publications of the United States, September 5, 1774 — March 4, 1881* (Washington: Government Printing Office, 1885).

12. U.S. Congress, Senate, Committee on Governmental Affairs, *Lack of Accountability in Government Public Information and Publishing Programs* (Washington: Government Printing Office, 1979), pp. 57-92 (Y 4.G74/9:Ac2/3).

13. Note 3, *supra*, p. 31.

14. *Scholars' Access to Information: Public Responsibility/Private Initiative: Minutes of the Ninety-ninth Meeting [of the Association of Research Libraries, October 29-30, 1981]* (Washington: The Association, 1982), p. 22.

15. *A Citizen's Guide on How to Use the Freedom of Information Act and the Privacy Act in Requesting Government Documents* (Washington: Government Printing Office, 1977), p. 3 (95-1:H.rp. 793).

16. Bernard M. Fry, *Government Publications: Their Role in the National Program for Library and Information Services* (Washington: Government Printing Office, 1978), p. 115 (Y 3.L61:2P96).

17. DttP 10: 154 (July 1982).

18. Charles R. McClure, "Online Government Documents Data Base Searching and the Use of Microfiche Documents Online by Academic and Public Depository Librarians," *Microform Review* 10: 245 (Fall 1981).

19. PDH 50:2 (February 1982).

20. In Saul K. Padover (ed.), *The Complete Madison: His Basic Writings* (New York: Harper, 1953), p. 337.

2

Government Printing Office

BACKGROUND

During the eighteenth century, printing was still an infant art; an expert printer, working hard, could hope to accomplish but two or three pages of composition a day. Printing for the early Congresses was handled entirely by private firms. Among these, the firm of Gales and Seaton dominated the printing of congressional proceedings from 1789 to 1818, but the imprint of several other establishments was carried on congressional documents for this period. In 1818 a congressional committee recommended the creation of a government printing office, in order "to produce promptitude, uniformity, accuracy and elegance in the execution of the public printing" for "the work of Congress ... and that of the various departments." The current system of low bidder, the committee reported, created delays and a product "executed in such an inelegant and incorrect manner, as must bring disgrace and ridicule on the literature, and the press of our country."[1] But nothing came of the proposal, and "half a century would pass before these words would be implemented by action."[2]

Despite a number of acts that Congress passed during the first half of the nineteenth century in an attempt to bring some integrity into the commercial printing of government documents, the system was increasingly beset with corruption and patronage. Profiteering, waste, and egregious inefficiency flourished until Congress passed and President Buchanan signed into law the Printing Act of 1860. The act created a Superintendent of Public Printing to manage the official printing and binding "authorized by the Senate and House of Representatives, the executive and judicial departments, and the Court of Claims." The officers of this new agency were enjoined not to "have any interest, direct or indirect, in the publication of any newspaper or periodical" or other binding, engraving, or procurement activities that would suggest a conflict of interest. If the new Superintendent were to "corruptly collude" with private publishers, a fine and penitentiary sentence awaited him.[3] With these sober warnings, the doors of the GPO were officially opened on March 4, 1861, the same day Abraham Lincoln was inaugurated, on the eve of the Civil War.

In the years following the end of the civil conflict, a number of amendments to the 1860 act attempted to effect firmer control over public printing. Congress in 1876 changed the title of the chief officer to that of Public Printer, the position to be filled by presidential appointment with the advice and consent of the Senate. By 1890, over 1,800 people were employed at the GPO, which was now being bruited in periodical accounts as "the largest printing office in the world." And in 1895 Congress passed a comprehensive act codifying the public printing laws in force and creating the office of Superintendent of Documents.

The Office of Superintendent of Public Documents was established in the Department of the Interior by the act of March 3, 1869 (15 *Stat.* 292). The Printing Act of 1895 transferred this position to the Government Printing Office and renamed it Office of Superintendent of Documents. While the Superintendent's responsibilities in the areas of bibliographic control and sales were expanded, the 1895 legislation consolidated the power of the Public Printer as the principal agent for the production of documents.

Despite the fact that the 1860 act vested the GPO with the authority to handle "all government printing," a number of agencies were still securing private firms for their publications. Since 1860, however, some units within the federal executive branch had been discovering that the GPO produced a better product at a lower cost, and they began to divert their printing to the young office. The new act placed all federal printing offices under the control of the Public Printer—"those then in operation and any that might be put in operation later." Certain agencies were excepted from this regulation, but the Printer was now empowered to abolish any other printing operations when in his judgment—with the approval of the Joint Committee on Printing—"the economy of the public service would be thereby advanced." With the act of 1895 the primacy of the GPO as printer and publisher for all congressional and much agency printing was clearly intended, and it was thought that the centralization of printing was accomplished.[4]

Over the years, the centralization and control which the Printing Act mandated rapidly deteriorated. Nevertheless, the act of 1895, with the usual amendments refining this and that procedure or introducing a nuance for expediency, served as the basic legal instrument for the activities of the Public Printer until 1962, when major changes in sections of the earlier act were effected. But these changes had more impact upon the depository library program than upon the functions of the Printer. With the passage of time, the GPO has undergone important, even crucial, changes that affect libraries apart from the role of the Assistant Public Printer (Superintendent of Documents) within the GPO's organizational structure. It is to these recent developments that our attention will be directed. In perspective, this brief sketch of GPO history does scant justice to the interesting and often colorful record of "the largest printing office in the world." Two authoritative accounts of the GPO are found in the authorized version, *100 GPO Years, 1861-1961: A History of United States Public Printing* (Washington: Government Printing Office, 1961), and in a work by Robert E. Kling, Jr., *The Government Printing Office* (New York: Praeger, 1970). The former is a chronological report of GPO activities, with numerous citations from the laws enacted over that period, plus accounts from newspapers and other secondary sources that described the unfolding drama. The latter, written by a former Superintendent of Documents, draws heavily upon *100 GPO Years* and carries the story up to 1970.

THE GPO TODAY

FUNCTIONS

The mission of the GPO is to provide the printing and binding services required by the Congress and the various government departments and agencies in accordance with law and with the *Government Printing & Binding Regulations*. That law has been codified in Title 44 of the *United States Code*, Public Printing and Documents. In order to accomplish this mission, the Public Printer is required to have sufficient equipment and an adequate complement of trained employees to meet the peak-load requirements for the Congress and the urgent needs of the departments. These services, which include the furnishing of blank paper, inks, and similar supplies to all governmental activities on order, cover specifically all congressional work, the bulk of which is produced on very close schedules in order to meet "must" delivery dates.

The GPO is officially an agency of the legislative branch. As early as 1875, Chief Justice Morrison R. Waite, ruling on the GPO's position within the federal establishment, declared:

> In short, the GPO superintendent seems to have a department of his own, in which he is in a sense supreme. Certainly he is not under control of any of the executive departments. Apparently he is more responsible to Congress than to any other authority.[5]

In 1932, a Comptroller General's decision stated that the GPO was indeed a part of the legislative branch not subject to legislation applicable only to the executive departments and independent establishments of the government.[6] The Public Printer "is required by law to be a practical printer versed in the art of bookbinding and is appointed by the President with the advice and consent of the Senate."[7] However, the president does not exercise direct or delegated control of the GPO's management.

The Congressional Joint Committee on Printing (JCP) acts as a functioning arm of Congress but serves the entire government. As the single voice of the Senate and House, it is, in effect, an active board of directors of the GPO and oversees printing, binding, and document distribution for Congress and other federal entities. The JCP "not only has statutory authority over the establishment of printing capabilities elsewhere in government, but contracts between the GPO and commercial contractors also must be approved by JCP." Moreover, the JCP is charged by law with employing "any measure it considers necessary to remedy neglect, delay, duplication, or waste in the public printing and binding and the distribution of Government publications."[8]

GPO officials are obliged to testify before House and Senate subcommittees on legislative branch appropriations and defend their budgetary requests for the forthcoming fiscal year. The published hearings of this annual ritual provide the best single source of information about the activities and plans of the GPO and Superintendent of Documents, and are available to depository libraries in hard copy or microfiche. The House hearings are usually more detailed than their Senate counterparts.

PRINTING POLICIES

Thirteen regional printing procurement offices function in ten regions throughout the country. They operate as brokerage houses; their officials are authorized to advertise for bids or establish an "open-end" contract with commercial printers in the region. Over the last two decades the amount of commercially procured printing has increased, and this trend has been justified as both good fiscal policy and good politics. Some 7,000 commercial printers enjoy contractual arrangements with GPO, and Public Printers have testified in committee hearings that the operation is efficient and inexpensive. An estimated 90 percent of commercial printers are categorized as "small businesses," and the GPO works in concert with the Small Business Administration to insure the viability of the arrangement.

The Federal Printing Procurement Program, which was established by the JCP to increase the amount of commercially produced printing, sets policy on the types of government materials that will be let out on contract or printed "in house" by GPO. Broadly, GPO will not print items determined to be commercially procurable. Orders which require completion faster than can be done commercially, orders requiring specialized capabilities, and orders needed to balance in-house workload are accomplished at the GPO facility. Most congressional documents, for example, are printed in house because of their urgency. Executive department and agency orders are generally less urgent and can often be accomplished by a commercial contractor.

Field printing constitutes a very small percentage of total GPO printing. A limited number of field printing facilities, located on federal property, handle minor requests, primarily of a local nature, that can be carried out more efficiently and with less cost than either commercial procurement or the main Washington plant could manage. Most field printing work consists of overnight or daily jobs in small quantities. With some exceptions, these publications are used locally or for internal consumption.

Documents produced for the GPO by commercial firms still carry the GPO imprint. However, one can tell if a particular publication was printed at GPO or by a contractor: a white star in front of the words "U.S. Government Printing Office" indicates that the publication was printed by a contractor. The absence of the star indicates that the job was done at the GPO's own facilities.[9]

Documents produced by or for the GPO are not to be confused with the large body of "non-GPO" documentation printed or processed at the facilities of departments and agencies. It has been estimated that as many as eight of ten federal publications are non-GPO produced at some 300 government printing facilities throughout the country. The role of non-GPO documents will be discussed later in this chapter in the section on micropublishing and in Chapter 4.

AUTOMATION AND COMPUTER TECHNOLOGY

In 1977 the Public Printer testified before a subcommittee of the House Appropriations Committee that "85 percent of the cost of congressional printing and binding is in the typesetting, not in the paper.... Most of the cost is in setting the type."[10] A book page can be set into type in about fifteen minutes by a competent linotype operator, but the composing process, including proofreading, correction, and verification, is lengthy and complex. Accordingly, technological emphasis has concentrated upon shortening and simplifying this process. In 1962 the Public Printer convened a committee to study and recommend a solution to the problems that stem from the reproduction of material produced by high-speed printers on automatic data processing equipment. The committee proposed "a high-speed electronic phototypesetting device operating from magnetic tapes which would produce a fully-formatted page of hard copy," and bids were invited. An award was made to the Mergenthaler Linotype Company, which teamed with CBS Laboratories on the project, and in 1967 the "Linotron" was born.[11]

The Linotron is a custom-made electronic phototypesetting machine that can almost effortlessly link the modern high-speed computer to the old art of printing. The material to be printed arrives at the machine in the form of encoded magnetic tape from other departmental computers. On instruction from the computer tape, the Linotron finds the character and typeface desired, and at computer speed sets the document a page at a time. Each 1,000 characters can be set electronically in any of eight print sizes in a second. What emerges is a filmstrip that is ready to be developed and turned into hard copy.

A second Linotron system was placed in operation in 1969. By 1970, a former Public Printer was able to state that the systems had saved enough money in two years of operation to be self-sustaining. The acceleration of the printing process by computerized composition has been dramatic. In 1974 the Superintendent of Documents noted that "a page of the Chicago Telephone Directory consisting of approximately 22,000 characters would be completed in about 20 seconds, or at the rate of three pages per minute."[12] Moreover, the system permits reduction of the number of printed pages almost 40 percent; this translates into fewer negatives, fewer plates, less presswork, less paper and, ultimately, lower costs.

The amount of photocomposing has grown every year. In fiscal year 1974 the GPO composed over three-quarters of a million pages on the two Linotron systems. During a fifteen-month period ending September 30, 1976, an additional million pages were set electronically. In FY 1978 GPO set 2.1 million pages and the following year 2.4 million pages by photocomposition. And in FY 1980 "there were about 400,000 pages set in hot metal and 2.8 million pages set by photocomposition."[13]

The conversion is cost effective. Without automation the appropriations requested for printing costs would be several million dollars greater. For example, in FY 1981 the cost of setting a page of hearings by the hot metal process would have been $76 compared to the $46 for photocomposition. On January 25, 1982, the *Congressional Record* for the first time was entirely composed using electronic photocomposition production processes. This milestone was duly reported in the February 11, 1982 issue of the daily *Record*, pp. S820-21. Composing the *Record* by the new processes effects savings of over $550,000 in a single year.

But conversion of major publications is not confined to congressional documents. The *Economic Report of the President* and the *Statistical Abstract of the United States* have been converted with cost savings. A system has been developed to update the *Code of Federal Regulations* whereby the entire full text database is now online and available for processing. In FY 1982 the *United States Code*, which is reprinted in its entirety every six years, was produced "using for the first time an automated method for the typesetting phase."[14] Indeed, most hot metal composition was phased out during FY 1982, and the estimated savings of some $2.6 million was factored into GPO's fiscal year 1982 request.

MICROPUBLISHING

In 1970 Public Printer A. N. Spence submitted a proposal to the JCP requesting permission to study the feasibility of making GPO publications available in microform "to customers either in addition to or in lieu of printing." JCP gave the Public Printer authority to form an advisory committee, which included representatives from the Library of Congress, the American Library Association, and industry. The advisory committee's recommendations included a questionnaire sent to depository libraries, wherein 75 percent of those responding indicated an interest in receiving some documents in microform.

Spence's death and an interregnum in appointment of a new Public Printer delayed implementation of the micropublishing venture. In the summer of 1973, Public Printer Thomas F. McCormick submitted a plan to the JCP to obtain new and additional data on the microform needs of the depository library community. Part II of the 1973 *Biennial Report of Depository Libraries* was another questionnaire designed to determine interest in receiving categories of publications in microform.[15]

The survey was mailed to libraries in late February 1974. When the responses were finally tabulated, the results were basically the same as the earlier survey: an overwhelming number of depository libraries desired that at least some categories of documents be received in microform. In June 1974 McCormick, in a formal letter to the JCP, requested approval to conduct a pilot microform project in cooperation with selected depository institutions. The purpose of the pilot project was "to examine the adequacy of bibliographic controls, attempt to measure user response, examine the quality of film manufacture, packaging and distribution of the film. The test would provide for system refinement to assure the best possible product in the hands of the Depository Librarians."[16]

On January 9, 1975, the chairman of the JCP approved the microform pilot project. The project called for the conversion of some 63,000 pages of the *Code of Federal Regulations* (CFR) to a 98-frame nominal 24:1 reduction ratio microfiche for distribution to twenty-two participating depository libraries for a period of about four months.[17] The final report on the pilot project was submitted to the JCP in June of 1976. Titled *Test Results, Government Printing Office Microform Pilot Project* (June 30, 1976), copies were furnished to members of the Depository Library Council to the Public Printer. Later the report was transmitted to all depository libraries with *Daily Depository Shipping List 9301* (November 16, 1976).

Results of the pilot project indicated that, with a few minor exceptions, the program was judged a success. Approval from the chairman of the JCP was transmitted by letter to the Public Printer on March 25, 1977. In that missive the Printer was given authority to "convert to microfiche, as necessary and as requested by individual depository libraries, that category of publications identified as 'non-GPO documentation' " and to "convert to microfiche, as necessary and as requested by individual depository libraries and when savings in costs are clearly demonstrable, that category of publications identified as 'GPO documentation.' "[18]

This policy established two separate microform programs proceeding along parallel tracks. Non-GPO documentation refers to titles produced by agencies using their own printing facilities. Because microform distribution of these titles saves the agencies a great deal of money, they became more cooperative. And the library community was content to secure those non-GPO publications that remained elusive so long as agencies had to supply quantities of them in hard copy. In this category, however, libraries electing to receive the item accepted the microform edition or none at all.

The second track is somewhat more controversial. GPO documentation refers to those titles and categories printed at GPO or by contract with GPO. Generally they are familiar to a larger audience and comprise the standard reference sources, most periodicals, congressional publications, court reports, census data, laws, and the like. Some of the titles are those that commercial micropublishers have been filming and selling to libraries for many years, and the GPO decision to give these microformatted documents to depository libraries has made members of the Information Industry Association exceedingly unhappy.

For GPO documentation, librarians began with a choice: they could receive the item in hard copy *or* microfiche. GPO officials at first agreed to proceed slowly in determining the categories of microfiche conversion of GPO documentation and to seek the guidance of the Depository Library Council, a representative group of librarians that was established in 1972 to advise the Public Printer on matters dealing with federal documents policy. In April 1979, for example, the Council recommended that "GPO convert to microfiche all series within the Congressional Serial Set (House and Senate reports, House and Senate Documents, and Senate Executive Documents)."[19] Following that, congressional hearings and committee prints were converted, but the choice remained for librarians to accept these series in either microform or paper copy. However, the pledge to offer GPO documentation in a choice of formats was abrogated when librarians read the following notice on *Depository Shipping List 16,085-M,* June 16, 1981: "We will no longer distribute Congressional House and Senate bills in paper format. Beginning with the 6th microfiche bill shipment, all depositories previously receiving paper will begin to receive microfiche. Shipments containing paper bills will discontinue." Public bills and resolutions, with their amendments, had heretofore been a standard GPO category and, since April 1979, librarians had been offered a choice of format. Now those who use depository libraries to research the language of legislation will have only the microform to work with.

In making their decision on bills and resolutions, GPO officials cited "severe budget constraints."[20] This shibboleth signals the beginning of a policy that is certain to metastasize throughout the depository library system whether or not it is in the best interest of the user. Conversion of GPO documentation to a microformat will accelerate because it is manifestly cost effective. Although guidelines for microfiche conversion have been promulgated by GPO and categories not suitable for filming have been established, no federal document remains immune from the microform disease.

Because GPO micropublishing is largely confined to the depository library system, the topic will be assayed again in Chapter 4. For whatever the immediate effects, it is obvious that the GPO micropublishing program has momentous and probably irreversible consequences for federal documents collection management and public use.

FACILITIES

Four buildings located on G to H North Capitol Street NW in the District of Columbia house the GPO printing and binding plant and administrative offices. This facility has long been considered inadequate. In addition, GPO leased facilities include warehouses located in Laurel, Maryland and Alexandria, Virginia, and these are used in the operations of the Superintendent of Documents (see Chapter 3). According to figures submitted at hearings before a House subcommittee on Public Buildings and Grounds, the total amount of square feet for GPO owned and leased facilities is 2,428,000.[21]

GPO has desired a new facility for decades, but gaining approval has been a frustrating experience. The author, in his 1978 edition of this text (pp. 36-38), provided an account of the search for a new location and the complex factors inhibiting approval. GPO officials insist that a new facility will pay for itself in reduced materials handling costs, in the maintenance of a large number of freight elevators, and in reduced payroll costs. The new structure, they argue, will pay for itself within ten years.[22]

To expand its operations in the interim, GPO wants to buy leased land adjacent to the present plant. The DC government, which owns the land, has expressed a desire to raise funds by selling it. Even if the new building becomes a reality, the operations on the adjacent properly could remain in place during the years before occupancy of the new facilities. And if the new building is not authorized and funded, the adjacent land would permit GPO to realign some of its present operations.[23]

The new site, east of the Rhode Island Metro station in a triangle bounded by Ninth Street, Rhode Island Avenue, and Brentwood Road, would be spacious enough to accommodate a modern, three-story building which would place the bulk of the production effort on one floor, thus increasing capabilities, productivity, and service while improving working conditions and employee safety. But even when approved, the facility would not be built and ready for occupancy for five or more years. In the meanwhile, an official testified, for every postponed month, inflation adds over $1 million to the eventual cost of the project.[24]

TITLE 44 REVISION

In June 1978 the chairman of the JCP announced that his committee was undertaking a review of Title 44 of the *United States Code*. To that end, an Ad Hoc Advisory Committee to the JCP on Revising Title 44 was convened, consisting of representatives from the AFL-CIO, American Paper Institute, departments of Commerce and Defense, American Library Association, and other groups. On May 23, 1979, the Advisory Committee published its report, which was organized into six chapters corresponding to six major topics. Following this report, H.R. 4572, The Public Printing Reorganization Act of 1979, was introduced on June 21, while a companion bill, S.1436, was introduced in the Senate on June 27. The legislation proposed a reorganization of the GPO into an independent agency governed by a board of directors, replacing the JCP, which would be abolished. Moreover, the Public Printer and Superintendent of Documents would be elevated to equal status, the one responsible for public printing services and the other for the distribution of public documents. Other major changes involved bibliographic control, depository libraries, and the redefinitions of critical terms such as "public document."

Joint hearings on H.R. 4572 and S.1436 brought a parade of witnesses with divergent viewpoints. Not surprisingly, the Public Printer strongly opposed the legislation. Witnesses for the American Library Association supported the bill. The witness for the American Paper Institute had no strong feelings on the bill one way or the other. And the representative from Coopers and Lybrand, a Chicago-based accounting and consulting firm, found some provisions of the legislation good, others not so good.[25]

Before the marking-up process on H.R. 4572 and its Senate counterpart, a "clean bill" (H.R. 5424) was introduced. Meanwhile, hearings on the earlier bills had been published and distributed to depository libraries. Entitled The National Publications Act of 1979, clean bill H.R. 5424 would revise the definition of a "public document," change the name of the Government Printing Office to the National Publications Agency (NPA), change the title of Superintendent of Documents to Director of Distribution Services and that of the Public Printer to Director of Production Services, and provide support services, including direct financial assistance if warranted, to depository libraries. When H.R. 5424 was introduced, the Senate postponed action on Title 44 revision, preferring to wait for the House to pass a bill and send it along.[26]

The Depository Library Council to the Public Printer voiced support for the new bill, identifying a number of features that would strengthen the depository library system and the availability of public information. But the critics of the legislation remained many and strong, and ultimately H.R. 5424 was pronounced dead for the Ninety-sixth Congress. Any hope of reviving the legislation for the Ninety-seventh Congress was dashed with the following interchange between the Acting Public Printer and the chairman of the subcommittee on legislative branch appropriations for fiscal year 1982:

> Congressman Fazio: Last year, Mr. Hawkins' subcommittee of House Administration reported, but the House did not approve, H.R. 5424, which would have amended Title 44. Do you expect to see the bill back? What would you recommend in terms of changes in it? How would it impact your operation?

> Public Printer Saylor: Mr. Chairman, let me say this. Do I expect it back? No, sir. You didn't ask me did I want to see it come back? Had you, I would have said no sir.

> Fazio: I am sure you can convey that in the answer.

> Saylor: Title 44 is a very, very old statute. By the same token, it is a very, very good statute.

> Fazio: Sometimes that goes hand in hand. Like an old shoe, it feels good.

> Saylor: I agree with you, sir.

> Fazio: You don't anticipate seeing any of those changes, not in piece-meal form or comprehensive form?

> Saylor: No, sir.[27]

But there are many things lacking in Title 44. Wholesale revision of this title of the *United States Code* was the wrong strategy at the wrong time. Piecemeal change must indeed be effected, either by amending specific provisions of Title 44 in Congress, or administratively by revising the JCP's *Government Printing & Binding Regulations*. The pity of the Title 44 revision fiasco is that so many talented librarians spent so much time and effort for naught.

GPO PUBLICATIONS

Current editions of the *List of Classes of United States Government Publications Available for Selection by Depository Libraries* (GP 3.24: date) show only two series from the GPO itself: General Publications (GP 1.2) and Handbooks, Manuals, and Guides (GP 1.23/4), both available under depository item 548. Andriot's *Guide to U.S. Government Publications*, however, lists a number of non-depository series like bulletins, safety pamphlets, posters, security procedures, etc. Few librarians see these publications, and there is probably little use for them in libraries.

Two publications within the Handbooks, Manuals, and Guides series are well known. *How to Do Business with the GPO: A Guide for Contractors* (GP 1.23/4: B96/yr.) is a booklet that assists commercial contractors in their dealings with GPO and is available on request from any of the regional printing procurement offices. The *U.S. Government Printing Office Style Manual* (GP 1.23/4: St 9/yr.) is a lengthy monograph, revised periodically, that sets forth standardized rules of grammar, punctuation, spelling, capitalization, citations, and other usage prescriptions.

The *Annual Report of the U.S. Government Printing Office* (GP 1.1) is not a depository item, but it is available to libraries. Its typical format is that of a softcover mimeographed pamphlet of some fifty pages in length. 44 U.S.C. 1117 allows government agencies to "discontinue the printing of annual or special reports" in order to "keep expenditures for printing and binding within appropriations." Covering the fiscal year activities of the agency, the *Annual Report* contains many useful facts and figures. And, like the *United States Government Manual*, it has a current organization chart of the GPO.

REFERENCES

1. *100 GPO Years, 1861-1961: A History of United States Public Printing* (Washington: Government Printing Office, 1961), p. 15 (GP 1.2: G74/7/861-961).

2. Robert E. Kling, Jr., *The Government Printing Office* (New York: Praeger, 1970), p. 12.

3. *100 GPO Years*, pp. 31-33.

4. Kling, pp. 33-34.

5. *100 GPO Years*, p. 162.

6. Ibid., p. 163.

7.   U.S. Office of the Federal Register, *United States Government Manual, 1980/81* (Washington: Government Printing Office, 1980), p. 61.

8.   Kling, p. 136.

9.   PDH 10: 1,3 (June 1975).

10.   *Legislative Branch Appropriations for 1978* (House), p. 428.

11.   Kling, pp. 197-200.

12.   W. H. Lewis, "Superintendent of Documents on the GPO and Its Plans," *Illinois Libraries* 56: 262 (April 1974).

13.   *Legislative Branch Appropriations for 1982, Part 2* (House), p. 886.

14.   Ibid., pp. 863, 867, 885.

15.   DttP 3: 32 (January 1975); PDH 3: 1-2 (April 1974).

16.   PDH 4: 1,4 (June 1974).

17.   A list of participating libraries is found in DttP 3: 37 (January 1975).

18.   PDH 21: 1 (April 1977).

19.   DttP 8: 292 (November 1980).

20.   PDH 46: 1,4 (June 1981).

21.   U.S. Congress, House, Committee on Public Works and Transportation, Subcommittee on Public Buildings and Grounds, *Proposed Relocation of the Government Printing Office in Washington, D.C.*, Hearings, 95th Cong., 1st Sess., May 17, 18, 1977 (Washington: Government Printing Office, 1977), p. 79.

22.   *Legislative Branch Appropriations for 1982, Part 2* (House), p. 900.

23.   Ibid., p. 879.

24.   Ibid., p. 900.

25.   Coopers and Lybrand conducted a management study of GPO during 1978. Entitled *Analysis and Evaluation of Selected Government Printing Office Operations*, it was published as a committee print (Y4.P93/1:G74/10) and distributed to depository libraries.

26.   Normally, a clean bill is introduced after a committee has made extensive revision of the original bill. Because H.R. 5424 was introduced *before* the marking-up process on H.R. 4572 had taken place, it was considered an unusual procedure.

27.   *Legislative Branch Appropriations for 1982, Part 2* (House), p. 887.

3

Superintendent of Documents

BACKGROUND

The Printing Act of 1895 created the Office of Superintendent of Documents to effect "a more intelligent distribution of Government publications," because the procedures in force at the time were hopelessly chaotic. The first Superintendent, F. A. Crandall, registered dismay at the "bewildering congeries of volumes, numbers, and parts ... of Congressional documents," and of the overall operation stated:

> Of course the present system was not devised by anybody. There was never anybody who could have devised it. Like Topsy, it "jist growed."[1]

Topsy's haphazard growth generated abuse in the dispersal of documents; the Congress was chiefly to blame for the distribution of its quota of publications in a manner "too promiscuous among persons who did not appreciate their true value." Documents had been turning up in secondhand bookstores for sale, "thus abusing the generosity of the Government." Some libraries "were overwhelmed by mountains of government publications, while others received no regular distribution at all." Moreover, "no standard system for titling government documents existed," rendering "practical cataloging ... virtually impossible."[2]

While the act of 1860 had endeavored to correct the several problems in the printing of documents, the act of 1895 sought to remedy the defects in distribution. It directed the Superintendent to

> receive and care for all surplus documents in the possession of Government offices; assort and catalog them; supervise their distribution and sale; catalog and index monthly and annually all documents published; in fine, to render accessible to librarian and the public generally the vast store of Government publications.[3]

To carry out this mission, a Public Documents Division was established within the GPO; the Superintendent was subordinate to the Public Printer but "was to exercise full authority over the tangled government documents situation."[4]

Established in leased quarters on the sixth floor of the Union Building on G Street, NW, near Seventh, accompanied by the usual lamentations of inadequate space, the Division began "the giant task of taking over 134,000 publications accumulated by the departments, hundreds of boxes from the House and Senate document rooms, and over 21,000 publications in the GPO."[5] Distribution to depository libraries was systematized, the enormous job of cataloging was begun, and the sales program was initiated. Thus 106 years after George Washington took the oath of office of president of the United States, a semblance of management was introduced into the dissemination of the publications of the federal establishment.

When the Printing Act of 1895 established the Office of Superintendent of Documents (SuDocs), it did not explicitly mandate the creation and maintenance of a library of federal documents. However, a collection developed in the Public Documents Division because of the requirements to "prepare and publish a comprehensive index of public documents" and "a catalog of government publications which shall show the documents printed during the preceding month, where obtainable, and the price." The fledgling "Library" retained at least one copy of every distinct document received for cataloging/indexing purposes. By 1898 the Superintendent had organized the Public Documents Division into six operational units: "Bookkeeping and Correspondence, Sales, Catalog, Library, Mail, and Stock."[6]

Joseph A. King, a former librarian of the Division, was unequivocal in discussing the genesis of the collection. The documents assembled, he noted, constitute "the by-product of one of the functions charged by law to the Superintendent of Documents," namely, the compilation of catalogs and indexes. Writing in 1951, he pointed out that the Library "was established to carry out the will of Congress by publishing this monthly catalog. Though its collection is a by-product, it has become one of the largest collections of United States Government Publications in the world."[7]

The Library was not open to the general public; a small area, however, had been set aside as a reference department for use by the staff for cataloging and by government officials and infrequent visitors doing research in the collection.[8] It is clear that the Library of the Public Documents Division was not a library in any traditional sense. It was, in King's phrase, a "publishing Library" whose physical characteristics were "strictly functional," unable to offer reference or research services because of space limitations, while accumulating materials for cataloging and indexing at a rate that only served to exacerbate the critical lack of space. Over three decades ago King was able to affirm that the Library "is believed to be the most complete collection of its kind in existence."[9]

THE RETROSPECTIVE PUBLIC DOCUMENTS COLLECTION

Because of concern for the preservation of this great collection of materials, it was transferred to the National Archives in 1972. Later in the decade, however, it was moved to what was thought to be a better location, the former Lansburgh's Department Store, located about one and one-half blocks from the Archives building across Pennsylvania Avenue on Eighth Street. But while this location was more spacious, it lacked an adequate sprinkling system. Indeed, while the collection was housed at Lansburgh's, the National Archives had been actively seeking yet another location for the publications.

In August 1979 the General Services Administration finally determined that it would be too expensive to renovate Lansburgh's to meet archival fire safety requirements, and it terminated the store's lease. A month later the collection was transferred to the Federal Records Center in Suitland, Maryland, a suburb of Washington. However, in early 1982 a reorganization within the National Archives which established a Library and Printed Archives Branch resulted in part of the collection being moved back to the National Archives in Washington. The ostensible purpose of all these changes in policy is to provide for the collection an adequate search room, a good photographic laboratory, and better mail service. All materials, with a few exceptions, are stored in standard archives boxes, marked and shelved in Superintendent of Documents classification order. Because the notation is based upon provenance, the idea of an archival order is philosophically acceptable.

After a government document is cataloged at the Library Division, Library and Statutory Distribution Service, it is sent to the Library of Congress to be filmed for the Readex Microprint edition. In the past, after filming, the documents were sent directly to the Archives. But current plans include retention at the Library Division for three years before being shipped to the appropriate facility.[10]

OFFICE OF THE SUPERINTENDENT OF DOCUMENTS

In 1974 the Public Documents Department was thoroughly reorganized. The Assistant Public Printer (Superintendent of Documents) reports directly to the Public Printer and is in charge of three major "Service" units: Documents Sales, Documents Support, and Library and Statutory Distribution. Within these service units there are "Divisions." For example, the Library and Statutory Distribution Service houses the Library Division, with "Branches" such as the Classification and Cataloging Branch. Similarly, the Depository Distribution Division consists of various subunits like the Depository Administration Branch, which in turn contains "Sections" responsible for micrographics, library services, non-GPO publications, etc.

This structure provides the framework for the accomplishing of four major programs:

1. The sale to the public of government publications produced by or through the Government Printing Office;

2. The compilation and publication of catalogs and indexes of government publications;

3. The distribution of government publications to designated depository libraries;

4. The mailing of certain government publications for members of Congress and other government agencies in accordance with specific provisions of law or on a reimbursable basis.[11]

The fourth function listed is called the "by-law" distribution program, in which the Superintendent of Documents provides certain mailings at no charge to agencies in accordance with specific provisions of law, while mailing and distribution services to government agencies on a reimbursable basis generate millions of dollars in fees. One of the better-known services is the distribution of free and inexpensive consumer information publications performed at the Pueblo, Colorado distribution center for the General Services Administration. Another noteworthy program involves the distribution of publications on behalf of the Smithsonian Institution and the Library of Congress according to covenants enacted at the Brussell's Convention in 1886. Known as the International Exchange Program, this activity involves almost 200 foreign libraries that receive materials on a reciprocal basis, although the volume of documents sent by the United States is six times the number received from other countries.[12]

The first three functions, however, are of central importance to documents librarians and will be examined in some detail.

THE SALES PROGRAM

The official purpose of the sales program is to make "the vast quantity of information published by the Federal Government more accessible to the general public."[13] It is the largest and, presumably, the most important responsibility of the Superintendent of Documents. In 1895 the Superintendent of Documents was empowered "to sell at cost any public document in its charge, the distribution of which is not specifically directed by law." His stock for the first years was acquired from extra copies that libraries had been sent or departments had received.[14]

Far from relying on the leftover largesse of libraries and agencies, the Superintendent today obtains sales publications from the GPO by submitting printing orders for the number of copies he estimates he will need to meet public demand. And demand for public documents is high. In FY 1980 total sales revenue showed a 14 percent increase over FY 1979 as sales exceeded $48 million. This increase was attributed to "a more aggressive marketing approach through advertising and closer cooperation with the publishing agencies." Moreover, with the renovation of mailing facilities at distribution centers in order to realize postage savings inherent in the third-class bulk sort rates, operating costs were held down.[15] In recent fiscal years, the total number of publications sold has exceeded 70 million. And in FY 1979 the Superintendent began, for the first time, to accept major credit cards (VISA, MasterCard) for mail order and bookstore purchase.

PRICES

The price of government publications is governed by 44 U.S.C. 1708, which reads:

> The price at which additional copies of Government publications are offered for sale to the public by the Superintendent of Documents shall be based on the cost as determined by the Public Printer plus 50 percent.

This formula permits GPO to recover costs, or as it is frequently called, to conduct a "self-sustaining" operation. Although Public Printers over the years were "less than candid in divulging to the Congress the specific pricing formula and the value of its components," nevertheless prices of government documents in the past remained inexpensive relative to commercial publications of comparable size and quality.[16]

During the 1970s, however, librarians and users alike were dismayed by several large price increases, which found some customers paying up to 450 percent more for certain subscriptions. The public must now pay for government information at prices no longer competitive with commercial monographs and journals. So long as the "self-sustaining" concept of GPO sales is upheld, prices will continue to rise with inflation. The danger is that prohibitive prices become a form of censorship when they adversely affect the ability of libraries to provide government information for an informed citizenry.

GPO BOOKSTORES

On March 21, 1967, the first retail bookstore for the sale of government publications outside the Washington, DC area was opened in the Everett McKinley Dirksen federal building in Chicago. By 1981 there were twenty-seven bookstores, seven in Washington, DC and vicinity and the rest in cities throughout the country. Most bookstores are located on federally owned or leased property, but as a new approach in marketing, the Birmingham, Houston, and Los Angeles bookstores are located in shopping centers.

Government bookstores are run along the lines of commercial bookstores, without such frills as gift shops, and patrons may browse and purchase what is available. If a publication is not available on the premises, forms are conveniently located for mail order service. Bookstores in the Washington, DC area generally do very well in sales, and bookstore sales "increased nearly 16 percent in fiscal year 1980."[17] Usually a statement of revenue and expense for each bookstore may be found in current legislative branch appropriations hearings covering the previous fiscal year.

In 1982 the Public Printer recommended that twenty-three of the twenty-seven GPO bookstores be closed, on the grounds that the program is neither cost effective nor essential to GPO's mission to insure that government publications are available to the general public. The Joint Committee on Printing, however, overruled that recommendation until further study of overall sales services could be made.

A current list of bookstores with addresses and phone numbers is found in issues of the *Monthly Catalog of United States Government Publications* and in the latest edition of *Price List 36*.

COMMERCIAL SELLERS

Although a 25 percent discount is allowed to individuals and libraries that purchase 100 or more copies of a single publication mailed to one address, bookdealers may receive the same discount regardless of quantity if the publications are mailed to their normal place of business. But this discount of 25 percent is not competitive with the private sector, which offers discounts to booksellers up to 50 percent. GPO officials have discussed plans to offer an amendment to 44 U.S.C. 1708 that would free the Superintendent of Documents from the 25 percent discount restriction to bookdealers and allow him to offer more competitive discounts.

In recent years the GPO has managed to get "certain large bookstore chains to carry some Government publications." Specifically, Walden Books and B. Dalton have carried documents on a selective basis. They buy directly from the

Superintendent on a cash basis but are confined to the 25 percent discount permitted by law. In most cases, they sell the publication for its listed price, but in some instances they may add a small handling charge. GPO officials have testified in hearings that they would like to see these arrangements with bookstore chains grow and flourish, because if successful, GPO will not be obliged "to open new Government [bookstores]."[18]

DEALERS AND JOBBERS

Because librarians have experienced some difficulties in locating dealers and jobbers to meet their specific acquisitions needs, a helpful service is published biennially in *Documents to the People*, which provides a list of those merchants who supply federal as well as other government materials. Entitled "Directory of Government Document Dealers and Jobbers," the listing includes name, address, phone number, "type of documents" (whether the dealer covers microform as well as hard copy), fees, existence of a dealer's catalog, and other pertinent information.

First published in the September 1975 issue of DttP (pp. 40-43), the "Directory" has appeared in September 1977 (pp. 209-212), July 1979 (pp. 159-63), and September 1981 (pp. 229-34) issues thus far. Compilers of this valuable service have been Linda Siler-Regan and Ed Herman.

DISTRIBUTION CENTERS

The distribution of sales publications is a decentralized operation. In addition to government bookstores and commercial booksellers, publications may be ordered by mail from the central office (Superintendent of Documents, U.S. Government Printing Office, Washington, DC 20402) or from the Consumer Information Center, Pueblo, Colorado 81009. Order forms are provided for each location, and remittance can be made by check, money order, credit card, or deposit account. The latter is a most convenient way for either individuals or institutions to order publications from the Washington office. With a deposit of $50 or more (as of 1982), a prepaid account may be opened. A deposit number is assigned, and deposit order forms are used to register the transactions.

The Pueblo, Colorado facility is used to process publications distributed under the aegis of the Consumer Information Center. The Center is actually under the jurisdiction of the General Services Administration, but the Pueblo facility handles all requests for publications under this program. In 1980, for example, the Center processed "over 2.9 million orders ..., and all expenses associated with this effort were reimbursed through GSA."[19] A *Consumer Information Catalog*, issued quarterly and available free, lists a number of consumer-oriented pamphlets and brochures (e.g., *Acne*, *Home Fire Safety*, *Spring Lawn Care*), over half of which are free.

But the Washington, DC address absorbs the bulk of mail order sales. This task is accomplished in two large warehouses in Laurel, Maryland. Automated computerized systems for bulk sales inventory and order processing permit relatively efficient procedures. Material is systematically arranged in stock number sequence in a single area, and retail distribution activities adjacent to bulk stock have reduced transportation expenses. Moreover, automated data processing systems provide improved management of one-time publication orders, inventory, processing subscriptions, refund control, and deposit account maintenance.

CONSIGNED AGENTS

Under the provisions of 44 U.S.C. 1708, the Superintendent of Documents "may designate any Government officer his agent for the sale of Government publications under regulations agreed upon by the Superintendent of Documents and the head of the respective department or establishment of the Government." These agents are located in most government bureaus and number over 125. According to GPO officials, some consigned agents "are the only source of government publications that they handle. As examples: Federal Aviation Agency Office in Oklahoma City handles all Airworthiness Directives. The Defense Logistics Support Center at Battle Creek, Michigan, handles the Department of Defense Federal Item Identification Guides and Supplements."[20] The concept of consigned agents accounts for the numerous publications that can be purchased directly from the "issuing agency" rather than from the Washington or Pueblo outlets.

STANDING ORDER SERVICE

In 1980 a standing order service was initiated for certain GPO sales publications. Subscribers to this service must submit a separate "Authorization for Standing Order Service" form for each title or series ordered; and VISA, MasterCard, or a deposit account may be used to charge the materials. The list of standing order publications includes a number of agency annual reports, Agriculture Yearbooks, budget documents, *Code of Federal Regulations* titles, reference sources like the *United States Government Manual, Social Indicators, Statistical Abstract of the United States,* and *United States Code,* and other series, primarily annual issuances. Bookdealers, as usual, are given the standard discount. At the time this service was launched, it did not accommodate periodicals or subscription services, although future plans may include the addition of such categories.

If an order cannot be filled, the Superintendent of Documents sends the customer a standard reply which includes a list of regional depository libraries that may have a reference copy of the title with a warning that these libraries do not sell government publications. Despite this caveat, customers have incorrectly inferred that regionals are authorized to function as sales agents for the Superintendent.[21]

Useful suggestions to aid customers in ordering GPO publications were published in the January 1980 issue of *Documents to the People* (pp. 25-26). They include the proper use of the latest quarterly issue of *Price List 36,* how to use the PRF, *Monthly Catalog,* and *Selected List* (*infra*), the importance of the GPO stock number, methods of payment, and the like.[22]

CATALOGS AND INDEXES

A number of agencies issue catalogs, or "lists," of their publications at specified intervals or on an irregular basis. But the Superintendent of Documents as an issuing agency is responsible for publishing several current awareness sources that have become basic bibliographic tools for libraries large and small. Some of these basic sources will be discussed in the following pages:

U.S. Government Books (GP 3.17/5; item 556-A)

New Books (GP 3.17/6; item 556-B)

Price List 36 (GP 3.9; item 554)

Subject Bibliographies (GP 3.22/2; item 552-B)

Publications Reference File (GP 3.22/3; item 552-B)

Monthly Catalog of United States Government Publications (GP 3.8; item 557)

U.S. GOVERNMENT BOOKS

In the fall of 1982 the Superintendent of Documents published the first issue of *U.S. Government Books*, a quarterly current awareness ordering tool. *U.S. Government Books* contains approximately 1,000 annotated entries of popular monographic and serial publications available for sale through the Superintendent. Each issue runs over sixty pages and contains illustrations; forms for ordering the materials are provided in each issue.

U.S. Government Books replaced *Selected US Government Publications* (GP 3.17; item 556), which was first issued as a weekly service in 1928, changed to semimonthly status in 1942, and became a monthly in 1974. The purpose of the *Selected List* (as it was popularly known) was to announce GPO sales publications of popular interest to individuals and institutions, and *U.S. Government Books* fulfills the same purpose. Rising costs made it uneconomical to continue a monthly listing, and with the combined August/September 1982 issue the *Selected List* ceased publication.

NEW BOOKS

A bimonthly catalog of approximately twenty-four pages, *New Books* was first published in late 1982. Unlike *U.S. Government Books*, this publication is an unannotated listing of all new titles placed on sale during the preceding two months. Its purpose is to provide professional users of government materials with a current source of information about new publications in their fields of interest. Launched jointly by GPO's director of marketing and the Superintendent of Documents, both catalogs were announced in *Depository Shipping List No. 17,299* (August 27, 1982) and in the August/September 1982 issue of *GPO Newsletter*.

PRICE LIST 36

When in 1973 the price structure of sales publications underwent dramatic changes, a series of subject pamphlets known as *Price Lists* became inoperative and were "recalled." For a time it was thought that they would simply be reissued reflecting the price increases. In March 1974, however, the Superintendent of Documents announced that, with the exception of *Price List 36*, called *Government Periodicals and Subscription Services*, publication of the series would be discontinued. Because of its unique features, *Price List 36* was retained.

As its title suggests, *Price List 36* is an annotated listing of over 500 recurring publications: dated periodicals, and publications which consist of a basic volume updated by changes or new material issued for a predetermined or indefinite period. These are all interfiled alphabetically by title. Although there is no subject index, there is a detailed agency index. Subscription order forms are included, as is a current list of GPO bookstores. Issued quarterly, *Price List 36* is free to individuals and institutions.

Dated periodicals, those subscriptions issued on a regular basis such as daily, weekly, monthly, quarterly, etc., include popular and technical journals and magazines and indexes like the *Monthly Catalog*. Subscription services are indicated by a bullet symbol (•) and include a number of regulatory series such as *Regulations of the Civil Aeronautics Board*, which are issued in looseleaf form, punched for a three-ring binder. The periodicals and subscription services listed in *Price List 36* constitute only those sold by the Superintendent of Documents, a small percentage of the total periodical publishing of the federal establishment.

Materials listed in *Price List 36* are ordered from the Superintendent of Documents in Washington, DC. Order forms and ordering information are provided in each quarterly issue. In addition, each issue announces changes which have occurred since publication of the previous *Price List 36*—new subscriptions available, changes in titles (for example, the useful periodical *Our Public Lands* was changed to *Your Public Lands* as announced in the spring 1982 list), and discontinued subscriptions. Remittance may be accomplished by check, money order, VISA or MasterCard, SuDocs deposit account, or Unesco coupons.

A memorandum from the Superintendent of Documents entitled *Dated Periodicals Retention List* (May 22, 1981) listed 287 regular periodicals and subscription services to be used in conjunction with *Price List 36*. Designed to assist customers who wish to purchase single issues of periodicals or irregularly issued subscriptions (except for basic and supplemental subscription issues), the *Retention List*, arranged in alphabetical sequence by title, included retention information, frequency of issuance, and subscription symbol. Librarians were advised to keep this list with their current edition of *Price List 36*. Retention information, however, is given in brackets following the single copy price as shown in the typical *Price List 36* entry on page 54.

YOUR PUBLIC LANDS. (Formerly *Our Public Lands.*) (Quarterly.) Subscription price: Domestic—**$9.50** a year; Foreign—**$11.90** a year. Single copy price: Domestic—$2.50 a copy; Foreign—$3.15 a copy [2].

[OPL]   I 53.12:
(File Code 2R)   S/N 024–011–80001–8

Features all news about the 460-million-acre public domain such as: How to buy public lands, where to hunt and fish, new laws and regulations, scenic and natural areas, new camping sites, conservation highlights, Alaskan opportunities, and ancient ruins.

SUBJECT BIBLIOGRAPHIES (SB)

With the exception of *Price List 36*, the several *Price Lists* were replaced by a series called *Subject Bibliographies* (SB). The first issue in this new series was called *Home Gardening of Fruits and Vegetables* (SB-001, April 7, 1975), a list of pamphlets and brochures in that ubiquitous category of didactic government literature. The SB series has grown rapidly to include over 250 bibliographies. The bibliographies are organized by topic (Air Pollution, SB-046), by series (Agriculture Yearbooks, SB-031), or by agency (Government Printing Office Publications, SB-244). Arranged alphabetically by title, many entries are annotated and the bibliographic information includes date, pagination, Superintendent of Documents class number, GPO stock number, and price.

Subjects cover the gamut of government interests: anthropology and archaeology (SB-205), the Civil War (SB-192), fossils (SB-143), motor vehicles (SB-049), school lunches (SB-071), violence (SB-096), zoology (SB-124). Order forms are included in the back of each SB; one may get on the mailing list for this series, including the *Subject Bibliography Index* (SB-999). And when an individual SB is revised, the same base number is continued, with a shilling mark preceding the number of the revision.

Despite the inconsistent pattern in compiling the various *Subject Bibliographies*, the series represents a considerable improvement over the old *Price Lists*. And it is certainly a more systematic and comprehensive account of government publications than was found in *Selected US Government Publications*. Figure 1 shows the first page of a typical *Subject Bibliography*.

PUBLICATIONS REFERENCE FILE

Originally developed as an in-house reference tool for filling publications orders, the *Publications Reference File* (PRF) has become one of the most popular and widely used of selection and current awareness sources. In 1976 it was made available to 100 depository libraries, including regionals, for a two-month evaluation period. Participating libraries were asked to respond to its 48X reduction ratio 270-frame microfiche format and its suitability as a sales item for general public use.[23] Both responses being favorable, the PRF today is available free to depository institutions, while for non-depository libraries and other subscribers an identical edition, the *GPO Sales Publications Reference File*, may be purchased from the Superintendent of Documents.[24]

The PRF is a *microfiche catalog* of all publications currently for sale by the Superintendent of Documents as well as forthcoming and recently out-of-stock titles. At any one time there are about 25,000 sales titles available from all the

Figure 1
Subject Bibliography

UNITED STATES GOVERNMENT PRINTING OFFICE

SUPERINTENDENT OF DOCUMENTS

WASHINGTON, D.C. 20402

SUBJECT BIBLIOGRAPHY (SB)

SB-150
April 23, 1981

NOTICE

Prices shown were in effect on the above date. Government documents' prices are subject to change without prior notice. Therefore, prices in effect when your order is filled may differ from prices on this list. Since it is not feasible to change prices shown in Government documents in print, the price printed in a document may differ from the price in effect when your order is processed.

LIBRARIES AND LIBRARY COLLECTIONS

Alternatives for Financing the Public Library. 1974. 70 p.
Y 3.L 61:2 F 49   S/N 052-003-00044-0 $ 1.05

American National Standards Committee Z39, Recommended Future Directions. *Prepared by Task Force on American National Standards Committee Z39, Activities and Future Directions. Voluntary consensus standards in library work, documentation, and related publishing practices are developed by American National Standards Committee Z39 operating under the procedures of the American National Standards Institute.* 1978. 63 p.
Y 3.L 61:2 Am 3   S/N 052-003-00518-2   2.40

American Revolution in Drawings and Prints, A Checklist of 1765-1790 Graphics in the Library of Congress. 1975. 455 p. Clothbound.
LC 1.2:Am 3/9   S/N 030-001-00050-8   14.35

Annual Report of the Librarian of Congress:

1974. 181 p. Clothbound.
LC 1.1:974   S/N 030-000-00078-1   6.40

1975. 177 p. il. Clothbound.
LC 1.1:975   S/N 030-000-00081-1   5.50

1977. 220 p. il. Clothbound.
LC 1.1:977   S/N 030-000-00096-0   7.50

1978. 191 p. il. Clothbound.
LC 1.1:978   S/N 030-000-00104-4   7.50

1979. 206 p. il. Clothbound.
LC 1.1:979   S/N 030-000-00118-4   10.00

1980. 232 p. il. Clothbound.
LC 1.1:980   S/N 030-000-00130-3   10.00

Arab World Newspapers in the Library of Congress. 1980. 91 p.
LC 41.9:Ar 1   S/N 030-000-00120-6   3.50

entities of the federal establishment, most of them having been issued within the last five years. Thus the 48X microfiche PRF is analogous to a *Books in Print* for GPO sales publications. Generated by computer output microfiche (COM) weekly for internal use within GPO, the PRF is produced in two segments: a master cumulative file of about 350 fiche is issued to subscribers and depository libraries bimonthly in January, March, May, July, September, and November; and a monthly supplement, called "GPO New Sales Publications," is included with each mailing of the master file and mailed separately in the other months. Consisting of one or two fiche, "GPO New Sales Publications" offered for sale during the past month are listed in only one sequence, alphabetically by title, and include 1) forthcoming publications with prices; 2) new publications in stock for the first time; and 3) reprints of older publications that have come back in stock.

For user access, the bimonthly master file has three sequences. First, there is a "stock number sequence," arranged numerically. The GPO "stock number" is a multi-digit number assigned to all sales publications. It is perhaps the most significant piece of information used by GPO sales personnel because of the Superintendent's automated order processing system. Next, there is the "catalog number sequence," arranged alphanumerically. This is simply an arrangement by Superintendent of Documents classification number, but the Sales Management Division of the Office of Superintendent of Documents has chosen to retain the old phrase "catalog number." Finally, there is an "alphabetical sequence," a dictionary index of interfiled titles, series, key words, key phrases, subjects, and personal authors.

The color stripe at the top of each microfiche is the header, which works like a telephone directory in giving the first and last entries on each fiche. A grid system is used to locate information on the fiche; each is divided into rows and columns, lettered A to O and numbered 1 to 18. Thus each frame is designated by a letter and a number, for example, A1, B6, J12, etc. There are 270 frames on one fiche and an average of two or three records to a frame. The last frame (O18) is the index frame.

A time-saving feature of the PRF is that each time the record is repeated on the fiche, all the available bibliographic information is present. Entries are very complete, and include, in addition to the three "sequence" points of access, stock status, location in the warehouse where copies of the title are stored, issuing agency, imprint, depository item number, price, SB number, ISSN or ISBN, and other relevant data.

For the convenience of librarians and users, the Records Branch, Sales Management Division, issued in 1981 a *PRF User's Manual: A Guide to Using the GPO Sales Publications Reference File* (GP 3.22/3: manual). For an example illustrating the search process in using the PRF, the *Manual* chose an eleven-page brochure called *Growing Peonies*. This pamphlet is indexed under 1) stock number 001-000-03807-9, 2) SuDocs class number A 1.77: 126/5, and in the alphabetical sequence under 3) the title *Growing Peonies*, 4) the author, Cathey, Henry M., 5) the series Home and Garden Bulletin 126, 6) the key word "Peonies," and 7) the subject heading "Floriculture."

A complete listing of GPO subscription services can be found on the PRF under the heading "Government Periodicals and Subscription Services," which is, of course, *Price List 36*. But each periodical or irregular issuance can be accessed by all the means available for other PRF titles.

A companion product to the PRF was issued in 1980 under the title *Exhausted GPO Publications Reference File* (EPRF) and covered titles that went out of print from 1972 to December 1978. Beginning with the 1981 edition, each annual EPRF cumulates all titles exhausted since the basic 1980 edition. At the beginning of each year, a number of exhausted (out-of-print) titles are removed from the *GPO Sales Publications Reference File* and merged into a separate index of exhausted titles. The EPRF is identical in its indexing and fiche format to the PRF and can be searched in the same way. If the user does not find a publication listed on the PRF, he or she should consult the out-of-print file to determine if the publication was sold by GPO in the past. Copies of exhausted publications may be found in regional and selective depository libraries, and copies of certain technical publications no longer sold by the Superintendent of Documents may be obtained from the National Technical Information Service (NTIS), Springfield, Virginia, at NTIS prices for microfiche or paper copy.

A problem of terminology arose with this file of "exhausted" titles. Stock status code number 15 in the PRF was changed from "exhausted" to "Out of Print-GPO" effective April 1982 because the former term, commonly understood by librarians, was creating confusion among customers using the PRF.

In 1982 the GPO announced that a DIALORDER service for customers subscribing to DIALOG Information Services, Inc. became operational. Users performing online searches using the PRF are able to order directly from GPO, thus greatly reducing order processing time. More traditional methods of securing titles from the information provided on the PRF are, of course, available: check, VISA or MasterCard, money order, or deposit account. Customers may also place orders by telephone or telex.

The PRF, on microfiche and online through DIALOG, is by far the best of the in-print GPO sales catalogs. Because of its updating frequency and comprehensive nature, it should be consulted for current price and availability in preference to any other official or unofficial announcements of SuDocs sales publications.

MONTHLY CATALOG OF UNITED STATES GOVERNMENT PUBLICATIONS

Known by its short title, the *Monthly Catalog* was first issued in 1895 and over the years has undergone six name changes. From January 1951 it has been published under its current title. As Schwarzkopf noted, the *Monthly Catalog* "established its distinctive character early and has witnessed relatively few major changes over the years."[25] Prior to 1976 the *Monthly Catalog* was arranged alphabetically by issuing agency, with the exception of the publications of the Congress, which were subdivided both by form and by issuing entity. Monthly and annual indexes were organized in an interfiled author-title-subject format until 1974 when the indexes were separated by subject, personal author, and title. Decennial indexes (1941-1950 and 1951-1960), quinquennial cumulations (1961-1965 and 1966-1970), and a cumulation covering the period 1971 through June 1976 made searching somewhat easier. Relatively simple and unsophisticated, the earlier *Monthly Catalog*'s size and format were as familiar to users as an old but comfortable shoe.

But that relative stability was rudely shattered with the appearance of the July 1976 issue, which presented to users of this primary bibliographic source the most far-reaching change in the publication's history. In the preface to the July 1976 issue of the *Monthly Catalog*, a modest statement appeared:

In response to requests by the library community and the Depository Library Council to the Public Printer, the Assistant Public Printer (Superintendent of Documents) in the summer of 1974 directed the Library Division to join the Ohio College Library Center's on-line cataloging network, convert to the MARC format, and catalog according to the Anglo-American cataloging rules (AACR).

The *Monthly Catalog* utilizes AACR and Library of Congress main entries. Subjects are derived from *Library of Congress Subject Headings* 8th edition and its supplements. The catalog consists of text and four indexes — author, title, subject, and series/report number.

The Government Printing Office considers the *Monthly Catalog* to be an evolving publication. Its scope and timeliness will continue to be of prime importance.

There was a calculated effort to schedule these sweeping changes for the July 1976 issue as GPO's contribution to the American Bicentennial, perhaps to rival the stately ships that streamed proudly into New York harbor. In a paroxysm of enthusiasm, the August 1976 issue of *Public Documents Highlights*, under the heading "Monthly Catalog in a Revolutionary Format," announced the glad tidings:

> The July issue of the *Monthly Catalog* is as revolutionary as 1776! New dimensions of 10¼"x7⅞" frame a MARC style format proceeding from the OCLC data base.... Entries in the text are blocked into two columns. Headings separate the larger organizational groupings. Text is arranged by order of SuDocs classification.[26]

Perhaps the Superintendent could be forgiven such unabashed joy, for it was a significant development, a confluence of technologies in which the new, sacred acronyms — MARC, OCLC, AACR — flowed together to create a *Monthly Catalog* that would have been unrecognizable by F. A. Crandall, the first Superintendent of Documents. After the revolution, however, the *Monthly Catalog* has evolved less dramatically. New indexes have been added to the original four, AACR has given way to AACR II, the ninth edition of *Library of Congress Subject Headings* replaced the eighth, and main entries have been "compressed" into paragraph form. Still, in bulk and shape, the "new" *Monthly Catalog* bears more resemblance to those indexing sources for scientific and technical literature than to its diminutive, pre-July 1976 forebear.

The salient characteristics of the *Monthly Catalog* are as follows:

- Entries are arranged alphanumerically by Superintendent of Documents classification notation.

- Each monthly issue consists of a main entry section followed by separate indexes for authors, titles, subjects, series/reports, stock numbers, and title key words. Beginning with the January 1982 issue, the Title Keyword Index includes the printing of "telephone" headers to provide easier access. Moreover, the January 1982 issue introduced a "compressed entry" in paragraph form which reduces the size and cost of the catalog without sacrificing bibliographic information.

- Semiannual and annual cumulative indexes retain all of the indexes listed above plus a SuDocs classification number index.

- A list of depository libraries by state and city, traditionally located in the September issue, was eliminated from the 1979 and 1980 *Monthly Catalog*. As if to overcompensate for this ill-advised omission, the list was reinstated in both the March and October 1981 issues.

- In the preliminary pages of each issue, detailed information on the GPO sales program, how to order publications, a current list of regional depository libraries, and other matters is provided. Much of this expanded information was introduced with the January 1982 issue.

- Other information includes new classification numbers, discontinued series, corrections for previous issues, an alphabetical list of government authors, and a sample entry (Figure 2, page 60). GPO bookstore locations are found on the inside back cover of each issue.

- The *Monthly Catalog* is online through DIALOG, Bibliographic Retrieval Services (BRS), and SDC Search Service (ORBIT).

Serials Supplement

A *Serials Supplement*, listing publications issued "three or more times per year and a select group of annual publications and monographic series titles,"[27] is published annually. It is not assigned a month; rather, its inclusive entry numbers indicate its place between monthly issues of the *Monthly Catalog*.[28] For example, the 1981 edition covered entries 81-7399 to 81-9523, falling between the July and August issues for that year. The *Serials Supplement* is a more robust version of the "old" (pre-July 1976) February appendix to the *Monthly Catalog* that listed periodicals and subscription services. Note that the *Serials Supplement* includes but is not confined to *Price List 36* periodicals sold by the Superintendent.

* * * * *

GPO's decision to become a member of the Online Computer Library Center (OCLC), formerly called the Ohio College Library Center, has had far-reaching consequences. For decades the Government Printing Office used its own system for cataloging publications involving the use of a locally produced cataloging manual and a locally maintained subject thesaurus. By joining the OCLC network, GPO was obliged to abandon its old cataloging practices and abide by Anglo-American Cataloging Rules and Library of Congress subject headings. The benefits of network participation include the use of computer tapes for *Monthly Catalog* production and the standardization of documents cataloging.

Catalogers at the GPO's Library Division were given intensive training in Library of Congress cataloging rules, and by 1981 LC began "accepting GPO as the authoritative source for descriptive cataloging for Federal Government Documents."[29] The assumption of authoritative responsibility for subject and serial cataloging will follow not long thereafter. In 1980 GPO became a member

Figure 2
Monthly Catalog: Sample Entry

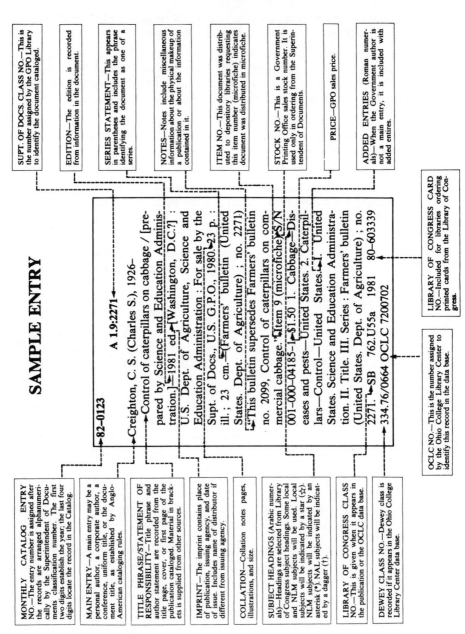

of the Conversion of Serials Project (CONSER), in which the agency cooperates with major libraries in the United States and Canada to maintain an authoritative and current file of serial records on OCLC. In January 1981 GPO began establishing monographic series for the Library of Congress through the Name Authority Cooperative Project (NACP), thus assuring uniform treatment of series by GPO and LC. And in 1981 GPO announced plans to develop an in-house online cataloging system (CATS) "in order to shorten the production cycle of the *Monthly Catalog.*"[30] As a result of internal improvements, GPO officials were able to announce a significant increase in cataloging production during the last three months of 1981.

Despite its innovative features and cooperative arrangements, the "new" *Monthly Catalog* is not without its critics. The late James Bennett Childs, an acknowledged authority on government publications, had this to say after looking at the July 1976 issue: "I feel far from impressed with it." It simply emphasizes "some of the mistakes in some of the author headings under AACR '67 and a lot of expanded entries at the expense of completeness of coverage of entries."[31] Another expert noted that Library of Congress cataloging results in a great deal of repetition. In the November 1977 issue, for example, 118 entries (77-14618 through 77-14736) "all have identical main entries, source notes, and tracings." Moreover, the 1977 *Monthly Catalog* "used three times as much paper as that of 1975 to list 12% fewer entries."[32] Problems have dogged the *Serials Supplement* from its inception. The author in a study found egregious errors in entries for the 1977 and 1978 editions.[33] And in the 1981 *Serials Supplement*, eighty-five classes listed in the "ERRATA" section were mysteriously omitted.

Figure 2 shows a *Monthly Catalog* sample entry in "compressed" paragraph form. A sample entry of a government periodical is also provided in annual issues of the *Serials Supplement.*

Commercial Sources to Aid Monthly Catalog Use

The shortcomings of the official *Monthly Catalog* over the years stimulated commercial publishers to create and market products that have corrected and enhanced some of these inadequacies. Carrollton Press originally issued three of these bibliographic sources that come to the rescue of *Monthly Catalog* users. They are now distributed by Research Publications, Inc. (RPI), a commercial publisher located in Woodbridge, Connecticut.

Edna A. Kanely (comp.), *Cumulative Subject Index to the Monthly Catalog of U.S. Government Publications, 1895-1899.* For these years, the *Monthly Catalog* had no indexing whatsoever from January 1895 through December 1897 and only monthly indexes from December 1897 through December 1899. Original entries were produced for the thirty-five issues which had no indexing and were merged with the entries for the twenty-five monthly indexes. The *Index* was issued in two hardcover volumes.

Edna A. Kanely and William Buchanan (comps.), *Cumulative Subject Index to the Monthly Catalog of U.S. Government Publications, 1900-1971.* Issued in fifteen hardcover volumes, this compilation represents "a massive merging of entries in all previously published official cumulative indexes to the *Monthly Catalog*: 49 annual indexes; the two decennial indexes; and one six-month index."[34]

Mary Elizabeth Poole (comp.), *The "Classes Added" Reprint Edition of the Monthly Catalog of U.S. Government Publications, 1895-1924.* For these years, the official *Monthly Catalog* did not include the SuDocs class numbers with its entries. The task of adding some 100,000 class notations was completed by Poole and her staff at the D. H. Hill Library of North Carolina State University, Raleigh. Fortunately, the pre-1925 notation symbols were being used by the Public Documents Library in Washington during that time, and Poole was able to assemble the class numbers for the 360 issues published before 1925.

The Pierian Press (Ann Arbor, Michigan) has published in five volumes a series of *Cumulative Personal Author Indexes to the Monthly Catalog of U.S. Government Publications, 1941-1975.* Edited by Edward Przebienda, the volumes include two decennial and three quinquennial indexes. They consist of alphabetical lists of all personal names that have appeared in the entries of the *Monthly Catalog* for those years, followed by volume and entry number in the catalog. Names include virtually every relationship of author to cited publication — editor, compiler, translator, researcher, lecturer, joint author(s), illustrator — including a systematic author approach to Joint Publications Research Service (JPRS) translations.

These author indexes are valuable because from September 1946 to December 1962 personal authors were omitted from the *Monthly Catalog* indexes, including the two decennial cumulative indexes (1941-1950 and 1951-1960). In other years the *Monthly Catalog* indexed by first author only. The *Document Catalog* (1893-1940) includes personal authors, and from July 1976 the *Monthly Catalog* has been thoroughly indexing personal authors, editors, illustrators, etc. However, for earlier searching, Pierian Press's contribution to a flawed *Monthly Catalog* is indispensable.

The cumulative subject indexes and "classes added" reprint were originally issued under the imprint of Carrollton Press. Pierian Press and Carrollton Press have published other bibliographic guides which will be noted in Chapter 6. The above publications represent a systematic effort to improve access to a *Monthly Catalog* whose bibliographic history has been less than illustrious.

Another commercial venture in support of *Monthly Catalog* access is the full text edition of entries filmed by Readex Microprint Corporation. In 1953 the company began filming and making available non-depository titles and in 1956 began offering the depository series of *Monthly Catalog* entries. The project is a cooperative enterprise involving the Library of Congress Photoduplication Service, where the publications are filmed at Readex's expense, and the Library Division of the Superintendent of Documents. The *Monthly Catalog* entry number serves as the basic unit of access, and the catalog serves as an index to the microprint collection.

Subscribing libraries receive the microprint cards in plastic boxes in the shape and size of a royal octavo volume, which permits shelving in the same manner as books. The specifications for paper and printing to insure archival permanence are set forth by the U.S. National Bureau of Standards. Readex sells an opaque viewer and an enlarger-printer for users of the microprint collection.

Although Readex tends to emphasize the sturdy archival quality of its microprint editions of *Monthly Catalog* publications, the growing time lag for delivery since 1978 has diminished its utility as a current awareness source.

SUPERINTENDENT OF DOCUMENTS CLASSIFICATION

The Superintendent of Documents classification system was established in the Library of the Public Documents Department sometime between 1895 and 1903. The first explanation of the system was given in 1903 by William Leander Post, then in charge of the Library, who gave credit for the concept to Adelaide R. Hasse. Ms. Hasse had used the system in assigning classification numbers to a Department of Agriculture List of Publications. The notation expanded as the federal establishment's quantity of publications and issuing units grew, and has changed in some details, but it has retained the principles upon which it was first based. For many years it served as the order or "catalog" number, until that function was replaced by the multi-digit stock number for GPO sales publications.

The SuDocs classification is an alphameric notation based on the principle of *provenance*, whereby the several publications of any government author — a department, bureau, agency, office — are grouped together under like notation. Basically, this sort of arrangement guarantees no inevitable grouping of similar subject matter, and in that sense the purist would argue that the notation is not truly a "classed" system. A book on children's poetry and a guide to the official publications of Swaziland are documents of the same government author (in this case the Library of Congress). In the system, the classification reflects the organizational structure of the United States government, and this is at once the scheme's strength and its weakness.

The concept of provenance avoids the tortuous Procrustean problems of a scheme like the Dewey decimal classification, but it is at the mercy of any government reorganization. Since reorganization happens not infrequently, the publications of many government authors are located in several places in the system. The *Budget of the United States Government*, for example, has undergone title changes, agency changes, and has, of course, been issued under different administrations. As a result it has been classed in T 51.5, Pr 32.107, PR 33.107, PR 34.107, and PrEx 2.8. The *Index-Catalog of the Library of the Surgeon-General's Office* has been classed in W 44.7/4, M 102.8, FS 2.210, and D 104.8 over the years, owing to its different provenances.

The reclassification that results from reorganization will always cause problems for both the catalogers at GPO and documents librarians and their clientele. When the Department of Health, Education, and Welfare was created in 1953 and the functions of the Federal Security Agency, which was thereby abolished, were transferred to the new cabinet-level entity, publications of the old agency were still designated "FS" for sixteen years before the letters were changed to "HE," thus reinstating a minor mnemonic advantage. In 1972 a reorganization placed the Census Bureau under a newly created entity called the Social and Economic Statistics Administration (SESA). This new hierarchical level obliged the Superintendent to change census classes from "C3" to "C56.200." In 1975, however, SESA was abolished, Census resumed its former place in the Department of Commerce hierarchy, and the publications reverted back to the familiar "C3." More recently the Secretary of Agriculture dismantled the Economics and Statistics Service and the Science and Education Administration organized by a previous administration. This 1981 "reverse reorganization" affected a number of class stems when the original agencies were restored, for the Superintendent reinstated the old symbols. This sort of reorganizational foofaraw plays havoc with depository library record keeping and shelf arrangements.[35]

When changes in reorganization require changes in the classification of documents, librarians have three basic options. They may continue the old notations; they may assign new notations as issued and change all the notations on the older publications to conform to the new notation; or they may assign new notations as issued and leave the old letters and numbers on the earlier materials. The last strategy appears to accommodate the fewest disadvantages, but librarians responsible for segregated documents collections have not formed a consensus as to which option is better. Indeed, the problem of reclassification is a vexing one, and the literature of librarianship is liberally sprinkled with debate on the issue.[36] Despite the fact that browsing is discouraged by the very nature of a provenance system of classification, users and librarians alike find it annoying to have the publications of the *Index-Catalog of the Library of the Surgeon-General's Office* shelved in four places. Whatever options librarians choose, the larger factor of the role of government publications in the overall collection will dictate the decision; in any case, rigidity in the decision-making process should be eschewed.

A BRIEF EXPLANATION OF THE SYSTEM

The explanation that follows is based primarily on *An Explanation of the Superintendent of Documents Classification System* (GP 3.2: C 56/8: yr.) and John L. Andriot, *Working with U.S. Government Publications, Preprint No. 1: The Superintendent of Documents Classification Scheme, an Explanation and Current Agency Outline* (McLean, VA: Documents Index, 1973). The former pamphlet is used in the Library Division of the Office of Superintendent of Documents and has been revised from time to time since 1963.

The basic arrangement is the grouping of subordinate units with the parent organization so that each full notation reveals the responsible *issuing agency* (provenance) and its place in the organizational structure of the federal establishment. But the classification scheme does not necessarily show "authorship" in the sense of an individual or, more commonly, a corporate body responsible for the *intellectual content* of the publication. Hence, issuing agency is not to be confused with corporate, or government, author, even though in many instances the two may be the same. A study prepared *by* the Congressional Research Service of the Library of Congress may be transmitted to a congressional committee. The committee in turn orders the publication to be printed, and it is issued under the committee's provenance with the appropriate SuDocs class notation.

The full class number can be divided into three major elements: author symbol, series designation, and book number. The combination of author and series designations is called the "class stem." The book number is that which gives the publication its unique identification and rounds out the notation. An example is shown on the following page. In this example, Bulletin 2057 is entitled *Occupational Employment in Manufacturing Industries, 1977*, which was published by the Bureau in 1980.

	Symbol	Designation	Hierarchy
	L	Parent Agency	Department of Labor
class stem	2	Sub Agency	Bureau of Labor Statistics
	.3	Series or generic type	Bulletin (series)
book number	:2057	Individual publication	Bulletin 2057

Letters are ascribed to the parent agency, as "A" for Agriculture Department, "Ju" for Judiciary, "FT" for Federal Trade Commission. To set off the subordinate bureaus and offices, numbers are added to the letters, the digit "1" assigned to the secretary's or administrator's office of the parent organization. Succeeding numbers are applied, in order, to the lesser agencies. This alphanumeric notation represents the bureau or office, for example:

Agriculture Department (Secretary's Office and Department Series)	A 1.
Forest Service	A 13.
Soil Conservation Service	A 57.
Rural Electrification Administration	A 68.

The next division in the scheme is assigned to the various series issued by a particular bureau or office. Numbers .1 through .8 are reserved for the following types of publications:

.1:   Annual reports
.2:   General publications
.3:   Bulletins
.4:   Circulars
.5:   Laws (administered by the agency)
.6:   Regulations, rules, and instructions
.7:   Press releases
.8:   Handbooks, manuals, guides

Any additional series issued by an agency are given the next numerical sequence. Thus "A 1.9:" was assigned within the Department of Agriculture to a series called "Farmers' Bulletins" to distinguish this type of publication from ".3:," which is set aside for ordinary "Bulletins." The well-known Yearbook of Agriculture became "A 1.10:" and so forth.

New series closely related to already existing series are designated by use of the shilling mark after the number assigned to the existing series, followed by a digit for each related series starting with "2". Separates are distinguished by use of a lowercase letter beginning with "a" rather than by numbers. A theoretical example of these "tie-in" classes is as follows:

.4:   Circulars
.4/a: Separates from Circulars (numbered)
.4/b: Separates from Circulars (unnumbered)
.4/2:   Administrative Circulars
.4/3:   Technical Circulars

Notations assigned to subunits of a large department like Health and Human Services (HHS) in multiples of ten still retain the eight "form" designations, for example:

National Institutes of Health

HE 20.3001:   Annual report
HE 20.3002:   General publications
HE 20.3006:   Regulations, rules, and instructions
HE 20.3008:   Handbooks, manuals, guides

By combining the "author" symbol and series designation, the class stems are obtained for the several series issued, for example:

A 1.10:   Yearbook of Agriculture
A 13.1:   Annual Report of Chief of Forest Service
A 57.38:   Soil Survey Reports

The individual book number follows the colon. For numbered series, these book numbers reflect a simple numerical sequence. For example, Department of Agriculture Leaflet No. 381 would be assigned the notation A 1.35:381. For revisions of numbered publications, the shilling mark and additional numbers beginning with "2" are added. Thus when Leaflet No. 381 first appeared in revised form, the notation read A 1.35:381/2.

General Publications (.2:), which are unnumbered publications of a miscellaneous nature other than continuations, are given a book number based upon the key word in the title, using the two-figure Cutter table. Revisions of unnumbered publications are usually identified by addition of the shilling mark and, if applicable, the last three digits of the year of revision. If necessary, shilling marks following the original Cutter number further distinguish the individuality of the work. The dash (−) has also been employed to extend the numbers within the SuDocs class system; it is often used to designate a reprint of an individual edition.

As Andriot points out, the SuDocs system follows the structure of the federal establishment. "Since the structure is a vertical step system from department to agency on through bureau, division, office, and even branch, one would have a complicated classification scheme if this were followed. Several methods have been used to effect a subdivision of at least one or two steps down the organizational ladder. One method is to divide a class into 100's.... The number for the Public Health Service was FS 2 until 1969 when HE classes were assigned to the Department of Health, Education, and Welfare. The National Office of Vital Statistics was assigned the class number of FS 2.100 and the National Library of Medicine FS 2.200. This meant that when all of the first 99 numbers were used, a jump to FS 2.300 had to be made for the Public Health Service publications. Since the classification scheme determines the position of publications on the shelves, this also meant a broken arrangement for the Public Health Service. Had the division been in 1000's instead of 100's, this would not have happened."

Another example of achieving a subdivision is "by assigning a class number to a regular sequential number and building from there in a normal manner. Staying within the Public Health Service in the old FS 2 numbers, we find that the various publications of the National Institutes of Health were classed together under FS 2.22. A brief review of the class shows at least 102 basic sub-classes entered under FS 2.22. When the FS classes were changed to HE numbers in 1969, the organization scheme of the Public Health Service under HE 20 was greatly expanded. Whether to subdivide by a group number of 10, 50, 100, or 1000 or expand on a single sequential number is probably decided on a case by case basis. Also, the rule on whether an agency is given its own agency class number or is assigned a sequential number within the parent class is not clear. One finds dozens of units of the Air Force classified within the D 301 number, while on the other extreme is the greatly expanded classification scheme for the Public Health Service under HE 20."[37]

Periodicals, too, are not immune to the effects of government reorganization. For example, when the bimonthly *Children* was the provenance of the Office of Child Development it was classed in HE 21.9. When its title was changed to *Children Today*, the class notation was changed to HE 21.9/2, another use of the shilling mark. Currently, *Children Today* is issued by the Children's Bureau, Department of Health and Human Services, where it has been assigned an HE 23.1209 notation.

The system described above governs the classification of most government publications. There are special forms employed by certain entities; these consist of classes assigned to

a) some series issued by the Interstate Commerce Commission, for example, IC 1 wat. (water carriers), IC 1 mot. (motor carriers), etc.;

b) boards, commissions, and committees established by act of Congress or under authority of act of Congress, not specifically designated in the executive branch of the government nor as completely independent agencies, for example, Y 3.Ad 9/7 (Advisory Commission on Information);

c) the several publications of the Congress and its working committees, for example, Y 4.P93/1 (Joint Committee on Printing);

d) multilateral international organizations in which the United States participates, for example, S 5.48 (National Commission for UNESCO Publications); and

e) publications of the president and the Executive Office of the President, including committees and commissions established by executive order and reporting directly to the president, for example, Pr 40.8 (Special Commissions and Committees), PrEx 1.10 (President's Committee on Employment of the Handicapped, General Publications).

The classification of the special forms will be noted in succeeding chapters as the publications themselves are discussed. A number of other minor wrinkles to the system will not be described here. The reader is referred to the latest revision of *An Explanation of the Superintendent of Documents Classification System*, for it was prepared by experts in GPO's Library Division and is used in the training of new personnel in that organization.

Utilizing the principles of the system set forth in the preceding pages, let us work through a specific title with its unique classification notation:

When You Work at a Job
HE 3.2: J 57/2/978

	Symbol	Provenance and Hierarchy
	HE	Department of Health and Human Services (Parent Agency)
class stem	HE 3.	Social Security Administration (Issuing Agency)
	HE 3.2:	General publications series
	J 57	Cutter table based on key word (*Job*) in title
book number	J 57/2	Second edition
	J 57/2/978	Issued in 1978

Although the SuDocs class system, like other notation schemes, conveys an initial appearance of difficulty, it becomes easily comprehensible with frequent use. Since the *Monthly Catalog* itself is organized in SuDocs class order, early familiarity with the system will enable the librarian to relate organizational structure to issuance, resulting in faster and more accurate service to the user.

DISTRIBUTION TO DEPOSITORY LIBRARIES

By the end of the year 1981 there were 1,355 designated depository libraries in the United States and its territories. The distribution of documents to these libraries, the last of the four major functions of the Superintendent of Documents to be noted in this chapter, is of paramount importance. Accordingly, the depository library system, its laws, regulations, and activities, will be fully discussed in the next chapter.

REFERENCES

1. *100 GPO Years, 1861-1961: A History of United States Public Printing* (Washington: Government Printing Office, 1961), pp. 75-76.

2. Robert E. Kling, Jr. *The Government Printing Office* (New York: Praeger, 1970), p. 112.

3. *100 GPO Years*, p. 75.

4. Kling, p. 112.

5. *100 GPO Years*, p. 75.

6. Ibid., p. 79. See also Kling, pp. 35, 112-14.

7. Joseph A. King, "The United States Government Printing Office Library," *D.C. Libraries* 22: 2 (January 1951).

8. Ibid., p. 4.

9. Ibid., pp. 3, 4. Cf. L. F. Schmeckebier and R. B. Eastin, *Government Publications and Their Use*, 2nd rev. ed. (Washington: Brookings, 1969), p. 132: "There is probably no complete collection of government publications in existence, but the one in the Public Documents Library is probably the most nearly complete."

10. DttP 7: 283 (November 1979).

11. *Legislative Branch Appropriations for 1981* (House), pp. 818-19.

12. *Legislative Branch Appropriations for 1982* (House), p. 903.

13. *Legislative Branch Appropriations for 1981* (House), p. 819.

14. *100 GPO Years*, p. 76.

15. *Legislative Branch Appropriations, Fiscal Year 1982* (Senate), p. 592.

16. DttP 3: 27-28 (September 1975). A useful summary of the pricing issue is found in Arthur D. Larson, "The Pricing of Documents by the Government Printing Office: Survival Response by an Agency in Crisis," *Government Publications Review* 4: 277-313 (1977).

17. *Supra*, note 15.

18. *Supra*, note 11, p. 887.

19. *Supra*, note 11, p. 821.

20. Bill Barrett, "Direct Sales by Other Agencies," *Government Publications Review* 5: 142 (1978).

21. DttP 10: 94 (May 1982).

22. DttP 8: 25-26 (January 1980).

23. *Daily Depository Shipping List 9343*, 3rd Shipment (December 3, 1976), contains a list of libraries by state and library depository number that received the PRF for the pilot project.

24. In 1981 an annual subscription to the *GPO Sales Publications Reference File* was $85.

25. LeRoy C. Schwarzkopf, "The Monthly Catalog and Bibliographic Control of U.S. Government Publications," *Drexel Library Quarterly* 10: 83 (January-April 1974).

26. PDH 17: 1 (August 1976).

27. From the "Preface" to the 1981 *Serials Supplement*.

28. The 1977 *Serials Supplement* in its first appearance was issued between the April and May issues of the *Monthly Catalog.* The following year it appeared between the February and March issues. In 1979 and 1980 the *Serials Supplement* was published before the January *Monthly Catalog.*

29. PDH 44:4 (February 1981).

30. PDH 47:3 (August 1981).

31. Letter, James Bennett Childs, to the writer, November 12, 1976.

32. Paul Axel-Lute, "Recent Developments in Federal Documents," *Law Library Journal* 71: 250 (May 1978).

33. Joe Morehead, "A Status Report on the Monthly Catalog and Serials Supplement," *The Serials Librarian* 4: 137-39 (Winter 1979).

34. From a review by LeRoy C. Schwarzkopf in *American Reference Books Annual* (1975), entry 102, pp. 47-48.

35. DttP 9: 246 (November 1981).

36. For comprehensive summaries of arguments concerning this enduring problem, see Forrest C. Palmer, "Simmons vs. Schwarzkopf: The Great Class(ification) Debate," *Southeastern Librarian* (Fall 1977), pp. 163-66; and Michael Waldo, "An Historical Look at the Debate over How to Organize Federal Government Documents in Depository Libraries," *Government Publications Review* 4: 319-29 (1977).

37. John L. Andriot (ed.), *Guide to U.S. Government Publications, Volume 1* (McLean, VA: Documents Index, 1978), p. ix.

4

Depository Library System

BACKGROUND

Before designated depositories were established, and before the Printing Act of 1895 established a systematic approach, special legislation was passed at various times which provided for the printing of copies of the House and Senate *Journals*. These were issued in sufficient number to be distributed to the executives of the several states and to each of the state and territorial legislatures. Provision was also made at times to supply the acts, documents, and reports, as well as the *Journals*, to incorporated universities and colleges in each state and to incorporated historical societies throughout the country.

During the Thirteenth Congress, second session, Joint Resolution 1 of December 27, 1813 (3 *Stat*. 140) directed that "for every future Congress" a limit of 200 copies in addition to the usual number were to be transmitted to institutions outside the federal establishment, "and this, of course, was more than sufficient for the needs of that early day."[1] That number was increased "from 200 to 250 by Joint Resolution no. 5 of July 20, 1840 (5 *Stat*. 409) and to 300 by Joint Resolution no. 5 of April 30, 1844 (5 *Stat*. 717). The depository library program was formally established by a series of two resolutions in 1857 and 1858 and an Act of 1859." The 1857 resolution transferred "responsibility for distribution of the journals and documents from the Department of State to the Department of Interior" and authorized the Secretary of Interior to distribute public documents to "such colleges, public libraries, athenaeums, literary and scientific institutions, boards of trade, or public associations as may be designated by him." The 1858 resolution provided for congressional designation and the Act of 1859 incorporated senatorial designation. Thus the principle of representative designation as the cornerstone of the depository library system was established.[2]

In 1869 legislation established a "position of Superintendent of Public Documents in the Department of the Interior with the responsibility for distributing public documents to depository libraries, and to other officials and institutions authorized by law." The landmark Printing Act of 1895 (28 *Stat*. 601) consolidated earlier laws concerning the preparation and distribution of public documents; its primary effect was "to increase the categories of materials which were distributed to depository libraries," but it also established a "systematic program for bibliographic control" by authorizing the creation of the *Monthly*

Catalog and the famous *Document Catalog* (see Chapter 6). This 1895 legislation also expanded the system to include other than senatorial and representative designation, establishing the first "by law" depositories that included state libraries, libraries within several executive departments, and the libraries of West Point and Annapolis. Other provisions of the 1895 Printing Act set the pattern for deposit and control.[3] Indeed, with several amendments over the years that were relatively minor, the 1895 legislation existed without comprehensive review and change for sixty-seven years.

By 1962 the scheme included 594 depository libraries located in all of the states and most of the territories. The mechanics of distribution allowed "at least one mailing a day" to every depository. But changes in the demographic pattern, owing to redistricting and to economic shifts, created the need for new depositories in areas where no vacancies for an additional designation existed. Moreover, depository libraries were unable to dispose of documents no longer needed or those that could not be housed properly, and some librarians complained that they lacked important "non-GPO" publications, which were excluded from depository distribution. On the other hand, they faulted the existing system for its inadequacies in supplying important GPO documents. In response to these and other complaints, the GPO and the Superintendent of Documents applied their efforts to effect new legislation. The result, the Depository Library Act of 1962, represented the most significant major changes in depository legislation since the Printing Act of 1895.[4]

The Depository Library Act of 1962 (76 *Stat.* 352), as amended, is codified as Chapter 19 of Title 44, *United States Code*, "Public Printing and Documents." In addition, a manual, *Instructions to Depository Libraries*, has been published and revised from time to time. According to the prefatory note, it is "designed to provide guidance regarding the duties and privileges of libraries designated as depositories for U.S. Government publications."

All documents librarians working in designated depository libraries must be familiar with the provisions of 44 U.S.C. 1901 *et seq.*, the *Instructions* as noted, and current information on depository developments. The latter may be found in issues of *Documents to the People, Public Documents Highlights, Administrative Notes* issued irregularly by the Library and Statutory Distribution Service, the annual legislative branch appropriations hearings of the House of Representatives and Senate, and notices found in the *Depository Shipping List*. In addition, articles, columns, and reviews that appear in library journals like *Government Publications Review, Drexel Library Quarterly, Microform Review, Law Library Journal*, and others become obligatory reading. Because developments and changes in the administration and procedures of the system tend to fluctuate with a rapidity not evident in earlier years, it is the professional task to keep abreast of current trends.

CURRENT DEVELOPMENTS AND PRACTICES

While our concern will focus on the general depository system, a number of agencies have specialized depository provisions. These include maps and charts issued by the Geological Survey, National Ocean Survey, and Defense Mapping Agency, HUD "planning reports," patents, and the like. One reason for special deposit arrangements has been to accommodate unusual handling or storage conditions. Thus the map-producing agencies established their own deposit systems with a number of libraries. Many libraries which participate in the general depository program administered by the Superintendent of Documents also serve as depositories for one or more of the specialized categories. Unfortunately, some of the special programs are no longer admitting new libraries into their system. Moreover, many of these agencies do not publish information about their arrangements with the consistency or specificity found in the general depository system.

The present general depository system is a twofold structure consisting of over 1,300 *selective* depository institutions and over 50 *regional* depository libraries. As the word suggests, *selective* depositories may choose from the thousands of items available those categories that will meet the needs of their customers. The creation of regionals, a distinctive achievement of the 1962 legislation, assures receipt of at least one copy of every available depository publication. Designated regionals have been chosen from already existing selective depository libraries and are governed by the provisions of 44 U.S.C. 1912 and Section 2 of the *Instructions to Depository Libraries* (1977 revision). They are obliged to serve the selective institutions within their region through interlibrary loan, reference service, and assistance in the disposal of unwanted government publications. And in 1979 the Superintendent of Documents determined "that regional libraries will be supplied with both hard copy and microfiche of converted GPO items. However, a regional must retain only one format of the document, as part of its permanent collection. It may dispose of the other format if desired, and should offer it to the other depositories in its region."[5]

In addition to the standard representative and senatorial designations, special legislation has given several kinds of institutions an opportunity to participate in the general depository system: libraries of executive departments, service academies, and independent agencies (44 U.S.C. 1907); highest state appellate court libraries (44 U.S.C. 1915); accredited law school libraries (44 U.S.C. 1916); and others. The majority of depositories, however, are academic libraries. Recent statistics have indicated that almost 60 percent of regional depositories and 65 percent of all depositories are affiliated with institutions of higher education.[6]

Under the provisions of 44 U.S.C. 1912, each state (and Puerto Rico) may have two regional depositories. But because nothing in Title 44 *requires* that states participate in the regional structure at all, the pattern of regional institutions is skewed. Most states have found that one regional serves the needs of their selective depositories adequately. Some states, however, have two regionals, while some states have none. The states of New Hampshire and Vermont are served by the University of Maine's regional depository in Orono. Since there is no legal requirement, the GPO can only resort to moral suasion. Officials would like to see this decade as one that will bring regional depository service to all fifty states. For states lacking regional service, GPO has offered to "have a specialist on the subject speak to library associations, documents round tables, and similar groups" in those recalcitrant states.[7]

One glaring weakness in the system involves the constitutional mandate for redistricting after each decennial census. In a number of instances one finds three or more depository libraries in the same congressional district, all designated by representatives. The 1962 legislation increased the number of congressional designations from one to two, but this did not meet the population needs in a shifting and changing demographic picture. As Nakata points out, while some districts carry more than the maximum number of depositories, "in other areas there are unused designations. This is because, once designated, a depository library remains one until the library wishes to discontinue its status or until the designation is removed by the Superintendent of Documents."[8]

COOPERATIVE ARRANGEMENTS

The Superintendent of Documents encourages the development of cooperative storage and access arrangements between depository and non-depository libraries as long as appropriate conditions for use are maintained. One such arrangement reported in the literature involves two New York State institutions. Troy Public Library, a selective depository, works closely with Rensselaer Polytechnic Institute (RPI), a distinguished private engineering school whose Richard G. Folsom Library is a non-depository institution. Scientific and technical items that Troy Public's clientele do not use are housed at Folsom Library, where they serve the extensive research programs of the school. Administratively, Troy Public "remains the sole official contact with the Superintendent of Documents," while those categories of publications held at RPI are as "accessible to the general public [as] they would be at the depository itself."[9] The arrangement has permitted Troy Public to increase its selection of non-scientific and technical series, and the savings to RPI, where tools like *Index Medicus* and *Government Reports Announcements and Index* remain expensive subscriptions, have been considerable. Similar cooperative endeavors expand the availability of government documents to user groups within the spirit and letter of Title 44, Chapter 19.

DEPOSITORY LIBRARY COUNCIL

The Depository Library Council to the Public Printer is a fifteen-member group of librarians appointed by the Public Printer to provide advice and practical assistance to the staff of the Government Printing Office. The Council operates under a charter and by-laws adopted in 1975 and holds open meetings, announced in the *Federal Register*, twice a year. Each year five new members are appointed to serve for a period of three years.

The Council issues an annual report based on the minutes of the semiannual meetings held during that period. It has a committee structure that deals effectively with bibliographic control, GPO operations, depository libraries, micrographics, and, of course, ad hoc committees for select problems. Travel and other expenses for Council members to attend meetings are borne by Superintendent of Documents appropriations.

A typical agenda at a semiannual meeting includes a report by the Superintendent on the status of resolutions passed at the previous meeting of the Council, and addresses and status reports by GPO staff members, Council members, and invited guests. Working sessions of the committees and discussion and approval of draft resolutions comprise the remainder of the two-and-one-half-day meetings.

In theory the Council advises the Public Printer on behalf of the larger community of documents librarians. But although Council resolutions and recommendations are studied by the Public Printer, he is not bound by the Council's deliberations.

STANDARDS AND GUIDELINES

The Council worked during 1974 on a statement of guidelines that would "provide an inspection tool for the Superintendent of Documents, a guide for the education of documents librarians, and a tool for communication with library administrators."[10] Two reports emerged from this effort, one covering minimum standards for the depository system and the other setting forth guidelines for the system. Published as a *Special Supplement* to the December 1975 issue of *Public Documents Highlights*, the two separate reports were brought together under the rubric *Proposed Standards & Guidelines*.

A number of individual librarians as well as professional groups responded to the first draft. Comments on the 1975 version were considered at the October 1976 meeting of the Council and changes were made. The revised *Proposed Standards & Guidelines* as adopted by the Council in October and amended in April 1977 were published as a *Special Supplement* to the August 1977 issue of *Public Documents Highlights*. The statements are designed to reflect a recommended level of conduct for both the GPO and for designated depository libraries in carrying out the objectives of the system. They were superseded by an official GPO publication, *Guidelines for the Depository Library System as Adopted by the Depository Library Council to the Public Printer, October 18, 1977* (GP 1.23/4: D44/978), and contain much useful information on the role of the Superintendent of Documents, designation of new depository libraries, cooperation with GPO, regional depository library requirements and obligations, and, in "Appendix A," a list of twenty-three titles of federal publications that all depository libraries should subscribe to.

MICROFORM DISTRIBUTION

The GPO micropublishing venture and some of its implications were discussed in Chapter 2. A *Policy Statement* issued by the Superintendent of Documents in August 1981 reaffirmed earlier decisions and set the tone for the future. The *Statement* unequivocally declared that distribution of categories "will be made in microfiche rather than paper format, whenever possible, to minimize the cost of printing and binding and help alleviate space problems in depository libraries." Moreover, the *Statement* reiterated GPO's ongoing policy of reviewing series published in paper format for suitability in converting to microfiche. "Primary considerations will be the physical characteristics of a publication, the nature of its content, and its relationship to other publications. Consistency of format and maintenance of the usability of depository collections will be continuing objectives." Following that declaration, the *Policy Statement* briefly outlined four types of publications "which usually will not be converted to microfiche."[11]

Expanded guidelines covering both publications suitable for microfiche conversion and those that should remain in a paper format were issued by the director of the Library and Statutory Distribution Service and published in the September 1981 issue of *Documents to the People*. Categories to be converted to a microformat include statistical publications "other than major reference works"; scientific, technical, and research publications; conference proceedings; annual reports; and telephone directories, indexes of research grant recipients, "or other such publications of a highly specialized nature."

Types of publications "which will normally not be converted to microfiche" include materials whose physical characteristics would make them unusable in microform or which would not be cost effective to convert, popular didactic pamphlets intended for the general public, standard reference works, and dated periodicals in a magazine or newsletter format. Explanations and examples of both categories followed in greater detail than the GPO had hitherto assayed, suggesting a specific blueprint for the future. Appended to these guidelines was a partial list of about eighty "reference tools that should stay in paper," a list that was to be updated in the future. The list contains familiar titles illustrative of the categories deemed inadvisable to be converted to microfiche.

One of the categories GPO exempted from microfiche conversion was materials "which are updated by changes, transmittals, etc. These will not be fiched because they are intended to be interfiled and would be hard to use on fiche."[12] This exempted class clearly included bills and resolutions, for without a computer-output-microfilm (COM) cumulation, bills with their numerous amendments and motions suffer a scattering effect among the fiche and even on scattered coordinates of the fiche. Despite this manifest inconvenience to users, the Depository Library Council to the Public Printer, with the enthusiastic endorsement of GPO, approved a resolution in April 1981 recommending that bills (and many other categories) be converted to a microfiche-only format. This recommendation became official in June 1981 (see Chapter 2), and as a result a number of depository libraries that wished to continue receiving this item in paper were denied that option.

During FY 1982 the number of titles distributed in paper copy declined 32 percent from 25,000 to an estimated 17,000. The reasons given for this decline by GPO officials were the moratorium on government publications established by presidential edict and the increased conversion of GPO titles to microfiche as a result of FY 1982 budget cuts.[13]

At the same time, depository libraries have been acquiring a greater number of non-GPO publications, those produced by the agencies using their own equipment and funds. Because of greater microfiche distribution of both GPO and non-GPO titles, GPO reported that in the spring of 1982 there were already "about 6,600 titles in the backlog for conversion to microfiche." And although the federal agencies reduced their output of individual titles or series, the amount of depository distribution has increased. For example, FY 1982 witnessed the distribution of about 70,000 titles as compared to 53,000 in FY 1981. "Besides the 17,000 paper copy titles, the microfiche titles include the 6,600 backlogged titles; 10,000 block statistics maps; 10,000 bills and resolutions; and 26,400 miscellaneous publications in microfiche."[14]

While regionals receive depository items in both formats, selective depository institutions, as noted, are able to receive certain categories in a paper or a microfiche format, but not both. GPO's newsletter, Library and Statutory Distribution Service *Administrative Notes*, in its April 1982 issue, listed titles to date that were offered in this choice of formats. The list included the *Code of Federal Regulations*, the bound edition of the *Congressional Record*, House and Senate *Journals*, Congressional Serial Set reports and documents, and a lengthy list of congressional committee issuances. There is little doubt that the future will see many additional series added to this list.

MICROFICHE MANAGEMENT

Concern among documents librarians about the proper care of microfiche prompted GPO to issue suggestions and guidelines. The depository library program uses diazo microfiche, which are durable and can last fifty years or longer. Although GPO does not contract for vesicular microfiche, it does receive some from government agencies and distributes them. At one time, GPO sent silver halide fiche to regional depositories only, but many commercial micro-publishers sell silver halide microforms and stress their archival quality.

The envelopes which hold GPO microfiche are acid-free, as are inserted dividers. Writing or using a rubber stamp on the envelopes requires the use of acid-free ink and removal of the fiche before writing or stamping. Other suggestions involve the appropriate temperature and humidity levels; removing fiche before painting a room; avoiding plastic boxes for storage; protecting the fiche from chemicals, urban and industrial air pollution, gas fumes, and the like.[15]

While management and organization of materials in a microformat are important considerations for libraries, user needs and preferences have been less well addressed. Few would deliberately choose microform over paper copy given similar or identical conditions. If government publications on microfiche are to serve the needs of library patrons, they must satisfy the criteria suggested by Charles R. McClure—bibliographic accessibility, physical availability, and a level of professional service for document and information retrieval at least equal to that for paper copy materials.[16]

Because distribution of government publications in a microformat is now the rule rather than the exception, serving the user wisely and well assumes an urgency. And because microfiche conversion is demonstrably cost effective, it is seen by GPO officials as a budgetary solution. Whether librarians and users envisage microform as a desideratum remains to be seen.

DISCARDING PROCEDURES

An important feature of the role of regional depository libraries is that by virtue of their mandatory retention of all depository categories, selective depositories may dispose of unwanted materials after a period of five years. Procedures for disposal are outlined in Section 2 of the *Instructions to Depository Libraries*. The *Instructions* state that the regional "may refuse to grant permission for disposal of any publication that it feels should be kept by one of its depositories for a longer period of time," but this interpretation of the statutes governing disposal is dubious.

However, Section 11 of the *Instructions* consists of a list of fourteen types of material that can be discarded by all depository libraries, including regionals. Note well that these categories of documents *have nothing to do* with the five-year disposal policy of selective depository libraries. The language of Section 11 preceding the list is important: "Below are listed some of the types of material which may be disposed of by all libraries." Because the list is exemplary rather than exhaustive, the need for a more definitive list prompted action. A "Superseded Documents Committee" composed of five documents librarians was formed at a meeting of regional depositories held in conjunction with the Depository Library Council in St. Paul, Minnesota in April 1980. A list was drafted and, after Council approval, was distributed to depository libraries by the Government Printing Office in June 1981. Entitled *List of Superseded Depository Documents*, it is a mimeographed, thirty-two page issuance containing about 500 categories arranged alphanumerically by SuDocs classification with reference to depository item number and series title and with brief instructions for discarding.

Most titles and series on this list are obvious candidates for discarding. For instance, one should keep the latest issue only of an agency telephone directory, discard looseleaf pages of a subscription service upon receipt of revised pages, throw out obsolete Civil Service examination announcements, etc. But because this is not a mandatory.disposal list, librarians must exercise care and judgment in discarding. For purposes of scholarship or archival control, a research library may wish to hold earlier editions of an important work. Again, concern for user needs must transcend any preconceived notions of the librarian's housekeeping convenience, however tempting.

INSPECTION PROGRAM

According to 44 U.S.C. 1909, "The Superintendent of Documents shall make firsthand investigation of conditions for which need is indicated and include the results of investigations in his annual report." But without adequate staffing, the Superintendent could not carry out even the spirit, much less the letter, of the law. 44 U.S.C. 1909 also requires that the "designated depository libraries shall report to the Superintendent of Documents at least every two years concerning their condition." This is accomplished by a biennial report, but before an adequate inspection program was developed, the Superintendent relied on the depository institutions themselves to judge the effectiveness of their operation.

Finally, appropriations permitted the creation of two depository library inspectors who assumed their duties in November 1974; and during FY 1975, 224 depository libraries in seventeen states were inspected. Subsequently, a third inspector was hired and a schedule was established that allowed the inspectors to visit approximately one-third of the designated depositories each year.

In general, the duties of the inspectors encompass the extent to which the depository library fulfills the obligations of the program as set forth in Chapter 19 of Title 44, the *Instructions*, and the *Standards & Guidelines* developed by the Depository Library Council. Librarians are notified in advance of the inspection visit, and criticism is proffered "in a spirit of helpfulness, rather than fault-finding." The inspections are designed in part to help documents librarians petition administrators for an upgrading of services.[17]

Nevertheless, in FY 1979-80 the inspectors found that "almost one-sixth of the depositories ... were unable to comply with the minimum" standards upon which they were evaluated. Significant problems included the "lack of or inappropriate kinds of staff and/or space," the need for cabinets and microfiche readers and reader-printers, and the absence of adequate record-keeping, the latter being in large part a problem of staff shortages.[18]

Severe deficiencies can result in a depository being placed on probation and reinspected. Occasionally a recidivous depository is shorn of its designation, but this occurs infrequently. Despite the shortcomings of inspections,[19] the program has been adjudged successful, and GPO hopes eventually to maintain the number of inspectors at five.[20]

LISTS OF DEPOSITORY LIBRARIES

As noted in Chapter 3, the *Monthly Catalog* sustained a long tradition of providing a list of depository libraries by state and city in its September issue. After having been dropped from the 1979 and 1980 *Monthly Catalog*, it was reinstated in the March 1981 and October 1981 issues. Another list was published as an appendix in the 1981/1982 issue of *The United States Directory of Federal Regional Structure*, pp. 151-202. Apparently, it was the first time this publication was used for such a purpose. Like the *Monthly Catalog* arrangement, depository libraries were organized by state and city.

The most complete list appears in *Government Depository Libraries: The Present Law Governing Designated Depository Libraries*, a Joint Committee Print issued by the JCP. Revised annually, the committee print lists depository libraries in two distinct ways: 1) by state and city, and 2) by state and within state by congressional district (including the at-large senatorial designations). Other parts of this publication include a narrative overview of the system, a statistical breakdown of the types of designations (e.g., state libraries, executive departments, law school libraries, etc.), and a list of GPO bookstores and distribution centers.

The directory information in the committee print includes address, phone number, year of designation, and a discrete depository library number supplied by GPO for each library. In the breakdown by congressional district, the type of designation is given as well. Although the committee print contains the most information, the user would be best served by the list in the *Monthly Catalog*, since the latter is found in numerous non-depository institutions and is visible to patrons who use government reference services.

SELECTION TOOLS AND PROCEDURES

Several bibliographic aids produced by the government and by commercial publishers are used by depository libraries for selection and control. A summary of their purpose and use follows.

ITEM CARDS

44 U.S.C. 1904 requires that the Superintendent of Documents "issue a classified list of Government publications in suitable form, containing annotations of contents and listed by item identification numbers to facilitate the selection of only those publications needed by depository libraries." Two sets of 3x5-inch cards are furnished depository libraries at the time of their designation. One set is retained by the library for its records; the other is used to make selections. The library returns to the Superintendent of Documents one item card for each series desired, properly identified with the library's assigned depository number. Ongoing item selections are made from the original deck and from special "Surveys" that are announced from time to time. The mimeographed numbered "Survey" is accompanied by item cards in duplicate for each category offered. If the depository institution wishes to subscribe to a newly offered item, it simply returns one of the enclosed item cards marked with the library's depository number to the Library Division of GPO. The "Survey" is issued as a

separate numbered *Shipping List* and whenever possible includes, in addition to an annotation of the item, a sample copy for evaluation.

In most instances the assigned item number remains the controlling designation for that category regardless of a change of title or reorganization of the issuing agency. Items do not reflect the number or ratio of publications to categories. For example, libraries selecting item 150 will receive one copy of the annual *Statistical Abstract of the United States.* On the other hand, choosing item 557 will insure receipt of all issues of the *Monthly Catalog* for the year. Other items cover series with an indeterminate number of individual issues: slip laws, treaties and agreements, Supreme Court reports, bills and resolutions. Moreover, an item number assigned to a series may also govern the distribution of a closely related series. Thus the Census Bureau's Computer Tape Series (C 3.240/3:) and Geography Series (C 3.240/6:) are both received under item 142-D even though the class notation for the two series differs slightly.

To distinguish between items available to depository libraries in paper copy or on microfiche, a system of letter suffixes has been adopted. Thus hearings of the House Committee on Education and Labor are received by libraries in paper copy under item 1015-A and on microfiche under item 1015-B. Many other items have both letter and number suffixes, but these were assigned for other purposes and do not necessarily signify a distinction between microfiche or paper copy distribution.

The Depository Distribution Information System (DDIS), an online automated program, enables GPO to produce item cards, the *List of Classes* and other printed guides, and the *GPO Depository Union List of Item Selections* (GP 3.32/2: yr./issue) published quarterly on microfiche and distributed to all depository libraries. Moreover, a computer printout, *List of Item Selections*, issued quarterly, permits selective depositories to add or drop item categories which become effective on a quarterly schedule.[21]

Automation of item selection records at GPO also permits faster claims verification. This is important because of the increase in the number of categories available to depository libraries. At the beginning of 1982 there were over 5,300 active items, and the average number of items selected by depository institutions exceeded 1,500.

Figure 3 shows typical annotated item cards that accompanied "Surveys."

DEPOSITORY SHIPPING LIST

The *Depository Shipping List* (sometimes entitled *Daily Depository Shipping List*) is a numbered series that registers the items mailed from GPO's Library and Statutory Distribution Service to depository libraries. Every depository library receives a copy of the same *Shipping List* with each shipment of depository publications. The list serves as an invoice for the shipment. Upon receipt of a shipment of materials, selective depositories must check the item numbers against their active item cards to determine whether any publications have been sent by mistake or have been inadvertently omitted from the shipment. Regionals, of course, are obliged to receive every item listed on every *Shipping List.*

Arranged by item number, the *Shipping List* includes SuDocs class number and title. Title entries indicate stock number and price for GPO sales publications. As mentioned, "Surveys" come with *Shipping Lists* and carry a *Shipping List* number as well as an individual survey number. Claims for

Figure 3
Item Cards

Item No. 0431-K-07

ENVIRONMENTAL PROTECTION AGENCY

Quarterly Progress Report, Nationwide EP 1.92:
  Urban Runoff Program
Summarizes the progress and status of the Program,
which functions to assess urban runoff and to support
regional State, and local program participants. Contains
tables, graphs, and project summary sheets on State and
local grantees.

Survey 80-68   Depository Library No.

Item No. 0300-E

    PERSONNEL MANAGEMENT OFFICE
Performance (vol. nos. and nos.)   PM 1.34:
Folder concerned with broadening and improving Fede-
ral productivity measurement. Will contain overviews
of productivity measurement documents published by the
Office on subjects such as measuring common administra-
tive services and assessing productivity of operating
personnel offices. Each issue is expected to contain
about 6 pages. Published 8 times a year by the
Office's Workforce Effectiveness and Development
Group.
Survey 80-71   Depository Library No.

(Item cards continue on page 82)

Figure 3 (cont'd)

Item No. 0900-C-09

    AGENCY FOR INTERNATIONAL DEVELOPMENT, State
       Department
<u>Technical Series Bulletins</u>   S 18.50:
   (numbered)
Series includes information papers, bibliographies, etc.,
on agricultural technology for developing world areas
such as Pacific and Indian Oceans, islands and tropics
in general, treating such subjects as rapid crop improvement using tissue culture technique. May contain
tables and many black and white photographs. Number
and pagination of publications to be issued a year cannot be anticipated.
Survey 80-66   Depository Library No.

nonreceipt of publications required in the past the submission of a separate "Claim Form." Today the claim form is located at the bottom of the list; missing titles are claimed by circling item numbers and SuDocs class numbers and returning the list to the Library Division (SLL) within a prescribed period of time.

Shipping Lists have been sequentially numbered since 1951 to include items issued in paper copy and microfiche. For a while, items sent in microform carried only the letter "M" following the *Shipping List* number. Thus, for example, *Depository Shipping List No. 16,568-M* (November 12, 1981), designated as "Microfiche Number 60," showed only those items sent to depositories in that format.

However, in 1982 a new numbering system was established for titles distributed on microfiche beginning with "Microfiche #1" and distinguished by the suffix "M" following the *Shipping List* number. The suffix "S" is used for *Shipping Lists* that register separate shipments; these usually record five to ten titles, and each title is shipped separately due to its large size.

Occasionally a depository library's request for items in paper copy cannot be honored because GPO has not received sufficient quantities for distribution. When this happens, a separate *Shipping List* is prepared by the Library Services Section of the Depository Administration Branch. These special *Shipping Lists* include a note from GPO to the effect that efforts to obtain enough paper copies of the title have been unsuccessful. As can be readily seen, this mix causes a problem for internal management and control of government publications in a library.

The *Shipping List* is perhaps the single most important internal working document for the management of depository collections. It is typically the first notification of new publications and projected series, is the "only convenient, publicly available source of information on individual pieces of many serial publications," provides immediate notice of agency reorganization and attendant reclassification of items, affords "instant processing with a minimum of cataloging" so that patrons can access the materials without waiting for the printed indexes,[22] and serves, along with GPO's monthly mimeographed *Administrative Notes*, as a vehicle for transmitting special policy announcements or news of importance to depository librarians. Although its chief and obvious function involves the depository library program, it is also available for sale from the Superintendent of Documents where non-depository libraries may use it to order sales publications.

Figure 4 shows two typical *Shipping Lists* announcing titles sent to libraries in paper copy and titles shipped on microfiche.

Figure 4
Depository Shipping Lists

GPO Form 3482
(R 9-81)

Box Number 78   **Depository Shipping List No.** __17,173__

__2nd__ Shipment of __June 15, 1982__   Page __1__ of __2__

Claims for nonreceipt of publications on this list under item numbers previously selected by a library must be postmarked within 60 calendar days of receipt of this shipment. When filing a claim for missing publications, please return a copy of the list on which they appear and circle the item numbers that are missing.

ITEM NUMBER	CLASSIFICATION NUMBER	TITLE
		WE ARE USING THE INFROMATION FROM THE RETURNED NOVEMBER 1981 (4TH QUARTER) COMPUTER PRINTOUTS.
14-A	A 1.68:1314	National Agricultural Library Online Training Classes, Program Aid No. 1314, June 1982
80-G	A 13.28:C 19/4	Caribbean National Forest, Puerto Rico, 1981 (Map)
142-A	C 3.158:M 20 J(82)-4	Current Industrial Reports: Fats and Oils - Oilseed Crushings, M20J(82)-4, April 1982
142-A	C 3.158:M 28 C(82)-3	Current Industrial Reports: Industrial Gases, M28C(82)-3, March 1982
142-A	C 3.158:M 30 E(82)-3	Current Industrial Reports: Plastics Bottles, M30E(82)-3, March 1982
142-A	C 3.158:M 36 D(82)-3	Current Industrial Reports: Electric Lamps, M36D(82)-3, March 1982
142-A	C 3.158:MQ-23 X(82)-1	Current Industrial Reports: Sheets, Pillowcases, and Towels, MQ-23X(82)-1, First Quarter 1982

Mail Claims to:

U.S. GOVERNMENT PRINTING OFFICE
SUPERINTENDENT OF DOCUMENTS
LIBRARY DIVISION (SLL)
WASHINGTON, D.C. 20402

Signature of librarian authorized to make claim: _____

CLEARLY PRINT OR TYPE ADDRESS AND INFORMATION ON MAILING LABEL.

U.S. GOVERNMENT PRINTING OFFICE
SUPERINTENDENT OF DOCUMENTS
WASHINGTON, D.C. 20402

OFFICIAL BUSINESS

Penalty for Private Use
$300

(LIB# _____) (SL# __17,173__)

Name _____

Street address _____

City and State _____ Zip Code _____

POSTAGE AND FEES PAID
U.S. GOVERNMENT PRINTING OFFICE
377
PRINTED MATTER

(Figure 4 continues on page 84)

Figure 4 (cont'd)

GPO Form 3452
(R 9–81)

Depository Shipping List No. <u>576-M</u>

<u>5th</u> Shipment of <u>October 20, 1982</u> Page <u>1</u> of <u>2</u>

> Claims for nonreceipt of publications on this list under item numbers previously selected by a library must be postmarked within 60 calendar days of receipt of this shipment. When filing a claim for missing publications, please return a copy of the list on which they appear and circle the item numbers that are missing.

Microfiche #576

ITEM NUMBER	CLASSIFICATION NUMBER	TITLE
		WE ARE USING THE INFORMATION FROM THE RETURNED APRIL 1982 (2ND QUARTER) COMPUTER PRINTOUTS.
208-C-1	C 55.13:EDIS 34	An Application of Stochastic Forecasting to Monthly Averaged 700-MB Heights, NOAA Technical Report EDIS 34, U.S. Department of Commerce, May 1982
429-H-4	E 1.89:0009/6	Geothermal Progress Monitor, Progress Report, DOE/CE-0009/6, U.S. Department of Energy, June 1982
	E 1.89:0023	The Fourth Report to Congress, Comprehensive Program and Plan for Federal Energy Education, Extension and Information Activities, DOE/CE-0023, U.S. Department of Energy, May 1981
429-P	E 1.18:20622-1	Putting Renewable Energy to Work in Cities, DOE/ET/20622-1, U.S. Dept. of Energy, June 1982, S/N 061-000-00591-9*$11.0(
431-I-11	EP 1.23:600/3-82-024	Methodology for Overland and Instream Migration and Risk Assessment of Pesticides, EPA-600/3-82-024, U.S. Environmental Protection Agency, May 1982
467-A-1	HE 20.8202:Ac 1	Drug Program Report, Academic Linkage and Credentialing, U.S. Department of Health and Human Services, 1982
483-E-9	EP 4.19:C 63	A Review of Standards of Performance for New Stationary Sources-Coal Preparation Plants, U.S. Environmental Protection Agency, December 1980
505-A	HE 20.7008:R 11/2	A Guide to Radiation Safety in the Laboratory, U.S. Department of Health and Human Services, June 14, 1982
507-L-2	HE 20.3502:R 31/4/981	Research Grants, October 1981 Data Book, U.S. Department of Health and Human Services, 1981

Mail Claims to:

U.S. GOVERNMENT PRINTING OFFICE
SUPERINTENDENT OF DOCUMENTS
LIBRARY DIVISION (SLL)
WASHINGTON, D.C. 20402

Signature of librarian authorized to make claim: _____

CLEARLY PRINT OR TYPE ADDRESS AND INFORMATION ON MAILING LABEL.

U.S. GOVERNMENT PRINTING OFFICE
SUPERINTENDENT OF DOCUMENTS
WASHINGTON, D.C. 20402

OFFICIAL BUSINESS

Penalty for Private Use
$300

(LIB# _____) (SL# _____)

Name _____

Street address _____

City and State _____ Zip Code _____

POSTAGE AND FEES PAID
U.S. GOVERNMENT PRINTING OFFICE
377

PRINTED MATTER

DOC/LIST

The value of a cumulated *Shipping List* has been manifest for many years and was formally recommended by a Government Documents Round Table (GODORT) Committee on Review of the Shipping List in 1980.[23] But it was left to a commercial publisher to package this concept. Transrep/Bibliographics of Denver, Colorado issues a biweekly cumulative record on microfiche of depository items listed on the *Shipping Lists*. Arranged by SuDocs classification notation, DOC/LIST is basically a shelflist and was first issued in a special cumulation of titles that were sent to depository libraries during the first six months of 1980. Currently, DOC/LIST is issued fortnightly with quarterly cumulations.

The publisher has included all the appropriate information found on the *Shipping Lists* and has added several features. Information on congressional hearings and committee prints has been expanded to include bill number and date of hearing or print. Certain series like Supreme Court reports have been rearranged to permit more effective access. A special feature includes a list of some sixteen periodicals mailed directly from the contractor or printer to subscribing depository libraries, serials which do *not* appear on the *Shipping Lists*.[24] Moreover, a complete listing of current titles within selected series like Country Study/Area Handbooks issued by the Department of the Army and Public Laws is found in the biweekly issues. An annual subscription to DOC/LIST includes the biweekly and quarterly cumulations.

LISTS OF DEPOSITORY ITEMS

Printed lists of classes of publications available to depository libraries are issued by the Office of the Superintendent of Documents, but they do not have the recency of the *Shipping Lists*. The well-known *List of Classes of United States Government Publications Available for Selection by Depository Libraries* (GP 3.24: yr./qtr.) is arranged by SuDocs classification number referencing series or item title and depository item number. Non-GPO items are noted on the *List of Classes*, and categories available in microfiche only are indicated by the symbol (MF).

A *List of Items for Selection by Depository Libraries* (GP 3.24: yr./app.) covers the same ground, but arrangement is by item number with reference to title and SuDocs class notation. *Inactive or Discontinued Items from the 1950 Revision of Classified List* (GP 3.24: yr./app.), issued as an "appendix" to the *List of Classes*, shows by item number those categories no longer available from the Superintendent. All these lists are revised periodically but between revisions must be updated by the *Shipping Lists* and "Surveys."

LOC/EX

A companion product to DOC/LIST published by Transrep/Bibliographics provides a current, expanded version of the *List of Classes*. Called LOC/EX, it is a monthly microfiche subscription that began July 1, 1980. Each monthly edition supersedes that for the previous month, while the January 1 edition includes a supplement showing all additions and deletions to the *List of Classes* for the previous year and should be retained for reference purposes.

Arranged like the *List of Classes*, LOC/EX includes several enhancing features. Series like County Business Patterns and Area Wage Surveys show state and item number. Other series such as Current Population Reports and Subject Bibliographies have been expanded by listing titles within the main series. There is a table of contents preceding the classified list, a section that cumulates additions and deletions, useful appendixes, and a government author/agency index. As one reviewer noted, those working with documents "have had the experience of having a publication or SuDocs number for a new series without being able to verify the name of the series or its predecessor, or of trying to determine the fate of a discontinued series. LOC/EX is a boon to the documents sleuth."[25]

CONCLUSION

In the years since the establishment of the Government Documents Round Table of the American Library Association, there have been several indications of growth and progress in the depository library program. Efforts have been made to include more maps and non-print materials into the general depository program. The Joint Committee on Printing has through its regulations given the program more support and visibility. The GPO has been responsive by virtue of its inspection program, workshops, creation of the Depository Library Council, and internal management improvements. And depository librarians, "no longer isolated in their institutions ..., have many means of communication and action open to them" through structured groups and associations.[26]

Nevertheless, all is not well. The collapse of Title 44 revision legislation in the Ninety-sixth Congress was a significant setback; provisions of H.R. 5424 (see Chapter 2) would have strengthened the program in several critical areas. Some sections of 44 U.S.C. Chapter 19 need to be rewritten and key terms redefined. Regional depositories, the linchpins of the system, have experienced space problems and, in LeRoy C. Schwarzkopf's judgment, are "in deep peril and in danger of collapsing from sheer volume." One solution is the establishment of "super regionals" situated on a "truly regional basis," which would dramatically reduce the present number but would allow those regionals not so designated to "weed their collections." Another proposal would create a regional network "built around existing computer-supported library networks." And there remains the perennial cry for "direct federal financial support," to which Congress has turned a deaf ear for many years.[27] None of these options are viewed as real possibilities for the near future.

It may still be true, as Schwarzkopf noted in 1978, that the present depository system — with all its faults — is generally an "effective and economical program to provide public access to official publications of the United States Government," publications used by a citizenry that would "have to buy or otherwise obtain" them "at far greater expense in time and money."[28] How effective this system of distribution continues to be in a decade where the political climate favors recision and retrenchment remains the central issue when one speaks of access to public information. The budget for administering the depository library program for FY 1983 was approximately $14.5 million, a minuscule federal expenditure. It is difficult to see how that sum can effectively discharge the mandate of 44 U.S.C. 1911, which states in part that depository libraries "shall make Government publications available for the free use of the general public."

REFERENCES

1. U.S. Congress, Joint Committee on Printing, *Government Depository Libraries: The Present Law Governing Designated Depository Libraries*, Joint Committee Print, 97th Cong., 1st Sess., rev. March 1981, pp. 3-4 (Y 4.P93/1:D44/yr.).

2. LeRoy C. Schwarzkopf, "Depository Libraries and Public Access," in *Collection Development and Public Access of Government Documents*, edited by Peter Hernon (Westport, CT: Meckler Publishing, 1982), pp. 9-10.

3. Ibid., pp. 10-12.

4. Carper W. Buckley, "Implementation of the Federal Depository Library Act of 1962," *Library Trends* 15: 27-28 (July 1966).

5. DttP 7: 140 (July 1979).

6. Yuri Nakata, *From Press to People: Collecting and Using U.S. Government Publications* (Chicago: American Library Association, 1979), pp. 20-21.

7. PDH 38: 1 (February 1980).

8. Nakata, p. 11.

9. Pat Molholt et al., "Cooperative Program for Collecting Government Documents between Depository and Non-Depository Libraries," *Science & Technology Libraries* 1: 36 (Winter 1980).

10. DttP 3: 21 (January 1975).

11. Superintendent of Documents *Policy Statement*, SOD 13, August 21, 1981. Subject: Format of Publications Distributed to Depository Libraries.

12. DttP 9: 217-20, 223 (September 1981).

13. DttP 10: 146 (July 1982).

14. Ibid.

15. *Administrative Notes* 2: 1 (March 1981); PDH 50: 12 (February 1982).

16. Charles R. McClure, "Administrative Integration of Microformated Government Publications: A Framework for Analysis," *Microform Review* 6: 267-69 (September 1977).

17. DttP 4: 18-19 (June 1976).

18. DttP 8: 301 (November 1980).

19. See *Government Publications Review* 7A: 449-52 (1980) for suggestions to improve the inspection program.

20. DttP 9: 259 (November 1981).

21. DttP 10: 68 (March 1982).

22. DttP 8: 217-19 (September 1980).

23. Ibid., p. 217.

24. A list of those periodicals was published in the June 1977 issue of *Public Documents Highlights*, p. 2.

25. DOC/LIST and LOC/EX were reviewed in *Government Publications Review* 8A: 368-70 (1981).

26. Bernadine E. Abbott Hoduski, "Federal Depository Library System," *Drexel Library Quarterly* 16: 7, 9-10 (October 1980).

27. LeRoy C. Schwarzkopf, "Regional Depositories in Peril: Or the Future Is Now," *Drexel Library Quarterly* 16: 19, 36-37 (October 1980).

28. LeRoy C. Schwarzkopf, "The Depository Library Program and Access by the Public to Official Publications of the United States Government," *Government Publications Review* 5: 155 (1978).

5

Technical Report Literature

BACKGROUND

Although the depository library system provides thousands of series to libraries, it does not encompass all federal publishing. For example, those publications in the *Monthly Catalog* lacking an item number and not distinguished by a "black dot" or bullet symbol (•) must be obtained by other than depository means. They may be GPO or non-GPO documentation; but whatever their provenance or publishing venue, they share a common lack of availability under the depository system. Broadly speaking, they may be identified as non-depository publications.

These issuances are available to individuals and institutions in several ways: from one's representative or senator, from the issuing agency, for sale by the Superintendent or other government agents, on subscription from Readex Microprint's non-depository series, from other commercial vendors like Congressional Information Service on microfiche or paper copy, from the Documents Expediting Project, and so forth. The latter, called DocEx, is located within the Exchange and Gift Division of the Library of Congress. For an annual fee, over 120 libraries and other organizations receive certain non-depository series. However, by arrangement the Expediter "continues to send the Superintendent of Documents one copy of each publication which it receives for inclusion in the *Monthly Catalog*."[1]

In addition to the publications produced by agencies that lie outside the depository program, there is a vast body of federally sponsored technical report literature that remains exempted from depository distribution. These publications reflect the federal commitment to research and development (R&D), a commitment made manifest by multitudes of contracts and grants awarded by federal agencies to corporations, universities, think tanks, specialized consultants, and professional associations and societies. This federal largesse in turn results in an outpouring of subsidized research reports whose bibliographic structure, sale, and distribution exist largely apart from the machinery of the Superintendent of Documents. Because the growth of this literature has been unsystematic, diffused, and rapid, it represents an often confusing domain. Indeed, as Fry suggests, the jungle of distribution systems at the federal level is nowhere more evident than in the dissemination of technical reports.... Commonly, each agency distributing its own reports started as a mission-oriented operation concerned with a limited body of information and with a limited clientele. This is reflected in the substantial differences in their operations that have developed during the past 25 years. The results have been confusion, sometimes duplication, and, not surprisingly, underutilization.[2]

To place the growth and diffusion of government-sponsored research literature in perspective, we must examine existing law and recognize that there is no clear consensus on the crucial matter of legislative intent, thus giving rise to interpretations that pit one interest group against another.

First, let us examine the provisions of 44 U.S.C. 1902. It states that publications of the federal government "shall be made available to depository libraries" with the following exceptions: "those distributed by their issuing components to be required for official use only or for strictly administrative or operational purposes which have no public interest or educational value and publications classified for reasons of national security." To these exemptions from the depository system, 44 U.S.C. 1903 adds another category: "so-called cooperative publications which must necessarily be sold in order to be self-sustaining."

Finally, let us review the brief and inadequate "definition" of a government publication found at 44 U.S.C. 1901, the beginning of Chapter 19 (Depository Library Program) of Title 44 of the *United States Code*: "Government publication, as used in this chapter, means informational matter which is published as an individual document at Government expense, or as required by law."

What does this mean? For one thing, the "definition" includes the phrase "at Government expense," which, though somewhat ambiguous, would seem *not to exclude* federally funded documentation from entry into the depository distribution system. On the other hand, 44 U.S.C. 1902 and 1903 appear to *exclude* the following categories no matter what their provenance:

1. Official use only;

2. Having no public interest or educational value;

3. Classified for national security;

4. "Cooperative" publications that need to be sold to be self-sustaining.

Fortunately, many publications produced by and for agencies have been and continue to be added to the depository system through the machinery of the "Survey." In recent years, a large number of items in the non-GPO documentation category have been added to the *List of Classes*, and these publications are scientific and technical in nature. Other important series, such as Senate executive reports and treaty documents, were removed from non-depository status. Is it to be presumed that these publications now possess an educational value or a public interest that for years they did not have? Moreover, publications classified for security reasons do become declassified and are made available to depository institutions. Internal administrative documents clearly having no public interest or educational value are not desired by depository libraries. But the cooperative publications of 44 U.S.C. 1903, those generated from subsidies "at Government expense," are still largely precluded from depository distribution.

The focus of this chapter will be on this subventionary literature. The systems discussed in the following pages comprise some of the major sources of acquiring and controlling these non-depository monographs, series, and serials. As Schmeckebier and Eastin pointed out, they "include many noteworthy and valuable contributions in almost every branch of the physical and social sciences" and "if approached by way of the subject matter ... would include almost every field of scientific inquiry and human interest."[3] Because they are sponsored by federal dollars or otherwise associated closely with government, the community of professional documents librarians includes them among its accepted responsibilities.

NATIONAL TECHNICAL INFORMATION SERVICE

The National Technical Information Service (NTIS) is a federal agency within the Department of Commerce. Established on September 2, 1970 to simplify and improve access to data files and scientific and technical reports produced by federal agencies and their contractors, it is obligated by law to recover its cost from sales to users. Its immediate predecessors were the Clearinghouse for Federal Scientific and Technical Information (1964-1970) and the Office of Technical Services (1946-1964).

NTIS is described in its promotional literature as the "central source for the public sale of U.S. Government-sponsored research, development, and engineering reports, as well as for foreign technical reports and other analyses prepared by national and local government agencies, their contractors or grantees." It purports to be a "cornerstone of the technological publishing structure in the United States," and is the central source for "federally generated machine processable data files." As of 1981 the NTIS collection exceeded 1.2 million titles, all of which are permanently available for sale, either "directly from the 80,000 titles in shelf stock or from the microfiche masters of titles less in demand." The sheer quantity of the operation permits NTIS to call itself "one of the world's leading processors of specialty information."[4]

THE NTIS CHARTER

NTIS is governed by the provisions of 15 U.S.C. 1151-1157. As an agency of the federal government dealing with so-called "cooperative publications" (44 U.S.C. 1903), NTIS consistently maintains that it is exempt from participation in the depository library program. The crucial provision is found at 15 U.S.C. 1153, which says in part:

> The Secretary [of Commerce] is authorized ... to establish ... a schedule or schedules of reasonable fees or charges for services performed or for documents or other publications furnished under this chapter.
>
> It is the policy of this chapter, to the fullest extent feasible and consistent with the objectives of this chapter, that each of the services

and functions provided herein shall be self-sustaining or self-liquidating and that the general public shall not bear the cost of publications and other services which are for the special use and benefit of private groups and individuals; but nothing herein shall be construed to require the levying of fees or charges for services performed or publications furnished to any agency or instrumentality of the Federal Government, or for publications which are distributed pursuant to reciprocal arrangements for the exchange of information or which are otherwise issued primarily for the general benefit of the public.

In 1974 the Public Printer asked the Comptroller General of the United States to decide whether the Depository Library Act of 1962 is applicable to publications sold by NTIS. His ruling (Decision Number B-114829, June 27, 1975) was lengthy, but the last paragraph, which expressed his conclusions, was published in *Documents to the People*:

> To summarize, we agree with NTIS that its publications may generally be regarded as "cooperative publications." We also agree that those NTIS publications of a specialized and limited interest nature are to be self-sustaining under 15 U.S.C. 1153 and are therefore exempt from the Depository Library Act under 44 U.S.C. 1903. At the same time, we conclude that both statutes, as well as the legislative history discussed herein, indicate a different treatment for NTIS publications that are "issued primarily for the general benefit of the public." Thus we agree with GPO that the latter are subject to the Library Act. It is recognized that it may be difficult to apply precisely the foregoing distinction; and this task must be left to resolution between NTIS and GPO. However, we are inclined to favor the general framework indicated in GPO's letter to us, which suggests coverage for "... certain serial publications (by NTIS); e.g., *Government Reports Announcements and Index* and the *GRA Annual Index*, which are of widespread public interest, most especially to the library community."[5]

Accordingly, the basic bibliographic tool of NTIS, *Government Reports Announcements & Index* (GRA&I), is available through the depository library system (C 51.9/3; item 270), but a large number of publications listed therein are excluded from depository distribution. In recent years, some technical report series, primarily those of the Environmental Protection Agency, Department of Energy, and Nuclear Regulatory Commission, have been printed by GPO and made available to depository libraries. This has been accomplished largely by the cost-effective characteristics of microfiche distribution. Still, the library community is not satisfied with the pace of deposit. That the problem must be resolved, by legislation if necessary, was underscored by a recommendation contained in the final report of the National Study Commission on Records and Documents of Federal Officials, dated March 31, 1977:

Most documents containing technical information ... remain outside the depository system.... NTIS does not participate in the Depository Library Program, holding that the act creating the Service provides that the public cannot bear the cost of its publications. Librarians, however, assert that NTIS can and should participate in the Depository Library Program because the same act states that NTIS can freely distribute information "for the general benefit of the public" (15 U.S.C. 1153).... Means should be found to assess the need by depositories for the kind of material processed by NTIS and a solution found to bring that material into the Depository Library System by, if necessary, clarifying the law.[6]

Moreover, NTIS over the years has extended its scope to include government magazines like *Business America* and many other titles and series not limited to scientific, technical, and engineering subjects. Asked why non-scientific and technical materials were included in GRA&I, an NTIS official replied that the service attempts "to make all possible useful information known to the users of all our products. We view many reports that may not be termed scientific or technical in the strictest sense as still being useful to our users. Research emphasis changes constantly and today research in Social or Behavioral Sciences is just as important in the scientific and technical community as research in Physics or Chemistry was a few years ago."[7]

As an agency sustained by its customers, NTIS operates very much as a public service business and has always been more aggressive in seeking to consolidate and expand its bureaucratic position than GPO. In 1981, however, cooperative agreements were struck between the two entities. "Selected scientific and technical documents published by the Government Printing Office will be announced in NTIS newsletters and journals.... The GPO documents will be announced as available hardbound from the Superintendent of Documents and available in microfiche from NTIS, as well as being searchable online through the NTIS Bibliographic Data Base." Another feature of the agreements permits NTIS "to sell both paper and microfiche copies of selected GPO documents that have been taken out of stock by [the Superintendent]," and both agencies may "honor orders charged to each other's deposit accounts, so that customers may use these accounts interchangeably."[8]

But these arrangements involve the sales functions of GPO and NTIS. The Comptroller General's decision remains the official interpretation of NTIS's legislative mandate, an understanding that the technical report literature it processes will continue to be exempted from the depository library program.

NTIS PRODUCTS AND SERVICES

The basic NTIS *Bibliographic Data Base* on magnetic tape is the resource from which NTIS designs and produces a number of services and the bibliographic tools by which they can be accessed. Following are some of the primary information packages available from the agency.

NTIS PUBLISHED SEARCHES

NTIS *Published Searches* are bibliographies containing full bibliographic citations developed by information specialists in subject areas most frequently requested by NTIS customers. Each *Published Search* provides up to 200 or more comprehensive research summaries, or abstracts. The *1982 Published Searches Master Catalog* listed over 3,500 published searches.

SRIM

SRIM is an acronym for *Selected Research in Microfiche*, a biweekly service that provides full text microfiche copies of research reports from among the numerous subject categories that the customer selects. A *SRIM Index* is published quarterly and cumulates into an annual index. Available to subscribers in paper copy or on microfiche, the *SRIM Index* is accessed by subject, personal author, title, contract or grant number, accession or report number, or corporate author.

TECH NOTES

Tech Notes summarizes on a monthly schedule digests of the latest applied technology developed by federal agencies and their contractors. Subscribers may choose any or all of ten categories: computers, energy, engineering, electrotechnology, life sciences, machinery and tools, manufacturing, materials, physical sciences, and testing and instrumentation.

ABSTRACT NEWSLETTERS

Abstract Newsletters, formerly called *Weekly Government Abstracts*, are summaries of current research in twenty-six categories of interest. The various newsletters include *Behavior & Society, Energy, Physics, Chemistry*, and *Library & Information Sciences*. In each area the final issue of the year is a special subject and order number index containing up to ten cross-references for each research summary indexed. Although *Abstract Newsletters* are not available for depository distribution, they are bibliographically noted in the *Serials Supplement* to the *Monthly Catalog*.

KEYWORD AUTHORITY SOURCES

Controlled language terms used by NTIS to index reports are taken from different authority lists. The authorized keywords are listed hierarchically in special publications called *thesauri*. Major thesauri are those used as an authorized source for all keywords for a particular agency or report series; minor thesauri are used only to assist analysts in vocabulary control for free language terms selected by NTIS to express concepts or terminology not covered by major thesauri. DoD-sponsored reports are indexed using the *DDC Retrieval and Indexing Terminology* thesaurus. DOE employs the *Energy Information Data Base: Subject Thesaurus*. NASA uses a two-volume authority, *NASA Thesaurus Volume 1: Alphabetical Listing* and *Volume 2: Access Vocabulary*. Minor thesauri include energy and environmental microthesauri and those of other agencies. Thesauri in use by NTIS and its contributing agencies are available for sale from NTIS or from the entity and are listed in the current edition of *A Reference Guide to the NTIS Bibliographic Data Base* (NTIS-PR 253).

DATABASE SERVICES

In addition to its master *Bibliographic Data Base* on magnetic tape, NTIS provides databases for energy, patents, and water resources. Moreover, the agency provides online access to databases processed by federal agencies when a comparable service is not offered by a commercial vendor. Batch services include custom reports from a database that contains all of the employment-related information of the 1980 census. Information on and lists of computer software applications are available from Product Management, NTIS, 5285 Port Royal Road, Springfield, Virginia 22161.

OTHER

In addition to the above services, NTIS announcements proclaim a number of bibliographic, full text, and online products. Among these are its *Catalog of Government Patents* and the *Energy Data Base*, available for lease through the agency but created and maintained by the Department of Energy's Technical Information Center (*infra*). NTIS issues a *General Catalog of Information Services* (NTIS-PR 154) annually which lists and describes the agency's current products and services.

GOVERNMENT REPORTS ANNOUNCEMENTS & INDEX

The basic bibliographic tool for libraries and information centers is *Government Reports Announcements & Index* (GRA&I), a semimonthly indexing and abstracting service containing current citations of all publications received by NTIS. Although sold through NTIS, it is available to depository libraries (C 51.9/3; item 270).

Entries are arranged by COSATI (Committee on Scientific and Technical Information) classification, a scheme using some twenty-two broad subject categories subdivided into almost 200 subcategories. The COSATI structure ranges from aeronautics to space technology. Category 5, "Behavioral & Social Sciences," includes subdivisions such as economics, humanities, linguistics, personnel selection, and sociology. Most subject categories, however, are scientific and technical. A *COSATI Subject Category List* is available from NTIS in paper copy or on microfiche.

The main entry section, "Reports Announcements," contains the basic bibliographic information, and each entry is arranged by subject category and subcategory. Within the latter the reports are organized alphanumerically by NTIS order number. Preceding the numerals is an "Accession Number Prefix" which indicates the entity from which the report was received. Commonly used prefixes and the source agencies they signify include AD (Department of Defense), ED (Educational Resources Information Center), JPRS (Joint Publications Research Service), N (National Aeronautics and Space Administration). The prefix "PB" is an acronym for "Publications Board." It was used by the predecessor agency of NTIS and has been continued despite reorganization and agency name changes. PB is employed to indicate reports entered by NTIS for other agencies. The Accession Number Prefix is used by subscribers as an order number for the documents.

In 1970 NTIS developed a new subject scheme to be used in conjunction with the COSATI system. The scheme, called "NTIS Subject Classification," provides useful sorting categories for both hard and soft sciences, particularly in areas such as environment, transportation, health, and urban technology. Unlike COSATI, which is academically oriented primarily for the "hard" sciences, the NTIS scheme contains 39 categories and over 300 subcategories. Twenty-six of the NTIS subject categories are used to sort reports in the NTIS *Abstract Newsletters.*

GRA&I index entries are by key word, personal author, corporate author, contract/grant number, and NTIS order/report number. The key word index functions as a subject approach, and most of the key words are selected from the controlled vocabularies of the Department of Defense, Department of Energy, NASA, or NTIS.

Government Reports Annual Index (C 51.9/4; item 270) is published in six sections. Section 1 is the key word index (A-L), and Section 2 concludes the listing (M-Z). Section 3 is the personal author index. Section 4 is the corporate author index. Sections 5 and 6 comprise the contract/grant number index and the NTIS order/report number index.

Because GRA&I and its annual index lack a title approach, the agency publishes a separate microfiche *NTIS Title Index.* This is a cumulation of new publications merged quarterly on a two-year cycle. The *NTIS Title Index* is issued within two weeks after the closing of the last GRA&I for the quarter. A *Retrospective Index* for titles covers July 1964 through December 1978 and includes over 750,000 publications on 1,332 sheets of microfiche. This product contains a Keyword Out of Context (KWOC) title index, an author index, and a report/accession number index.

In 1982 NTIS published in two volumes its *Corporate Author File* (CAF). The file, updated by quarterly supplements, standardizes corporate author names for documents cataloged by NTIS and for documents from other agencies like NASA and DOE received by NTIS on magnetic tape.

SSIE DATABASE

In October 1981 the Smithsonian Science Information Exchange (SSIE) ceased operation and NTIS assumed responsibility for SSIE's research-in-progress database. SSIE had operated under contract to NTIS through congressional appropriations with the provision that SSIE become self-sustaining. Owing to financial problems, this goal was not realized, and the SSIE Board of Directors recommended abolition of the corporation.

SSIE had been a central source of information on federally supported research in progress for several years, and its database included over 300,000 current projects funded by federal agencies. Monthly updates of the former database are now leased by NTIS to online vendors, thus assuring continued public accessibility but probably resulting in higher prices.

ONLINE SERVICES

The bibliographic data contained in GRA&I and in part for the weekly *Abstract Newsletters* (and including SSIE) are online through SDC Search Service (ORBIT), Bibliographic Retrieval Services (BRS), and DIALOG Information Services, Inc.

Figure 5 shows a sample main entry found in each issue of GRA&I.

Figure 5
Government Reports Announcements & Index: Sample Entry

REPORTS
ANNOUNCEMENTS

The full bibliographic report entries in this section are arranged by subject category and subcategory. Within each subcategory the reports are arranged alphanumerically by NTIS order number; the Ebcdic character set sort is used.

SAMPLE ENTRY

Field 12—MATHEMATICAL SCIENCES
Group 12A—Mathematics and Statistics
PB80-104045   PC A02/MF A01
Massachusetts Inst. of Tech., Cambridge. Constructed Facilities Div.
Computation of Hankel Transforms Using the Fast-Fourier Transform Algorithm,
E. Kausel, and G. Bouckovalas. Aug 79, 49p
R79-12, NSF/RA-79-12, NSF/RA-790206
Grant NSF-ENV77-18339

An efficient numerical procedure is presented for the computation of Hankel Transforms. The algorithm is based on the expression of the Hankel Transform in terms of a two-dimensional Fourier Transform, which is then reduced to only one dimension. The latter is then evaluated with the Fast Fourier Transform algorithm. Examples are presented, and a listing of the computer program included.

NTIS Subject Category
NTIS Subcateogry
  NTIS order number Availability/Price codes
Corporate or Performing Organization

Report title

Personal authors Report date   Page count
Report number(s)
Contract or grant number(s)

Abstract

1.

AERONAUTICS

1A. Aerodynamics

AD-A110 495/9   PC A04/MF A01
Virginia Polytechnic Inst. and State Univ., Blacksburg. Dept. of Engineering Science and Mechanics.

On the Aerodynamics of Windblast.
Final technical rept.,
Daniel J. Schneck. 13 Nov 81, 51p VPI-E-81-31, AFOSR-TR-82-0031
Grant AFOSR-78-3706

In two previous reports (Schneck, 1976, 1979) a mathematical theory was developed in order to calculate the aerodynamic loading to which a pilot is exposed during high speed ejections. Neglecting the effects of flow separation, preliminary results suggested that the pilot's musculo-skeletal resistance is not likely to withstand the tendency for dislodgement from a restraining surface if he is ejecting at Mach numbers exceeding 0.72. Recently (Schneck, 1979) the mathematical theory of windblast was modified to include some effects of flow separation. In the report that follows, these effects are examined in greater detail, particularly as they affect the time-course of limb dislodging forces after the onset of windblast.

AD-A110 660/8   PC A07/MF A01
Naval Air Development Center, Warminster, PA. Aircraft and Crew Systems Technology Directorate.
Statistical Review of Counting Accelerometer Data for Navy and Marine Fleet Aircraft from 1 January 1962 to 30 June 1981.
Semiannual summary rept. 1 Jan 62-30 Jun 81, Warren J. Williams. 1 Nov 81, 149p Rept no. NADC-13920-2
Supersedes report dated 1 May 81, AD-A102 495.

This is a semi-annual progress report, and it presents a specialized summary of the data in the counting accelerometer program. Statistics describing Navy and Marine aircraft cumulative g-count exceedances are calculated and tabulated. These tabulations are separated by calendar time and into four major categories of fleet experience: Navy Training, Navy Combat, Marine Training, and Marine Combat. These data show that the load rate distributions (counts at 1000 hours) for most models and most g-levels have a non-

SUMMARY

The National Technical Information Service is not without its critics. In a perceptive analysis of the agency's practices, Meredith sets forth the major limitations of NTIS: It is a passive acquisitions system; coverage of materials in subject fields is uneven; "soft" discipline categories diminish the "scientific and technical" nature of the services. As a "secondary depository apparatus" of the federal government, NTIS "exercises virtually no control over input." Passive acquisition results in an absence of quality control. Input does not fall "neatly within conceptual boundaries." Thus within the subcategory "Personnel Selection, Training and Evaluation" of Category 5, one finds non-scientific documents on education, titles which belong in other databases and indexing services. As Meredith points out, the criticism of GRA&I reflects faults of the system rather than defects intrinsic to the index itself.

Meredith notes that NTIS "has always had a problem of domain ... conferred on it by the looseness of the enabling legislation." It "accepts almost anything and everything that is submitted by a Federal agency, contractor, or grantee, as long as it is accompanied by a nominal fee." The fuzzy language of the law permits the director of NTIS to "disregard the needs and expectations of anyone not identified with 'industry and business,' including many of the people who generated the information in the first place." The author is constrained to summarize his analysis with these harsh words: "It is impossible to describe NTIS without a degree of asperity bordering — at times — on censure."[9]

A former NTIS director was quoted as expressing a desire that the agency become a quasi-government corporation. "I don't think NTIS can be a private firm like McGraw-Hill. It's still got to have Government involvement in one way or another because it serves Government agencies. My point is that I don't think NTIS operates as effectively as it could while entirely in a Government department."[10] The Information Industry Association, however, would like to see NTIS abolished and its functions taken over by private companies. While this would be a boon for commercial distributors of government information, it would doubtless result in greater price increases, an irony that is not lost on other private firms which purchase this technical report literature.

It is clear that NTIS and GPO represent antithetical positions in a philosophy of public service and public access, and this issue is exacerbated by ambiguous enabling legislation. Indeed, NTIS has complained about the distribution of GRA&I and its annual index to depository libraries, thus representing a loss of income to NTIS. "The result is that those who buy NTIS publications are paying the cost" of free distribution by GPO.[11] The National Study Commission on Records and Documents of Federal Officials suggested a resolution of this problem, a recommendation that bears repeating: "Means should be found to assess the need by depositories for the kind of material processed by NTIS and a solution found to bring that material into the Depository Library System by, if necessary, clarifying the law."

NATIONAL AERONAUTICS AND SPACE ADMINISTRATION

The National Aeronautics and Space Administration (NASA) is a major agency for in-house and sponsored research. Its chief bibliographic tool is *Scientific and Technical Aerospace Reports* (STAR), a semimonthly indexing/abstracting service. STAR is available for sale by the Superintendent of Documents and to depository libraries (NAS 1.9/4; item 830-K). There is an annual index volume (NAS 1.9/5; item 830-K).

STAR announces current publications in the following areas: 1) NASA, NASA contractor, and NASA grantee reports; 2) reports issued by other federal government agencies, domestic and foreign institutions, universities, and private firms; 3) translations in report form; 4) NASA-owned patents and patent applications; and 4) dissertations and theses. In addition, NASA cooperates with the private sector in that book, journal, and conference literature, journal translations, and selected foreign dissertations are announced in a companion service, *International Aerospace Abstracts* (IAA), which is available to subscribers from the American Institute of Aeronautics and Astronautics in New York City.

On-Going Research Reports are inserted into each issue of STAR. These provide titles of active NASA grants and university contracts, summary portions of recently updated *NASA Research and Technology Objectives and Plans* (RTOPs), and notices of non-NASA research projects that were funded in the most recent or current fiscal year.

The subject scope of STAR, IAA, and *On-Going Research Reports* includes all aspects of aeronautics and space research and development, supporting basic and applied research, and applications. Also covered are aerospace aspects of earth resources, energy development, conservation, oceanography, environmental protection, urban transportation, and other topics of national priority and public policy. Other NASA publications and information services are described in the publication *The NASA Scientific and Technical Information System ... and How to Use It*, which is available free from the NASA Scientific and Technical Information Facility, P.O. Box 8757, B.W.I. Airport, Maryland 21240.

STAR uses ten major subject divisions further organized into over seventy specific subject categories and one general category/division. The major subject divisions are listed in the table of contents, together with a note for each that defines its scope and provides cross-references. STAR abstracts are grouped by specific category, and the categories appear in sequential order.

Documents announced in STAR are available either in paper copy or microfiche from several sources: NTIS, SuDocs, NASA Public Document Rooms (Washington, DC), NASA research centers, University Microfilms (dissertations), U.S. Geological Survey field offices (for examination), the U.S. Patent and Trademark Office, and other sources listed in the introductory pages of STAR. Because NASA is an important participating agency in the NTIS database registry, there is duplication of indexing information in STAR and GRA&I.

STAR's semimonthly issues consist of main entries arranged by subject divisions and categories followed by indexes for subjects, personal authors, corporate sources, contract numbers, and report/accession numbers. The annual index supersedes the semimonthly and semiannual indexes previously issued and appears in two bound volumes. The first volume contains the subject index. The second contains the indexes by personal author, corporate source, contract number, and report/accession number.

An online database called NASA, produced by the agency and the American Institute of Aeronautics and Astronautics, is available through ESA-IRS (Paris, France). However, because the agency participates in the NTIS system, information on publications announced in STAR heavily overlaps with that published in GRA&I and may be accessed through DIALOG, BRS, and ORBIT.

Figure 6, page 100, shows a sample main entry in *Scientific and Technical Aerospace Reports*.

Figure 6
Scientific and Technical Aerospace Reports: Sample Entry

TYPICAL CITATION AND ABSTRACT

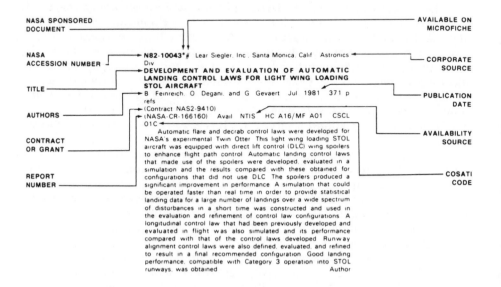

DEPARTMENT OF ENERGY

One of the large producers of information whose contract report literature found its way into the NTIS apparatus was the Atomic Energy Commission (AEC). It was abolished by the Energy Reorganization Act of 1974 (88 *Stat.* 1237; 42 U.S.C. 5814) and its functions transferred to the Energy Research and Development Administration and the Nuclear Regulatory Commission. While the Nuclear Regulatory Commission (NUREG), an independent agency, awards contracts for research, its primary purpose is focused on the use of nuclear energy to generate electrical power, and it fulfills its responsibilities through a system of licensing and regulating nuclear reactors and other nuclear facilities. The Energy Research and Development Administration (ERDA), however, became the primary research entity for all other energy technologies. And during its brief life, ERDA registered reports with NTIS.

On August 4, 1977, the president signed PL 95-91 (91 *Stat.* 565; 42 U.S.C. 7101), establishing a Department of Energy (DOE) and bringing the number of departments of the federal government up to twelve. On September 13, 1977, Executive Order 12009 was signed, prescribing October 1, 1977 the effective date of the Department of Energy Organization Act, and directing that the transfer of functions commence.

And quite a transfer it was! The new department, pursuant to Title III of the Act, consolidated all functions of the Federal Energy Administration (FEA), Federal Power Commission (FPC), and ERDA, and these entities ceased to exist. Moreover, energy-related functions were transferred from the departments of Interior, Housing and Urban Development (HUD), Transportation, Defense, and Commerce; and from two independent regulatory agencies, the Interstate Commerce Commission (ICC) and the Securities and Exchange Commission (SEC). And the Department of Energy participates in the energy activities of other federal agencies such as the Rural Electrification Administration.

Disaffection over the role and functions of DOE has resulted in a great deal of discussion to abolish the entity and transfer its functions to the Department of Commerce. In 1982, however, DOE still survives and continues to issue a large number of federally funded research reports. Two major sources issued by DOE provide coverage of these materials, *Energy Research Abstracts* (ERA) and *Energy Abstracts for Policy Analysis* (EAPA).

ENERGY RESEARCH ABSTRACTS

ERA is a semimonthly service that provides abstracting and indexing coverage of all scientific and technical reports, journal articles, conference papers and proceedings, books, patents, theses, and monographs originated by the Department, its laboratories, energy centers, and contractors. ERA also covers other energy information prepared in report form by federal and state government agencies, foreign governments, and domestic and foreign universities and research organizations. Non-report literature, however, is limited to that generated by DOE activity.

Published by DOE's Technical Information Center (TIC), ERA is available for sale through the Superintendent of Documents and to depository libraries (E 1.17; item 474-A-6). ERA used to provide semiannual and annual printed indexes, but beginning with Volume 7 (1982) TIC issued a microfiche-only edition of the cumulated index. However, with Volume 7 of ERA, coverage was broadened by some 10,000 additional abstracts with the inclusion of all unclassified, publicly available reports processed by TIC. It is expected that discontinuing the printed cumulative indexes will offset the cost of this additional coverage.

ERA consists of a main entry section and indexes by personal author, corporate author, subject contract number, and report number. The reports abstracted in ERA are available from NTIS, the Superintendent of Documents, TIC, and other DOE offices and centers. An increasing number of TIC reports are being made available to depository libraries in microfiche-only distribution item categories.

The Energy Data Base (EDB) maintains the total content of ERA and is available for searching through the DOE/RECON online system. Commercial online services include BRS (Department of Energy Database), DIALOG (DOE Energy), and ORBIT (EDB). Because the online services provide a continually cumulating index to ERA information, the editor of *Energy Research Abstracts* believes that printed cumulative indexes have become increasingly impractical.

ENERGY ABSTRACTS FOR POLICY ANALYSIS

EAPA is a monthly abstract journal devoted to information on the analysis and evaluation of energy research and public policy. It is limited primarily to non-technical articles or reports having significant reference value, leaving the "hard" scientific and technical literature to ERA. Like ERA, EAPA is published by TIC, Oak Ridge, Tennessee.

EAPA is a depository item and a SuDocs sales publication (E 1.11; item 474-A-2). Abstracts are created from congressional publications, department and agency reports, regional commission studies, reports of state and local governments, periodicals, conference proceedings, books, and documents from industry, private foundations, universities, societies, and associations. The monthly issues consist of a main entry section and indexes by personal author, corporate author, subject, and report number. There is an annual cumulative index.

The contents of EAPA are available through NTIS, Superintendent of Documents, TIC, or the appropriate publisher, in paper copy or microform. As with ERA, sources for ordering EAPA publications are listed in the report number index.

GPO/DOE COOPERATION

In 1979 the microfiche collection of DOE's Energy Information Administration (EIA) was made available to depository libraries under item 429-T-56. The quarterly *EIA Publications Directory* (E 3.27; item 429-T-49) serves as a bibliographic guide to the collection. A number of these reports were received by depositories in paper copy under other DOE items. Access to individual titles is principally through *American Statistics Index* (ASI) and, to a lesser extent, through the *Monthly Catalog* and PRF. A useful correlation list of EIA report numbers and titles to their SuDocs class notations and ASI accession numbers was compiled by Steven D. Zink and published in the fall 1981 issue of *Microform Review*, pp. 261-70. Moreover, the information corresponding to *EIA Publications Directory* citations is online in FEDEX (Federal Energy Data Index), a database available through BRS.

From March 1981 to January 1983 Contractor Research and Development Reports, classed in E 1.28, were made available to depository libraries in forty TIC subject categories. The depository item designation for this series was changed from 429-T-4 to 430-L-1 through 430-L-40. Thus libraries wishing only technical reports on fusion fuels would subscribe to item 430-L-6; energy storage, 430-L-18; geosciences, 430-L-36; etc. The categories issued during this time period did not have the class notation printed on the fiche.

However, after January 1983, the same subject categories were not only reclassified but reassigned another depository item number. All TIC Contractor R&D Reports issued after January 1983 are classed in E 1.99 and assigned item categories 430-M-1 through 430-M-40. For this series, the class notation is printed on the fiche. These changes, announced in Surveys 82-100 and 82-101 accompanying the depository shipments of August 27, 1982, demonstrate that GPO can bedevil the library community with reclassification even when government reorganization does not occur. However, the advantages of being able to choose specific subjects tailored to the needs of users are obvious. In addition, the E 1.99 class stem, followed by the alphanumeric DOE/TIC report number assigned to each document, allows the integration of the microfiche with an existing collection, whether the series is filed by SuDocs class number or DOE/TIC report number.

Figure 7 shows a sample main entry in *Energy Research Abstracts.*

Figure 7
Energy Research Abstracts: Sample Entry

● ABSTRACTS IN *ENERGY RESEARCH ABSTRACTS*

The principal elements of abstract entries for a typical research and development report and a typical technical journal article are illustrated below.

Report number   Date of publication   Contract number

Availability   Author(s)   Title   Corporate

24582 (LA–8830-MS) Nucleonic analysis of the ETF neutral-beam-injector-duct and vacuum-pumping-duct shields. Urban, W.T.; Seed, T.J.; Dudziak, D.J. (Los Alamos Scientific Lab., NM (USA)). May 1981. Contract W-7405-ENG-36. 82p. NTIS, PC A05/MF A01. Order Number DE81023986.

Abstract
A nucleonic analysis of the Engineering Test Facility neutral-beam-injector-duct and vacuum-pumping-duct shields has been made using a hybrid Monte Carlo/discrete-ordinates method. This method used Monte Carlo to determine internal and external boundary surface sources for subsequent discrete-ordinates calculations of the neutron and gamma-ray transport through the shields. Confidence was provided in both the hybrid method and the results obtained through a comparison with three-dimensional Monte Carlo results.

Journal citation   Date of publication

Author(s)   Title

24033 Semi-empirical prediction of bubble diameter in gas fluidized beds. Bar-Cohen, A.; Glicksman, L.R.; Hughes, R.W. (Ben Gurion Univ. of the Negev, Beer Sheva, Isr). *International Journal of Multiphase Flow;* 7: No. 1, 101-113 (Feb 1981).

Abstract
Theoretical expressions for bubble diameter in both small and large particle fluidized beds are derived by the application of two phase theory and gas flow continuity. Comparison with experimental data suggests that the numerical and analytical solution of these expressions, combined with empirical bubble frequency relations, can provide an accurate prediction of bubble size and its parametric trends. 25 refs.

NUCLEAR ENERGY DOCUMENTATION

For many years librarians and their public enjoyed the free use of *Nuclear Science Abstracts* (NSA) through the depository library system. Issued by the defunct Atomic Energy Commission, NSA was a semimonthly indexing/abstracting service for the literature of nuclear science and engineering. Quinquennial cumulative indexes were published by GPO and made available to depository libraries from 1948 to 1973.

The final issue of NSA was that of June 30, 1976. It was replaced by *INIS Atomindex*, which is published by the International Atomic Energy Agency, Vienna, Austria, a specialized agency within the United Nations family. *Atomindex* is a product of the International Nuclear Information System (INIS) and is available for sale in the United States through UNIPUB, 345 Park Avenue South, New York, NY 10010. A semimonthly abstracting journal, *INIS Atomindex* identifies publications relating to nuclear science and its peaceful applications. Although it is claimed that the literature coverage in ERA does not duplicate the material indexed in *Atomindex*, the subject categories in both services suggest that some duplication may be impossible to avoid.

Each issue of *INIS Atomindex* consists of a main entry section and indexes by personal author, corporate entry, subject, report, standard and patent number, and conference. Most United States reports announced in *Atomindex* are available through NTIS, and some reports are available from the Superintendent of Documents.

DEFENSE TECHNICAL INFORMATION CENTER

The Defense Technical Information Center (DTIC), formerly known as the Defense Documentation Center (DDC), is a unit within the Defense Logistics Agency of the Department of Defense (DoD). Located in Alexandria, Virginia, DTIC acts as a clearinghouse for DoD-sponsored research and development reports in scientific and technical fields. By contractual arrangement with NTIS, the Center provides copies of unclassified and unlimited DoD reports which are then announced in GRA&I. According to Carlynn J. Thompson, writing in the July 1979 issue of *Documents to the People*, almost "40% of the NTIS Technical Report collection" consists of reports of this kind that are channeled through the Center.

Classified and limited DoD reports are announced in the Center's *Technical Abstract Bulletin* (TAB) and its indexes. In 1967 TAB was given a "confidential" security classification, and in 1971 that security label was placed on the *TAB Indexes*. However, Thompson notes that TAB is "now unclassified," but it remains a non-GPO publication which is not sent to depository libraries. DTIC maintains almost 1,000,000 technical reports; over 100,000 work unit summaries, which are descriptions of ongoing R&D efforts; 20,000 independent research and development summaries performed by DoD contractors; and almost 30,000 program planning summaries, project and task-level R&D activities in the planning stages. DTIC's users comprise DoD agencies, other federal departments and agencies, and their contractors, subcontractors, and grantees. "Access is granted only to those organizations which have registered their official requirements" with the Center.[12]

The NTIS order number (or "accession/report number") assigned to DoD research reports is prefixed by the letters "AD." This symbol is a holdover from the old *Astia* (*Armed Services Technical Information Agency*) *Document* designation.[13]

DUPLICATION OF INFORMATION

NASA, DOE, and DoD account for most of the technical reports in the NTIS bibliographic system, and, as we have observed, most of them are not available to depository libraries. But so vast is the bibliographic net cast by NTIS that a *partial list* of entities that register reports with the service shows hundreds of federal units as well as state and local government agencies, councils, conferences, boards, foreign governments, and companies worldwide.[14]

The result is information overload and duplication of material indexed elsewhere, a subject of concern to the federal government. A report to the Congress by the General Accounting Office presents that agency's views on how the government can improve the management of scientific, technical, and other specialized information. As far back as 1969 studies by the National Academy of Sciences and other entities identified duplication as a problem in need of a resolution. Indeed, the report alludes to a 1976 American Society for Information Science publication that listed

> 57 publicly available, computerized data bases in the environmental field, 99 in the chemistry and chemical engineering fields, and 51 in the medicine field. While the existence of numerous data bases in one field does not necessarily indicate duplication, the greater the number of data bases, the greater the likelihood that it will occur.[15]

One can identify duplication of bibliographic database information virtually at random. A modest, sixteen-page document called *Our Prodigal Sun*, for example, was indexed in GRA&I, STAR, *Nuclear Science Abstracts*, and the *Monthly Catalog*; myriad examples of this kind exist. It may be argued that duplication ultimately benefits the user, who may not know precisely what index to search. Saturation bombing was said to hasten the allied victory in World War II, but is saturation indexing an appropriate strategy for winning the information contest?

EDUCATIONAL RESOURCES INFORMATION CENTER

The administration's federal budget proposal for FY 1983 called for the abolition of the Department of Education, an entity that was established in 1980 (90 *Stat.* 668), and its reorganization as a subcabinet foundation with reduced regulatory power and funds. As of 1982, however, the Department (ED) survives. The Educational Resources Information Center (ERIC), a nationwide information network, is a unit of the National Institute of Education (NIE) within the Education Department. Its purpose is to acquire, index, and disseminate timely education-related materials for the use of teachers, administrators, researchers, students, and other interested persons. This is accomplished by a central coordinating staff in Washington, DC, and sixteen clearinghouses located at universities or professional organizations across the country. Each clearinghouse is responsible for a particular subject area of education and for collecting all relevant unpublished, noncopyrightable material of value in that area. Clearinghouse areas include rural education; adult, career, and vocational education; reading and communication skills; and information resources. The latter, known as ERIC/IR, is located at Syracuse University in New York and is sponsored by the university's School of Information Studies and School of Education.

BIBLIOGRAPHIC TOOLS

Two major indexing/abstracting services provide the bibliographic control of educational materials screened by the clearinghouses and accepted into the ERIC database. *Resources in Education* (RIE) announces "document" literature, and *Current Index to Journals in Education* covers "journal" literature.

RESOURCES IN EDUCATION

RIE, a monthly abstract journal, is sold through the Superintendent of Documents and is distributed to depository libraries (ED 1.310; item 466-A). It consists of a main entry section composed of "resumes" and indexes by subject, author, institution, publication categories (books, dissertations, reports, audiovisual materials, etc.), and clearinghouse number/ED number cross-references. Other features of RIE include New Thesaurus Terms, ordering information, and a current list of ERIC clearinghouses. Semiannual indexes (January-June; July-December) are available for sale or on deposit. An annual cumulative index by subjects, authors, and institutions is available for sale from the Oryx Press, Phoenix, Arizona.

On July 19, 1982, Survey 82-16 that accompanied *Depository Shipping List No. 17,246* offered depository libraries the opportunity to subscribe to *Education Documents Announced in RIE* (ED 1.310/2; item 466-A-3). The annotation for this new category conveyed the impression that *all* the documents listed in RIE would be made available on microfiche. The September 1982 issue of *Administrative Notes* apologized for this inaccuracy, stating that "only those publications printed by the National Institute of Education or otherwise federally funded will be distributed to depository libraries. Thus you will not receive all of the documents announced in RIE. Under Title 44, section 1903, GPO is only authorized to distribute Government publications." Unfortunately, even this putative clarification was misleading. It remained for ERIC officials to provide the correct information. The fact is that *Education Documents Announced in RIE* comprise somewhat less than 10 percent of ERIC's total announcements. The 100 or so documents per issue of RIE obtained from ERIC by GPO for this microfiche shipment represent *only* those Department of Education prepared or sponsored documents that have been issued by the entity *and* that have met ERIC selection criteria. They do not necessarily represent the total departmental output.

CURRENT INDEX TO JOURNALS IN EDUCATION

CIJE is a monthly guide to current periodical literature in education. Articles published in almost 800 education and education-related journals are indexed and abstracted by the sixteen clearinghouses plus the San Mateo (California)

Educational Resources Center (SMERC), which provides information on journals that do not fall within the subject disciplines of the regular clearinghouses. Copies of many of the articles included in CIJE are available from University Microfilms International, Ann Arbor, Michigan, indicated by the words "(Reprint: UMI)" in the main entry section.

The main entry section of CIJE includes full bibliographic information and an "annotation" (abstract) of the article, followed by indexes for subjects, authors, and journal contents. Prior to 1982, CIJE was not a depository library item; the monthly issues and semiannual cumulations were and continue to be published by Oryx Press and sold to libraries in a printed edition. Beginning in January 1982, however, CIJE became a depository item (ED 1.310/4; item 466-A) and was made available to depository institutions in a microfiche format.

THESAURUS OF ERIC DESCRIPTORS

The *Thesaurus of ERIC Descriptors*, ninth edition, was published in a clothbound edition by Oryx Press in 1982. In addition, it is distributed through GPO on microfiche to depository libraries. The *Thesaurus* is a controlled vocabulary of educational terms called "descriptors" which conform to the major terms used in the subject indexes of both RIE and CIJE. Subjects can be located through a main Alphabetical Display providing a variety of information including terms no longer valid; a Rotated Descriptor Display grouping related terms in an alphabetical index; a Hierarchical Display providing "generic trees" for each descriptor; and Descriptor Groups serving as a "table of contents" for the *Thesaurus*. The *Thesaurus* is kept current by the section in both RIE and CIJE called New Thesaurus Terms until a new revision of the basic *Thesaurus* is published.

IDENTIFIER AUTHORITY LIST

In addition to descriptors, "identifiers" (which are *not* found in the *Thesaurus*) are semi-controlled retrieval terms intended to add a depth to indexing that is not always possible with descriptors alone. An identifier is usually the name of a specific entity like a project, public law, organization, item of equipment, group, person, or place. It may also be a new concept, under consideration for descriptor status once its scope, definition, and "staying power" have been established. Transitory identifiers or those represented in the literature infrequently do not achieve descriptor status.

The *Identifier Authority List* (IAL) is an alphabetical arrangement of preferred identifier forms that are used to achieve consistency in indexing and searching alike. Issued semiannually in printed form, it serves as a companion volume to the *Thesaurus*. Additional identifiers continue to be added to the IAL as a result of the monthly RIE and CIJE input to the database, and items are purged from the IAL as they are upgraded to descriptor status and shifted to the *Thesaurus*. The IAL is available for sale from the ERIC Processing and Reference Facility, Bethesda, Maryland.

DUPLICATION OF INFORMATION

While a few documents in RIE are also found in GRA&I in COSATI Subject Category 5 (Behavioral and Social Sciences), the "incursion is numerically insignificant."[16] Approximately 4 percent of RIE duplicates information found in *Dissertation Abstracts International*. However, there is a 25 percent overlap in the journals regularly scanned and indexed in CIJE and *Psychological Abstracts*. A much greater duplication is found "between CIJE and *Education Index* ... though CIJE covers about three times the number of journals as does *Education Index*."[17]

ONLINE SEARCHES

The documents and journals in RIE and CIJE may be searched online via DIALOG, ORBIT, and BRS.

Figures 8 and 9 show, respectively, sample main entries for RIE and CIJE. Main entry arrangement is by ERIC accession number; there is also a clearinghouse accession number which identifies the clearinghouse responsible for the preparation of the bibliographic information in each entry.

Figure 8
Resources in Education: Sample Entry

SAMPLE RESUME

ERIC Accession Number—identification number sequentially assigned to documents as they are processed

Clearinghouse Accession Number.

Author(s).

Title.

Organization where document originated.

Date Published.

Contract or Grant Number.

Alternate source for obtaining document.

Language of Document.

ERIC Document Reproduction Service (EDRS) Availability "MF" means microfiche; "PC" means reproduced paper copy. When described as "Document Not Available from EDRS", alternate sources are cited above. Prices are subject to change; for latest price code schedule see section on "How to Order ERIC Documents", in the most recent issue of RIE.

Publication Type—broad categories indicating the form or organization of the document, as contrasted to its subject matter. The category name is followed by the category code.

Sponsoring Agency—agency responsible for initiating, funding, and managing the research project.

Report Number—assigned by originator.

Descriptive Note (pagination first).

Descriptors—subject terms which characterize substantive content. Only the major terms, preceded by an asterisk, are printed in the subject index.

Identifiers—additional identifying terms not found in the *Thesaurus of ERIC Descriptors*. Only the major terms, preceded by an asterisk, are printed in the subject index.

Informative Abstract.

Abstractor's Initials.

ED 654 321   CE 123 456
Smith, John D.   Johnson, Jane
Career Education for Women.
Central Univ., Chicago, Ill.
Spons Agency—National Inst. of Education
  (ED), Washington, D.C.
Report No—CU-2081-S
Pub Date May 73
Contract—NIE-C-73-0001
Note—129p.; Presented at the National Conference on
  Career Education (3rd, Chicago, IL, May 15-17,
  1973).
Available from—Campus Bookstore, 123 College
  Ave., Chicago, IL 60690 ($3.25).
Language—English; French
EDRS Price MF01/PC06 Plus Postage.
Pub Type—Dissertations/Theses (040)
Descriptors—*Career Opportunities, Career Planning, Careers, *Demand Occupations, *Employment Opportunities, Females, Labor Force, Labor Market, *Manpower Needs, Occupational Aspiration, Occupational Guidance, Occupations, Vocational Counseling, *Working Women
Identifiers—Consortium of States, *National Occupational Competency Testing Institute, Illinois
  Women's opportunities for employment will be directly related to their level of skill and experience but also to the labor market demands through the remainder of the decade. The number of workers needed for all major occupational categories is expected to increase by about one-fifth between 1970 and 1980, but the growth rate will vary by occupational group. Professional and technical workers are expected to have the highest predicted rate (39 percent), followed by service workers (35 percent), clerical workers (26 percent), sales workers (24 percent), craftsmen and foremen (20 percent), managers and administrators (15 percent), and operatives (11 percent). This publication contains a brief discussion and employment information concerning occupations for professional and technical workers, managers and administrators, skilled trades, sales workers, clerical workers, and service workers. In order for women to take advantage of increased labor market demands, employer attitudes toward working women need to change and women must: (1) receive better career planning and counseling, (2) change their career aspirations, and (3) fully utilize the sources of legal protection and assistance which are available to them. (SB)

Figure 9
Current Index to Journals in Education: Sample Entry

Main Entry Section

Complete information about each article included in CIJE is given in the Main Entry Section, which is arranged by Clearinghouse and sequential EJ numbers.

Accession No. ——	**EJ 123 465** RC 503 097 —— Clearinghouse No.
Article Title ——	**Native American Techniques of Survival in the**
	Country. Price, John A. *Indian Historian;* v11 n4 —— Issue No.
Author ——	p3-11 Dec 1978 (Reprint: UMI) —— Volume No.
	Descriptors: *American Indians; Fire Science
Pages ——	Education; *Foods Instruction; *Medicine; —— Journal Title
	*Outdoor Education; *Plant Identification; —— Availability
Major and Minor Descriptors (major descriptors are starred)	*Safety; Trees
	Identifiers: American Indian Education; *Survival —— Publ. Date
	Techniques
Major and Minor Identifiers (major identifiers are starred)	Presenting a review of basic information, this article presents the following: (1) building a shelter, (2) making a fire, (3) finding and keeping food, (4) safety and medicine, (5) orientation to directions, and (6) aids in traveling in the country. (RTS) —— Annotator's Initials

OTHER ERIC PRODUCTS AND SERVICES

Most documents announced in RIE may be purchased from the ERIC Document Reproduction Service (EDRS) in Arlington, Virginia, in paper copy or microfiche. Each issue of RIE contains an order form, which one can photocopy, that gives the current unit price schedules for paper copy and microfiche.

EDRS special microfiche products include *RIE Cumulative Subject Index, 1977-1980, RIE Cumulative Institution Index, 1977-1980, RIE Cumulative Title Index, 1966-1980, RIE Cumulative Author Index, 1966-1980,* and *RIE/CIJE Cumulative Descriptor/Identifier Usage Report, 1969-1980.* The latter is a concise cumulative index containing in four separate lists all the terms used in each publication with the ED or EJ numbers for the documents or articles to which they were assigned. The fiche provides the only published access to minor identifiers. A *Directory of ERIC Microfiche Collections*, revised periodically, lists subscribers to the collections alphabetically by state and name of institution.

In addition to collecting the literature of education for announcement in RIE and CIJE, the ERIC clearinghouses analyze and synthesize information into research reviews, bibliographies, state-of-the-art studies, and interpretive studies on topics of interest to users. Called *Information Analysis Products* (IAPs), these studies are usually available directly from the appropriate clearinghouse. When announced in RIE, they are available in paper copy or microfiche from EDRS. Periodically, ERIC prepares bibliographies of its IAPs, and these are assigned an accession number and abstracted in RIE.

Microfiche cumulations of RIE (1966-1980) and CIJE (1969-1980) are available from Oryx Press. The fiche consist of separate RIE and CIJE main entry cumulations and a combined RIE/CIJE subject index containing the major descriptors and identifiers assigned to all abstracts. The combined subject index is based on the ninth edition of the *Thesaurus of ERIC Descriptors* and references the titles of the items indexed rather than simply the ED or EJ accession numbers. Moreover, a fiche index is included in the combined subject index, a feature which guides the user from any given subject index term to the exact fiche number and location of that term. The basic RIE and CIJE cumulations are updated annually.

These and many other products and services are announced in issues of RIE and CIJE, in brochures issued by the National Institute of Education, in *Users Interchange*, a mimeographed newsletter prepared by the staff of the ERIC Processing and Reference Facility, Bethesda, Maryland, and in announcements from the clearinghouses. For example, *ERIC/IR Update*, a bulletin issued periodically by the Clearinghouse on Information Resources, contains useful news of ERIC products and services, trends, and developments for library and information science professionals.

DOCUMENTS EXPEDITING PROJECT

Mentioned earlier in this chapter, the Documents Expediting Project (DocEx) is located within the Exchange and Gift Division of the Library of Congress. It provides member libraries a centralized service for acquiring non-depository publications generally not available for purchase either through GPO or from the issuing agency.

In 1980 membership in DocEx included 124 university, public, and special libraries and other organizations. Thirteen new libraries joined the project during the year. Moreover, in 1980 DocEx sent 4,022 titles to member libraries, "an increase of 1,000 titles over the previous year."[18] Annual subscriptions range from $225 to $750 in increments of $25; members paying the higher rates enjoy priority in distribution of titles when a limited number of copies are available.

Although DocEx affirms that one copy of every publication it receives for distribution to subscribers is sent to the Superintendent of Documents for inclusion in the *Monthly Catalog*, a number of libraries have complained that "shelves of materials" distributed by DocEx await the assignment of SuDocs classification numbers.[19]

Every new item offered by the Superintendent of Documents reduces the attractiveness of DocEx to depository libraries. Over the years, depository institutions that have looked to the Project for acquiring series like committee prints, Senate executive reports, Senate treaty documents, and CIA Reference Aids, have found that these titles are now available for deposit in either paper copy or on microfiche. Nevertheless, the Project continues to serve a useful purpose for libraries, and it is patently a boon for non-depository institutions.

CONCLUSION

In addition to federal agencies involved in the sale, distribution, and bibliographic control of information produced by or for other federal entities, a growing number of commercial firms supply libraries and other institutions with non-depository publications. For example, Congressional Information Service provides many congressional and statistical non-depository series on microfiche, numerous federal district and appellate court decisions no longer published by the federal government are issued by several private companies, and the Readex Microprint Corporation offers all non-depository titles listed in the *Monthly Catalog* since 1953.[20]

The only significant way in which non-GPO titles produced by federal agencies have added to the *List of Classes* in recent years is through the "microfiche-only" component of the GPO micropublishing venture. Thus the analytical reports of the Foreign Broadcast Information Service and the foreign-language translations and abstracts of the Joint Publications Research Service, as well as some contract reports series noted in this chapter, are now microfiche-only depository items. GPO officials take pride in asserting that the number of former non-GPO and non-depository categories now available in the depository system is rapidly expanding. The stimulus to this trend was the addition of paragraph 41-2 to the April 1977 revision of the JCP's *Government Printing & Binding Regulations*, which stated:

> To meet the requirement of *Monthly Catalog* listing of Government publications by the Superintendent of Documents, each agency printing officer shall forward copies of those types of Government publications cited in Section 1902, Title 44 U.S.C. which are produced or procured through other than GPO sources to the Director, Library and Statutory Distribution Service (SL), Government Printing Office, Washington, D.C. 20401.[21]

Accordingly, agencies need furnish only two copies to the Service. One copy is used to catalog the title; the other is used to prepare a microfiche master from which to produce additional copies for distribution to subscribing depository institutions.

Despite these gains, there remains a large amount of information produced for government agencies which must be purchased. The provision of 44 U.S.C. 1903 which precludes "so-called cooperative publications which must necessarily be sold in order to be self-sustaining" obliges individuals and institutions to "buy back" from the government information which has already been paid for in the general taxation schedules. Thus public information subsidized by government agencies, whether scientific, technical, or educational, remains largely exempt from free deposit by legislative intent.

REFERENCES

1. *Annual Report of the Librarian of Congress, 1980* (Washington: Library of Congress, 1981), p. 62.

2. Bernard M. Fry, *Government Publications: Their Role in the National Program for Library and Information Services* (Washington: Government Printing Office, 1978), pp. 32-33.

3. Laurence F. Schmeckebier and Roy B. Eastin, *Government Publications and Their Use*, 2nd rev. ed. (Washington: Brookings, 1969), p. 443.

4. National Technical Information Service, *General Catalog of Information Services No. 7* (1981), p. 1.

5. DttP 3: 41 (November 1975).

6. *Final Report of the National Study Commission on Records and Documents of Federal Officials*, March 31, 1977, p. 46 (Y 3.R24/2: 1/977).

7. DttP 3: 41-42 (November 1975).

8. *NTIS NewsLine No. 5* (Spring 1981), p. 1.

9. J. C. Meredith, "NTIS Update: A Critical Review of Services," *Government Publications Review* 1: 344-46, 357-58 (1974).

10. Catherine Ettlinger, "NTIS: The Nation's Biggest Publisher," *Government Executive* (February 1974), p. 48.

11. "New Plan for NTIS?," *American Libraries* 5: 285-86 (June 1974).

12. DttP 7: 148 (July 1979).

13. Meredith, p. 346.

14. National Technical Information Service, *General Catalog of Information Services No. 7* (1981), pp. 30-31.

15. U.S. General Accounting Office, *Better Information Management Policies Needed: A Study of Scientific and Technical Bibliographic Services* (Washington: Government Printing Office, 1979), pp. 10-11, 13 (GA 1.13: PAD-72-62).

16. Meredith, p. 346.

17. Katherine Clay, "Searching ERIC on DIALOG: The Times They Are a'Changing," *Database* 2: 47-48 (September 1979). See also Jane Caldwell and Celia Ellingson, "A Comparison of Overlap: ERIC and Psychological Abstracts," *Database* 2: 62-67 (June 1979).

18. *Annual Report of the Librarian of Congress, 1980*, p. 62.

19. DttP 7: 111 (May 1979); DttP 7: 130 (July 1979).

20. Diane H. Smith, "Analysis of Readex Microprint and Alternate Sources of Non-Depository Publications," DttP 8: 28-29 (January 1980).

21. U.S. Congress, Joint Committee on Printing, *Government Printing & Binding Regulations, No. 24*, rev. April 1977 (Y 4.P93/1: 6/24).

6

Selected Information Sources for Federal Government Publications

INTRODUCTION

The bibliographic apparatus of United States public documents is as complex and variegated as the unwieldy corpus of materials it attempts to encompass. Indexes, lists, guides, bibliographies, whatever the name assigned to them, exhibit — like the materials they enumerate — a pattern that is irregular and often confusing. This should come as no surprise to the user of federal public documents. The bibliographic enterprise always falls short of its ideal.

A note of optimism, however, must be sounded when one compares recent bibliographic efforts with early nineteenth-century endeavors. The federal government waited until 1883 before charging Ben Perley Poore with the unenviable task of finding and cataloging all publications bereft of bibliographic existence since the beginning of the republic. He and his inexperienced, "incompetent" helpers dredged up 63,063 titles, only to be later accused of generating an unsatisfactory product.[1] In part, the history of current federal indexing and bibliographic publishing, especially in the private sector, has been a largely successful attempt to correct the errors and omissions of former efforts while enhancing the whole.

We have indeed come a long way since Poore compared his task to that of "Christopher Columbus when he steered westward on his voyage of discovery."[2] Developments in micropublishing and computer-generated information have created a revolution in bibliographic control and retrieval. Yet we still share Poore's feeling of helplessness in the face of the huge production of documentation which must be brought swiftly and accurately under control. Moreover, the distribution of government materials, such as those of the Census Bureau, in different formats exacerbates the problem of information management. By definition, the bibliographic ideal is unattainable, and attempts to achieve it will forever challenge the ingenuity of publisher and librarian.

This chapter will survey some of the more important retrospective and current sources of information that purport to organize this vast and sometimes bewildering mass of information.

PROFESSIONAL LITERATURE

Consistent with the growth of government information, there has been a steady increase in the size and variety of professional literature reporting and commenting on the federal publishing enterprise. The following titles represent a selection of basic sources that have withstood the test of time and more recent contributions that attempt to classify and evaluate government materials.

GENERAL WORKS

Anne M. Boyd, *United States Government Publications*, 3rd ed. rev., by Rae E. Rips (New York: Wilson, 1949), and Laurence F. Schmeckebier and Roy B. Eastin, *Government Publications and Their Use*, 2nd rev. ed. (Washington: Brookings, 1969) remain outstanding resources. Yuri Nakata, *From Press to People: Collecting and Using U.S. Government Publications* (Chicago: American Library Association, 1979) provides information on government printing and libraries, the depository library program, collection development, cataloging, classification, reference sources, and record-keeping, with appendixes, figures, and tables. James Bennett Childs, "Government Publications (Documents)," in Allen Kent, et al. (eds.), *Encyclopedia of Library and Information Science, Vol. 10* (New York: Marcel Dekker, 1973) presents a summary of federal documents in his survey of the bibliographic structure of worldwide government publishing. J. J. Cherns, *Official Publishing: An Overview* (New York: Pergamon, 1979) examines the organization and effectiveness of the publishing activities of national governments; Chapter 22 of this study analyzes United States government official information policy.

BIBLIOGRAPHIC GUIDES

Alexander C. Body, *Annotated Bibliography of Bibliographies on Selected Government Publications and Supplementary Guides to the Superintendent of Documents Classification System* was first published in 1967, and the author has been issuing supplements ever since. The *Sixth Supplement* (Greeley, CO: Gabor Kovacs, 1981) contains over 1,000 bibliographies, thoroughly annotated, including appendixes and a dictionary index; arrangement is by SuDocs class notation.

Roberta A. Scull, *A Bibliography of United States Government Bibliographies, Vol. I: 1968-1973* (Ann Arbor, MI: Pierian Press, 1974) has been updated by *Vol. II: 1974-1976* (Pierian, 1979). Over 2,600 bibliographies covering the period 1968 through 1976 are grouped within broad subject categories, with a subject and title index. Most entries are annotated and include full bibliographic information.

Vladimir M. Palic, *Government Publications: A Guide to Bibliographic Tools,* 4th ed. (Washington: Library of Congress, 1975) covers official publications worldwide, including the United States. A compilation of catalogs, checklists, indexes, accession lists, and bibliographies issued by federal agencies is found on pp. 11-80. Palic's *Government Organization Manuals: A Bibliography* (Washington: Library of Congress, 1976) lists official manuals and other publications that set forth the organization and structure of national governments, including the United States. Both works were combined and republished in one volume in 1977 by Pergamon Press.[3]

David W. Parish, *Changes in American Society, 1960-1978: An Annotated Bibliography of Official Government Publications* (Metuchen, NJ: Scarecrow Press, 1980) contains over 1,100 entries for federal and state publications that reflect social change in the United States. Arranged by broad subjects, the annotated entries for federal documents include SuDocs class number and availability. Frederic J. O'Hara, *A Guide to Publications of the Executive Branch* (Ann Arbor, MI: Pierian Press, 1979) describes the function and operation of executive departments and agencies and many of the publications they issue; evaluative annotations make this guide a most useful source.

Walter L. Newsome, *Government Reference Books 80/81: A Biennial Guide to U.S. Government Publications* (Littleton, CO: Libraries Unlimited, 1982) is the seventh volume in this series. It contains some 1,600 entries covering atlases, bibliographies, dictionaries, directories, guides, handbooks, indexes, and manuals issued by federal agencies during 1980 and 1981. Entries are annotated and include a complete list of GPO's Subject Bibliography (SB) series. Alice J. Wittig, *U.S. Government Publications for the School Media Center* (Littleton, CO: Libraries Unlimited, 1979) is an annotated, subject arrangement of over 350 maps, pictures, basic lists, and other titles available from the GPO and from individual agencies. Steven D. Zink, *United States Government Publications Catalogs* (New York: Special Libraries Association, 1982), number 8 in the SLA Bibliography series, contains over 200 annotated entries of the current publication lists of federal agencies; included are descriptions of agency catalogs of audiovisual and other non-print materials. Nancy Patton Van Zant, *Selected U.S. Government Series: A Guide for Public and Academic Libraries* (Chicago: American Library Association, 1978) is an annotated selection of about 600 federal government series. Arrangement is by broad topics with a title and subject index; the entries include depository item number and SuDocs class notation.

Popular guides include Walter L. Newsome, *New Guide to Popular Government Publications: For Libraries and Home Reference* (Littleton, CO: Libraries Unlimited, 1978), and W. Philip Leidy, *A Popular Guide to Government Publications* (New York: Columbia University Press, 1976). The former lists and annotates some 2,500 titles chosen for their currency or long-term popular interest. The latter lists several thousand titles selected from materials issued by government units between 1967 and 1975.

AGENCY HISTORIES

The Westview Library of Federal Departments, Agencies, and Systems is a series issued by Westview Press (Boulder, Colorado). Formerly called the Praeger Library of U.S. Government Departments and Agencies, each title in the series deals with a government entity. Studies include William C. Everhart, *The National Park Service*; Michael Frome, *The Forest Service*; Paul H. Oehser, *The Smithsonian Institution*; Theodore W. Taylor, *The Bureau of Indian Affairs*; and Charles A. Goodrum and Helen W. Dalrymple, *The Library of Congress*. A partial list of titles in the earlier Praeger series is included in Palic's *Government Organization Manuals: A Bibliography*, pp. 79-80.

EDUCATIONAL AIDS

Gladys Sachse, *U.S. Government Publications for Small and Medium-sized Public Libraries: A Study Guide* (Chicago: American Library Association, 1981) consists of a series of independent lessons designed for library assistants in small and medium-sized libraries. Modules include selection aids; acquisition, processing, and housing; frequently used reference sources; and the like. There are many useful sample illustrations of the *Monthly Catalog*, shelflist cards, and other forms. *Draft Syllabus of Resources for Teaching Government Publications* (Education Task Force, Government Documents Round Table, 1976) contains a section on federal publications which includes citations to abstracting and indexing services, background readings, cataloging and classification, the depository library system, Congress, laws, maps, microforms, and other topics. Issued to GODORT members in paper copy, it is available from EDRS in both paper copy and microfiche (ED 125 668; IR 003 784).

PERIODICAL LITERATURE

As Schorr's bibliography demonstrates, the literature of librarianship contains numerous accounts of writings on or about government publications.[4] These take the form of recurring columns, bibliographic roundups, annual updates, reviews, general commentary, news notes, and specialized articles on topics of interest to the profession. Magazines that contain these features include *Wilson Library Bulletin, Reference Services Review, Booklist, RQ, The Serials Librarian, Legal Reference Services Quarterly, Microform Review, Law Library Journal*, and many more. Some journals, notably *Illinois Libraries* and *Drexel Library Quarterly*, from time to time devote an entire issue to an aspect or theme related to federal government documents. For a full range of secondary source materials, one must consult indexes like *Library Literature*.

Documents to the People and *Government Publications Review* (GPR) are periodicals devoted entirely to the publications and activities of governments at all levels. The former is the official bimonthly publication of GODORT and provides a wealth of information for the documents librarian. Its issues feature new publications, columns, current activities, and periodic bibliographies of materials relating to government publications and documents librarianship. The latter, a refereed journal, was renamed *Government Publications Review: An International Journal of Issues and Information Resources* and began appearing bimonthly with Volume 9 (1982). The last issue of each volume is devoted entirely to columns identifying notable documents of the year. The magazine often devotes an entire issue to a common theme or topic, and the scholarly articles and several columns "provide a forum for current practice, new developments, trends, and issues associated with the production, distribution, processing, and use of government publications/information from all levels of government."[5]

CITATION MANUALS

There is no single uniform way in which writers cite the many forms of federal government materials. Generally, a citation should contain sufficient bibliographic data to lead the reader to the cited source and should be consistent in the citing of like materials.

Specific citation manuals include the *U.S. Government Printing Office Style Manual* (GP 1.23/4: St 9; item 548), George D. Brightbill and Wayne C. Maxson, *Citation Manual for United States Government Publications* (Philadelphia: Center for the Study of Federalism, Temple University), and *A Uniform System of Citation* (Harvard Law Review Association, et al.).

General citation manuals that include government and legal references include the *MLA Handbook for Writers of Research Papers, Theses, and Dissertations* (New York: Modern Language Association), *The Chicago Manual of Style for Authors, Editors and Copywriters* (Chicago: University of Chicago Press), Kate L. Turabian, *A Manual for Writers of Term Papers, Theses, and Dissertations* (Chicago: University of Chicago Press), and *Publication Manual of the American Psychological Association* (Washington: American Psychological Association). Some of these are revised periodically and new editions prepared.

CATALOGS, INDEXES, AND CHECKLISTS

Some of the sources that follow will be discussed again in later chapters as their utility impels more detailed analysis. Other important instruments of bibliographic control not included in this section will be given coverage in the chapters that ensue, for the bibliographic mosaic must be assembled piece by piece.

GOVERNMENT PUBLISHING

Benjamin Perley Poore, *Descriptive Catalogue of the Government Publications of the United States, September 5, 1774—March 4, 1881*, issued as Senate Miscellaneous Document 67, Forty-eighth Congress, second session, was the first attempt to make a complete list of all government publications—executive, legislative, and judicial. Lack of a good index makes the chronological arrangement of publications difficult to access. Moreover, Poore's *Catalogue* omitted many departmental publications.

John Griffith Ames, *Comprehensive Index to the Publications of the United States Government, 1881-1893*, issued in two volumes as House Document 754, Fifth-eighth Congress, second session, omitted a number of departmental publications but was a manifest improvement over Poore's *Catalogue*. Arrangement is alphabetical by subject with a personal name index at the end of Volume 2. Within subjects, author or department and title by key word reference Congress, session, and series volume for the Congressional Serial Set; serial volume numbers are given in tables under the subject "Congressional Documents" in Volume 1.

Adolphus Washington Greely, *Public Documents of the First Fourteen Congresses, 1789-1817 – Papers Relating to Early Congressional Documents*, issued as Senate Document 428, Fifty-sixth Congress, first session, overlaps somewhat with Poore, but no attempt was made to include departmental publications as such. Arrangement is chronological by Congress, followed by a forty-five page index of names (but not subjects). Greely's efforts, too, were marred by omissions. A supplement was published in Volume 1 of the 1903 *Annual Report* of the American Historical Association.

Superintendent of Documents, *Checklist of United States Public Documents, 1789-1909* reproduced the shelflist of the Public Documents Department Library. It is arranged in three sections: congressional edition by serial number; departmental edition by SuDocs class notation; and miscellaneous publications of Congress. Planned in two volumes, the index volume was never issued. The *Checklist's* inclusion of departmental publications marks a significant improvement over Poore and Ames, and those conversant with government structure have found the *Checklist* to be a most useful retrospective bibliography.

Superintendent of Documents, *Tables of and Annotated Index to the Congressional Series of United States Public Documents* continues Greely's work and lists publications of the Fifteenth to the Fifty-second Congresses, 1817-1893. The first section of the book, the "Tables," gives series information, with notes on contents and on omission or duplication in the Congressional Serial Set. The second section, the "Index," is a useful reference by subject and name, with the accompanying serial number of the bound congressional set. Unfortunately, the work covers little more than half of the numbered documents and reports issued from 1817 to 1893. The compilers expressed their disdain for many congressional materials and managed "to extricate the more important documents from the scattered mass of worthless matter which composes nearly one half the congressional set."[6] Like Greely's compilation, the *Tables and Annotated Index* includes only congressional publications. However, because many executive publications transmitted to Congress were ordered to be issued in their "congressional edition," the guide has some usefulness in this area. The peculiarities of issuing publications in more than one edition will be discussed in Chapter 7.[7]

Superintendent of Documents, *Catalogue of the Public Documents of the* [Fifty-third – Seventy-sixth] *Congress and of All Departments of the Government of the United States for the Period from March 4, 1893 to December 31, 1940* is a biennial dictionary catalog with entries for both personal and government author, subject, and, frequently, title. Proclamations and executive orders are indexed, as are periodicals that were issued regularly. A list of government offices appears at the end of each catalog to serve as a guide to government organization. Beginning with the Fifty-sixth Congress, the serial volume number is included in brackets to permit easy access to the bound volumes of the Congressional Serial Set. Known by its short title, the *Document Catalog* is renowned for its bibliographic thoroughness and accuracy. However, production of the *Catalog* fell woefully behind, and it was finally discontinued with Volume 25, issued in 1947 but covering the Seventy-sixth Congress (1939-1940).

Superintendent of Documents, *Index to the Reports and Documents of the* [Fifty-fourth – Seventy-second] *Congress, with Numerical Lists and Schedule of Volumes, 1895-1933* is an alphabetical subject (or inverted title) listing for congressional documents and reports only. Libraries that have the *Document*

Catalog rarely need to use the *Document Index* (its short title) unless the client has only the number of the document or report. This publication was discontinued with No. 43 for the second session of the Seventy-second Congress and replaced by the *Numerical Lists and Schedule of Volumes.*

Superintendent of Documents, *Numerical Lists and Schedule of Volumes* began in 1933 and is simply that section of the *Document Index* consisting of the reports and documents in numbered sequence (the "Lists") and a grouping of numbered reports and documents by volumes (the "Schedule") of the Congressional Serial Set. Lists and schedules were included in the biennial *Document Catalog*, but owing to its increasingly tardy appearance, libraries that subscribed to the congressional set needed a more current key. With the discontinuance of the *Document Catalog*, the *Numerical Lists* (its short title) assumed a more important role in accessing the bound serial set volumes. Because of its essential value in this respect, the *Numerical Lists* will be considered in more detail in the next chapter.

Superintendent of Documents, *Monthly Catalog of United States Government Publications* was created by the Printing Act of 1895, which directed the Superintendent of Documents "to prepare and publish a Monthly Catalog of Government Publications, which shall show the publications printed during a month, where obtainable, and the price thereof." However, the same act instructed the Superintendent "to prepare and print at the close of each Congress a Comprehensive Index [*Document Catalog*] of public documents [and] to prepare and print at the close of each regular session of Congress a Consolidated Index [*Document Index*] of congressional documents."[8] The *Monthly Catalog* began as little more than an in-print list, designed to remedy the haphazard system of distribution and sales of public documents. The *Document Catalog*, a "retrospective" tool virtually from its inception, was to be the exemplary bibliographic achievement. But as the cost of compiling and printing the biennial work grew ever more burdensome, and as the *Monthly Catalog* expanded its coverage, the Superintendent of Documents was compelled to reexamine both programs. Upon his recommendation to the Joint Committee on Printing, the latter index became the single official source of publications as mandated by Section 62 of the 1895 Printing Act.

A privately published work in ten volumes known as *Hickcox's Monthly Catalogue* was the precursor of the monthly publication.[9] Between 1941 and 1947 three supplements to the *Monthly Catalog* were issued "to cover publications which had been omitted from the *Monthly Catalog* and which would have appeared in the biennial *Document Catalog.*"[10] The internal improvements beginning with the September 1947 issue, the reemergence of personal authors in 1963, the decennial indexes, and, of course, the great evolution of the work discussed in Chapter 3 – all have been measures designed to make the *Monthly Catalog* a guide fully justifying the discontinuance of the *Document Catalog*. Yet, ironically, even today the *Monthly Catalog* does not exhibit the bibliographic excellence and sophistication of the magnificent *Document Catalog*.

A microfiche collection of Poore, Ames, the *Checklist*, the *Tables and Annotated Index*, and the *Monthly Catalog* (to 1980), accompanied by a user guide, is available from Information Interchange Corporation, a Washington, DC based commercial publisher.

COMMERCIAL PUBLISHING

Because of the limitations inherent in the bibliographic guides and indexes described above, librarians have been obliged to direct the client to more than one source, especially for citations prior to 1893. However, recent endeavors by enterprising commercial publishers have brought the publications of the federal government under better control, thus enhancing access and accuracy.

One commercial source that has attempted, with singular success, to rectify the bibliographic shortcomings of retrospective and current guides to federal congressional and statistical publications is Congressional Information Service, Inc. (CIS). Currently located in Bethesda, Maryland, CIS began auspiciously in 1970 with the publication of *CIS/Index* and has been issuing a series of products and services ever since. Distinguished by their quality and accuracy, they employ largely a "dual media" technique by which paper copy indexes are accompanied by the full text microfiche of the publications identified in the index.

CIS/INDEX

CIS/Index appears monthly and provides abstracts and indexing information for congressional hearings, committee prints, reports, documents, Senate executive reports, and Senate treaty documents. The indexes cumulate quarterly, and there is an annual cumulation that includes index and abstracts volumes (*CIS/Annual*). A *CIS Five-Year Cumulative Index* (1970-1974) and a *CIS Four-Year Cumulative Index* (1975-1978) provide ease of use.

Direct access to abstracts is furnished by subjects and names, titles, bill, report and document numbers, and names of committee or subcommittee chairpersons. The abstracts provide full bibliographic information, a description of the publication's subject matter and purpose, and an outline of specific contents. The *CIS/Annual* includes citations to multivolume hearings and legislative histories. The *CIS/Microfiche Library* provides the text of the publications listed in *CIS/Index* (except interim legislative calendars) as well as all public laws of the session.

In 1982 Congressional Information Service published a *Conversion Table: SuDocs Number to CIS/Index and CIS/Microfiche Number, 1970-1979*. Edited by Alice N. McGarvey, Government Documents Service, University Library, Arizona State University, the *Conversion Table* is a ten-year list of congressional hearings and committee prints in SuDocs class order referencing the CIS abstract notation. Thus users with only the classification notation can readily locate the CIS abstract and proceed to the full text in the *CIS/Microfiche Library*.

CIS/Index is online through DIALOG and ORBIT. A *CIS Online User Guide and Thesaurus* is available for purchase from Congressional Information Service. The *User Guide*, a two-volume looseleaf manual, provides numerous examples and illustrations showing the easiest and most cost-effective online searching techniques. The manual contains all of the subject terms used to create the *CIS/Index*, thus enabling users to focus their searches more precisely by selecting the narrowest term under which specific information can be found.

Figure 10 shows a sample abstract in *CIS/Index*.

Figure 10
CIS/Index: Sample Abstract

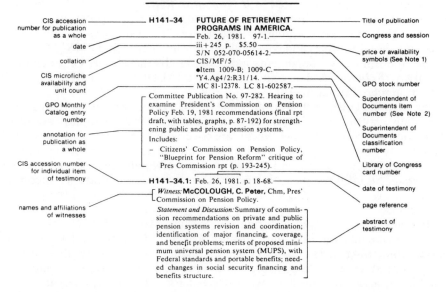

SAMPLE ABSTRACT

The following sample entry shows the information contained in a typical abstract.

H141   **Hearings**
AGING,
Select Committee on, House

CIS accession number for publication as a whole — **H141-34**   **FUTURE OF RETIREMENT PROGRAMS IN AMERICA.** — Title of publication

date — Feb. 26, 1981. 97-1. — Congress and session

collation — iii+245 p. $5.50 — price or availability symbols (See Note 1)

S/N 052-070-05614-2.

CIS microfiche availability and unit count — CIS/MF/5

•Item 1009-B; 1009-C. — Superintendent of Documents item number (See Note 2)

GPO Monthly Catalog entry number — °Y4.Ag4/2:R31/14. — Superintendent of Documents classification number

MC 81-12378. LC 81-602587. — GPO stock number

annotation for publication as a whole — Committee Publication No. 97-282. Hearing to examine President's Commission on Pension Policy Feb. 19, 1981 recommendations (final rpt draft, with tables, graphs, p. 87-192) for strengthening public and private pension systems.
Includes:
— Citizens' Commission on Pension Policy, "Blueprint for Pension Reform" critique of Pres Commission rpt (p. 193-245). — Library of Congress card number

CIS accession number for individual item of testimony — **H141-34.1:** Feb. 26, 1981. p. 18-68. — date of testimony

— page reference

names and affiliations of witnesses — *Witness:* **McCOLOUGH, C. Peter,** Chm, Pres' Commission on Pension Policy.

Statement and Discussion: Summary of commission recommendations on private and public pension systems revision and coordination; identification of major financing, coverage, and benefit problems; merits of proposed minimum universal pension system (MUPS), with Federal standards and portable benefits; needed changes in social security financing and benefits structure. — abstract of testimony

NOTE 1 — AVAILABILITY: Publications that have a price are sold by the U.S. Government Printing Office, Superintendent of Documents, Washington, D.C. 20402. Publications marked "price not given" are also sold by the Superintendent of Documents, but the actual sale price has not yet been made available. *Prices are subject to change without notice.*

Publications marked with a single dagger (†) may be requested in writing from the issuing committee; such requests are honored when possible, but these publications usually are available only in limited quantities. Reports and documents are also distributed by the House and Senate Document Rooms. It is suggested that requests be accompanied by a return address label. Write to Senate committees at Washington, D.C. 20510, and to House committees at Washington, D.C. 20515.

Publications marked with a double dagger (‡) are printed for official use. These documents may be requested from the issuing committee, but they are generally not available for distribution to the public.

Publications marked with a diamond (◆) are specifically designated by the issuing committee as not available for distribution.

Microfiche copies of all publications abstracted in the CIS/Index are sold by Congressional Information Service, Inc., in either complete collections, or individually. For details, see your librarian or write the publisher.

NOTE 2 — ITEM NUMBERS: Publications marked with a bullet (•) and an Item Number are sent to Depository Libraries. (Not all Depository Libraries collect all Item Numbers, however.)

In the case of a double item number, the first item number is for paper copy and the second is for microfiche.

NOTE 3 — IDENTIFICATION NUMBERS: Wherever possible, a Superintendent of Documents classification number (identified by a ° symbol), a Library of Congress card number, a GPO stock number, and a GPO monthly catalog entry number have been given for each publication. However, not all Congressional publications have been assigned these identification numbers.

Publications (particularly committee prints) which do not appear in the GPO Monthly Catalog do not receive entry numbers or Superintendent of Documents classification numbers. Even if such identification numbers are assigned they are not always available to us at press time. If they subsequently become available, they will be noted in the next List of Bibliographic Data Additions and Revisions published in each quarterly index, and included in document abstracts published in the CIS/Annual.

AMERICAN STATISTICS INDEX

American Statistics Index (ASI) identifies indexes, and provides abstracts for the statistical publications of the executive branch, Congress, and other federal entities. Like *CIS/Index*, ASI is issued monthly with quarterly cumulated indexes and an *ASI/Annual Supplement* consisting of index and abstracts volumes. It is by far the single most comprehensive finding aid to federal government statistics in existence.

Indexes by subjects and names, categories (demographic and geographic characteristics), titles, and agency report numbers refer the user to abstracts that provide bibliographic information and specific content information. A clothbound "base edition" titled *ASI Annual & Retrospective Edition* provides indexing and abstracting information on a selective basis for publications issued from the early 1960s to January 1974. Thereafter *ASI Annual Supplements* replace the monthly issues and cover calendar years. Through the *ASI Microfiche Library*, the full text of documents indexed and abstracted may be purchased.

Like *CIS/Index*, ASI is online through DIALOG and ORBIT. Figure 11 shows a sample abstract in ASI.

As Figure 11 demonstrates, an outstanding feature of ASI is the in-depth abstracting given to government periodicals which contain statistical information. Over 800 such periodicals are covered by ASI on a continuing basis. The monthly issues index and abstract each entirely new periodical but only the new articles, special tables, and format changes of established periodicals. The *ASI Annual Supplement* fully abstracts and indexes each periodical. Therefore, search strategy requires using both the current monthly issues and the previous year's annual.

In 1981 Congressional Information Service offered *CIS Periodicals on Microfiche*, a collection of some 250 statistical titles from the mid-1970s to the present containing data on economics, finance, trade, natural resources, industrial production, employment, and other topics. The periodicals and series available through this collection were selected for their primary research value from the total periodicals available from the *ASI Microfiche Library*. In 1982 the company offered *CIS Energy Periodicals on Microfiche*, a smaller, specialized collection of twenty-five periodicals that contain statistical information on all major aspects of energy supply, production, consumption, and pricing. Subscribers may purchase individual periodical titles and volumes for the current year or previous years, or comprehensive current and backfile collections.

CIS & ASI Documents on Demand Service will provide almost any publication described in the indexes on an individual order basis. Prices depend on the number of pages reproduced and whether the publication is requested in paper copy or on microfiche. While the cost of an individual publication on microfiche is reasonable, the price of the paper edition is very expensive.[11]

Figure 11
American Statistics Index: Sample Abstract

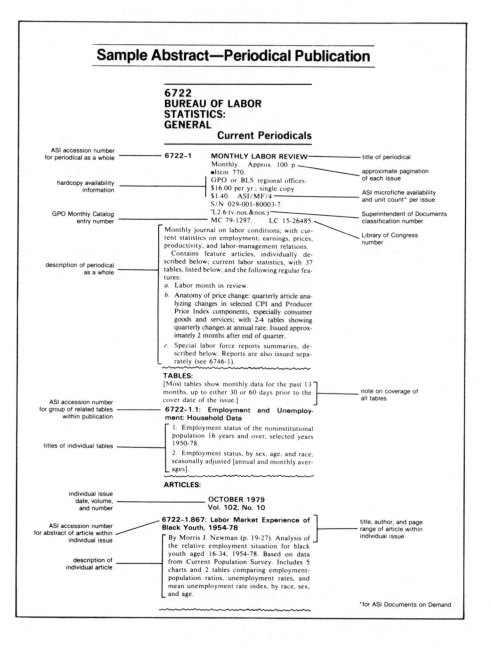

Sample Abstract—Periodical Publication

6722
BUREAU OF LABOR STATISTICS: GENERAL
Current Periodicals

ASI accession number for periodical as a whole — **6722-1**   **MONTHLY LABOR REVIEW** — title of periodical

Monthly. Approx. 100 p. — approximate pagination of each issue
● Item 770.

hardcopy availability information — GPO or BLS regional offices: $16.00 per yr.; single copy $1.40. ASI/MF/4 — ASI microfiche availability and unit count* per issue

S/N 029-001-80003-7.

GPO Monthly Catalog entry number — *L2.6:(v.nos.&nos.) — Superintendent of Documents classification number

MC 79-1297.   LC 15-26485. — Library of Congress number

description of periodical as a whole — Monthly journal on labor conditions; with current statistics on employment, earnings, prices, productivity, and labor-management relations.
Contains feature articles, individually described below; current labor statistics, with 37 tables, listed below; and the following regular features:

a. Labor month in review.

b. Anatomy of price change: quarterly article analyzing changes in selected CPI and Producer Price Index components, especially consumer goods and services; with 2-4 tables showing quarterly changes at annual rate. Issued approximately 2 months after end of quarter.

c. Special labor force reports summaries, described below. Reports are also issued separately (see 6746-1).

TABLES:
[Most tables show monthly data for the past 13 months, up to either 30 or 60 days prior to the cover date of the issue.] — note on coverage of all tables

ASI accession number for group of related tables within publication — **6722-1.1: Employment and Unemployment: Household Data**

titles of individual tables — 1. Employment status of the noninstitutional population 16 years and over, selected years 1950-78.

2. Employment status, by sex, age, and race, seasonally adjusted [annual and monthly averages].

ARTICLES:

individual issue date, volume, and number — **OCTOBER 1979**
Vol. 102, No. 10

ASI accession number for abstract of article within individual issue — **6722-1.867: Labor Market Experience of Black Youth, 1954-78** — title, author, and page range of article within individual issue

description of individual article — By Morris J. Newman (p. 19-27). Analysis of the relative employment situation for black youth aged 16-34, 1954-78. Based on data from Current Population Survey. Includes 5 charts and 2 tables comparing employment-population ratios, unemployment rates, and mean unemployment rate index, by race, sex, and age.

*for ASI Documents on Demand

CIS US SERIAL SET INDEX, 1789-1969

This massive undertaking permits users to bypass the earlier, flawed bibliographic guides that covered those publications which comprise the Congressional Serial Set from its beginning through 1969. From 1970, coverage of serial set publications, as well as other congressional materials, is provided by *CIS/Index*. Thus the *CIS US Serial Set Index* is the definitive retrospective tool, encompassing some 330,000 publications issued over a 180-year period.

The indexes consist of twelve parts totaling thirty-six volumes. Access is provided by subjects and key words, private relief and related actions (private legislation affecting persons or organizations), numerical lists of report and document numbers, and a schedule of serial volumes. The bibliographic information thus provided can be effectively used to access a library's collection of the volumes, or the full text is available for purchase from the *CIS US Serial Set on Microfiche*.

CIS US CONGRESSIONAL COMMITTEE HEARINGS INDEX

This inspired effort covers published hearings from the early 1800s through 1969, after which the user is directed to *CIS/Index*. Distributed in eight parts, the index encompasses over 30,000 publications. The "Reference Bibliography" section provides full bibliographic information, annotations, microfiche notes, issuing committee and subcommittee, bill numbers, and witness names and affiliations. Moreover, access is provided by subjects and organizations, personal names, titles, bill numbers, SuDocs class numbers, and report or document numbers. A *US Congressional Committee Hearings on Microfiche Full Collection* contains a full text microfiche copy of each publication identified in the *Index*.

CIS US CONGRESSIONAL COMMITTEE PRINTS INDEX FROM THE EARLIEST PUBLICATIONS THROUGH 1969

Owing to inconsistent distribution and depository practices, a library's collection of committee prints is apt to be less complete than its hearings or serial set volumes. This guide, issued in five volumes, covers approximately 15,000 titles issued from the mid-1800s through 1969; thereafter *CIS/Index* provides excellent coverage of prints.

The *Index* consists of a "Reference Bibliography" in two volumes, which gives full bibliographic information; a two-volume index by subjects and names; and a single volume with indexes by titles, Congress and issuing committee, bill numbers, and SuDocs class numbers. An appendix to this latter volume contains summary histories of the establishment, jurisdictional assignments, and jurisdictional interrelationships of all standing committees that issued publications appearing in the *Index*. The full text of prints is provided by *US Congressional Committee Prints on Microfiche*, a project that was begun by Greenwood Press (Westport, Connecticut) before it became a division of Congressional Information Service.

OTHER COMMERCIAL SOURCES

The remaining commercial publications include ambitious retrospective projects of a bibliographic nature, John L. Andriot's well-known *Guide to U.S. Government Publications*, and the indispensable *Directory of Government Document Collections & Librarians*. Although they may not enjoy the reputation of Congressional Information Service publications, they serve an important function in the control and access of government documents information.

In Chapter 3 we noted some commercial ventures in support of the *Monthly Catalog* that were published by Carrollton Press and are now distributed by Research Publications, Inc. Other Carrollton issuances now handled by RPI include the following:

The Declassified Documents Reference System. In a dual-media, self-contained package, the *System* consists of top secret, secret, and confidential federal documents declassified under mandatory review procedures and amendments to the Freedom of Information Act.[12] The declassified documents include telegrams, correspondence, field reports, minutes of cabinet meetings, national security policy statements, and intelligence estimates. Documents have been secured from a number of departments and agencies, including State, Defense, CIA, FBI, Presidential Libraries, and the National Archives.

Abstract Catalogs are published quarterly with a subject index cumulated annually. There are annual collections from 1975 and a *Declassified Documents Retrospective Collection* containing two volumes of abstracts of over 8,000 documents, a one-volume subject index, and over 1,000 microfiche containing the full text of the documents.

Once entries are identified in the index or abstracts, users can immediately consult the fiche where the text of the materials is found. Access to this collection provides the student and scholar the means for critical reevaluation of historical events of great magnitude.

The National Union Catalog of U.S. Government Publications Received by Depository Libraries, 1974. This is a four-volume set showing the depository libraries in the United States and the depository items they subscribed to as of November 1973. At one time this work may have had some value as an interlibrary loan tool or locating directory, but current item changes among depository institutions diminish its usefulness today.

Cumulative Subject Guide to U.S. Government Bibliographies, 1924-1973. A useful spin-off from the *Cumulative Subject Index to the Monthly Catalog of U.S. Government Publications, 1900-1971*, this seven-volume hardcover compilation describes all bibliographic references in the *Monthly Catalog* for those years. Entries include not only separate bibliographies taken from the subject "Bibliography" used by the *Monthly Catalog* during those years, but thousands of entries of proceedings, journal articles, and the like, with references appended. The latter information was not indexed in the *Monthly Catalog* from 1948 on. The result is a total of more than 40,000 entries covering "bibliographies" in the broadest sense of the word for fifty years of *Monthly Catalogs*. A "dual media" package, the *Guide* is an index to *U.S. Government Bibliography Masterfile, 1924-1973*, which contains the full text of the references on microfiche. The *Masterfile*, however, has been discontinued and is no longer available.

Edna A. Kanely (comp.), *Cumulative Index to Hickcox's Monthly Catalog of U.S. Government Publications, 1885-1894*. As noted, the precursor of the official *Monthly Catalog* was published under the direction of John H. Hickcox in ten annual catalogs. Kanely's edition provides cumulative subject and author access to Hickcox's valuable historical work. Her decennial index is published in three hardcover volumes.

Mary Elizabeth Poole (comp.), *The "Classes Added" Reprint Edition of Hickcox's Monthly Catalog of U.S. Government Publications, 1885-1894*. As we noted in Chapter 3, Poole added SuDocs class numbers to the first thirty years of the official *Monthly Catalog*, and she has provided the same service for Hickcox's work. Thus all *Monthly Catalog* entries have been assigned SuDocs class numbers from 1885 to the present. This edition was published in six hardcover volumes.

The United States Historical Documents Institute, Inc. (USHDI), formed in 1970, was affiliated with Carrollton Press and has issued some useful dual-media products that provide retrospective control over publications cataloged in the library of the Superintendent of Documents over the decades.

Checklist of United States Public Documents, 1789-1976. This is a microfilm edition of the shelflist of GPO's Public Documents Library. It contains some 1,300,000 bibliographic entries for over 2,000,000 publications issued during these years. Thus *Checklist '76* contains in one place all the bibliographic information found in the *1789-1909 Checklist*, the *Document Catalog* (1893-1940), and the *Monthly Catalog* (1895-1976), plus shelflist entries never listed in any catalog. The 118 microfilm reels are accompanied by five hardcover index volumes arranged by government author/organization.

Cumulative Title Index to U.S. Government Publications, 1789-1976. Compiled by Daniel Lester and Sandra Faull, this is a sixteen-volume hardcover listing of all titles included in the microfilm. Bibliographic data provided include, in addition to the title, the SuDocs class notation, the date, and the microfilm reel section where the full description can be found in *Checklist '76*.

Mary Elizabeth Poole (comp.), *Documents Office Classification, Fifth Edition, 1977*. Now distributed by RPI, this original USHDI issuance is correlated with *Checklist '76*. It consists of thousands of entries arranged by SuDocs number with title and reference to earlier and later class numbers. An alphabetical index appears at the end of each of the three hardcover volumes listing the names of over 2,000 author-organizations. Because *Checklist '76* is arranged by SuDocs classification, the indefatigable Ms. Poole was able to accomplish her *Documents Office Classification*.

John L. Andriot (McLean, VA: Documents Index) has published guides to federal statistics and major United States government series over the years. These have been widely used and their value justly acknowledged. Of Andriot's several efforts, his *Guide to U.S. Government Publications* is the most prominent and the one which he has consistently updated.

Andriot's *Guide* has undergone format changes during its publication history. Early editions were issued as a looseleaf service, and later editions were published in hardcover volumes. The 1981 edition of the *Guide* was issued on microfiche in three volumes. Volume 1 lists in SuDocs class order all federal entities currently in existence as well as those agencies that were abolished subsequent to January 1, 1975. Many of the series and periodicals are annotated and include periodicity, depository item number, and a statement of purpose. Some entries, such as the Yearbook of Agriculture (A 1.10), provide a valuable historical annotation with a complete list of Yearbook titles. Volume 2 consists of a SuDocs class arrangement of publications for agencies abolished prior to January 1, 1975. Volume 3 provides alphabetical agency and title indexes to entries in Volumes 1 and 2 and a valuable new feature called "Agency Class Chronology." Arranged alphanumerically by the symbols representing parent agency and provenance, the chronology shows the history of all agency class numbers assigned. Also included in Volume 3 is a detailed explanation of the Superintendent of Documents classification scheme. Periodic cumulative supplements on microfiche are issued to keep the basic volumes current.

However, in 1982 Andriot reverted to a hard copy format. Volume 1 of the 1982 *Guide* is divided into separate sections. The first part is arranged by SuDocs classification and lists current agency series. The second section retains the innovative "Agency Class Chronology" introduced in Volume 3 of the 1981 microfiche sequence. The third and fourth sections comprise an agency index and a title index. Volume 2 consists of superseded and abolished agencies. Andriot's inability to stay with a consistent format for his editions has diminished the utility of this valuable product.

Omnibus guides include *United States Government Publications* (London: Mansell Publishing) and *Bibliographic Guide to Government Publications — U.S.* (Boston: G. K. Hall & Co.). The former is a sixteen-volume corporate author index representing the pre-1956 holdings of over 900 American libraries reported to the *National Union Catalog* at the Library of Congress. It was previously published as Volumes 609-624 of *The National Union Catalog, Pre-1956 Imprints*. The latter is an annual subject bibliography which brings together publications cataloged by the Research Libraries of the New York Public Library with additional entries from Library of Congress MARC tapes. Access is by main entry, added entries, titles, series titles, and subjects.

An important non-bibliographic source is the *Directory of Government Document Collections & Librarians, Third Edition*. Issued in June 1981, the *Directory* was compiled by members of the Government Documents Round Table, ALA, and can be purchased from Congressional Information Service, Inc. Eight sections provide information on the holdings of federal, state, local, foreign, and international documents for some 2,700 libraries in the United States. Previous editions of this valuable *Directory* were issued in 1974 and 1978. The 1981 edition includes sections on government documents instructors in library schools, libraries which have special collection strengths in categories of documents, state document authorities, an alphabetical list of individuals working with government publications, and directory information for key people and organizations in the government documents professional community.

CONCLUSION

This represents a selection of guides to federal government materials. Other lists, indexes, and finding aids will be discussed in the chapters that follow. Moreover, new products or updated editions of existing sources will appear at a steady rate, for the production of bibliographic services in this field has become a growth industry. Owing to technological advances, bibliographic control has traveled great distances since the heroic but inadequate efforts of individuals like Poore and Ames. Yet as microform collections and online services expand the scope and enhance the quality control of government information, the result seems only to reveal the need for more and better systems. Indeed, the sheer amount of information continually threatens to overwhelm the bibliographic apparatus that seeks to contain it and render it manageable. The task often resembles the one designed to punish Sisyphus.

REFERENCES

1. Laurence F. Schmeckebier and Roy B. Eastin, *Government Publications and Their Use*, 2nd rev. ed. (Washington: Brookings, 1969), p. 7.

2. Ibid.

3. Vladimir M. Palic, *Government Publications: A Guide to Bibliographic Tools Incorporating Government Organization Manuals: A Bibliography* (New York: Pergamon Press, 1977).

4. Alan Edward Schorr, *Government Documents in the Library Literature, 1909-1974* (Ann Arbor, MI: Pierian Press, 1977). The guide is a comprehensive bibliographic coverage of literature on federal, state, municipal, United Nations, and League of Nations documents.

5. *Government Publications Review* 9: 1 (1982).

6. Schmeckebier and Eastin, p. 33.

7. For the convenience of users, Poore, Ames, Greely, the *Checklist*, and the *Tables and Annotated Index* have been reprinted by various publishers.

8. Section 68, Printing Act of 1895 (28 *Stat*. 610).

9. John H. Hickcox, *United States Government Publications: A Monthly Catalog* (Washington: W. H. Lowdermilk, 1885-1894). Irregularly issued over this period, it contains many entries not listed elsewhere.

10. Schmeckebier and Eastin, p. 26.

11. For example, a 273-page hearing issued by the Senate Foreign Relations Committee entitled *The Situation in El Salvador* was made available on microfiche for $6.50 and in paper copy for $65.52.

12. See *Executive Order 11652* (March 8, 1972), 3 CFR 1971-75 Comp., pp. 678-90.

7

Legislative Branch Materials

INTRODUCTION

"The basic architecture of American government," Telford Taylor wrote, "is trinitarian: three separate and distinct though interlocked segments of power, the operations of which are guided by a written document, the Constitution."[1] It is clear that the framers regarded the legislative branch as *primus inter pares*. Article I, Section 1 of that basic instrument bears the unequivocal statement, "All legislative powers herein granted shall be vested in a Congress of the United States, which shall consist of a Senate and House of Representatives." Indeed, James Burnham points out that "the Founding Fathers believed that in a republican and representative governmental system the preponderating share of power [was to be] held and exercised by the legislature." Moreover, that belief was "rather a self-evident axiom than a conclusion to be argued."[2]

In historical fact Congress antedates both the presidency and the judicial branch. The first federal Congress made the arrangements for counting the ballots of the first electoral college and for inaugurating George Washington and John Adams as the first executive officers. The office of Attorney General and the departments of War, Foreign Affairs, and Treasury were established by acts of the first Congress. Furthermore, the first Congress "established the judicial courts of the United States," and "more than threescore major statutes were the legislative fruits of its effort." Included in that burst of law-giving were bills on tariffs, appropriations, patents and copyrights, the punishment of crimes, uniform militia, succession to the presidency, reduction of the public debt, rates of foreign exchange, naturalization, harbors, the establishment of hospitals, and the progress of the useful arts.[3] The crown jewel in the diadem of the first Congress was the submission of the first ten amendments to the Constitution, the Bill of Rights.

The word "Congress" was taken from the Articles of Confederation, while the words "House of Representatives" and "Senate" emerged from the 1787 Constitutional Convention. In addition to its committee structure and staff, both House and Senate are served by agencies which are sometimes called "supporting arms of Congress." These entities include the by now familiar Government Printing Office, Congressional Budget Office, Architect of the Capitol, Cost

Accounting Standards Board, General Accounting Office, Library of Congress, United States Botanic Garden, and Office of Technology Assessment. Brief descriptions of the activities of these agencies are found in the current edition of the *United States Government Manual*, and detailed accountability is set forth in the annual House and Senate legislative branch appropriations hearings.

This chapter will examine some of the principal sources of information produced by or for the Congress of the United States pursuant to its duties and activities and the specialized bibliographic systems for current and retrospective research. The reader will discover that the multiplicity of bibliographic tools published by government and the private sector permits ready access to the voluminous materials generated by the legislative branch of this trinitarian federal establishment.

THE LEGISLATIVE PROCESS

A knowledge of the process by which a bill becomes a law is a prerequisite to a comprehension of its underlying bibliographic structure. Useful guides to both process and structure include Walter J. Oleszek, *Congressional Procedures and the Policy Process* (Washington: Congressional Quarterly Press, 1978), Robert Goehlert, *Congress and Law-Making: Researching the Legislative Process* (Santa Barbara, CA: Clio Press, 1979) and *How Our Laws Are Made*. The latter was first issued by the House Judiciary Committee in 1953, and since that time it has undergone many revisions and editions. Published in the House documents series and prepared by the Law Revision Counsel of that chamber, it provides a detailed explanation of the legislative process with numerous illustrations of a bill in its several parliamentary stages, committee reports, and enactment into law. A companion publication, *Enactment of a Law: Steps in the Legislative Process*, is issued in the Senate documents series and illustrates the progress of legislation originating in that body.

The chart, "How a Bill Becomes Law," is shown as Figure 12. Published by Congressional Quarterly, Inc., it traces the passage of legislation in both houses of Congress and will provide the reader with a graphic account of the legislative process from introduction to enactment or veto. What follows are the several congressional publications associated with this process, a crucial activity that, while often tortuous and frustrating, manifests and encourages "deliberation, collegial decisionmaking, dissent, openness, participation, and accessibility."[4]

INTRODUCTION OF LEGISLATION

Many are the ways in which legislation originates. In modern times the "executive communication" has become a prolific source of legislative proposals. Article II, Section 3 of the Constitution obliges the president to report to the Congress from time to time on the state of the Union and to recommend for consideration such measures as he deems necessary and expedient. This takes the form of a letter from a member of the president's cabinet or the head of an independent agency—or even from the president himself—transmitting a draft of a proposed bill to the Speaker of the House and the president of the Senate. The communication is then referred to the standing committee having jurisdiction over the subject matter embraced in the proposal.

Figure 12
How a Bill Becomes Law

HOW A BILL BECOMES LAW

This graphic shows the most typical way in which proposed legislation is enacted into law. There are more complicated, as well as simpler, routes, and most bills fall by the wayside and never become law. The process is illustrated with two hypothetical bills, House bill No. 1 (HR 1) and Senate bill No. 2 (S 2).

Each bill must be passed by both houses of Congress in identical form before it can become law. The path of HR 1 is traced by a solid line, that of S 2 by a broken line. However, in practice most legislation begins as similar proposals in both houses.

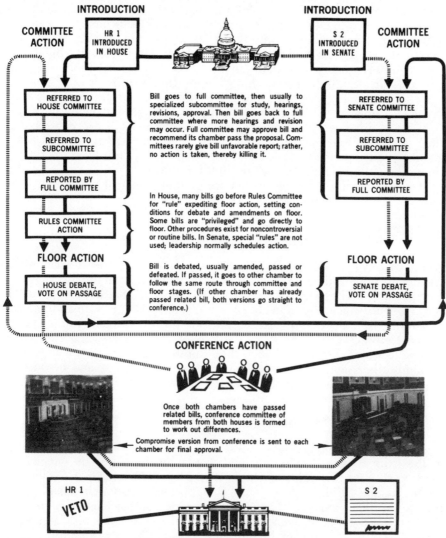

INTRODUCTION

COMMITTEE ACTION

HR 1 INTRODUCED IN HOUSE

REFERRED TO HOUSE COMMITTEE

REFERRED TO SUBCOMMITTEE

REPORTED BY FULL COMMITTEE

RULES COMMITTEE ACTION

FLOOR ACTION

HOUSE DEBATE, VOTE ON PASSAGE

INTRODUCTION

S 2 INTRODUCED IN SENATE

COMMITTEE ACTION

REFERRED TO SENATE COMMITTEE

REFERRED TO SUBCOMMITTEE

REPORTED BY FULL COMMITTEE

FLOOR ACTION

SENATE DEBATE, VOTE ON PASSAGE

Bill goes to full committee, then usually to specialized subcommittee for study, hearings, revisions, approval. Then bill goes back to full committee where more hearings and revision may occur. Full committee may approve bill and recommend its chamber pass the proposal. Committees rarely give bill unfavorable report; rather, no action is taken, thereby killing it.

In House, many bills go before Rules Committee for "rule" expediting floor action, setting conditions for debate and amendments on floor. Some bills are "privileged" and go directly to floor. Other procedures exist for noncontroversial or routine bills. In Senate, special "rules" are not used; leadership normally schedules action.

Bill is debated, usually amended, passed or defeated. If passed, it goes to other chamber to follow the same route through committee and floor stages. (If other chamber has already passed related bill, both versions go straight to conference.)

CONFERENCE ACTION

Once both chambers have passed related bills, conference committee of members from both houses is formed to work out differences.

Compromise version from conference is sent to each chamber for final approval.

HR 1 VETO

S 2

Compromise version approved by both houses is sent to President who can either sign it into law or veto it and return it to Congress. Congress may override veto by a two-thirds majority vote in both houses; bill then becomes law without President's signature.

Legislation may be conceived and drafted by interest groups—bar associations, labor unions, chambers of commerce, professional societies—or indeed by individuals. If a member is favorably disposed toward the drafted legislation, he may introduce such measures. Of course, legislative ideas come also from members themselves, initially arising from campaign pledges made or, after taking office, experience learned in the need for amendments to existing statutory law or the repeal of laws.

Whatever the origin, *introduction* of legislation can be made only by a member of Congress. Bills and resolutions are the forms of legislation, and they may be introduced in either chamber. Of the thousands of pieces of legislation introduced in each Congress, only about 20 percent are ever reported out of committee and often less than 5 percent become law. The voyage of a bill through Congress begins when it is introduced by a member. Both House and Senate permit unlimited multiple sponsorship of a bill. In the House it is no longer the custom to read bills, even by title, at the time of introduction. The bill is introduced simply by placing it in the "hopper" provided for the purpose at the side of the clerk's desk in the House chamber. The Senate's procedure is more formal: A senator may introduce a bill or resolution by presenting it to the clerks at the desk of the presiding officer without commenting on it from the floor, or he may rise and introduce the measure from the floor.

Measures or proposals introduced are of four principal forms: bills, joint resolutions, concurrent resolutions, and simple resolutions.

BILLS (H.R.; S.)

The term *bill* is used for most legislative proposals whether in enacting new legislation or in amending previous legislation, and appear in the form shown in Figure 13. Bills may originate in either the House or the Senate, except for bills raising revenue, which, according to Article I, Section 7 of the Constitution, shall originate in the House. It is also customary, but not necessary, that general appropriation measures originate in the House. They are assigned a number in the order in which they are introduced during the two-year congressional term. The number is retained throughout all parliamentary stages and becomes the most useful piece of bibliographic data for tracing legislation.

JOINT RESOLUTIONS (H.J. Res.; S.J. Res.)

At one time the joint resolution was used for purposes of general legislation; but the two houses finally concluded that a bill was the appropriate instrumentality for this purpose. However, the legal effect of joint resolutions is the same as that of bills—they require the approval of both chambers and the signature of the president. They may be used for "incidental or inferior" legislation, such as establishing the date for the convening of Congress, or "unusual" legislation, such as the infamous Tonkin Gulf Resolution (H.J. Res. 1145, adopted August 7, 1964). They are assigned a sequential number and use the word "resolved" rather than the phrase "be it enacted." Amendments to the Constitution are proposed in the form of a joint resolution, as Figure 14 (page 134) shows. Constitutional amendments approved by two-thirds of both chambers are not signed by the president. They are sent directly to the administrator of general services for submission to the several states for

Figure 13
Bill: Introduced Print

97TH CONGRESS
1ST SESSION **H. R. 3712**

To establish the national space policy of the United States, to declare the goals of the Nation's space program (both in terms of space and terrestrial applications and in space science), and to provide for the planning and implementation of such program.

IN THE HOUSE OF REPRESENTATIVES

MAY 28, 1981

Mr. BROWN of California introduced the following bill; which was referred to the Committee on Science and Technology

---

A BILL

To establish the national space policy of the United States, to declare the goals of the Nation's space program (both in terms of space and terrestrial applications and in space science), and to provide for the planning and implementation of such program.

1   *Be it enacted by the Senate and House of Representa-*

2 *tives of the United States of America in Congress assembled,*

3 That this Act may be cited as the "National Space Policy

4 Act of 1981".

ratification. After ratification by the legislatures of three-fourths of the states, the amendment is filed with the administrator, who is responsible for its certification and publication.

Figure 14
House Joint Resolution

97TH CONGRESS
1ST SESSION

H. J. RES. 16

Proposing an amendment to the Constitution of the United States relative to freedom from forced assignment to schools or jobs because of race, creed, or color.

IN THE HOUSE OF REPRESENTATIVES

JANUARY 5, 1981

Mr. ASHBROOK introduced the following joint resolution; which was referred to the Committee on the Judiciary

---

JOINT RESOLUTION

Proposing an amendment to the Constitution of the United States relative to freedom from forced assignment to schools or jobs because of race, creed, or color.

1   *Resolved by the Senate and House of Representatives of*

2   *the United States of America in Congress assembled (two-*

3   *thirds of each House concurring therein),* That the following

4   article is proposed as an amendment to the Constitution of

5   the United States, which shall be valid to all intents and

6   purposes as part of the Constitution when ratified by the leg-

7   islatures of three-fourths of the several States:

CONCURRENT RESOLUTIONS (H.Con.Res.; S.Con.Res.)

The term "concurrent" does not necessarily signify simultaneous introduction and consideration in both chambers. Concurrent resolutions are not normally legislative in character and do not require the signature of the president. They are numbered in sequence and are used to express an opinion, purpose, fact, principle, or "sense of" the Congress. Figure 15 shows a typical House concurrent resolution.

Figure 15
House Concurrent Resolution

97TH CONGRESS
1ST SESSION

H. CON. RES. 131

To express the sorrow of the Congress upon the death of former world heavyweight boxing champion Joe Louis.

IN THE HOUSE OF REPRESENTATIVES

MAY 12, 1981

Mr. SAVAGE submitted the following concurrent resolution; which was referred to the Committee on Post Office and Civil Service

---

CONCURRENT RESOLUTION

To express the sorrow of the Congress upon the death of former world heavyweight boxing champion Joe Louis.

Whereas Joe Louis, who was born the son of a black sharecropper, overcame the barriers of racial bigotry to become the longest reigning world heavyweight boxing champion in history;

Whereas Joe Louis was a man of exceptional talent, pride, and determination, both inside and outside of the boxing ring;

Whereas the life and career of Joe Louis continue to serve as inspirations for people of all races throughout the world and as models of courage and achievement for all Americans; and

RESOLUTIONS (H.Res.; S.Res.)

Known as "simple" resolutions, they govern the action of only one body and are used for the concern only of the legislative chamber passing them. They are used to initiate procedures of the body to which they relate or express the "sense of" one body. They need no presidential signature and, like the other forms above, are numbered in sequence throughout the two-year term of the Congress. Figure 16 is an example of a House resolution.

Figure 16
House Resolution

97TH CONGRESS
1ST SESSION

H. RES. 16

To reaffirm the use of our national motto on currency.

IN THE HOUSE OF REPRESENTATIVES

JANUARY 5, 1981

Mr. GUYER submitted the following resolution; which was referred to the Committee on Banking, Finance and Urban Affairs

---

RESOLUTION

To reaffirm the use of our national motto on currency.

1   *Resolved*, That it is the sense of the House that the

2   national motto, "In God We Trust", shall be reaffirmed and

3   shall continue to be engraved and printed on our currency.

O

The first printing is known as the "introduced print" (Figure 13), but when reported from committee there is a "reported print" with calendar number and House report number assigned. "Engrossed bills" are printed on blue paper. When passed by one chamber and sent to the other body, the bill becomes known as a "referred (Act) print." When reported out of a Senate committee, the bill is called a "Senate reported print" and carries a calendar and report number for that chamber. A bill that contains an error is designated a "star print"; the corrected bill has a small star in its lower left-hand corner. Other published forms include "motions," requests by members for any one of a variety of parliamentary actions. Illustrations of the parliamentary stages of a House bill as it makes its way in the legislative process are found in the current edition of *How Our Laws Are Made*, and a detailed analysis of these legislative instruments is found in Jerrold Zwirn, "Congressional Bills," *Government Publications Review* 7A: 17-25 (1980).

Congressional bills, resolutions, and amendments are sent to depository libraries in a microfiche-only format under item 1006-A. They are classified and designated as follows:

Y 1.4/1: (Cong.-no.)   Senate Bills
Y 1.4/2: (Cong.-no.)   Senate Resolutions
Y 1.4/3: (Cong.-no.)   Senate Joint Resolutions
Y 1.4/4: (Cong.-no.)   Senate Concurrent Resolutions
Y 1.4/5: (Cong.-no.)   Senate Printed Amendments
Y 1.4/6: (Cong.-no.)   House Bills
Y 1.4/7: (Cong.-no.)   House Resolutions
Y 1.4/8: (Cong.-no.)   House Joint Resolutions
Y 1.4/9: (Cong.-no.)   House Concurrent Resolutions

For the Ninety-sixth Congress a set of 1,929 fiche containing 20,685 House and Senate public and private bills was sent to subscribing depository institutions.[5] The microfiche bill shipments are now accompanied by a *Microfiche User's Guide* (sometimes called the *Bill Finding Aid*). Issued in paper copy, the *Guide* is divided into the nine distinct groups noted above and provides instructions for locating the grid coordinates for bills and resolutions. The category "Senate Printed Amendments" (Y 1.4/5) includes Senate amendments to bills, resolutions, and treaty documents, and for the Ninety-sixth and Ninety-seventh Congresses was listed in the Amendment section of the *Guide*. However, beginning with the Ninety-eighth Congress, first session (January 1983), amendments are listed directly under the corresponding bill or resolution which they amend, thus eliminating the need to check a different section of the *Guide* and the fiche file for amendments to bills. A *Final Cumulative Finding Aid, House and Senate Bills, Microfiche Format, Annual* (GP 3.28: 97/1; item 1006-A) covered the Ninety-seventh Congress, first session, and was distributed on March 26, 1982. Four days later, the Superintendent of Documents resumed issuing the *Microfiche User's Guide* in printed format covering the first microfiche bill shipment for the Ninety-seventh Congress, second session.

One salutary effect of the distribution of bills and resolutions on microfiche will be their preservation in libraries for future researchers. Bills and resolutions were not authorized for distribution to depository libraries until 1938 (52 *Stat.* 126). Moreover, the *Instructions* permit all depository libraries, including regionals, to dispose of bills and resolutions one year after the adjournment of a

Congress. As a consequence there are few depository institutions in the country that boast of a substantial retrospective collection of these valuable publications. Fortunately, the Library of Congress houses a reasonably complete collection of the printed versions of public and private bills and resolutions in each parliamentary stage.

Access to the most complete collection of bills and resolutions in their several forms, including amendments and revisions, is available through *CIS/Congressional Bills, Resolutions, & Laws on Microfiche.* For each Congress the publications are filed sequentially by bill number within bill category with pre-printed divider cards included. The different versions of a bill are arranged chronologically behind the introduced version. Microfiche of the *United States Statutes at Large* are included with bills from the Eighty-sixth through Ninety-first Congresses, and public and private slip laws on fiche accompany the Ninety-third through Ninety-sixth Congresses. The collection is updated every two years, several months after the adjournment of the latest Congress; and at the same time Congressional Information Service is filming materials issued by earlier Congresses. As of 1981 the collection covered bills, resolutions, and laws from the Eighty-sixth through the Ninety-sixth Congresses.

COMMITTEE ACTION

After introduction, the bill is referred to the appropriate committees of House and Senate. Both chambers practice multiple referral of complex legislation to two or more committees. There are three categories of multiple referral: "joint referral of a bill concurrently to two or more committees; sequential referral of a bill successively to one committee, then a second, and so on; and split referral of parts of a bill to several committees for consideration of each part."[6] The bill may be considered by the full committee, but the common practice is for the bill's assignment to a subcommittee. There are over 250 subcommittees in the House and Senate. The proliferation of subcommittees and the legislative maze created by overlapping jurisdictions have generated controversy. Many senators and representatives complain that "they spend so much time dashing from one panel meeting to another that they can't do a proper job of drafting bills." For example, the House "has at least five subcommittees that deal exclusively with consumer affairs, six with energy matters, a half dozen that handle housing bills and as many as a dozen with a hand in setting welfare policy."[7]

Subcommittees usually schedule public hearings on the bill, following which they engage in the "marking-up" process, a section-by-section analysis of the bill in which major or minor revision occurs. If a measure is extensively revised, it may emerge as a "clean bill" with a new number. The subcommittee makes its recommendations to the full committee, which may repeat wholly or in part the same procedures, or it may simply accept the work of the subcommittee.

Out of this critical committee process important government publications are generated. Hearings which provide testimony by interested parties are published; committee prints provide background information for the committee's consideration; and the committee report informs the plenary chamber of the committee's oversight findings and recommendations. These three congressional forms deserve further discussion.

HEARINGS

Although hearings pursuant to legislation are perhaps the most familiar category of this congressional activity, they are held by committees for other purposes. Hearings may be exploratory, providing testimony and data about general topical areas. Evaluative hearings provide information about the economy and efficiency of program operations. Appropriation hearings provide testimony and information about department or agency operations, oversight activities, and comparative fiscal information. Investigatory hearings explore the need for legislation, inform public opinion, or uncover scandal. From the Army-McCarthy hearings to Watergate, this type represents a powerful congressional forum.

Classed in the Superintendent's "Y 4" notation, hearings are available to depository libraries in paper copy or on microfiche. Although they do not constitute a real series, some committees have serialized their hearings for their own convenience. Some hearings are designated alphabetically, some numerically. Some series run through a session, others through a Congress. Hearings are also designated by other devices. The Watergate hearings, for example, were conducted in phases, and the issuing notation read: Y 4.P92/ phase 1/bk.4, etc. That Congress considers hearings an important component of the legislative process is demonstrated by their scope and frequency of publication.

COMMITTEE PRINTS

Committee prints are publications prepared for the use and reference of a given committee, either as staff or consultant research studies, activity reports, or compilations of materials for the committee's background information. Studies are frequently prepared by the Congressional Research Service (CRS) of the Library of Congress for the use of the committee. Because many committee prints are studied in the course of formulating legislation, they are valuable to members and, later, to the general public.

Although more committee prints have been made available to depository libraries in recent years, the series is not automatically distributed. Under the "administrative or operational purposes" provision of 44 U.S.C. 1902, a committee chairperson is not obliged to authorize all committee prints for distribution or sale. Moreover, the series is characterized by a pattern of discontinuity and inconsistency, and many of the individual issuances do not have numbering or series designations. Sometimes a print, in revised form, is reissued as a document or report in the numbered Congressional Serial Set. Other odd variations in distribution and form occur. Committee prints have been published in the *Congressional Record*, and the occasional study has been issued as a House or Senate document while made available for sale by the Superintendent of Documents in its "committee print edition."[8]

Like hearings, committee prints are classed in "Y 4" and if available are sent to depository libraries in paper copy or on microfiche. Despite their somewhat erratic publishing and distribution pattern, they are valuable sources of information often not available in any other form.

COMMITTEE REPORTS

Reports which accompany public and private bills voted out of committee describe the purpose and scope of the bill and the reasons for approval of the measure. Few bills are reported unfavorably. In a few instances, a committee may report a measure "without recommendation," which has the effect of an unfavorable report. When a committee declines to report a bill, that measure is effectively killed. Thus in general the report is a recommendation to the House or Senate to vote passage of the legislation. Reports on public bills include, in addition to the committee's oversight findings and recommendations, a statement indicating new budget authority or an estimate of new or increased expenditures. Cost estimates or revenue to be raised (or lost) cover the current fiscal year and the five succeeding fiscal years.

Reports on public bills are of great significance in the legislative process because they provide the courts with the best documentation of legislative intent. But Richard A. Givens notes that reports "in the future may provide less guidance to the courts than some of those in prior years when Congress allowed itself the luxury of more expansive committee documents."[9] If committee reports are indeed being drafted with less detail and specificity, that policy is ill-considered. As Supreme Court Justice Robert H. Jackson averred, "Resort to legislative history is only justified where the face of the Act is inescapably ambiguous, and then I think we should not go beyond Committee reports, which presumably are well considered and carefully prepared."[10]

House and Senate reports are assigned a report number and carry the reported bill number. Issued at first in slip form, they later comprise in bound volumes a portion of the Congressional Serial Set. House and Senate reports are classified in Y 1.1/8: and Y 1.1/5; respectively, and are designated by Congress and report number. Both series are available to depository libraries in paper copy (item 1008-C) or on microfiche (item 1008-D). A useful discussion of the role of these important publications in the legislative process is found in Jerrold Zwirn, "Congressional Committee Reports," *Government Publications Review* 7A: 319-27 (1980).

Committee reports on bills and resolutions always carry that indispensable piece of bibliographic information, the bill or resolution number. In Figure 17, the House report is pursuant to H.Res. 378, which is shown in brackets.

FLOOR ACTION

No specific Senate committee is involved in scheduling bills for floor debate, but the House Rules Committee regulates the process for expediting floor action. A rule, or special order, issued by the Rules Committee "sets the conditions under which a measure is to be considered, determining whether amendments will be permitted and how much debate will be allowed."[11] Following committee action, a new version of the bill, called a "reported print," is ordered to be printed. The bill in this stage has the calendar number and committee report number on the bill. The date of the "introduced print" is given, along with the name of the bill's sponsor and the date of the report out of committee.

To expedite the consideration of bills and resolutions, the House resolves itself into the Committee of the Whole House on the State of the Union. Known popularly as the *Committee of the Whole*, this parliamentary device permits the

Figure 17
House Committee Report

97TH CONGRESS *2d Session*	HOUSE OF REPRESENTATIVES	REPORT No. 97–470

PROVIDING AMOUNTS FROM THE CONTINGENT FUND OF THE HOUSE FOR EXPENSES OF INVESTIGATIONS AND STUDIES BY STANDING AND SELECT COMMITTEES OF THE HOUSE IN THE 2D SESSION OF THE 97TH CONGRESS

MARCH 24, 1982.—Referred to the House Calendar and ordered to be printed

Mr. ANNUNZIO, from the Committee on House Administration, submitted the following

REPORT

[To accompany H. Res. 378]

The Committee on House Administration submits the following report in explanation of the accompanying resolution, as amended, Providing Amounts from the Contingent Fund of the House for Expenses of Investigations and Studies by Standing and Select Committees of the House in the 2d session of the 97th Congress.

By unanimous consent, on March 23, 1982, the committee adopted a motion to report the accompanying resolution with an amendment.

AMENDMENT

The amendment strikes out all after the resolving clause and inserts in lieu thereof a substitute text which appears in italic type in the reported resolution.

REQUIREMENT OF RULE X

There were no oversight findings or recommendations submitted pursuant to clause 2(b)(1) of Rule X.

No statement was deemed necessary under section 308(a) of the Congressional Budget Act of 1974.

The Director of the Congressional Budget Office did not submit an estimate and comparison under section 403 of the Congressional Budget Act of 1974.

The Committee on Government Operations did not submit a summary of oversight findings and recommendations pursuant to clause 4(c)(2) of Rule X.

GENERAL DISCUSSION

House Resolution 378, as amended, provides $32,163,548 for investigations and studies by all standing, special and select committees of the House of Representatives with the exception of the Committees

House to act with a quorum of only 100 members instead of the usual majority of 218 representatives. The nature of the measure dictates the length allowed for debate, and the conduct of debate is governed largely by rules adopted by that chamber at the opening of each Congress and precedents set forth in the House *Manual*.

On the floor, amendments to the reported bill are debated. Sometimes members introduce "riders" into the amending process, provisions not germane to the subject matter of the bill. The crucial amending process can take the form of the amendment itself, an amendment to the amendment, a substitute amendment, or an amendment to the substitute. With complex or controversial legislation, it is not unusual to find hundreds of amendments to a measure. The principal congressional publication that reflects the consideration and passage of legislation is the *Congressional Record*, a controversial and often fascinating account of congressional activity.

CONGRESSIONAL RECORD (CR)

The predecessors of the present series were the *Annals of Congress* (1789-1824), *Register of Debates* (1824-1837), and the *Congressional Globe* (1833-1873), the first five volumes of which overlap the *Register*. The CR today appears in a daily edition when Congress is in session and a permanent bound edition later. The daily *Record* consists of four sections: the proceedings of the House and of the Senate; the Extensions of Remarks; and the Daily Digest. Each section is paged continuously and separately during each session, and each page in each section is preceded by a letter prefix as follows: "S" for Senate, "H" for House, "E" for Extensions of Remarks, and "D" for Daily Digest. Due to revision and rearrangement, the pagination of the bound *Record* differs from that of the daily edition. The permanent, bound CR consists of one continuous sequence which drops the separate "H," "S," and "E" designations from the daily edition. A cumulated index volume and a cumulated Daily Digest section form the last volumes of the bound *Record*.

In the proceedings sections and the Extensions of Remarks are found thousands of reprints of articles, editorials, book reviews, tributes, and sheer trivia inserted by members; an estimated 70 percent of what is found in the CR is never actually uttered on the floor.[12] Egregious misuse of this privilege has been documented, and the types of items that get "read into" the *Record* have been the subject of numerous studies in schools of journalism and public affairs.[13] In theory the Extensions of Remarks section contains traditionally extraneous material, although "germane" material does appear in this section if printing requirements and deadlines necessitate its appearance. In 1972 the Joint Committee on Printing was obliged to remind members not to include extraneous matter in the proceedings sections. Exceptions included "(a) excerpts from letters, telegrams, or articles presented in connection with a speech delivered in the course of debate; (b) communications from State Legislatures; and (c) addresses or articles by the President and the members of his cabinet, the Vice President, or a Member of Congress."[14] Members, however, find it excruciatingly difficult to abide by these modest guidelines.

Until the Ninetieth Congress, second session, the Extensions of Remarks was called the Appendix. Separately paged, it formed a part of both the daily and the permanent editions from the Seventy-fifth Congress, first session, through the

Eighty-third Congress, second session. Beginning with the Seventy-seventh Congress, first session, each page number was preceded by the designation "A." With the Eighty-fourth Congress, first session, the Appendix pages were *omitted* from the permanent edition. Thus from 1955 to 1968, material in the Appendix could be consulted only in the daily edition. The *index* to the permanent edition, however, cited references to Appendix material appearing in the daily edition. Libraries were required to retain the Appendix pages from the daily edition and shelve them in proper sequence with the permanent edition or purchase them on microfilm from University Microfilms International, Ann Arbor, Michigan. After the Appendix was omitted from the permanent edition, materials considered germane to legislation were inserted in that edition at the point when the legislation was under discussion. With the Ninetieth Congress, second session, the Appendix, renamed the Extensions of Remarks, was restored to the permanent edition of the *Record*. Moreover, beginning with that Congress and session, the last page of each daily edition has carried an alphabetical listing of members whose extended remarks appear in that issue, with page numbers.

The Daily Digest section includes "Highlights" of the legislative day, chamber action which summarizes bills introduced and reported, resolutions agreed to, quorum calls, bills signed by the president, committee meetings, and a schedule of House and Senate meetings for the following day.

Members of Congress are permitted to edit their remarks. House rules suggest that this privilege is not to be used to change the thought or substance of that which was spoken, but merely "the grammar, construction, or rhetoric of the remarks."[15] Senate rules also forbid substantive changes in remarks. But guidelines for revision lack specificity. Accordingly, "although the rule provides that there should be no substantive changes in the transcript, because of varied interpretation of the word 'substantive,' the degree to which changes are made varies."[16] In both chambers, altering the transcript of a colloquy in such a way as to place the response of the other member in an improper perspective is anathema. In the event the chief reporter is not successful in prevailing upon the member, he must take the matter to the parliamentarian.

Studies have shown that generally the editing privilege is not abused; the great majority of revisions are within the bounds of propriety. Of the two bodies, House revision occurs more frequently than Senate editing. However, one study concluded that "until Congress takes action to either prohibit the practices of revision and insertion, or clearly identify them when and where they occur, the *Record* will continue to be a less desirable source of speech texts than it might otherwise be."[17]

Members used to be permitted to insert "speeches" not actually delivered on the floor in such a way that the reader had no way of determining that the member was absent. However, on March 1, 1978, JCP regulations were amended to identify statements or insertions in the *Record* where no part of them was spoken. A few variations between House and Senate procedures were noted, but common to both bodies the significant ruling was qualified as follows:

(a) When, upon unanimous consent or by motion, a prepared statement is ordered to be printed in the Record and no part of it is spoken, the entire statement will be "bulleted."

(b) If a Member verbally delivers the first portion of the statement (such as the first sentence or paragraph), then the entire statement will appear without the "bullet" symbol.

(c) Extemporaneous speeches supplemented by prepared statements will not be "bulleted."[18]

The bullet device (•) is, of course, no stranger to documents librarians. It is the symbol used to signify a depository item in a *Monthly Catalog* entry, and a basic manual in a subscription service announced in *Price List 36*. Look closely, however, at paragraph (b) of the new rules. A member need only speak *one sentence* to avoid the bulleting of remarks. Many members of the press and, indeed, a number of senators and representatives ridiculed this provision as constituting "not a wholehearted embrace of truth and accuracy, but more a flirtation."[19] Yet it was a step in the right direction, and, in the words of one member, the "reputation of one of the most dishonest and mistrusted publications in the world may yet be saved."[20] It is interesting to note that the author of these remarks, Representative Laurence Coughlin (R-PA), chose to delete this sentiment from the permanent, bound *Record*, an instructive example of a member's privilege to expunge and an argument for retaining the daily CR in libraries.

After a few years of debate and discussion, the House of Representatives began televising its proceedings and debates. Deciding against coverage by the commercial networks or public television, the House installed its own system, at a cost of over $1 million, which gives it complete control. Fixed cameras, operated by remote control by House employees, focus on individual lawmakers as they deliver speeches. Thus viewers see no frenetic activity on close votes, no reaction shots of a backbencher booing a fellow member, no camera panning across the chamber to catch a sleeping solon. It is all very proper and sterile.

With a trial run on February 22, 1979 to see if the equipment worked, the House began official TV coverage March 19. About six months later, House Speaker Thomas P. O'Neill (D-MA) complained that the *Congressional Record* was "25 percent fatter than it was last year at this time, though the House passed fewer bills." To O'Neill that clearly meant only one thing: "Television is encouraging more talk and less work."[21] Moreover, the Speaker charged some members with abuse of TV coverage. He had in mind the "special order" speeches that may be made on the floor after the conclusion of the day's regular legislative business. Such speeches are "often directed at home town audiences, have little to do with House business, and are often presented to an empty floor and gallery."[22] It appears that the combination of incumbency and access to the TV camera has proven irresistible to a number of representatives.

Of perhaps greater import is the impact of television on the *Congressional Record*. One House member pointed out that by establishing cameras in the chamber, "we are creating a new official record of floor proceedings.... In the very near future, it can be anticipated that some bright lawyer will appear in Federal court and argue that the tapes are a more accurate reflection of congressional intent" than the revised and edited *Record*. A knowledgeable attorney noted that "courts rely on floor debates only when the legislation or [committee] reports are ambiguous." He concluded that the "archival tapes might eventually supersede [the *Congressional Record*] for the courts, just as West Publishing Company's private reporting system has taken over coverage of lower court opinions."[23] Moreover, the House will be virtually forced to adopt a truly verbatim *Record*. Otherwise, "the press will highlight instances of discrepancies between the audiotapes and the printed version whenever anything significant is involved to the discomfiture of the Members.... The dignity of Congress will suffer when invidious comparisons are made between the printed and taped record."[24]

As of 1982 the Senate has avoided the joys and tribulations of televising its debates and proceedings. One day after the convening of the Ninety-seventh Congress, first session, Senator Howard Baker (R-TN) introduced Senate Resolution 20 "to provide for television and radio coverage (including videotapes and radio broadcast recordings) of proceedings in the Senate Chamber," said coverage to be "carried out in such manner as the Committee on Rules and Administration shall prescribe."[25] But although S.Res. 20 has the support of many senators, other members of that body are adamantly opposed to live TV coverage. Senator Russell B. Long (D-LA), for example, points out that the experience of the House alone argues against the idea: "Since television was installed in the House [it] has passed a smaller number of substantive bills. It has taken about an hour longer to handle an average bill. Also, House members have the privilege of speaking on any subject for one minute at the start of sessions. That type of thing has increased by 120 percent." Long believes that TV would exacerbate the senatorial penchant for logorrhea. The presence of the cameras "would impede the Senate's work, drastically change the nature of the Senate, and not for the best."[26]

Cable-Satellite Public Affairs Network (C-SPAN) is the network that carries the House proceedings to a potential audience of millions of subscribers. A survey conducted by C-SPAN in February 1981 showed a majority of senators favoring or leaning toward TV coverage.[27] But, as Senator Long's comments suggest, the desire to be televised in the "upper house" is far from unanimous.

Voting on a measure is accomplished by voice vote, the division, the teller vote, the recorded vote, and the yea-and-nay vote, the latter used only in the House. Recorded votes are listed by name of member in the *Record*.

The daily CR has a fortnightly index, and there is a master index for the bound edition. The *Congressional Record Index* is composed of two parts: an index by subject and individual to the proceedings and debates, including material in the Extensions of Remarks, and a History of Bills and Resolutions. The History is arranged by chamber and within chamber by bill and resolution number. Bill and resolution number references are cumulative, however, so that with the latest biweekly index one can trace current legislation in page references to the measure's introduction, referral to committee, reported stage, debate, amendment(s), and enactment or defeat.

In 1981 the Joint Committee on Printing authorized the distribution on a trial basis of a cumulated edition of the twenty-four printed biweekly indexes for the Ninety-sixth Congress, first session, in a microfiche format. Responses from depository libraries were largely favorable, citing reduced space requirements, a decrease in time required to locate information, and increased public access to the *Record*.

The daily CR, issued when Congress is in session, carries an X/a class notation, is designated by volume and number, and is sent to depository libraries in paper copy (item 994). The permanent bound edition, also classed (X.), is designated by Congress and session with individual book numbers made of volume and part, and is made available to depository institutions in hardcopy (item 993) or on microfiche (item 993-A). A commercial edition of the *Congressional Record* and its predecessors from 1789 to the present is available on microfiche from Information Handling Services (IHS) accompanied by a *Congressional Record Checklist* in hard copy to supplement the fiche file.

When Congress is in session, the visitor in the gallery of either chamber sees the proceedings and debates being taken down by official reporters. By law the *Congressional Record* is supposed to be substantially a verbatim report of floor action, but the privileges of "leave to print," editing, and even expunging of members' remarks serve to qualify the word "substantially." Although committee reports are more faithful guides to legislative intent than remarks chronicled in the *Record*, both are important sources of information. As Zwirn notes, "Reports establish the contours of debate and are keys to understanding the views expressed and amendments proposed. Debate serves to disseminate and elaborate the arguments and explanations of proponents and opponents that appear in the committee report."[28]

SENATE ACTION

When the House passes a bill, an enrolling clerk in that chamber prepares an engrossed bill containing all the amendments agreed to and it is delivered to the Senate. The bill is then referred to the appropriate standing committee, where it is reprinted and called the "Act print" or "Senate referred print." The bill must now follow the same process as described for the House: subcommittee action, Senate committee report, consideration on the floor of the Senate, with proceedings, debate, and voting duly recorded in the CR. Keep in mind that the Senate referred print and Senate reported print continue to bear that crucial piece of bibliographic data, the House bill number. The Senate reported print, however, includes the Senate calendar number and Senate report number. The Senate committee report is presumed to reflect the same careful analysis of the measure as does the House committee report. All of the relevant activities—hearings, committee prints if appropriate, reports, debate, etc.—are accomplished in the Senate as they were in the House.

THE CONFERENCE COMMITTEE

Differing versions of the measure must be resolved before it can be sent to the president. Resolution may be accomplished without a conference, but the formal machinery for reconciling differences involves the conference committee, a strategy adopted by the first Congress and used ever since.

Conference committees have been referred to as the "Third House of Congress." Managers, or conferees, are appointed from each body; and they attempt to effect a compromise satisfactory to both chambers. When the conferees reach agreement, they embody their recommendations in a report made in duplicate that must be signed by a majority of the conferees appointed by each chamber. Beginning with the Ninety-second Congress in 1971, the conference report is required to be printed in both houses and is accompanied by an explanatory statement prepared jointly by the conferees. Because this report reflects final agreement and reconciliation of House and Senate amendments, it becomes perhaps the most important publication in the legislative process for determining legislative intent.

Conference committee reports must be printed in the daily *Congressional Record* before consideration on the floor of each chamber, and they are usually approved by both houses. Upon approval, a copy of the bill is enrolled for presentation to the president. Conference reports are classed in the same notation as House reports (Y 1.1/8:) and Senate reports (Y 1.1/5:) and are sent to depository libraries in paper copy or fiche; later they are incorporated into the bound volumes of the Congressional Serial Set. Figure 18 shows a conference report issued by the House.

Figure 18
Conference Committee Report

97TH CONGRESS	HOUSE OF REPRESENTATIVES	REPORT
1st Session		No. 97–401

EXPORT ADMINISTRATION AMENDMENTS ACT OF 1981

DECEMBER 11, 1981.—Ordered to be printed

Mr. BINGHAM, from the committee of conference,
submitted the following

CONFERENCE REPORT

[To accompany H.R. 3567]

The committee of conference on the disagreeing votes of the two Houses on the amendment of the Senate to the bill (H.R. 3567) to authorize appropriations for the fiscal years 1982 and 1983 to carry out the purposes of the Export Administration Act of 1979, and for other purposes, having met, after full and free conference, have agreed to recommend and do recommend to their respective Houses as follows:

That the House recede from its disagreement to the amendment of the Senate and agree to the same with an amendment as follows:

In lieu of the matter proposed to be inserted by the Senate amendment insert the following:

That this Act may be cited as the "Export Administration Amendments Act of 1981".

SEC. 2. (a) Section 18(b)(1) of the Export Administration Act of 1979 (50 U.S.C. App. 2417(b)(1)) is amended to read as follows:

"(1) $9,659,000 for each of the fiscal years 1982 and 1983; and".

(b) The amendment made by subsection (a) shall be effective as of October 1, 1981.

SEC. 3. Section 12(c) of the Export Administration Act of 1979 (50 U.S.C. App. 2411(c)) is amended by adding at the end thereof the following:

"(3) Departments or agencies which obtain information which is relevant to the enforcement of this Act shall furnish such information to the department or agency with enforcement responsibilities under this Act to the extent consistent with the protection of intelligence, counterintelligence, and law enforcement sources, methods,

PRESIDENTIAL ACTION

The enrolled bill, prepared by the enrolling clerk of the chamber that originated the measure, is signed by the Speaker of the House and the president of the Senate and sent to the president for veto or signature into law. Copies of the bill are usually transmitted by the White House to the various departments interested in the subject matter so that the president may be advised on the merits of the legislation. The bill may become law without the president's signature if he does not veto it within ten days after it has been presented to him. However, if the Congress adjourns before that ten-day period ends, a "pocket veto" takes place and the bill does not become law. In a regular veto, the president returns the bill to its originating chamber with his stated objections. To override a veto requires a two-thirds vote in both chambers. Veto messages are published as House or Senate documents; and a retrospective volume, *Presidential Vetoes, 1789-* (Y 1.3:P92/5; item 998) cumulates every few years.

PUBLICATION

When a bill becomes law either by presidential inaction, approval, or congressional override, publishing provenance shifts from Congress to the Office of the Federal Register, General Services Administration. Its first appearance as a "slip law" takes the form of an unbound pamphlet, printed by photoelectric offset process from the enrolled bill. A number is assigned for public and private laws, and this notation runs sequentially through a Congress. The slip law carries the *Statutes at Large* citation, bill number, and effective date. The Office of the Federal Register provides marginal notes which may include, if applicable, citations to prior statutes or treaties and citations to the *United States Code*. There is a "Legislative History" which appears at the end of a slip law and provides citations to House and Senate reports, conference reports if applicable, dates of consideration and passage in the *Congressional Record*, and any presidential statements relevant to the legislation that were published in the *Weekly Compilation of Presidential Documents*.

Public laws in slip form are assigned a class notation and distributed to depository libraries in that form (GS 4.110; item 575). Figure 19 shows a typical "slip law" with "Legislative History."

STATUTES AT LARGE (Stat.)

A chronological arrangement of the slip laws in bound sessional volumes is published as the *United States Statutes at Large*. Included in these compilations are public and private laws, joint and concurrent resolutions, presidential proclamations, reorganization plans, and proposed amendments to the Constitution. Various lists of bills enacted into law, reorganization plans, public laws, and the like serve as handy finding aids to the textual material in the volumes. A useful "Guide to Legislative History of Bills Enacted into Public Law" provides tabular data by public law number, referencing date, volume and page of *Statutes at Large*, bill number, House and Senate report number and name of committee, and *Congressional Record* dates of consideration and passage. When depository libraries receive the *Statutes at Large* (GS 4.111; item 576), the slip laws covered for that volume may be discarded.

Figure 19
Slip Law with Legislative History

PUBLIC LAW 97-114—DEC. 29, 1981   95 STAT. 1565

Public Law 97-114
97th Congress

An Act

Making appropriations for the Department of Defense for the fiscal year ending September 30, 1982, and for other purposes.

Dec. 29, 1981
[H.R. 4995]

Be it enacted by the Senate and House of Representatives of the United States of America in Congress assembled, That the following sums are appropriated, out of any money in the Treasury not otherwise appropriated, for the fiscal year ending September 30, 1982, for military functions administered by the Department of Defense, and for other purposes, namely:

Department of Defense Appropriation Act, 1982.

TITLE I

MILITARY PERSONNEL

MILITARY PERSONNEL, ARMY

For pay, allowances, individual clothing, subsistence, interest on deposits, gratuities, permanent change of station travel (including all expenses thereof for organizational movements), and expenses of temporary duty travel between permanent duty stations, for members of the Army on active duty (except members of reserve components provided for elsewhere), cadets, and aviation cadets; $12,447,827,000.

MILITARY PERSONNEL, NAVY

For pay, allowances, individual clothing, subsistence, interest on deposits, gratuities, permanent change of station travel (including all expenses thereof for organizational movements), and expenses of temporary duty travel between permanent duty stations, for members of the Navy on active duty (except members of the Reserve provided for elsewhere), midshipmen, and aviation cadets; $9,117,956,000.

SEC. 789. So far as may be practicable Indian labor shall be employed, and purchases of the products of Indian industry may be made in open market in the discretion of the Secretary of Defense.

Indian labor and products.

SEC. 790. Of the funds appropriated by this Act for strategic programs, the Secretary of Defense shall provide funds for the Advanced Technology Bomber program at a level at least equal to the amount provided by the committee of conference on this Act in order to maintain priority emphasis on this program.

Advanced Technology Bomber program.

SEC. 791. It is the sense of the Congress that—

10 USC 7291 note.

(1) A larger and stronger American Navy is needed as an essential ingredient of our Armed Forces, in order to fulfill its basic missions of (A) protecting the sea lanes to preserve the

---

LEGISLATIVE HISTORY—H.R. 4995 (S. 1857):

HOUSE REPORTS: No. 97-333 (Comm. on Appropriations) and No. 97-410 (Comm. of Conference).
SENATE REPORT No. 97-273 accompanying S. 1857 (Comm. on Appropriations).
CONGRESSIONAL RECORD, Vol. 127 (1981):
    Nov. 18, considered and passed House.
    Nov. 30, Dec. 1-4, considered and passed Senate, amended.
    Dec. 15, House and Senate agreed to conference report.
WEEKLY COMPILATION OF PRESIDENTIAL DOCUMENTS, Vol. 17, No. 53 (1981):
    Dec. 29, Presidential statement.

UNITED STATES CODE (U.S.C.)

Statutes of a permanent and general character in force are consolidated and codified in the *United States Code*. Since 1926 editions of the *U.S. Code* have been published at intervals of six years; cumulative annual supplements appear between editions. The Office of the Law Revision Counsel of the House of Representatives is engaged in a comprehensive project to enact the several titles of the *Code* into positive law. When the task is finally completed, the *Code* will be legal evidence of the general and permanent laws, and recourse to the *Statutes at Large* for this purpose will then be unnecessary.

Originally composed of fifty titles, Title 34 (Navy) has been eliminated by the enactment of Title 10 (Armed Forces). As of 1981 twenty titles and one subtitle have been enacted into positive law, the rest being considered prima facie evidence of the law. That is, if a conflict were to arise between the wording of the *Code* and the language in the *Statutes at Large*, the latter would take precedent.[29]

The *United States Code* includes tables covering presidential documents, conversion tables from the *Statutes at Large* to the *Code*, *District of Columbia Code* sections classified to the *U.S. Code*, an "Index of Acts Cited by Popular Name," and a general subject index. Formerly, the *U.S. Code* was classed in Y 4.J89/1:Un3/3. However, beginning with the 1976 edition, the classification notation was changed to Y 1.2/4: (yr./vols.). The *United States Code* and *Supplements* are available to depository libraries under item 991. A microfiche edition of the *Code* and *Supplements* from 1925 to the present is commercially available from William S. Hein & Company, Buffalo, New York.

UNITED STATES CODE ANNOTATED (U.S.C.A.)

Published by West Publishing Company (St. Paul, Minnesota), U.S.C.A. presents the identical wording and language of the official edition and is arranged in the same manner by titles, chapters, and sections. However, it cites judicial opinions construing provisions of the *Code*, historical notes indicating the sources of various sections and their amendments, digest, encyclopedia, and other references to West's sister publications, and other editorial aids. A general subject index and subject indexes in volumes; useful tables; and supplementation by pamphlet supplements, annual pocket supplements, and replacement volumes enhance the capability for extensive research.

UNITED STATES CODE SERVICE, LAWYERS' EDITION (U.S.C.S.)

Published by the Lawyers Co-operative Publishing Company and the Bancroft-Whitney Company, U.S.C.S. follows the exact language of the *Statutes at Large*. When clarification is necessary, bracketed words or references in text notes are inserted. Like U.S.C.A., the *Lawyers' Edition* contains editorial features that facilitate research. These features include extensive cross-references to the *Code of Federal Regulations*, references to decisions of major federal administrative agencies, the history of each section with amendment notes tracing the development of the law, selective citation to cases that construe the provisions of the *Code*, cross-references to the sister publications of Lawyers Co-operative

Publishing Company, and a cumulative later case and statutory service issued three times a year.

U.S.C.S. has general index volumes and supplementation by monthly Advance Service pamphlets, annual pocket supplements, and replacement volumes. While U.S.C.A. is useful for its comprehensive citations to case law, U.S.C.S. excels in references to journal articles, regulations, and "Annotations" in the *American Law Reports* series of Lawyers Co-operative Publishing Company (see Chapter 10). Both are preferable to the official edition for their currency and editorial references.

SHEPARD'S UNITED STATES CITATIONS: STATUTE EDITION

To trace the history and treatment of a relevant statute which has cited or construed the statute under consideration, use this unit of *Shepard's Citations*. Included are citations to the U.S. Constitution, *Statutes at Large, United States Code* (official and commercial editions), and U.S. treaties. The several units that comprise *Shepard's Citations* are explained more fully in Chapter 10.

ONLINE SERVICES

The *United States Code* is online through LEXIS. U.S.C.A. is online through WESTLAW. All units of *Shepard's Citations* are online through both LEXIS and WESTLAW (Chapter 10).

PRIVATE LEGISLATION

Private bills are introduced for the purpose of providing relief to individuals and institutions from the unanticipated implications of existing public laws that were not intended to apply to them. The only statutory definition given for a private bill appears in a 1905 act concerning the printing and distribution of bills in Congress: "The term 'private bill' shall be construed to mean all bills for the relief of private parties, bills granting pensions, bills removing political disabilities, and bills for the survey of rivers and harbors." The renowned parliamentarian Asher C. Hinds proposed this definition: "A private bill is a bill for the relief of one or several specified persons, corporations, institutions, etc., and is distinguished from a public bill, which relates to public matters and deals with individuals only by classes." However, he went on to quote this warning from the House *Manual*: "The line of distinction between public and private bills is so difficult to be defined in many cases that it must rest on the opinion of the Speaker and the details of the bill."[30]

Comparative data found in the final edition of the House *Calendars* show that several decades ago private laws far outnumbered public laws. For example, during the Fifty-ninth Congress, 6,248 private laws were enacted as opposed to only 692 public laws. By contrast, the Ninety-sixth Congress saw the enactment of 613 public laws and only 123 private laws.[31] This turnabout was effected by the passage of legislation giving executive agencies the authority to act on private matters previously handled by Congress and by streamlining congressional procedures to investigate the merit of private relief actions.

Immigration and naturalization bills and claims against the government constitute the two major categories of private legislation. These measures are referred to the House or the Senate judiciary committees. The House Judiciary Committee has subcommittees on Administrative Law and Governmental Relations to review claims, and Immigration, Refugees, and International Law to process immigration and naturalization bills. The House schedules private measures for deliberation on a private calendar. The Senate's simpler procedure involves scheduling on the Senate calendar of business. After a private bill is reported out of committee, floor action takes place and is reflected in the *Congressional Record*. A measure passed by both chambers goes to the president for signature or veto.

Thus private legislation follows the same process as public legislation. The critical piece of bibliographic data is the bill number. Depository libraries receive private bills on microfiche and committee reports on private measures in paper copy or on microfiche. Private laws, which are not sent to depository libraries in slip form, are listed in *Price List 36*, as are private bills. The following is a typical listing in the spring 1982 edition of *Price List 36*.

▶**PRIVATE BILLS.** (Irregularly.) Subscription price: Domestic—**$810.00** per session of Congress; Foreign—**$1,012.50** per session of Congress; no single copies sold; no back issues furnished.

[*PRB*]   X 97-2: Priv. bill
(File Code 1L)   S/N 052-070-81004-1

No discounts allowed on this subscription.

▶**PRIVATE LAWS.** (Irregularly.) Subscription price: Domestic—**$75.00** per session of Congress; Foreign—**$93.75** per session of Congress; no single copies sold; no back issues furnished.

[*PRLA*]   X 97-2:Priv.law
(File Code 1L)   S/N 052-070-81005-0

No discounts allowed on this subscription.

Private laws are published in the *Statutes at Large* in a section separate from public laws. The current edition of *How Our Laws Are Made* provides illustrations of a typical reported print of a private relief bill, the House and Senate committee reports on the bill, and the private law in slip form.[32]

Matters other than immigration and claims have been the subject of private legislation: land titles, exempting religious foundations from taxation, rewarding an inventor, waiving citizenship procedures for poignant, hardship cases, and the like. Oleszek cites an example of a private bill that "authorized payment to the family of a Central Intelligence Agency (CIA) agent who died while testing LSD for the agency."[33] Congress is also empowered to refer a private bill to the Court of Claims to make a determination of facts. Opinions of the Court have been published as an appendix to the committee report on the private measure.

The practice of dealing with grievances through enactment of private laws has existed since ancient Rome; and owing to the shimmering ambiguities of language embodied in public legislation, it is likely that the need for private measures will endure.

TRACING PUBLIC LEGISLATION

Users are fortunate to have several guides published by the federal government and by commercial firms that determine the current status of legislation. The following represents a selection of the more prominent bibliographic sources.

CCH CONGRESSIONAL INDEX

Commerce Clearing House, a Chicago-based commercial publisher of topical law reports, issues a weekly looseleaf service entitled *Congressional Index*. Because of its recency and comprehensive coverage, it is perhaps the most widely used source for current information.

Congressional Index is organized by divisions. The Subject Index division is updated by a Current Subject Index, and reference to both is necessary. Similarly, the Author Index division is supplemented by a Current Author Index. A separate index for "Headline Legislation" covers the handful of bills that have received widespread media attention. Divisions for House Bills, House Resolutions, Senate Bills, and Senate Resolutions are listed by date of introduction and number, followed by a descriptive title, and name of the author and original sponsors, a summary of the provisions of the legislation, and the committee to which it was referred. Private bills are listed only by number to account for the bill number sequence.

The "Status of House Bills" division reports House measures from the time hearings are held on them through the various stages to enactment or veto. The "Status of Senate Bills" division shows, in tabular form, what becomes of Senate-originated bills from the time hearings are held on them to final enactment or rejection. Within these divisions are current status tables which are used to update the main listings as the session progresses.

New laws can be located in the "Enactments — Vetoes" division by public law number, original bill number, subject, and author. The "Vetoes" section of this division lists by bill number every measure disapproved by the president as well as action in each chamber sustaining or overriding the veto.[34]

Other divisions list individual members of the House and Senate; standing, joint, special, and select committees and subcommittees; reorganization plans, treaties, and nominations; and roll call and recorded teller votes. A companion publication, *Congressional Legislative Reporting Service*, offers subscribers a daily report on public bills and resolutions in selected subject areas of interest to them. In addition to "active reports," subscribers receive full-text copies of introduced and reported bills, committee reports, and laws.

DIGEST OF PUBLIC GENERAL BILLS AND RESOLUTIONS

Issued since 1936 and currently prepared by the Congressional Research Service of the Library of Congress (LC 14.6; item 807), the *Digest of Public General Bills and Resolutions* provides summaries of the essential features of public bills and resolutions during the legislative process. The *Digest* is usually published during each session of a Congress in two cumulative issues with occasional supplements and a final edition at the conclusion of the session.

Each cumulative issue is divided into three parts:

Part 1. Action Taken during the Congress. This part reflects action taken on measures throughout the Congress, including first session action in second session publications. It consists of two sections, "Public Laws" and "Other Measures Receiving Action." The "Public Laws" section contains digests of public laws in numerical order of enactment, their legislative histories, and a cross-index of law to bill or resolution number. The section "Other Measures Receiving Action" lists by number the latest revised digests with their legislative histories.

Part 2. Digests of Public General Bills and Resolutions. This section includes by chamber and form of measure digests of all public bills and resolutions in numerical order as introduced. For identical bills, reference is made from higher numbered measures to the earlier bill or resolution. For measures having multiple sponsors, only the member whose name appears first on the bill is indicated. Where a measure is described only by the bill title as it appears in the *Congressional Record*, a digest will be described in a later supplement or cumulation. Private measures are identified by bill number only.

Part 3. Indexes to Digested Bills and Resolutions. This part consists of the following indexes:

1) Index by Sponsor and Cosponsor. This index furnishes a reference to all public and private bills and resolutions measures sponsored and cosponsored by each member of the House and Senate. Members' names, listed alphabetically by chamber, are followed by the subjects of the bills sponsored or cosponsored. This comprehensive listing supplements Part 2, where only the originating sponsor's name is given.

2) Index of Identical Bills. This index includes all measures which are identical in both language and content introduced during the Congress. Arranged by chamber and within chamber by form of measure, the number of the first identical bill or resolution is given with a "See" reference to the identical measure.

3) Short Title Index. This is an alphabetical index of short titles of bills containing such titles in their texts referencing the bill number.

4) Subject Index. The Subject Index is preceded by a list of "Principal Subject Headings" under which more detailed index entries may be found. Measures which have received action and appear in either the "Public Laws" section or the "Other Measures Receiving Action" sections of Part 1 are denoted by an asterisk.

Neither the Short Title Index nor the Subject Index includes entries for measures which are revised during the legislative process. The digests are brief or quite lengthy, depending on the size of the bill itself. Each supplement to the *Digest* contains the summaries, or bill titles when appropriate, of bills introduced since the previous cumulative issue or supplement, as well as a subject index to those measures. And when a cumulative issue is published, all previous issues may be discarded, but the final issue for a session should be permanently retained.

HOUSE CALENDARS

Prepared under the direction of the clerk of the House, this important source carries the full title *Calendars of the United States House of Representatives and History of Legislation* (Y 1.2/2; item 998-A). It is published daily when the House is in session, and in every Monday issue there is a subject index; each issue is cumulative so that libraries need retain only the Monday issue or that issue and one other day's *Calendars* until the following Monday.

Although its provenance is the House of Representatives, it serves as an index to all legislation, both House and Senate, that has been reported by the committees and acted upon by either or both chambers, with the exception of Senate resolutions not of interest to the House and special House reports.

The section entitled "Numerical Order of Bills and Resolutions Which Have Passed Either or Both Houses, and Bills Now Pending on the Calendars" provides by chamber and within chamber by form of measure the current status and legislative history of all actions on each bill. It is arranged by bill or resolution number, with similar or identical bills and bills having reference to each other indicated by number in parentheses. Tables of public and private laws are organized by law number referencing the bill number. A "Status of Major Bills" table is arranged by bill number with reference to title, committee report numbers, reported dates, dates of passage in both chambers, conference report dates, and public law numbers.

Tables of "Bills in Conference" and "Bills through Conference" provide number and date, brief title of measure, names of House and Senate conferees, and report numbers and dates. The several "calendars" of the House are arranged by date with bill or report number, sponsor and committee, title of measure, and calendar number.

Unlike the Senate, the House has five calendars for the scheduling of legislation provided by Rules XIII, XXIV, and XXVII of the House *Manual*. Of most value to the documents librarian for public legislation are the Union Calendar and House Calendar, the former for bills raising revenue, general appropriations bills, and bills of a public nature, the latter for bills of a public character not raising revenue or appropriating money or property. Tables are also provided for the Private Calendar, the Consent Calendar, and the Calendar of Motions to Discharge Committees.

The *Final Edition* of the House *Calendars* for a Congress should be permanently retained. It becomes a most valuable retrospective source for the information noted above as well as tables of acts vetoed while Congress was in session, acts which were vetoed but became laws, acts which became laws without presidential approval, pocket vetoes, constitutional amendments submitted to the states for ratification, and statistical tables and recapitulations for the Congress just completed and previous Congresses.

SENATE CALENDAR OF BUSINESS

Less important than the House *Calendars* in tracing legislation, the Senate *Calendar of Business* (Y 1.1/3; item 998-B) is prepared under the direction of the secretary of the Senate, but it is not cumulative and does not have an index. The Senate *Calendar* has a section called "General Orders" covering all major or minor legislation which is organized by calendar order number, bill number and sponsor, title, and report number. The "Bills in Conference" section is arranged by date sent to conference, with bill number, brief title, Senate and House conferees, Senate report number, and current status. A separate table gives "Status of Appropriations Bills" and is arranged by bill number with brief title and legislative history to date. While depository libraries ought to subscribe to this item, the House *Calendars* should be used to access current status information for both chambers.

CONGRESSIONAL RECORD

As we noted, the biweekly index to the *Congressional Record* has a section called "History of Bills and Resolutions," which cumulates and is arranged by chamber, form of measure, and number. Accordingly, the current index provides legislative status information from a bill's introduction to enactment or veto, referencing the page numbers in the CR where the activity is recorded. To provide more current and comprehensive access to the official *Record*, Capitol Services, Inc. (CSI), a Washington, DC commercial publisher, offers to subscribers a range of products and services.

CONGRESSIONAL RECORD REPORT

A personalized, customized daily report on a topic or topics selected by the subscriber, the *Report* covers speeches, debate, amendments, new bills, cosponsorships, and committee schedules. The subscription includes a binder and user guides.

CONGRESSIONAL RECORD ABSTRACTS, MASTER EDITION

Also published daily, the entire issue of the *Record* is organized by over 40 major topic divisions and more than 250 subjects within those divisions, with edited abstracts of the various congressional activities. There are extensive cross-references. Included in the subscription are a binder, topic finder, and other useful finding aids. Moreover, subscribers can purchase "Sector Editions" from the *Master Edition* for broad topics such as energy, health, national defense, welfare, foreign affairs, and education.

In 1982 CSI made available the daily *Record* in a microfiche format to be mailed to subscribers the same day the official daily printed edition sold by the Superintendent of Documents is sent to its subscribers.

CRECORD

The CSI Congressional Record Data Base has been online through ORBIT since January 1976 and more recently through DIALOG. Pronounced "C-Record," CRECORD is updated weekly and can be searched for legislative histories, current political issues, new bills, current status of legislation, roll call votes, public laws, members' remarks on issues, executive communications, and even humor (from CSI's file "The Lighter Side of the Record").

FEDERAL INDEX

CSI operates the monthly *Federal Index*, formerly a database of Predicasts, Inc. (Cleveland, Ohio). The online edition of the printed *Federal Index* used to be called FEDEX, but that acronym duplicated another database called FEDEX: Federal Energy Data Index, which is online through BRS. Therefore, *Federal Index*, which includes the *Congressional Record*, is the appropriate name for the database in this instance, and is online through ORBIT and DIALOG.[35]

ROLL CALL VOTING

Another organization, Policy Review Associates, Inc., provides online coverage of roll call votes. The accompanying information includes bills and resolutions, treaties, nominations, and other legislative action pursuant to a roll call vote. Record units in this database—called VOTES—include member profiles (specific votes cast by individual representatives and senators) and legislative histories (total roll results). VOTES covers the Ninety-sixth Congress, first session (1979) to the present, is updated twice a month while Congress is in session, and may be accessed by bill number, title, subject, sponsor, congressional district, state, political party affiliation, congressional session, and roll call number. VOTES is online through ORBIT.

ONLINE LEGISLATIVE SEARCH SYSTEMS

Since February 1981 Commerce Clearing House (CCH), whose *Congressional Index* was discussed above, has been providing its congressional and state legislative reporting services online through General Electric Information Services Company. The service, called *Electronic Legislative Search System* (ELSS), provides daily information on legislative activity for all fifty states and the U.S. Congress. For federal legislation, ELSS furnishes online descriptions of bills and resolutions, including short titles; sponsors; dates of introduction and committee referrals; committee and floor actions; vote counts; and final disposition. Overnight processing of the printed products of ELSS permits full text distribution. ELSS represents the first in a series of CCH computer-based products which have, in the past, been produced manually and continue to be distributed to subscribers in their numerous Topical Law Reports in looseleaf form.

LEGISLEX, produced by Legislex Associates (Columbus, Indiana), contains federal and state bill information. Data on bills by specified key words are reported, as are legislative histories, amendments, and votes in committee and on the floor. LEGISLEX is online through National CSS, Inc. (Wilton, Connecticut).

LEGI-SLATE, produced by Legi-Slate, Inc. (Washington, DC) covers the history of bills and resolutions of the Congress and the Texas legislature. LEGI-SLATE is online through Source Telecomputing Corporation (McLean, Virginia).

CIS/INDEX

Although *CIS/Index* (see Chapter 6) is not a current status tool, its monthly issues and annual volumes index and abstract those congressional publications related to the legislative process: hearings, committee prints, committee reports, and presidential statements (including veto messages) in the House and Senate documents series. The index of subjects and names includes names of witnesses at hearings and their affiliations. Supplementary indexes provide access to the abstracts by bill, report, document, and public law number. *CIS/Index* is online through ORBIT and DIALOG.

TRACING PRIVATE LEGISLATION

Because private bills are assigned a bill number and deal with the relief of individuals and institutions, they are not difficult to follow from introduction to enactment or veto. Some of the more useful status tools are as follows:

HOUSE CALENDARS

The "Private Calendar" section of the House *Calendars* indicates private legislation by date/bill number referencing committee referral and report number, title, and calendar number. A cumulative table of private laws cites private law number with reference to bill number. The status table, "Numerical Order of Bills and Resolutions Which Have Passed Either or Both Houses, and Bills Now Pending on the Calendars," includes private legislation by bill number, with all appropriate citations through private law number and date. The Subject Index in the Monday edition of the *Calendars* provides access to individuals and institutions alphabetically by name under the subject heading "Private Relief." The *Final Edition* of the House *Calendars* includes other tables showing by bill number and title private measures that became law during that Congress. Comparative statistical tables in the *Final Edition* show the total number of private laws enacted for the latest Congress and similar figures for Congresses going back several decades.

MONTHLY CATALOG

From July 1976 to the present, the *Monthly Catalog* provides information on private measures in its Subject Index by name of person or institution, in its Title Keyword Index under the word "relief," and in its Series/Report Index by House or Senate committee report number.

STATUTES AT LARGE

In the *Statutes at Large* there is a "List of Bills Enacted into Private Law" organized by bill number with reference to the private law number. In addition, the "Individual Index" at the end of the volumes lists alphabetically the names of individuals and institutions whose private measures have been enacted into law with reference to the page number in the *Statutes* where the text of the private law is published. Because the *United States Code* is a consolidation and topical arrangement of the *general* and permanent laws of the United States, the text of private legislation is not included in this source.

OTHER SOURCES

The "History of Bills and Resolutions" section of the *Congressional Record Index* includes private measures, arranged by bill number. Both the House and Senate *Journals* also have a "History of Bills and Resolutions" part organized by bill number in their sessional volumes; private measures indicate the date of proceedings. Moreover, the "Index" part of the *Journals* provides the name of the individual or institution seeking relief referencing the bill or resolution number. Committee reports on private bills can be accessed using the index volumes "Private Relief and Related Actions: Index of Names of Individuals and Organizations" in the *CIS US Serial Set Index, 1789-1969*.[36]

LEGISLATIVE HISTORIES

Legislative histories comprise citations to and the text of those intrinsic documents that permit executive agencies and the courts to determine legislative intent when the meaning or purpose of a statute is ambiguous. As we pointed out, the "Legislative History" printed at the end of the slip law (see Figure 19, *supra*) includes citations to committee reports, dates of consideration and passage in the *Congressional Record*, and apposite presidential statements published in the *Weekly Compilation of Presidential Documents*. Other sources include citations to hearings, committee prints, related measures, and ancillary documentation. However limited or comprehensive, legislative histories play an important role in research. Fortunately, there are several useful sources available to librarians and users. Some of the more prominent ones will be assayed below.

BIBLIOGRAPHIC GUIDE

The beginner would do well to consult Nancy P. Johnson (comp.), *Sources of Compiled Legislative Histories: A Bibliography of Government Documents, Periodical Articles, and Books* (AALL Publ. Series No. 14; Littleton, CO: Fred B. Rothman & Co., 1979). Issued in looseleaf binder, the basic volume and supplementary pages (1981) cover major compilations of legislative histories from the First through the Ninety-sixth Congresses. The contents include significant compilations arranged by publisher, looseleaf and online services, collections dealing with specific subject matter arranged by topic, sources arranged by public law, useful appendixes, and author, title, and act indexes.

SELECTED SOURCES

The several sources described in this chapter for tracing current legislation – CCH *Congressional Index, Digest of Public General Bills and Resolutions*,[37] House *Calendars, Congressional Record Index* – have cumulative features that encompass the process from bill to law or veto. Tabular accounts include the

"Guide to Legislative History of Bills Enacted into Public Law" in the *Statutes at Large* and a "History of Bills Enacted into Public Law" in the final sessional issue of the *Daily Digest* section of the *Congressional Record*. The sessional volumes of the House and Senate *Journals* have sections called "History of Bills and Resolutions," which are arranged by number and within number by date.

Voluminous legislative histories are issued on a selective basis by a House or Senate committee. Usually prepared by the Congressional Research Service of the Library of Congress and issued as committee prints, they are indexed in the *Monthly Catalog* and *CIS/Index*. Examples include *A Legislative History of the Clean Air Act Amendments of 1977* (Y 4.P96/10:95-16/v.8; item 1045) and *Legislative History of Public Law 96-88, Department of Education Organization Act* (Y 4.G74/9:Ed 8/3/pt.1-2; item 1037-A).

United States Code Congressional and Administrative News (U.S.C.C.A.N.), is issued monthly and cumulates into several bound sessional volumes. Although it can be used to keep track of documents in the legislative process, its value as a retrospective source is manifest. Included in the bound volumes are the text of the public laws paginated to the volumes of the *Statutes at Large* and the text of the committee reports pursuant to legislation. U.S.C.C.A.N. has an alphabetical list of legislative histories and several valuable tables. Table 1 ("Public Laws and Legislative History") lists public laws by number referencing the pages of the text of the law and the legislative history section. Table 2 ("U.S. Code and U.S. Code Annotated Classifications") shows sections of the public law referencing title and section of the *U.S. Code*. Table 3 ("U.S. Code and U.S. Code Annotated Sections Amended, Repealed, New, Etc.") reverses the information in Table 2, with *U.S. Code* citations referencing pages in U.S.C.C.A.N. Table 4 ("Legislative History") provides public law numbers with reference to pagination in the *Statutes at Large*, bill number, House and Senate committee report numbers and names of committees, and *Congressional Record* dates of consideration and passage. Table 5 ("Bills and Joint Resolutions Enacted") gives bill number referencing U.S.C.C.A.N. pagination to the text of the public law. Table 9 ("Major Bills Enacted") lists by title of measure references to bill number, dates reported and passed House and Senate, and dates of approval, with public law number, or veto. Table 10 ("Popular Name Acts") lists alphabetically by popular title of act with reference to pagination of text in U.S.C.C.A.N. Other tables provide information on presidential initiatives and will be discussed in Chapter 8. Each volume of U.S.C.C.A.N. has a detailed index with page references to the text of the laws and committee reports.

CIS/Annual includes a useful section on legislative histories of bills that have been enacted into public law in the *Abstracts* volume of the yearly *CIS/Index* cumulation. Citations include reports, hearings, committee prints, debate, and presidential messages. A separate section entitled "Revised Legislative Histories" includes any earlier laws supplementing the information already noted in the current annual volumes. Access to this information is through the *Index* volume of *CIS/Annual* by subjects and names, titles, bill, report and document numbers, and committee and subcommittee chairpersons. The public law number serves as the CIS accession number, and the text of the cited materials is available on microfiche. Figure 20 shows a sample legislative history from *CIS/Annual*.

Figure 20
CIS/Annual: Sample Legislative History

SAMPLE LEGISLATIVE
HISTORY CITATION

The following sample entry shows the information contained in a typical Legislative History Citation.

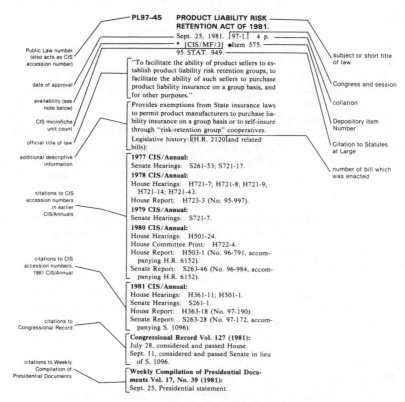

NOTE—AVAILABILITY: All public laws are sold in "slip law" form by the Superintendent of Documents, U.S. Government Printing Office, Washington, D.C. 20402. The price varies from law to law, ranging usually between $1.50 and $5.00 per law. After the close of every session, all the public laws passed during that session and approved by the President are compiled in the Statutes at Large.

LEGISLATIVE HISTORIES ON MICROFICHE

Commerce Clearing House publishes a service called *Public Laws—Legislative Histories on Microfiche*, in which the documentation for all laws enacted are sent to subscribers on 42X fiche shortly after enactment. The package usually includes the text of House or Senate bills as introduced and reported, committee reports (including the conference reports), debates in the *Congressional Record*, and the slip law. The materials on fiche are accompanied by looseleaf indexes on paper, and subscribers receive a CCH ring binder with pocketed pages to hold the microfiche and paper indexing.

Information Handling Services (IHS), located in Englewood, Colorado, offers an *IHS Legislative Histories Program*, in which the filming of important general legislation for current Congresses and retrospective sessions is being accomplished. Tax legislation goes back to 1909, and ultimately the coverage will include major landmark legislation of the twentieth century. The documentation on microfiche includes the text of the public law, bills, reports, hearings, committee prints, *Congressional Record* debates, and relevant presidential messages. A *Legislative Histories Indexed Guide* in hard copy provides access to the fiche by Congress, *Statutes at Large* citation, bill number, popular name, and subject. A table of contents is provided for each legislative history and includes the Congressional Serial Set number for reports, SuDocs class notation for hearings, and any citations to the *United States Code* that appear in the public law.

CIS Legislative History Service supplements the legislative history citations and microfiche text discussed in *CIS/Annual* above. This project offers two categories of subscription service: basic and comprehensive. The *Basic Legislative History Service*, available as an annual subscription, includes the text in paper copy or on microfiche of the following publications for current or prior Congresses: the slip law, bills (including similar bills), reports, debates, hearings, committee prints, and presidential messages and statements. The *Comprehensive Legislative History Service*, available as an annual subscription or by individual history "on demand," includes all the documentation mentioned above plus a number of related materials. These include reports on similar subjects by legislative committees or "study" committees of both chambers; alternative or similar bills, Senate printed amendments, and resolutions providing for consideration of bills; debate on similar or related measures; hearings on similar subject matter; related committee prints and documents; and other apposite publications from the Comptroller General, Congressional Budget Office, and concerned executive agencies.

Each law's microfiche collection is accompanied by an *Annotated Directory* that provides full bibliographic information for all the documents in each history along with abstracts of the public law and all reports, hearings, committee prints, and messages included in the history. These are provided in ring binders until the end of the session when the annotations are cumulated into a printed clothbound *Legislative History Annual*. A newsletter called the *Public Law Reporter* announces public laws for which legislative histories are available through the *Service* with summaries of available histories and a list of forthcoming legislative histories. All significant public laws are covered in this ambitious project, while laws of lesser import may be found in *CIS/Annual*. For example, subscribers to the CIS *Comprehensive Legislative History Service* for the Economic Recovery Tax Act of 1981 (P.L. 97-34) received the full text of about one thousand official publications pertinent to this landmark legislation, with the *Annotated Directory* consisting of a detailed table of contents and abstracts of major items in the history.

THE CONGRESSIONAL SERIAL SET

The Congressional Serial Set has been known variously as the serial number set, congressional edition, congressional set, congressional series, and sheep set (owing to its distinctive sheepskin binding). Throughout its history it has included a number of establishment publications: House and Senate *Journals*, executive and miscellaneous publications, reports on private and public legislation, the annual reports of the executive and independent agencies, reports on audits of federally charted private corporations, investigative and background studies, proceedings of certain societies and associations, and much more. Schmeckebier and Eastin present a thorough account of the historical serial set,[38] and the author described the series for the 1970s.[39] Some significant changes occurred in the format and distribution of the serial set beginning with the Ninety-sixth Congress, and the following account will be concerned with the present use and control of the publications that comprise the series.

The serial set consists of three categories of congressional publications issued in six distinct series: House reports, Senate reports, House documents, Senate documents, Senate executive reports, and Senate treaty documents. These publications may be described as follows.

HOUSE AND SENATE REPORTS

House and Senate reports on public and private measures have been described in this chapter in some detail. Pursuant to legislation, they constitute the majority of reports. In addition, "special reports" include investigative activities of committees, summaries of committee oversight activities, studies of matters relating to public policy, and the like. From the Eighty-fourth Congress through the Ninety-fifth Congress, House and Senate reports on public and private bills were bound separately in volumes entitled "Miscellaneous Reports on Public Bills" or "Miscellaneous Reports on Private Bills." Beginning with the second session of the Eighty-eighth Congress, special reports were also bound separately and thus indicated. With the Ninety-sixth Congress, all House and Senate reports are bound in numerical sequence.

HOUSE AND SENATE DOCUMENTS

Throughout this text, the word "documents" has been largely used in a generic sense, synonymous with "publications" or "materials." For serial set publications in this series, however, the word assumes a specificity not encountered elsewhere.

The kinds of materials ordered to be published as House or Senate documents are many and varied. Prior to the Ninety-sixth Congress, documents labeled "Miscellaneous" were bound in serial volumes bearing the same base serial number with the issues in the group differentiated (e.g., 13145-1, 13145-2, 13145-3, etc.). In these volumes one finds presidential messages, including vetoes;

reports on rescissions and deferrals of budget authority; budget amendments; the president's State of the Union Address; and the like. Reports on audits of government corporations like the Federal Home Loan Bank Board and Tennessee Valley Authority were usually grouped into a serial volume. These reports are required by law to set forth the scope of financial audit, documentation of the entity's assets and liabilities, income and expenses, and activities for the fiscal year. Other titles issued in the House and Senate document series included the annual reports of federal agencies and reference works such as *How Our Laws Are Made, Biographical Directory of the American Congress, Statistical Abstract of the United States*, and House and Senate *Manuals*.

An odd category of documents includes the annual reports of organizations like the Boy and Girl Scouts of America, proceedings of the American Legion Convention, national report of the Disabled American Veterans, and proceedings of the United Spanish War Veterans. Listed with statutory authority in a pamphlet entitled *Reports to Be Made to Congress* (itself issued as a House document), the reports of these societies, associations, and other non-governmental bodies provide a lively mix to the House and Senate documents series.

Like House and Senate reports, beginning with the Ninety-sixth Congress all House and Senate documents are bound in numerical sequence.

SENATE TREATY DOCUMENTS

Senate treaty documents were formerly called Senate executive documents and were issued in a *lettered* series. In 1977 this series was made available to depository libraries for the first time. The series became part of the serial set for the first time beginning with the Ninety-sixth Congress. For the Ninety-seventh Congress the title change became effective and the treaty documents became a *numbered* series throughout a Congress. Thus the unratified "Salt II Treaty" (*Treaty on Limitation of Strategic Offensive Arms and Protocol Thereto*) was issued as 96-1: Senate Executive Document Y and bound with a number of other executive documents in serial volume 13235.[40] However, in the following Congress, the *Tax Convention with the Federal Republic of Germany* was designated 97-1: Senate Treaty Document 1.

Treaty documents are messages from the president to the Senate Foreign Relations Committee transmitting the text of treaties. In accordance with Article II, Section 2, Clause 2 of the Constitution, the president may make treaties only with the advice and consent of two-thirds of the Senate. Since the Foreign Relations Committee exercises jurisdiction over treaties, its reports pursuant to treaty documents are of great significance (see Chapter 8).

SENATE EXECUTIVE REPORTS

Like treaty documents, Senate executive reports were first made available to depository institutions in 1977 and became part of the serial set beginning with the Ninety-sixth Congress. They too are a *numbered* series and appear to serve two purposes: 1) when issued by the Senate Foreign Relations Committee, they recommend to the full Senate that a treaty proposed by the president (in a Senate treaty document) be approved; 2) when issued by any Senate committee with the appropriate oversight function (including the Foreign Relations Committee), they recommend confirmation of presidential nominations of high officials in the executive and judiciary. Thus the *Treaty with Colombia Concerning the Status of Quita Sueno, Roncador, and Serrana*, reported out of the Foreign Relations Committee, was designated 97-1: Executive Report 16. But 95-1: Executive Report 7 was issued by the Senate Committee on Agriculture and carried the title *Nominations of Carol Tucker Foreman as Assistant Secretary of Agriculture and Member of the Board of Directors, Commodity Credit Corporation*. For executive reports on nominations there is no prior "executive document" series.

Treaty documents and executive reports are indexed in the *Monthly Catalog* by subject, title, and series/report notation, and in *CIS/Index* by the several access points discussed in Chapter 6 and *infra*. The Senate also issues a journal of its executive proceedings that contains useful treaty information and will be discussed in Chapter 8.

NUMERICAL LISTS AND SCHEDULE OF VOLUMES

Known by its short title, the *Numerical Lists* (GP 3.7/2; item 553) bridges the gap between the numerical designation of individual reports, documents, executive reports, and treaty documents and their subsequent appearance in serial set binding. They are issued sessionally and compiled under the direction of the Superintendent of Documents.

The title of the publication literally identifies its two-part arrangement. The first part, the "Numerical Lists," arranges the three categories by individual number, title, and serial-volume designation. A serial volume number may include several bound volumes within that base number. Thus 96-1: H.rp. 157 (*Consideration of H.R. 2295*) is found in Volume 5 of serial 13292, and this is indicated in the "Numerical Lists" section as "5; 13292." Figure 21 (page 166) shows a page from the "Numerical Lists" for the Ninety-sixth Congress, first session.

The second part, the "Schedule of Volumes," arranges the individual numbered publications by serial volume. The "Date of Receipt" column is a handy place for clerical personnel in depository libraries to note receipt of the serial volumes, after which all inclusive reports, documents, and Senate executive issuances received in slip form may be discarded. Figure 22 (page 167) shows a page from the "Schedule of Volumes" for the Ninety-sixth Congress, first session. Note that Figure 22 indicates "Senate Executive Documents" with Letters A-II. Until the Ninety-seventh Congress, these were assigned letters A through Z and then began again with AA, BB, etc. The new designation Senate Treaty Documents, with numbers instead of letters, appears in sessional *Numerical Lists and Schedule of Volumes* beginning with the Ninety-seventh Congress.

Users will discover that the "Schedule of Volumes" section of the *Numerical Lists* before the Ninety-sixth Congress reflected the grouping of like reports and documents in the bound serial volumes and, of course, did not include treaty documents and executive reports. Moreover, the bound set in its entirety as shown in the "Schedule of Volumes" was sent *only* to the Senate and House libraries, the Library of Congress, the National Archives, and the office of the Superintendent of Documents. This practice of providing two "editions" of the Congressional Serial Set was confusing to librarians and users alike, but with the

Ninety-sixth Congress all congressional materials listed in the "Schedule of Volumes" are sent to depository libraries that subscribe to the appropriate depository items.

Figure 21
Numerical Lists

34   NUMERICAL LISTS

No.	HOUSE REPORTS	Vol.; serial
537.	Earnings test for social security beneficiaries. 2 pts ____	15; 13302
538.	Reduce unemployment compensation by retirement benefits ____	15; 13302
539.	Unemployment compensation, employees of National Oceanic and Atmospheric Administration. 3 pts____	15; 13302
540.	Civil Service authorization act of 1979 ____	15; 13302
541.	2d concurrent resolution on budget, fiscal 1980 ____	15; 13302
542.	Appropriations for Department of Housing and Urban Development ____	15; 13302
543.	Designate birthday of Martin Luther King, Jr., as legal holiday ____	15; 13302
544.	Amend act of Dec. 22, 1974, 88 Stat. 1712____	15; 13302
545.	Tax administration provisions revision act of 1979 ____	15; 13302
546.	Department of Defense authorization act, fiscal 1980 ____	15; 13302
547.	Consideration of H.J. Res. 430 ____	15; 13302
548.	Civil suits for violations of civil rights ____	15; 13302
549.	Amend District of Columbia redevelopment act of 1945__	15; 13302
550.	Extend borrowing authority for District of Columbia ____	15; 13302
551.	Conveyance to Little Sisters of the Poor ____	15; 13302
552.	Low-income energy assistance supplemental appropriation. 2 pts ____	15; 13302
553.	Appropriations for Agriculture, Rural Development, and related agencies programs, fiscal 1980 ____	15; 13302
554.	Consideration of H.R. 4904 ____	15; 13302
555.	Consideration of H.R. 5192 ____	15; 13302
556.	Maritime appropriation authorization act, fiscal 1980 ____	15; 13302
557.	Indiana Dunes National Lakeshore ____	15; 13302
558.	Report by Permanent Select Committee on Intelligence pursuant to sec. 108(b), Foreign intelligence surveillance act ____	15; 13302
559.	Revitalize passenger ship industry ____	15; 13302
560.	Relief of Ohio Wesleyan University, Delaware, Ohio ____	15; 13302
561.	Relief of St. Paul's Episcopal Church, Riverside, Conn. 2 pts ____	15; 13302
562.	Temporary duty suspension on certain alloy steels used for making chipper knives ____	15; 13302
563.	Temporary reduction of duty on strontium nitrate ____	15; 13302
564.	Temporary suspension of duty on fluorspar ____	15; 13302
565.	Temporary duty reduction on titanium sponge ____	15; 13302
566.	Tariff classification of cold finished steel bars ____	15; 13302
567.	Temporary suspension of duty on pillow blanks of latex foam rubber____	15; 13302
568.	Child health assurance act of 1979____	15; 13302
569.	Miscellaneous tariff schedules amendments____	15; 13302
570.	Establish Legionville National Historic Site in Pennsylvania ____	15; 13302
571.	Consideration of H.R. 4985 ____	15; 13302
572.	Term of Federal Reserve Board Chairman ____	15; 13302
573.	Further expenses of investigations, etc., by Permanent Select Committee on Intelligence ____	15; 13302
574.	National Archives film-vault fire, Suitland, Maryland, Dec. 7, 1978 ____	15; 13302
575.	Express sense of Congress with respect to Baltic States and Soviet claims of citizenship over U.S. citizens __	15; 13302
576.	Consideration of H.R. 2603 ____	15; 13302
577.	Consideration of H.R. 2608 ____	15; 13302
578.	Consideration of H.R. 3994 ____	15; 13302
579.	Consideration of H.R. 2063 ____	15; 13302

Figure 22
Schedule of Volumes

40   # SCHEDULE OF VOLUMES

SENATE EXECUTIVE DOCUMENTS—SENATE REPORTS SENATE EXECUTIVE REPORTS—HOUSE DOCUMENTS	Serial no.	Date of receipt
SENATE EXECUTIVE DOCUMENTS		
Letters A–II: **Senate executive documents**	13235	
SENATE REPORTS		
Vol. 1. Nos. 1–47: **Senate miscellaneous reports** _	13236	
Vol. 2. Nos. 48–65: **Senate miscellaneous reports_**	13237	
Vol. 3. Nos. 66–104: **Senate miscellaneous reports**	13238	
Vol. 4. Nos. 105–155: **Senate miscellaneous reports** _	13239	
Vol. 5. Nos. 156–195: **Senate miscellaneous reports** _	13240	
Vol. 6. Nos. 196–237: **Senate miscellaneous reports** _	13241	
Vol. 7. Nos. 238–250: **Senate miscellaneous reports** _	13242	
Vol. 8. Nos. 251–299: **Senate miscellaneous reports** _	13243	
Vol. 9. Nos. 300–330: **Senate miscellaneous reports** _	13244	
Vol. 10. Nos. 331–374: **Senate miscellaneous reports** _	13245	
Vol. 11. Nos. 375–394: **Senate miscellaneous reports** _	13246	
Vol. 12. Nos. 395–423: **Senate miscellaneous reports** _	13247	
Vol. 13. Nos.424–471: **Senate miscellaneous reports** _	13248	
Vol. 14. Nos. 472–547: **Senate miscellaneous reports** _	13249	
SENATE EXECUTIVE REPORTS		
Nos. 1–26: **Senate executive reports** _ _ _ _	13250	|
HOUSE DOCUMENTS		
Vol. 1. Nos. 1–15: **Miscellaneous documents** _ _ _	13251	
Vol. 2. Nos. 16–20: **Examinations of rivers and harbors** _	13252	
Vol. 3. Nos. 21–23: **Examinations of rivers and harbors** _	13253	
Vol. 4. Nos. 24–26: **Examinations of rivers and harbors** _	13254	
Vol. 5. Nos. 27–39: **Miscellaneous documents** _ _ _	13255	

SERIAL SET "EDITIONS"

Prior to the Ninety-sixth Congress, certain publications, primarily in the *House Documents* series, were sent to depository libraries in their "departmental edition" only and were sent in their "congressional edition" to the five libraries mentioned above. Notification of this procedure was given in every sessional issue of the *Numerical Lists*. In the "Schedule of Volumes" section, preceding the titles of these "departmental" documents, there is this explanatory statement:

> Note.—The documents listed below originated in executive departments and agencies. They were or will be furnished to depository libraries and international exchanges at the time of printing in the format used by the departments and agencies. They will not be furnished as Congressional documents nor in the volumes as indicated hereby.

These publications typically consisted of annual reports of departments and agencies, including the independent and regulatory entities, and recurring reference sources such as the *Budget of the United States Government, Examinations of Rivers and Harbors, Army Register*, and *Economic Report of the President*. Pursuant to statutory authority, these executive branch publications are transmitted to the Congress. When ordered to be printed by the legislative branch, they become a part of the "congressional edition" of the serial set with an assigned document number and later a serial volume number. But because of their executive branch provenance, they were also assigned a SuDocs class notation and sent to depository libraries or sold by the Superintendent of Documents in their "departmental edition." To insure receipt of these several publications, depository libraries had to subscribe to the appropriate depository item number in advance. Under procedures initiated with the Ninety-sixth Congress, depository libraries are supposed to receive only one "edition" of the bound serial set. The "Schedule of Volumes" no longer notes departmental editions removed from the set. Moreover, as a strategy to reduce the cost of congressional printing, the so-called "posterity" edition (one with red, green, and black ink labels, stamped with imitation gold) was eliminated and the traditional, less elaborate "depository library" edition is now sent to depository institutions and all other authorized recipients alike.[41]

Despite this aim, duplication of editions continued for a reduced number of series, such as the *Budget of the United States*, the *Budget Appendix*, the *Economic Report of the President*, and the U.S. Army Corps of Engineers' *Examinations of Rivers and Harbors*. Thus libraries subscribing to the printed version of the serial set received the *Budget of the United States Government, Fiscal Year 1980* in its departmental edition (PrEx 2.8:980; item 853), in the "slip" form of the congressional edition (96-1: H.doc. 41; item 996-A) and in bound serial form (13257; item 996-C). The *Economic Report of the President* for 1981 was available in the departmental edition (Pr 39.9:981; item 848) and as 96-1: H.doc. 3 (item 996-A). Other inconsistencies are reflected in the main entry section of the *Monthly Catalog* where bibliographic information for serial set publications includes the availability of other editions. Thus a General Accounting Office study titled *Audit of the Rural Telephone Bank* was issued as 96-2: H.doc. 297, but in its "departmental edition" was titled *Examination of the Rural Telephone Bank's Financial Statements*.[42]

As we mentioned, the "new" printed version of the serial set mandates that all reports and documents be bound strictly in numerical order. The sizes and shapes of publications in this series have caused problems which were clearly foreseeable. As LeRoy C. Schwarzkopf noted,

> Documents are issued in several sizes without regard to grouping of numbers. Thick Reports or Documents which warrant separate binding may also appear haphazardly with the result that several thin publications may be numbered between two thick publications. Another problem ... is the new practice of numbering all reports on the same bill within one House with a single number and issuing in parts (example: House Report 96-836, pts. 1,2,3 on the National Publications Act of 1980). Binding cannot be scheduled until all parts of a report have been issued.[43]

THE SERIAL SET ON MICROFICHE

In 1979 the Joint Committee on Printing authorized an advisory committee to study methods to improve the serial set and to reduce its production costs. The committee, composed of representatives from JCP, GPO, the House and Senate libraries, the Library of Congress, the National Archives, and GODORT, recommended among other things that the serial set be offered to depository libraries on microfiche as an alternative to paper copy. A preliminary survey of libraries interested in a microfiche edition of the set indicated that about $1,500,000 could be saved in a two-year Congress through microfiche distribution. In December 1979 depository institutions were offered the choice of microfiche or paper copy distribution, and the far-reaching changes in serial set production and distribution were thus effected.[44]

Libraries choosing the microfiche are provided with dividers indicating the serial volume number with the number of reports and documents included in that volume. Accordingly, the initial sequence of materials issued in fact *becomes* the "bound" edition. Libraries choosing paper copy distribution receive the miscellaneous series in slip form and later in bound volumes. That all printed materials are bound in numerical order is clearly an accommodation to the decision to issue a microfiche edition, a policy based on economics rather than user convenience.

In 1982 GPO announced that it would resurvey depository libraries on their choice of serial set item selection for the Ninety-eighth Congress, and in so doing would offer an additional option: bound serial volumes on microfiche. This will occupy one-third less space than the microfiche of individual reports and documents and will not require dividers.

SERIAL SET CLASSIFICATION

The new distribution system eliminated a number of depository items that had been used to receive bound and unbound House and Senate reports on public and private bills, including special reports; bound and unbound House and Senate "miscellaneous" documents; and series like the House and Senate *Manuals*, annual reports of the Boy Scouts, Girl Scouts, Daughters of the

American Revolution, Disabled American Veterans, Veterans of Foreign Wars, etc. (see the author's 1978 edition, p. 188). The present classification scheme is shown in current editions of the *List of Classes* and is organized in the following manner:

PAPER COPY DISTRIBUTION

SuDocs Class Number	Category	Depository Item Number
Y 1.1/2: (Serial Volume Number)	Serial Set Volumes, H & S rpts., S. Exec. rpts.	1008-E
Y 1.1/2: (Serial Volume Number)	Serial Set Volumes, H & S docs., S. Treaty docs.	996-C
Y 1.1/3: (Cong.-no.)	S. docs.	996-A
Y 1.1/4: (Cong.-no.)	S. Treaty docs.	996-A
Y 1.1/5: (Cong.-no.)	S. rpts.	1008-C
Y 1.1/6: (Cong.-no.)	S. Exec. rpts.	1008-C
Y 1.1/7: (Cong.-no.)	H. docs.	996-A
Y 1.1/8: (Cong.-no.)	H. rpts.	1008-C

MICROFICHE DISTRIBUTION

SuDocs Class Number	Category	Depository Item Number
Y 1.1/2: (Serial Volume Number)	Serial Set Volumes, H & S rpts., S. Exec. rpts.	1008-D
Y 1.1/2: (Serial Volume Number)	Serial Set Volumes, H & S docs., S. Treaty docs.	996-B
Y 1.1/3: (Cong.-no.)	S. docs.	996-B
Y 1.1/4: (Cong.-no.)	S. Treaty docs.	996-B
Y 1.1/5: (Cong.-no.)	S. rpts.	1008-D
Y 1.1/6: (Cong.-no.)	S. Exec. rpts.	1008-D
Y 1.1/7: (Cong.-no.)	H. docs.	996-B
Y 1.1/8: (Cong.-no.)	H. rpts.	1008-D

Prior to the Ninety-sixth Congress, the serial set was simply designated without a SuDocs classification symbol. Thus the committee report for the Extension of Library Services and Construction Act was designated 95-1: H.rp. 97. But during the Ninety-sixth Congress, the classification "X" was *incorrectly* assigned by the Superintendent, in that it conflicted with an earlier assignment of that symbol for the *Annals of Congress, Register of Debates*, and *Congressional Globe*, the eighteenth- and nineteenth-century predecessors of the *Congressional Record*. Issues of the *Monthly Catalog* carried along this X-rated disaster until the reports and documents of the Ninety-seventh Congress began to appear. Thus in the January 1982 *Monthly Catalog* we find the incongruous spectacle of the semiannual *Report of the Secretary of the Senate* (April 1-September 30, 1980) *improperly* classed in X 96-2: S. doc. 65/pt.1-2, while on the very same page the following semiannual *Report of the Secretary of the Senate* (October 1, 1980-March 31, 1981) *correctly* classed in Y 1.1/3: 97-4/pt.1-2.

ACCESSING THE SERIAL SET

CIS/Index provides current comprehensive coverage of House and Senate reports and documents, Senate executive reports, and Senate treaty documents in one place. Access to the abstracts is provided by indexes for subjects, names, titles, and report and document numbers. For retrospective coverage, the *CIS US Serial Set Index, 1789-1969* (see Chapter 6) is the definitive tool replacing the earlier bibliographic efforts. The index volumes provide access to the printed serial volumes or the text in the *CIS US Serial Set on Microfiche*. From 1970, online access through DIALOG and ORBIT is possible for bibliographic and ordering information, with full text available through the *CIS/Microfiche Library*. Thus the user has, for the first time in our history, complete and accurate access to the wealth of materials in this renowned series.

OTHER LEGISLATIVE SOURCE MATERIALS

Publications issued by the Congress and its committees, by other federal entities, by commercial publishers and micropublishers not discussed in the preceding pages provide supporting documentation for the legislative process. A selective account of these several sources follows.

LEGISLATIVE CALENDARS

Individual committees issue calendars on an irregular schedule. Most committee calendars cumulate so that the final edition covers an entire Congress. They are classed in "Y 4." followed by a Cutter symbol for the specific committee. Following the Cutter symbol, they are designated by Congress and calendar numbers.

A typical legislative calendar includes information on presidential messages referred to committee; status of bills referred to committee on which action has been taken; notice of miscellaneous publications by the committee; nominations before the committee and committee action; hearings held, arranged by bill number; House and Senate bills and resolutions referred to committee, arranged by date; and separate author and subject indexes.

Unfortunately, legislative calendars are not depository items; they are, however, indexed in *CIS/Index* and shown in the *Serials Supplement* to the *Monthly Catalog*, where main entry information appears in this form:

BUDGET, Committee on the,
Senate
Washington, DC 20510

81-9442

Y 4.B 85/2:(Cong./cal.nos.)
United States. Congress. Senate. Committee on the Budget.
    Legislative calendar / Committee on the Budget, United States Senate. [Washington, D.C.] : U.S. G.P.O.,
    v. ; 29 cm.
    Cover title.
    Cumulative.
    Description based on: 96th Congress, no. 1 (1980).
    Indexed by: CIS/Index to publications of the United States Congress ISSN 0007-8514
    1. United States. Congress. Senate. Committee on the Budget — Periodicals. 2. Calendars — Periodicals. I. Title.
OCLC 03455510

JOURNALS OF THE HOUSE AND SENATE

The journals of the Congress are the only publications required by the Constitution. Article I, Section 5 states: "Each House shall keep a Journal of its Proceedings, and from time to time publish the same...." Consequently, the *Journals*, not the *Congressional Record*, are the official documents for the proceedings of Congress, but the *Journals* do not include the speeches of members.

Both House and Senate *Journals* are published at the end of a session. Their contents include the proceedings, rules, questions of order, motions, actions taken, voting information, memorials and petitions received, the text of communications from the president, and a "History of Bills and Resolutions" section. The indexes are arranged by interfiled names, subjects, and bill titles and numbers.

The House *Journal*, classed XJH and designated by Congress and session, is available to depository libraries in hard copy (item 1030-A) or on microfiche (item 1030-B). Similarly designated, the Senate *Journal* is classed XJS and is available to depository institutions in hard copy (item 1047-A) or on microfiche (item 1047-B).

CIS Congressional Journals on Microfiche, 1789-1978 permits libraries to fill the gaps in their collections. The retrospective collection will be updated every few years.

CUMULATIVE INDEX OF CONGRESSIONAL COMMITTEE HEARINGS

This official series began with *Index of Congressional Committee Hearings Prior to January 3, 1935 in the United States Senate Library* and is available in a 1968 Kraus reprint. The *Cumulative Index of Congressional Committee Hearings* for the Seventy-fourth through the Eighty-fifth Congresses (1935-1959) was followed by *Supplements* issued periodically and made available to depository libraries (Y 1.3: H35/2/yr./supp. no.; item 998). Hearings are listed by subject, committee, and bill number. Some of the editions have included an index to committee prints as well as hearings.

With the publication of *CIS US Congressional Committee Hearings Index* and *CIS US Congressional Committee Prints Index* (see Chapter 6) and the text of these congressional publications on microfiche, and with the current issues of *CIS/Index*, coverage of hearings and prints is accomplished with more sophistication and greater bibliographic and indexing detail than in the official Senate series.

HOUSE AND SENATE MANUALS

The full title of the House *Manual* is *Constitution, Jefferson's Manual, and Rules of the House of Representatives of the United States.* It is published biennially as a House document and contains the fundamental source material for parliamentary procedure used in that chamber. The full title of the Senate *Manual* is *Senate Manual, Containing the Standing Rules, Orders, Laws, and Resolutions Affecting the Business of the United States Senate, Articles of Confederation and the Constitution of the United States.* Published biennially as a Senate document, it provides an account of the standing rules of that body. Both *Manuals* also contain much miscellaneous information. For example, the Senate *Manual* has a section of statistical data on electoral votes for president and vice-president, 1789 to the present, lists of Supreme Court justices and cabinet officers, apportionments of representatives, and the like. As part of the serial set, both *Manuals* are available to depository libraries in hard copy or on microfiche.

HOUSE AND SENATE PROCEDURE

Deschler's Precedents of the United States House of Representatives is a distinguished series of volumes analyzing the precedents of the House. 88 *Stat.* 1777 requires that the precedents be updated every two years. The early precedents of the House, dating from the First Congress, are found in Asher Hinds' monumental work and Clarence Cannon's comprehensive study.[45] The current volumes are issued in the serial set as House documents. The author, Lewis Deschler, was parliamentarian of the House from 1928 to 1974.

Senate Procedure: Precedents and Practices, prepared by Floyd M. Riddick, parliamentarian emeritus of the Senate, is a large compilation of the rules of that chamber, portions of laws affecting Senate procedure, rulings by the presiding officer, and established Senate practices. The work is organized into chapters and arranged alphabetically. The author has been granted copyright under the provisions of 91 *Stat.* 115. *Senate Procedure* is issued in the serial set as a Senate document.

CONSTITUTION ANNOTATED

The Congressional Research Service of the Library of Congress is required by law to issue a new edition of the *Constitution of the United States of America, Analysis and Interpretation* every ten years, with biennial supplements between editions. Known by its short title, the *Constitution Annotated* provides commentary on its articles, sections, and clauses with selected decisions of the Supreme Court discussed and cited in footnotes. Useful tables include proposed constitutional amendments pending and unratified, acts of Congress declared unconstitutional by the high court, state and local laws held unconstitutional, Supreme Court decisions overruled by subsequent decisions, and a table of cases. The base edition and supplements are issued in the serial set as Senate documents. For example, the 1976 *Supplement* was issued as 94-2: S.doc. 200 [13140-2], and the 1978 *Supplement* was issued as 96-1: S.doc. 26 [12;13231].

MEMORIAL ADDRESSES

Eulogies delivered in the House or Senate upon the death of a member of Congress or former member are classed in Y 7.1. Depository libraries subscribing to item 1005 receive these addresses in handsome, bound volumes with the Y 7.1: notation. Following the colon, individual book numbers are assigned by using the three-figure Cutter table based on the name of the deceased member.

When presidents, vice-presidents, or presidential appointees who have held high office in the executive or judiciary are memorialized, the compilation of tributes is issued in the serial set as House or Senate documents. Memorial issuances in the case of persons who have enjoyed careers in both the Congress and in other government positions may be found in both series, for issuing patterns have not always been consistent.

For example, memorial services in Congress for General Eisenhower were issued as 91-1: H.doc. 195 [12852-9]. Eisenhower, of course, never served in the Congress. Tributes in eulogy of John F. Kennedy, who served in the House and Senate before becoming president, appeared as 88-2: S.doc. 59 [12624]. Memorial tributes for Harry S. Truman, senator and president, were issued as 93-1: H.doc. 131 [13034-3]. And addresses in Congress with various articles and editorials relating to the life and work of Vice-President Nelson A. Rockefeller appeared as 96-1: S.doc. 20 [13228].[46]

MAJOR LEGISLATION OF THE CONGRESS

Major Legislation of the Congress (MLC), an irregularly issued periodical, is designed to provide summaries of topical congressional issues and major legislation introduced in response to those issues. Compiled by the Congressional Research Service of the Library of Congress (LC 14.18; item 807-A-1), MLC is an automated by-product of the CRS Major Issues System, a special online program which extracts selected background material on key legislation. Copies of each issue are usually distributed following each month the Congress is in session. MLC is also sold by the Superintendent of Documents, and subscription information is found in the current edition of *Price List 36*.

CODE FINDING AID

How to Find U.S. Statutes and U.S. Code Citations (GS 4.102:St 1; item 574), an eight-page pamphlet revised periodically, enables the user who has a reference to the *Revised Statutes*, date of law, title or popular name, public law number, or citation to the *Statutes at Large* to find the appropriate citation to the *United States Code* or to its *Supplements*. Moreover, the guide makes note of commercial publications like U.S.C.C.A.N., *United States Code Annotated, United States Code Service*, and *Shepard's Acts and Cases by Popular Names*.

POPULAR NAME LISTING

Shepard's Acts and Cases by Popular Names, Federal and State (Colorado Springs, CO: Shepard's/McGraw-Hill) lists federal acts by their popular name, with citations to the *United States Code* and *Statutes at Large*. It is supplemented annually in cumulative paper form.

DIRECTORIES

The *Biographical Directory of the American Congress* has been issued under different names since 1859. Cumulative issues covering the years 1774-1949 and 1774-1961 were issued as House documents. The 1774-1971 compilation was issued as 92-1: S.doc. 8 [12938], and future cumulations will be forthcoming. The *Biographical Directory* includes thousands of short biographies of members of the House and Senate, and a feature of the 1774-1971 compilation is biographies of presidents who were not members of Congress.

Members of Congress since 1789, Second Edition (Washington: Congressional Quarterly, Inc., 1981) provides basic biographical data on all who have served in the Congress. The first section, "Facts on Members of Congress," includes statistics and summary material on membership such as age, religion, occupations, women, and blacks, and this summary is followed by thumbnail biographies. A final section, "Congressional Statistics," contains information on congressional sessions, party lineups, and leaderships.

The *Official Congressional Directory*, issued annually, updates the *Biographical Directory of the American Congress* and contains current biographical information as well as much useful reference material on committees and subcommittees, foreign representatives and consular offices in the United States, press representatives, state delegations, and statistical data on the sessions of Congress. Classed in Y 4.P93/1:1, it is available to depository libraries that select item 992.

Charles B. Brownson (ed.), *Congressional Staff Directory* (Mount Vernon, VA: Congressional Staff Directory, Ltd.) is also published annually. Here the emphasis is on the staffs of the members and of the committees and subcommittees together with almost 3,000 staff biographies. The staffs of congressional agencies like the General Accounting Office and Library of Congress are included, as are key personnel of executive departments and agencies. A list of almost 10,000 cities with their congressional districts and members is also included. A companion volume, *Federal Staff Directory*, updates and expands the information on the executive branch in the *Congressional Staff Directory* with biographical sketches of key personnel.

The *Congressional Yellow Book* (Washington: The Washington Monitor, Inc.) is issued in looseleaf form with quarterly updating. Directory information rather than biographical data is emphasized, with sections on names, addresses and phone numbers of senators and representatives, their office and committee aides, state delegations, district offices, and congressional agencies like GPO.

CONGRESSIONAL ROLL CALL

Congressional Roll Call (Washington: Congressional Quarterly, Inc.) is an annual chronology and analysis of all roll call votes taken in the House and Senate for a session of Congress. It provides a complete voting record of every member on every issue.

CONGRESSIONAL QUARTERLY SERVICE

CQ Service, as it is called, consists of research reports on topics of current interest plus two publications that are widely used in libraries and highly regarded by librarians and their users.

CQ WEEKLY REPORT

Mailed to subscribers every Saturday, *CQ Weekly Report* contains detailed coverage of Congress, the presidency, the Supreme Court, and national politics. Discussion includes major legislation; presidential legislative requests, press conferences, statements and messages; roll call votes of members; and other relevant activities. Quarterly indexes by subjects and names cumulate throughout the year. The *CQ Weekly Report* is online through NEXIS, a full text service available to users of LEXIS (see Chapter 10).

CQ ALMANAC

CQ Almanac is a voluminous hardbound volume published shortly after each congressional session. It distills, reorganizes, and cross-indexes the events of the year in Congress, politics, and government as reported in the *CQ Weekly Report* issues. Features include detailed summaries of all major legislation for the session, charts of all recorded votes, and an account of lobby activities for the previous calendar year.

OTHER CONGRESSIONAL QUARTERLY SERIES

Some publications formerly published by The Washington Monitor, Inc., are now published by Congressional Quarterly, Inc. The following deal with congressional activities:

CONGRESS DAILY

Congress Daily is a brief newsletter that provides concise accounts of committee action, highlights of House and Senate hearings, important bills introduced, and presidential messages on budgetary and other legislative concerns.

THE CONGRESSIONAL MONITOR

The Congressional Monitor, published daily with a weekly edition, reports on present and forthcoming activities of congressional committees; it is especially useful for its listing of committee hearings with the names of witnesses and the dates they are scheduled to give testimony. Floor action and future House and Senate committee action are also presented.

CONGRESS IN PRINT

Congress in Print is a weekly list of all hearings, committee reports, committee prints, and staff studies that have been released for public distribution. The publications listed are abstracted and arranged by committee. Room number and telephone number are provided so that the publication can be requested from the document clerk of the committee.

THE CONGRESSIONAL RECORD SCANNER

The Congressional Record Scanner is an abstract and edited outline of each day's *Congressional Record*. The *Scanner* categorizes substantive House and Senate actions and enables the user to locate quickly the reference to the full text in the CR.

THE CRS SERIES

A number of research studies and issue briefs prepared by the Congressional Research Service of the Library of Congress are neither sold by the Superintendent of Documents nor made available to depository libraries. Many of the reports in this CRS series, however, are available on microfilm from University Publications of America, Inc., a commercial publisher located in Frederick, Maryland.

The series includes *Major Studies of the Legislative Reference Service/Congressional Research Service: 1916-74, Major Studies of the Congressional Research Service: 1975-76 Supplement*, and *Major Studies and Issue Briefs of the Congressional Research Service* with *Supplements* covering 1976-78, 1978-79, 1979-80, 1980-81, 1981-82, etc. The original 1916-74 compilation has two printed guides: a title/author guide and a subject index. The *Supplements* have single printed *Guides*, pamphlets which are organized by a Reel Index section and a Subject Index section. The Reel Index section is arranged by reel numbers, broad topics (Legal and Constitutional Issues, Foreign and Defense Issues, etc.), and more specific topics (School Busing and Desegregation, Abortion, Weapons

Systems, etc.) of the studies and briefs giving frame number, title, author(s), date, and number of pages. The Subject Index is usually limited to one reference and, sometimes, one cross-reference for each study. This section provides reel and frame numbers, enabling the user to access the microfilm directly.

CONCLUSION

Because of the complexity of the legislative process, a multitude of individual actions and possible paths are open to each measure introduced before either chamber. House legislative experts created from a list of over 250 legislative steps a centralized, computer-based operation for information processing and dissemination called the Legislative Information and Status System (LEGIS), a superior version of the outdated Bill Status System, which was in use from 1973 to 1977. Each database in the LEGIS system contains a specific body of information. For each item in any database, three types of data are recorded: 1) identification data such as bill number, sponsor, date introduced, and title; 2) content data, updated whenever the item is altered by an amendment, such as a description of the bill's subject matter; 3) and status data consisting of the series of legislative steps through which the item has moved.

Although the system was designed and implemented in the House, Senate coverage is included. Items which are the peculiar province of the Senate—treaties, nominations, memorials, and petitions—are added to the system. Improvements and enhancements are under continual review by the House, Senate, and Library of Congress and have resulted in refinement and standardization of legislative status step definitions, improved subject tracking, improved cross-referencing information, inclusion of amendment digests, and inclusion of information on the disposition of rescissions and deferrals submitted by the president.

Before the advent of the original Bill Status System, there was no centralized and comprehensive source of legislative information, nor was there a systematic method of collecting, storing, or retrieving such information. Members and their staffs relied on experience and personal contacts. Their research was often subject to delays inherent in the publication of traditional indexes and digests. Efforts to seek current information resulted in duplication and extreme variations in the accuracy and timeliness of the information obtained. Moreover, the manual processes employed were not conducive to sharing information among offices.

LEGIS not only has eliminated most of these ineffective processes, but has also permitted several types of timely printouts for members and their staffs. Immediate printed status reports on measures are available within minutes. Overnight reports are ready for the next legislative day. Automatic tracking reports are prepared especially for offices that express long-term interest in specific subjects. And legislative profiles provided to members for measures they have sponsored or cosponsored may be requested. All the customized products and services that exemplify the manifold capabilities of the computer are available in greater depth of information and more convenient access than ever before.[47]

A policy group on information and computers of the Committee on House Administration proposed public distribution of the LEGIS databases on magnetic tape with daily updates. Questions of distribution by GPO or a commercial vendor, fees to be charged, private versus tax-supported institutional recipients, and other matters have provoked controversy. The idea has intriguing implications for depository libraries. If 44 U.S.C. 1901, the "Definition of [a] Government Publication," were amended to include "machine readable data files," and if other provisions of the depository laws were generously construed, library patrons in depository institutions would enjoy the free use of LEGIS as a *public document*. Thus employed, the system would provide a powerful source of current status information and legislative histories, as a complement to or replacement for the printed tools and commercial online services we must now rely upon. But to prophesy that something like this will come to pass in the near future would be foolhardy indeed.

REFERENCES

1. Telford Taylor, *Grand Inquest: The Story of Congressional Investigations* (New York: Simon and Schuster, 1955), p. 285.

2. James Burnham, *Congress and the American Tradition* (Chicago: Henry Regnery, 1965), p. 92.

3. George B. Galloway, "Precedents Established in the First Congress," *The Western Political Quarterly* 11: 462-63 (September 1958).

4. Walter J. Oleszek, *Congressional Procedures and the Policy Process* (Washington: Congressional Quarterly Press, 1978), p. xiv.

5. *Administrative Notes* 2: 4 (March 1981).

6. Oleszek, p. 57.

7. *U.S. News & World Report*, April 2, 1979, p. 45.

8. For example, 94-2: S.doc. 247 was sent to depository libraries as Serial 13140-5 but was made available for sale in the "committee print edition" only under S/N 052-070-03373.

9. *Congressional Record* (daily edition), January 19, 1978, p. E48.

10. *Schwegmann Bros. v. Calvert Distillers Corp.*, 341 U.S. 384 at 395 (1951).

11. Oleszek, pp. 106-107.

12. *Congressional Record* (daily edition), March 1, 1978, p. H1623.

13. For example, see Craig H. Grau, "What Publications Are Most Frequently Quoted in the Congressional Record," *Journalism Quarterly* 53: 716-19 (Winter 1976).

14. *Congressional Record* (daily edition), 92/2: 118/84, H4951.

15. U.S. Congress, Joint Committee on Printing, *Current Procedures and Production Processes of the Congressional Record*, Committee Print (Washington: Government Printing Office, 1978), p. 67.

16. Ibid., p. 13.

17. David F. Quadro, "The Congressional Record: Another Look," *Western Journal of Speech Communication* 41: 259 (Fall 1977).

18. *Congressional Record* (daily edition), February 20, 1978, p. H1193.

19. *Congressional Record* (daily edition), March 2, 1978, p. H1638.

20. *Congressional Record* (daily edition), March 1, 1978, p. H1623.

21. *U.S. News & World Report*, September 17, 1979, p. 75.

22. DttP 7: 188 (September 1979).

23. *Congressional Record* (daily edition), January 19, 1978, pp. E47, 48.

24. Ibid., p. E48.

25. *Congressional Record* (daily edition), January 6, 1981, p. S121.

26. *U.S. News & World Report*, March 8, 1982, p. 53.

27. *CQ Weekly Report*, March 7, 1981, p. 430.

28. Jerrold Zwirn, "Congressional Debate," *Government Publications Review* 8A: 183 (1981).

29. A list of titles enacted into law may be found in the preface to the editions of the *U.S. Code* and *Supplements*. Among the enacted titles is Title 44, Public Printing and Documents.

30. *Guide to the Congress of the United States: Origins, History and Procedure* (Washington: Congressional Quarterly Service, 1971), p. 331. Pages 329-52 of this work contain the best short analysis and summary of private legislation in existence.

31. *Calendars of the United States House of Representatives and History of Legislation, Final Edition, Ninety-Sixth Congress* (Washington: Government Printing Office, 1980), p. 326.

32. 96-2: H.doc. 352 (1980), pp. 70-73; 97-1: H.doc. 120 (1981), pp. 70-73.

33. Oleszek, p. 85.

34. Beginning with the Ninety-seventh Congress, *Congressional Index* discontinued its Index to Companion Bills.

35. The *Federal Index* also includes the *Federal Register, Weekly Compilation of Presidential Documents*, and other governmental and commercial sources of information.

36. For daily current information on the status of any bill or resolution when Congress is in session, a telephone call may be placed with the House Office of Legislative Information (202/225-1772). Inquiries may be accommodated by means of bill number, sponsor or cosponsor, referral committee, date introduced, or subject matter.

37. Cumulative issues of the *Digest of Public General Bills and Resolutions* in Part 1 contain a list of digests of measures that have become public law in numerical order of enactment.

38. Laurence F. Schmeckebier and Roy B. Eastin, *Government Publications and Their Use*, 2nd rev. ed. (Washington: Brookings, 1969), pp. 109-116; 124-29; 150-66.

39. Joe Morehead, *Introduction to United States Public Documents, Second Edition* (Littleton, CO: Libraries Unlimited, Inc., 1978), pp. 181-89.

40. The Senate Foreign Relations Committee favorably reported "Salt II" (96-1: Exec. Rpt. 14; serial volume 13250), but the full Senate failed to ratify.

41. PDH 42: 1 (October 1980).

42. *Monthly Catalog*, July 1980, Entry No. 80-15307, p. 310.

43. DttP 9: 42 (January 1981).

44. *Daily Depository Shipping List*, No. 13,540, Survey 79-27 (December 7, 1979).

45. *Hinds' Precedents of the House of Representatives* (1907) and *Cannon's Precedents of the House of Representatives* (1936) are justly famous and simply known by their short titles, *Hinds' Precedents* and *Cannon's Precedents*.

46. Senator Edward Kennedy's brief tribute to his brother Robert, which was delivered not in the Congress but at St. Patrick's Cathedral on June 8, 1968, was issued as 90-2: S.doc. 86 (12798-2).

47. See the committee print *The Legislative Information and Status System for the United States House of Representatives* (Washington: Government Printing Office, 1979). Appendix B, "Legislative Status Steps" (pp. 17-41), lists the over 250 defined steps.

8

Publications of the Presidency

INTRODUCTION

Article II of the Constitution states that "the executive power shall be vested in a President of the United States," who is charged "to take care that the laws be faithfully executed." The brevity of this constitutional injunction belies the complexity of the administrative task. When Jefferson was president, the entire federal government consisted of just over 2,000 persons—from the despised tax collectors to the marshalls of film and television immortality—whereas today there are at least that many units of federal administration. These agencies are organized in the familiar pyramid; each has its own hierarchical structure. Orders theoretically flow from the president, as the chief executive, to the department heads, and down to the lesser units—bureaus, agencies, offices—where the work of government is carried out and where most of the publications of government are produced.

Inherent in any large administrative entity is a line and staff organization. Of the total number of government employees, only a small percentage are presidential appointees. The control and direction of the vast administrative machinery in practice must be delegated by the president. However, the president has a staff whose job it is to advise and assist him in managing the affairs of state, and over this group the president has a large measure of control. Indeed, presidents often choose their staff on the basis of loyalty first and competence second.

Presidential control abides in what has come to be known as the White House Office; this inner locus of power extends outward to what is called the Executive Office of the President, a complex of administrative units that reports directly to the president. In the organization of his staff the president enjoys great flexibility. Moreover, presidents have used their staffs to execute responsibilities of greater moment than the corresponding duties of the cabinet.

For purposes of this chapter, the publications of the presidency include not only those which emanate from the Oval Office and the Executive Office of the President but also those associated with a president's treaty-making powers. Moreover, several kinds of presidential publications are transmitted to the Congress and are ordered to be published in the congressional edition. As we saw in Chapter 7, the relationship between executive and congressional authority is circular.

Because of this pattern of multiple provenance in the issuing of publications relating directly or indirectly to presidential action and decisions, there is duplication of materials. The multiplicity is sometimes confusing, but, when sorted out, it is manageable if not uniform. What follows is a discussion of selected publications related to the duties of the presidency as mandated by the Constitution and the laws of the land.

THE WHITE HOUSE OFFICE

Publications of the inner circle of presidential control and authority have been assigned the rubric "President of the United States" and bear a "Pr" notation in the SuDocs classification system. The number following the letters *Pr* indicates the chronology of persons who have held the office; for example, Ford (Pr 38), Carter (Pr 39), Reagan (Pr 40), etc.[1] Although there are few categories available to depository libraries in the Pr series, several noteworthy publications are included. For example, the general publications series (Pr -.2; item 850) occasionally carries documents of importance, such as *Submission of Recorded Presidential Conversations to the Committee on the Judiciary of the House of Representatives by President Richard Nixon* (Pr 37.2: C76).

A significant annual in the Pr series is the *Economic Report of the President.* Transmitted to the Congress in January of each year, the *Economic Report* includes the Annual Report of the Council of Economic Advisers, a panel established by the Employment Act of 1946 to provide economic analysis and advice to the chief executive. Classed in Pr -.9, it is sent to depository libraries in both the departmental and congressional editions (see Chapter 7). Thus the 1981 *Economic Report of the President* (Pr 39.9:981; item 848) was also issued as House document number 3 of the Ninety-seventh Congress, first session (Y 1.1/7: 97-3) and made available to depository institutions on microfiche (item 996-B) or in paper copy (item 996-A) as part of the Congressional Serial Set. The Council of Economic Advisers itself is a unit within the Executive Office of the President (*infra*) and has its own general publications series (PrEx 6.2; item 857-E-1).

ADVISORY COMMITTEES

Advisory committees have existed since Washington's presidency, and throughout the decades they have been established to assist a president, the departments and agencies, and the Congress on matters of greater or lesser moment. The Federal Advisory Committee Act (FACA) of 1972 as amended (86 *Stat.* 770) requires the president to submit an annual report to the Congress on the activities, status, and changes in the composition of federal advisory committees; the report is classed in Pr -.10 (item 848-C). For more detailed information on the Federal Advisory Committee Act and its implications, see the author's 1978 edition (pp. 282-88) and Brian C. Murphy, "Implementation of the Federal Advisory Committee Act: An Overview," *Government Publications Review* 9: 3-27 (1982).

Special commissions and committees appointed by presidents (Pr -.8; item 851-J) is a series that covers reports of ad hoc bodies established by executive order for a particular purpose. A Cutter designation in the SuDocs classification scheme is assigned each report; for example, *Report of President's Commission on the Assassination of President John F. Kennedy* (Pr 36.8: K38/R39).

Main entry information in the *Monthly Catalog* for presidential advisory committees appears in this form:

President of the United States

PRESIDENT OF THE UNITED STATES

82-777

Pr 39.8:W 84/2/v 87/980

United States. President's Advisory Committee for Women.

Voices for women : 1980 report of the President's Advisory Committee for Women. — [Washington, D. C.?] : President's Advisory Committee for Women : For sale by the Supt. of Docs., U.S. G.P.O., [1980]   192 p. : ill. ; 28 cm. ●Item 851-J S/N 029-002-00061-4 @ GPO $7.00 1. Women — Services for — United States 2. Women's rights — United States. I. Title. OCLC 07088431

82-778

Pr 40.8:N 88/G 74

Governance of nuclear power / by Graham Allison ... [et al.] ; submitted to the President's Nuclear Safety Oversight Committee. — [Washington, D.C.?] : The Committee, [1981]   49 p. ; 28 cm. Cover title. "September 1981." Includes bibliographical references. ●Item 851-J 1. Atomic energy policy — United States. I. Allison, Graham, T. 1940- II. United States. President's Nuclear Safety Oversight Committee. OCLC 07868135

And, as Figure 23 shows, a president may authorize or amend an advisory body by promulgating an executive order citing the Federal Advisory Committee Act as authority.

Frequently, the news media will use the name of the chairperson of an advisory committee. The more newsworthy the committee becomes, the more the popular name is used. And indexing tools like the *Monthly Catalog* are not likely to include popular names of reports. Thus *Popular Names of U.S. Government Reports: A Catalog* (LC 6.2:G74/976; item 818-F) has proved helpful in identifying popular name reports.

A selective listing, the *Popular Name Catalog* arranges the reports alphabetically by popular name. Coverage includes not only advisory bodies but also selected congressional committee reports, committee prints, or hearings known by the name of the chairperson or chief investigative officer. Entries include SuDocs class number and citation to the *Checklist of United States Public Documents, 1789-1909, Document Catalog*, or *Monthly Catalog*. Entries are indexed by the main subject of the report.

The third edition of the *Popular Name Catalog* (1976) includes a section under the heading "Impeachment Inquiry." This section includes reports, hearings, and miscellaneous documents printed by the GPO pertaining to the Watergate affair and related matters. Subdivisions include presidential documents, bills and resolutions, and hearings and reports.

Figure 23
Executive Order: Federal Register

23135

Federal Register
Vol. 47, No. 103
Thursday, May 27, 1982

Presidential Documents

Title 3—

The President

Executive Order 12366 of May 25, 1982

Presidential Commission on Broadcasting to Cuba

By the authority vested in me as President of the United States of America, and in accordance with the Federal Advisory Committee Act, as amended (5 U.S.C. App. 1), in order to permit an increase in the membership of the Presidential Commission on Broadcasting to Cuba by one member, Section 1(b) of Executive Order No. 12323 of September 22, 1981, is hereby amended to read as follows:

"(b) The Commission shall be composed of twelve members appointed by the President from among citizens of the United States."

THE WHITE HOUSE,
May 25, 1982.

Ronald Reagan

[FR Doc. 82-14684
Filed 5-26-82; 9:03 am]
Billing code 3195-01-M

The *Encyclopedia of Governmental Advisory Organizations* (Detroit: Gale Research Company) provides directory information for presidential advisory committees, public advisory committees (those serving departments and agencies), interagency committees, and other bodies that function in an advisory capacity. The third edition (1980), edited by Linda E. Sullivan, describes over 3,400 organizations organized into ten subject sections (Agriculture to Transportation). Within each section, committees with similar interests are grouped by subject key words contained in their names or supplied by the editor. Entries include the body's official name, acronym, popular name, address, telephone number, name of executive secretary, date of establishment and termination, description of activities, membership, size of staff, subsidiary units, frequency or location of meetings, and publications (with popular names of reports if known). Entries are accessed through a combined alphabetical and key word index. The basic volume is updated by periodic supplements entitled *New Governmental Advisory Organizations.*

Richard I. Korman (comp.), *Guide to Presidential Advisory Commissions, 1973-1981* (Westport, CT: Meckler Books, 1982) provides information on advisory bodies in existence or established since FACA was enacted. Section I of the *Guide* is a chronological presentation of commissions with directory information similar to that given in the *Encyclopedia.* Section II is an alphabetical listing of members with dates of service and position held on the commission. Section III is a list of all titled reports issued or sponsored by each commission with date, availability, and an abstract.

Over the years, presidents and Congresses have expressed concern over the number of advisory groups that no longer serve a useful function. To this end, the General Services Administration conducts an annual review of existing advisory committees as required by Section 7(b) of FACA. Nevertheless, the proliferation of these entities has led to the description "government by committee," and they have been called the "fifth arm of the federal establishment," taking their place alongside the constitutionally created legislative, executive, and judicial arms and the independent regulatory agencies possessing administrative, judicial, and executive functions.

EXECUTIVE OFFICE OF THE PRESIDENT

The several entities within the Executive Office of the President are under greater presidential control than is the civil service in the line organization. Under authority of the Reorganization Act of 1939 (53 *Stat.* 561), various agencies were transferred to the Executive Office by the president's Reorganization Plans I and II, effective July 1, 1939. Executive Order 8248 (September 8, 1939) established the components of the Office and defined their functions. Subsequent legislation permitted creation of new units or a reordering of existing agencies.

In terms of national policy, some of these agencies within the Executive Office of the President exercise substantial power and influence, while others have less impact on our lives. Beginning with the administration of President Kennedy, the agencies within the Executive Office are assigned a "PrEx" notation by the Superintendent of Documents, followed by the appropriate series and book numbers.

OFFICE OF MANAGEMENT AND BUDGET

A strong case can be made that this agency is the most important arm of executive power and intent in the presidency. Article II, Section 3 of the Constitution requires that the president "shall from time to time give to the Congress Information of the State of the Union, and recommend to their consideration such measures as he shall judge necessary and expedient." Furthermore, presidential initiative was expanded in the Budget and Accounting Act of 1921, which imposed on the president the duty to submit to Congress a plan of proposed expenditures for the executive agencies, including their financing. But a budget is not merely a mass of figures; it is a blueprint of public policy.

When the Congress specifically passed this duty to the chief executive, it acquiesced to presidential initiative in substantive policy measures. Unlike the statements in campaign rhetoric, the budget is an indication of exactly where the president is willing to spend funds. Almost a year in advance of the fiscal year, the Office of Management and Budget (OMB) begins securing from the departments and agencies requests for review. When the budget is finally submitted, the Congress is, of course, not required to accept it. But it is an authoritative statement of executive intent.

For many years the agency was known as the Bureau of the Budget. When first created by the 1921 Act, it was located in the Treasury Department, although under the president's immediate direction. The 1939 Reorganization Act transferred it to the Executive Office. By Reorganization Plan 2 of 1970 the Bureau was redesignated (Executive Order 11541, July 1, 1970) and its mission was delegated to the director of the renamed Office of Management and Budget. The several functions of the Office demonstrate the power and scope of this unit, and the chief publications of the agency symbolize the importance of its duties.[2]

THE BUDGET DOCUMENTS

The federal budget is probably this nation's most significant public document. It represents a continuous process, involving analysis and discussion among the president, OMB, the Treasury Department, the Federal Reserve Board, and the Congress, specifically the Joint Economic Committee and the Congressional Budget Office. When profound philosophical differences over revenues and expenditures divide the executive and legislative branches, the battle of the budget consumes an inordinate amount of time, often to the neglect of other legislative matters.

Several budget publications are issued for a fiscal year, two of them basic to the process, others that are published as special supplements or comprise special themes.

The *Budget of the United States Government* (PrEx 2.8; item 853) contains the budget message of the president and presents an overview of his budget proposals. It also includes explanations of spending programs in terms of national needs, agency missions, and basic programs, an analysis of estimated receipts, a discussion of the president's tax program, a description of the budget system, and various summary tables. The *Budget* is also issued in its congressional edition; for example, the *Budget of the United States Government, Fiscal Year 1983* (PrEx 2.8:983) was issued as 97-2: H.doc. 124.

The *Budget of the United States Government, Appendix* (PrEx 2.8/App; item 853) is a massive volume that contains detailed information on the various appropriations and funds that comprise the budget. The information includes the proposed text of appropriation language, budget schedules for each account, new legislative proposals, explanations of the work to be performed and the funds needed, proposed general provisions applicable to the appropriations of entire agencies or groups of agencies, and schedules of permanent positions. The *Budget Appendix* is also issued in the serial set edition; for example, the fiscal 1983 *Appendix* (PrEx 2.8:983/App.) was issued as 97-2: H.doc. 125.

Several related budget documents may be published during a fiscal year. *The United States Budget in Brief* (PrEx 2.8/2; item 855-A) is designed for use by the general public; it is less technical and contains summary and historical tables with graphic displays. *Major Themes and Additional Budget Details* (PrEx 2.8/Themes; item 853) is a supplementary report describing ways in which the budget implements important aspects of the president's program and the effects of specific programmatic changes. *Special Analyses* (PrEx 2.8/5; item 855-B) highlights specific program areas with alternate views of the budget. *Budget Revisions* (PrEx 2.8/7; item 853) presents additional budget details on presidential proposals. And various supplements, amendments, rescissions, and deferrals are published, usually in the House documents series.

CATALOG OF FEDERAL DOMESTIC ASSISTANCE

An extremely useful reference source issued by OMB is the *Catalog of Federal Domestic Assistance* (PrEx 2.20; item 853-A-1). Published annually in looseleaf binder, the *Catalog* provides information on federal assistance programs such as grants, scholarships, loan guarantees, technical assistance, exchange programs like Fulbright-Hays, and other service activities. Program descriptions are indexed by department and agency name, applicant eligibility, functional classification, subject, popular name, and deadlines. And program information is also available on machine-readable magnetic tape, microfiche, and paper copy from NTIS. The *Catalog* is the single, authoritative source for categories of federal assistance.

CENTRAL INTELLIGENCE AGENCY

The Central Intelligence Agency (CIA) provides several useful series to depository libraries. CIA Maps and Atlases (PrEx 3.10/4; item 856-A-1) cover a large number of countries, show relief by shading and spot heights, and include population, economic activity, land use, etc. Numbered publications of the National Foreign Assessment Center (PrEx 10.7; item 856-A-4) issued on microfiche include valuable research reports and directories. A semiannual publication, *The World Factbook* (PrEx 3.10; item 856-A-2), formerly titled the *National Basic Intelligence Factbook*, is a compilation of basic data on political entities worldwide arranged alphabetically by countries with some maps and much useful political, sociological, and economic data. Some of these series are commercially available on microfiche from Updata Publications, Los Angeles, California.

FOREIGN BROADCAST INFORMATION SERVICE

The Foreign Broadcast Information Service (FBIS) issues a Daily Report series covering Asia and the Pacific, the Middle East and Africa, the People's Republic of China, the Soviet Union, South Asia, and Western Europe (PrEx 7.10; items 856-B-3) through 856-B-10) on microfiche to depository libraries or for sale through NTIS. These reports consist of translations and analyses of information collected daily from foreign broadcasts, news accounts, commentaries, newspapers, periodicals, and government statements. In addition, the Joint Publications Research Service (JPRS) of FBIS issues a number of translations of current political and social documentation from various countries and continents. These valuable studies are available on microfiche to depository libraries in various PrEx 7.- series by subscribing to items 1067-L-1 through 1067-L-17.

OFFICE OF THE FEDERAL REGISTER

The Office of the Federal Register, a unit within the National Archives and Records Service, General Services Administration, is the provenance for a number of important publications that contain presidential materials. The following represents a selection of the more important titles and series.

FEDERAL REGISTER

This significant publication, classed in GS 4.107, was for many years available to depository libraries in paper copy only (item 573-C). However, beginning in October 1982, the daily *Federal Register* (FR) was made available to depository institutions on microfiche (item 573-D) as an alternate option. Although the bulk of the FR consists of the rules, proposed rules, and notices promulgated by the executive departments, agencies, and independent entities, there is a section entitled "Presidential Documents" that appears at the beginning of the *Register*. The most common kinds of presidential documents are Executive Orders (EO) and Proclamations (Proc.).

EXECUTIVE ORDERS

Executive orders generally relate to the conduct of government business or to the organization of executive agencies. They have "never been defined by law or regulation," thus "in a general sense every act of the President authorizing or directing that an act be performed is an executive order."[3] Authority for executive orders is claimed by a president in virtue of his office, in his role as commander in chief of the armed forces, under the Constitution, or under existing legislation.

Early presidential orders took the form of hastily scribbled endorsements on legal briefs or upon the margin of maps. The earliest chief executives would write "approved," "let it be done," or other terse comments which were sufficient to provide the authority for action. It was not until 1907 that the State Department began numbering executive orders which it had on file and later received. Since that time, many directives have been uncovered and assigned suffixes such as A, B, C, 1/2, etc.; they have been filed with the executive order corresponding to the nearest date when issued. It is estimated that many executive directives still lie in the files of agencies or in presidential papers.[4]

Earlier executive orders are indexed in Clifford L. Lord, *Presidential Executive Orders, Volume II* and cover the period 1862 to 1938. Volume I of Lord's work is a chronological list of the orders. Covering executive orders 1-8030, the volumes have been reprinted by Michael Glazier, Inc. (Wilmington, Delaware) under the title *Presidential Executive Orders: Numbered Series (1862-1938): List and Index.* Another Glazier publication, *List and Index of Presidential Executive Orders: Unnumbered Series (1789-1941)*, is a one-volume calendar and index of over 1,500 "unnumbered" orders. Presidential executive orders, June 26, 1845-June 26, 1936 (Nos. 1-7403) are available on 35mm. microfilm from Trans-Media Publishing Company, Dobbs Ferry, New York.

Figure 23 (page 185) shows an executive order as published in the *Federal Register.*

PROCLAMATIONS

In practice, the distinction between calling a presidential action an "Executive Order" or a "Proclamation" has never been clear. Generally, however, the occasion for this form is one of widespread interest, a decree addressed to the public at large. Some proclamations have legal effect while others do not have the force of law.[5] In the latter category we find the many hortatory designations of a ceremonial or celebratory nature: Mother's Day, Thanksgiving, Fire Prevention

Week, etc. Authority for proclamations is claimed by a president in virtue of his office, under existing legislation, or in response to a congressional joint resolution. Presidential proclamations covering the period 1789-1936 are available on 35mm. microfilm from Trans-Media. Figure 24 shows a proclamation as published in the *Federal Register*.

Figure 24
Proclamation: Federal Register

Federal Register / Vol. 47, No. 32 / Wednesday, February 17, 1982 / Presidential Documents   6815

Presidential Documents

Proclamation 4898 of February 13, 1982

National Patriotism Week, 1982

By the President of the United States of America

A Proclamation

National Patriotism Week affords all Americans a special opportunity to consider the meaning of an honorable term which has sometimes been misunderstood and misused.

True patriotism is a love of country, but it must be an intelligent love and not blind devotion to one's nation without regard to its ideals. Abraham Lincoln recognized this when, speaking in tribute of Henry Clay, he said:

"He loved his country partly because it was his own country, but mostly because it was a free country; and he burned with a zeal for its advancement, prosperity and glory, because he saw in such, the advancement, prosperity and glory, of human liberty, human right, and human nature."

The patriotism of Clay, Lincoln, and generations of Americans was of this nature. They loved their country because it was theirs but even more because it was a land where liberty, justice, and opportunity flourished. They did not love it because of its government but because of its people; not because of the role its government played in world affairs but because of the inspiration the very idea of America gave to every person, great and small, who made this blessed land his home, and to every person in the less fortunate lands of the world who, amid oppression, tyranny, and injustice—as in Poland today—looked to America as the land of freedom.

Americans today should dedicate themselves again to that true patriotism. We should dedicate ourselves again to the enduring values of family, neighborhood, work, peace, and freedom which have characterized our country these past two centuries. Let us do this, and our patriotism will be strong and fulfilling.

The Congress, by joint resolution (S.J. Res. 34), designated the week commencing with the third Monday in February of 1982 as "National Patriotism Week" and requested the President to issue a proclamation calling upon the people of the United States to commemorate that week with appropriate celebrations and observances.

NOW, THEREFORE, I, RONALD REAGAN, President of the United States of America, do hereby designate the week beginning February 15, 1982, as National Patriotism Week.

I invite all primary and secondary schools to conduct programs of study which are dedicated to those bedrock principles of national greatness devoted to rekindling the patriotic flame in all Americans.

I call upon all citizens of the United States of America to commemorate National Patriotism Week with appropriate celebrations and observances.

IN WITNESS WHEREOF, I have hereunto set my hand this thirteenth day of February, in the year of our Lord nineteen hundred and eighty-two, and of the Independence of the United States of America the two hundred and sixth.

Ronald Reagan

[FR Doc. 82-4477
Filed 2-16-82; 11:08 am]
Billing code 3195-01-M

CODIFICATION OF EXECUTIVE ORDERS AND PROCLAMATIONS

The *Codification of Presidential Proclamations and Executive Orders, January 20, 1961-January 20, 1981* (GS 4.113/3; item 574-A) provides in one convenient reference source executive orders and proclamations which have general applicability and continuing effect. An earlier edition covered the period January 20, 1961-January 20, 1977.

This volume contains the text of each executive order and proclamation and all amendments in effect on January 20, 1981 with citations to the *Federal Register* and *Code of Federal Regulations*. Arrangement is by chapters representing broad subject areas similar to the title designations of the *Code of Federal Regulations* and the *United States Code*. Each presidential directive is assigned an appropriate subject chapter, and if an executive order or a proclamation relates to more than one topic, the most appropriate chapter is selected.

The *Codification* includes a comprehensive index and a "Disposition Table." The latter lists proclamations and executive orders by number with reference to all amendments regardless of their current status and a "disposition" column indicating promulgations that were revoked, superseded, temporary, or hortatory. Directives issued before January 20, 1961, are included if they were amended or otherwise affected by documents issued during the 1961-1981 period.

. The value of the *Codification* is that one can use it to determine the latest text of a document without having to reconstruct it through extensive research.

OTHER PRESIDENTIAL DOCUMENTS

Rulings other than proclamations and executive orders published in the *Federal Register* include memorandums, usually to the heads of departments and agencies; directives, designating matters such as assignments for officials of agencies; presidential determinations, resolving that certain provisions of law are or are not in the national interest; letters, such as instructions to chiefs of diplomatic missions; and reorganization plans. The latter are instruments by which the president proposes changes in the structure of agencies below the departmental level. They automatically take effect unless disapproved by the Congress within a specified period of time.

Access to these presidential initiatives published in the FR is through a separately published *Federal Register Index*, which cumulates monthly into an annual issue.

TITLE 3, CODE OF FEDERAL REGULATIONS

Title 3 of the *Code of Federal Regulations* (CFR) is called *The President* and contains the full text of documents signed by the president during a calendar year which were published in the *Federal Register*. Title 3 is issued annually with periodic cumulations. Classed in GS 4.108: 3, it is sent to depository libraries in paper copy (item 572-B) or on microfiche (item 572-C). The Title 3 series began with Proclamation 2161 (March 19, 1936) and Executive Order 7316 (March 13, 1936).

During the years 1971-1975, the designation for the annual compilations was changed to Title 3A, *The President, Appendix*. Title 3 for those years contained Executive Office of the President directives and a codified text of selected presidential documents. With the 1976 volume, the editors returned to the use of Title 3 — *The President*. Fortunately, this ill-advised change for those years was corrected with the publication of a cumulation called *Title 3, 1971-1975 Compilation*. Other compilations cover the years 1936-1938, 1938-1942, 1943-1948, 1949-1953, 1954-1958, 1959-1963, 1964-1965, and 1966-1970. For user convenience, *Title 3, 1936-1965 — Consolidated Indexes* and *Title 3, 1936-1965 — Consolidated Tables* are available. The former consists of a consolidated subject index covering the period; the latter contains various tables and finding aids to facilitate searching presidential documents during this period.

An annual issue of Title 3 typically contains proclamations and executive orders in numbered sequence, other presidential documents arranged by date, and regulations of the Executive Office of the President. Tables include proclamations and executive orders by number with date, subject, and citation to the FR page number; other presidential documents by date, subject, and FR citation; presidential documents affected by documents published during the year; statutes cited as authority for presidential documents; and *United States Code* titles and sections referencing presidential documents. Other finding aids include a table of CFR titles and chapters, an alphabetical list of agencies appearing in the CFR, and a list of CFR sections affected. An index appears at the end of the volume.

UNITED STATES STATUTES AT LARGE

As indicated in Chapter 7, the *Statutes at Large* is primarily a compilation of public and private session laws; however, it does include presidential materials. A list of reorganization plans by number, topic, and date and a list of proclamations by number, title, and date are included in the *Statutes*, as well as the full text of those materials. The subject index of the *Statutes* refers the user to these presidential directives.

WEEKLY COMPILATION OF PRESIDENTIAL DOCUMENTS

The *Weekly Compilation* (GS 4.114; item 577-A) is called a "special edition" of the *Federal Register*. The first issue, dated August 2, 1965, covered documents for the week ending July 30. Since then, the *Weekly Compilation* has become the single most useful current collection of presidential activities in the public record.

Issued each Monday, the *Weekly Compilation* includes the text of proclamations and executive orders, addresses and remarks, communications to Congress, letters, messages, telegrams, news conferences, reorganization plans, resignations and retirements. Supplementary materials include acts approved by the president, nominations submitted to the Senate, a digest of other White House announcements, and a checklist of White House press releases. Each issue includes a cumulative index to prior issues up to the end of a quarter. Other index cumulations include quarterly plus semiannual and annual indexes separately issued.

PUBLIC PAPERS OF THE PRESIDENTS OF THE UNITED STATES

In response to a recommendation of the National Historical Publications Commission, an annual series of *Public Papers of the Presidents* was begun with the 1957 volume covering the Eisenhower administration. While contemporaneous compilations were mandated, provision was also made for a retrospective collection.

Volumes of the *Public Papers* go back to Herbert Hoover (1929-1933) and forward to the present, with the exception of Roosevelt. However, *The Complete Presidential Press Conferences of Franklin Delano Roosevelt* (New York: Da Capo Press, Inc.) was published in twelve volumes covering the years 1933-1945. Accompanying the Hoover series is a two-volume set of *Proclamations and Executive Orders: Herbert Hoover, March 4, 1929 to March 4, 1933* (GS 4.113/2:H76; item 574-A) issued in 1974. Because the Hoover period predates the *Federal Register* and *Code of Federal Regulations*, it represents the first official printed compilation of these documents.[6]

Prior to 1977 the *Public Papers* was an edited version of the *Weekly Compilation of Presidential Documents*, thus proscribing discard of the weekly issues upon receipt of the annual volumes. However, beginning with the administration of Jimmy Carter, the *Public Papers* were expanded to include all materials as printed in the *Weekly Compilation*. Current volumes in this series (issued as Book I, Book II, etc., for the calendar year) arrange presidential materials in chronological order within each week; the dates shown in the headings are the dates of the documents or events. Textnotes, footnotes, and cross-references are provided by the editors for purposes of identification or clarity. All materials are fully indexed by subject entries and by categories reflecting the type of presidential activity or document.

Classed in GS 4.113 (item 574-A), the *Public Papers*, along with the timely *Weekly Compilation*, provide comprehensive documentation of presidential actions.

DEPARTMENT OF STATE

The Constitution vests in the president command of two major instruments of foreign policy—the armed services and the diplomatic corps. Although presidents can and do rely on their staff for foreign policy implementation, the duly constituted line organization has the machinery in place for the administration of foreign relations.

The Department of State is the oldest executive body of the federal government. Its predecessors had limited functions and little real power until the creation, in 1781, of a separate Department of Foreign Affairs. In 1789, following the election of Washington, the Department was reconstituted, its name was changed to Department of State, and with Jefferson as the first Secretary of State its functions were expanded to make it one of the most important of the government offices within the executive establishment.

State Department publications are many and varied, but a few important materials issued by the Department are presidential in nature. Among these are publications that reflect the power of the president to enter into treaties and agreements.

TREATIES AND AGREEMENTS

Article II, Section 2(2) of the Constitution states that the president "shall have power, by and with the advice and consent of the Senate, to make treaties, provided two-thirds of the Senators present concur." The making of treaties involves a series of steps which generally include negotiation, signing, approval by the Senate, ratification by the president, deposit or exchange of ratifications with the other party or parties to the treaty, and proclamation. The Senate is associated with this process only at the "advice and consent" to ratification stage. "Contrary to popular impression, the Senate does not ratify treaties; the President ratifies treaties upon receiving the advice and consent of the Senate to this act."[7]

If the Senate approves, a president proclaims the pact to be law. If the Senate disapproves, the treaty can be returned to the president, who may renegotiate it or abandon it. Conversely, a rejected pact can be held by the Senate Foreign Relations Committee until that body decides to recommend it once again for passage. Other options open to the Senate include limiting actions that in recent years have been called amendment, reservation, understanding, interpretation, declaration, and statement. These may be offered at any time during consideration in the full Senate prior to the presentation of the resolution of ratification, and only a majority vote is required in committee and in the Senate for their adoption.[8]

Executive agreements, on the other hand, are not specifically mentioned in the Constitution — "Yet the executive agreement has been used since 1817 when the Rush-Bagot Agreement was reached with Great Britain, limiting naval forces to be kept on the Great Lakes."[9] In recent decades the number of executive agreements concluded has been about fifteen times that of formal treaties. The distinction between treaty and executive agreement in practice is the "submission or nonsubmission of an international instrument to the Senate.... Any international agreement which is not submitted to the Senate for its advice and consent is not considered a treaty, even though it may have legislative sanction, whereas any agreement which is submitted to the Senate, be it called a protocol, convention, treaty, agreement, articles, or by some other name, is considered a treaty."[10]

Fortunately, from a bibliographic point of view, both treaties and executive agreements are published in the same numbered series. The following is a selection of the more useful publications that provide information on treaties and other international agreements.

DEPARTMENT OF STATE BULLETIN (DSB)

From its inception in 1939 until 1977, the *Department of State Bulletin* (S 1.3; item 864) was issued weekly with semiannual indexes. Beginning with the January 1978 issue, this official record of United States foreign policy became a monthly with an annual index. The contents of DSB include major addresses and news conferences of the president and the Secretary of State; statements made before congressional committees by the Secretary and other senior State Department officials; special features and articles on international relations; selected press releases issued by the White House, the State Department, and the United States Mission to the United Nations; presidential proclamations relevant to foreign policy; and information on treaties and agreements to which the United States is or may become a party.

Unofficial notice of treaty or agreement action is often in the form of a press release, and sometimes the text of the pact is published in the DSB. Activities of the president in the field of foreign affairs are listed under the heading "Presidential Documents" in the DSB index. Toward the end of each monthly issue of the *Department of State Bulletin*, multilateral and bilateral current actions are bibliographically cited.

TREATIES IN FORCE (TIF)

Treaties in Force (S 9.14; item 900-A) is an annual volume that contains a list of treaties and other international agreements in force as of January 1 of the date of the compilation. The foreword to each volume of TIF sets forth the distinction between treaties made by the president with the advice and consent of the Senate, and agreements in force between the United States and foreign countries "which have been made by the Executive (a) pursuant to or in accordance with existing legislation or a treaty, (b) subject to Congressional approval or implementation, or (c) under and in accordance with the President's Constitutional power." Thus the word "Treaties" in the title of this document is used in its generic sense as referring to all international agreements of the United States.

TIF is arranged in two parts, followed by an appendix. Part 1 includes bilateral treaties and agreements listed by country or other political entity, with subject headings under each country or other entity. Part 2 includes multilateral treaties and agreements, arranged by subject headings, together with a list of the states which are parties to each agreement. The appendix contains a consolidated tabulation of documents affecting international copyright relations of the United States. Citations are provided for the appropriate current or retrospective series in which the text of the treaties or agreements is published. The current issue of TIF is updated and supplemented by current status information published in the *Department of State Bulletin*.

TREATIES AND OTHER INTERNATIONAL ACTS SERIES (TIAS)

Pursuant to PL 89-479, approved July 8, 1966 (80 *Stat.* 271; 1 U.S.C. 113), this numbered series is issued singly in pamphlet form and is known by the acronym TIAS (S 9.10; item 899). It represents competent evidence of the force and effect of the concluded treaty or agreement and includes the full text of the pact.

This series replaced an earlier *Treaty Series* (TS) and *Executive Agreement Series* (EAS) in 1945, but the numbering of treaties and agreements was continued. Accordingly, TIAS begins with treaty number 1501 and executive agreement number 506. The TIAS number, like the bill number for conventional legislation, becomes an important piece of bibliographic data, and is cited in the *Department of State Bulletin*, TIF, and other related publications.

UNITED STATES TREATIES AND OTHER INTERNATIONAL AGREEMENTS (UST)

Just as public laws are bound together chronologically in the *Statutes at Large*, so the TIAS pamphlets are collected into *United States Treaties* (S 9.12;

item 899-A). UST volumes published on a calendar year basis beginning January 1, 1950 are accessed by a subject and country index. Before 1950, the full text of treaties was published in the *Statutes at Large*.

TREATIES AND OTHER INTERNATIONAL AGREEMENTS OF THE UNITED STATES OF AMERICA, 1776-1949 (Bevans)

Earlier collections of treaties have been issued in separate sets and are known by the names of the compilers — Miller, Malloy, Redmond, Trenwith. With the definitive edition of *Treaties ..., 1776-1949*, compiled under the direction of Charles I. Bevans, the text of treaties and agreements for those years is easily accessed in one twelve-volume set with Volume 13 serving as the index volume.

SENATE EXECUTIVE SERIES

As noted in Chapter 7, Senate treaty documents and Senate executive reports are numbered series that became part of the Congressional Serial Set beginning with the Ninety-sixth Congress. Treaty documents consist of presidential messages transmitting the text of treaties to the Senate Foreign Relations Committee. They are reported out of that committee in the form of a Senate Executive Report. Thus, 97-1: S. Treaty Doc. 13, *Treaty with Canada on Pacific Coast Albacore Tuna Vessels and Port Privileges*, was reported out of committee as 97-1: S. Exec. Rpt. 15. Treaty documents and executive reports are indexed and abstracted in *CIS/Index* and *CIS/Annual*.

Senate printed amendments (Y 1.4/5) are issued as a component of the Congressional Bills, Resolutions, and Amendments series and sent to depository libraries on microfiche only (item 1006-A). They consist of proposals to treaties in the form of amendments, understandings, declarations, or reservations pursuant to the resolution of ratification of the treaty.

The *Journal of the Executive Proceedings of the Senate of the United States of America* (Y 1.3/4:) is issued in sessional volumes to depository libraries in hard copy (item 1047-C) or on microfiche (item 1047-D). The volumes contain the parliamentary proceedings of executive sessions of the Senate together with lists of treaties received during the session, lists of treaties of former sessions pending in the Senate, a list of Senate executive reports, tables of nominations, and an index to nominations including those of the diplomatic and foreign service corps.

INTERNATIONAL LAW DIGESTS

The *Digest of United States Practice in International Law* (S 7.12/3; item 864-A) is the latest in a distinguished series which began with Cadwalader and continued through a number of compilers. The present series began in 1973 and consists of an analysis of significant developments in the field of international law with especial reference to United States practice. The voluminous annual issues contain extensive, scholarly documentation. The current *Digest* is the successor to Marjorie M. Whiteman's well-known fifteen-volume set called *Digest of International Law* (S 7.12/2; item 864-A).[11]

COMMERCIAL SOURCES

Christian L. Wiktor (ed.), *Unperfected Treaties of the United States, 1776-1976* (Dobbs Ferry, NY: Oceana, 1976) is an annotated, multivolume set of treaties which have not received Senate approval or have not been ratified by the president.

Igor I. Kavass and M. A. Michael (comps.), *United States Treaties and Other International Agreements Cumulative Index, 1776-1949* (Buffalo, NY: William S. Hein, 1975) is a four-volume index which provides access to the treaties and agreements by TIAS number, date, country or intergovernmental organization, and subject.

Igor I. Kavass and Adolph Sprudzs (comps.), *UST Cumulative Index, 1950-1970* (Buffalo, NY:.William S. Hein, 1973), also in four volumes, provides similar access to treaties for this period. A *1971-75 Supplement* has been issued, and the set is updated by a looseleaf volume with bound five-year cumulations.

SHEPARD'S CITATIONS

To locate subsequent amendments, revisions, court decisions, extensions, or other changes to a treaty or executive agreement, consult *Shepard's United States Citations: Statute Edition.* Use the section "United States Statutes at Large" for treaties prior to 1950 and the section "United States Treaties and Other International Agreements" after 1950. The bound volumes of this unit of *Shepard's Citations* are supplemented by semiannual and monthly pamphlets. By "Shepardizing" treaties it is often possible to avoid searching the monthly issues of the *Department of State Bulletin* to determine current status.

INDIAN LAWS AND TREATIES

There are several useful sources for the specialist in Indian laws, treaties, and other congressional and presidential actions. Because the serial set contains a wealth of information on American Indian affairs, the *CIS US Serial Set Index, 1789-1969* is a valuable guide. Charles J. Kappler (comp.), *Indian Affairs: Laws and Treaties* (Y 4.In2/2:L44/v.1-5) was published in five volumes by the GPO and reprinted by GPO in 1975. It lists "all ratified and unratified treaties, all executive agreements, major federal court decisions relating to Indians, and tribal cases considered by the U.S. Court of Claims." Felix S. Cohen, *Handbook of Federal Indian Law*, issued by the GPO in 1942 and in a 1972 AMS Press reprint, is a useful synthesis that covers topics such as "citizenship, tribal membership, allotments, water rights, taxation, guaranteed health services, and countless other matters."[12]

Volume 7 of the *Statutes at Large* contains the text of Indian treaties from 1778 to 1842, and thereafter treaties and agreements with Indian tribes appear in the regular volumes of the *Statutes*. Current law is codified in Title 25 of the *United States Code*, and the regulations of agencies like the Bureau of Indian Affairs and the Indian Claims Commission are found in Title 25 of the *Code of Federal Regulations*. Current information on legislative and executive actions concerning Indian affairs may be accessed through several sources, among them *CIS/Index*, the *Monthly Catalog*, and the *Congressional Record*.[13]

Although the formal treaty process with the American Indian ended in the latter part of the nineteenth century, debates, reports, studies, administrative rulings, and court cases continue today. Therefore, the bibliographic and textual materials discussed above and elsewhere in the text serve to provide information on our government's role in its dealings with the American Indian.

OTHER SOURCES OF PRESIDENTIAL ACTIONS

In addition to the above sources, some of the official and commercial bibliographic tools discussed in Chapter 7 may be used for researching presidential materials. A brief account of these sources follows.

CCH CONGRESSIONAL INDEX

Congressional Index contains a division entitled "Reorganization Plans-Treaties-Nominations." Action on these presidential initiatives is reported in this division, preceded by a special index in which reorganization plans and treaties are entered by topic, and presidential nominations for Senate confirmation are listed by appointee and agency or branch of the military service to which appointed.

U.S.C.C.A.N.

Tables 7 and 8 of *United States Code Congressional and Administrative News* list by number, date, and subject proclamations and executive orders, respectively. References in these tables are to the pages in U.S.C.C.A.N. where the text of these materials can be located. Moreover, the text of reorganization plans is published in the U.S.C.C.A.N. volumes.

UNITED STATES CODE

Reorganization plans are published in the *United States Code* and its commercial editions in the appendix to Title 5. Indeed, Title 5 includes "all pertinent documents, such as the enabling act, text of the plan, presidential messages pertaining to the plans, any necessary executive orders implementing them, historical and revision notes, and editorial notes and cross-references for all plans in force."[14] The Advance Reports of *United States Code Service, Lawyers' Edition* include the text of proclamations, executive orders, and reorganization plans.

CONGRESSIONAL RECORD

The index entry for actions of the chief executive is "President of the United States," and there is also an approach by subject. The kinds of presidential materials printed in the *Record* include proclamations, executive orders, addresses, messages, statements, and the like. Because a member of Congress can request that virtually anything be printed in the *Record*, it is reasonable to assume that at one time or another any presidential document may appear in its pages.

HOUSE AND SENATE JOURNALS

Presidential materials in the *Journals* include addresses (for example, the State of the Union address), communications to the Congress, messages transmitting legislation, treaty messages (published in the Senate *Journal*), and veto messages (published in the *Journal* of the chamber where the bill originated). The quadrennial inaugural address of a president is customarily printed in the Senate *Journal*. The index entry in the House *Journal* for presidential materials is "President"; in the *Journal* of the Senate, "President of the United States."

CONGRESSIONAL SERIAL SET

With the addition of Senate treaty documents and Senate executive reports on treaties and on presidential nominations in the serial set, this series contains a number of presidential actions. As noted in Chapter 7 and this chapter, messages, addresses, reorganization plans, budget documents, and economic reports are among the materials sent by a president to Congress and ordered to be printed in the House or Senate documents series.

CAPITOL SERVICES, INC.

It was noted in Chapter 7 that Capitol Services, Inc., a Washington, DC-based commercial publisher, offers to subscribers printed reports and abstracts of the *Congressional Record* and an online database called CRECORD. Therefore, any presidential materials published in the *Record* can be accessed through CSI's printed and online services.

The same company, a sister company of Indian Head (New York City), provides similar services for *Federal Register* materials. The *Federal Register Report* is a customized daily service providing abstracts from the FR in topic areas pre-selected by the subscriber. The *Federal Register Abstracts, Master Edition* summarizes each issue of the FR and organizes the abstracted material into major topic divisions. Moreover, an online database called FEDREG, through ORBIT and DIALOG, provides weekly updating of *Federal Register* materials, including all presidential documents published therein.

In addition, CSI operates the monthly *Federal Index*, a bibliographic service formerly published by Predicasts, Inc., of Cleveland, Ohio. *Federal Index*, online through ORBIT and DIALOG, includes presidential documents from the *Federal Register, Congressional Record*, and *Weekly Compilation of Presidential Documents*.[15]

SHEPARD'S CFR CITATIONS

Finally, *Shepard's Code of Federal Regulation Citations* (Shepard's-McGraw Hill) shows citations to the CFR, including Title 3 proclamations, executive orders, and reorganization plans, as cited by federal and state cases reported in units of the *National Reporter System, Lawyers' Edition* reports, selected law review articles, and the *American Bar Association Journal*.

SUMMARY

The foregoing has been an attempt to categorize the various publications that are generated by or for the presidency through official provenance or under commercial imprints. Although the duplication of materials that carry the public record of presidential activity may seem wasteful, such duplication does provide one clear advantage to libraries and other institutions that require this information. By the very duplication, libraries large and small, non-depository and depository, may participate in the acquisition of at least some of these publications.

It is within the budget of a small library, for example, to subscribe to the *Department of State Bulletin, Weekly Compilation of Presidential Documents*, or *Public Papers of the Presidents* series. Depository libraries should select the full range of these materials according to their several item categories. Moreover, commercial products and services in support of official documentation are usually available in the larger libraries.

The following in tabular summary are official sources of public documents containing the text of major presidential activities.

Type of Activity	Sources
Addresses and Remarks	Department of State Bulletin Congressional Record House and Senate Journals Congressional Serial Set Weekly Compilation Public Papers
Executive Orders	Federal Register Title 3, Code of Federal Regulations Congressional Record Weekly Compilation Public Papers
Messages	Department of State Bulletin Congressional Record House and Senate Journals Congressional Serial Set Weekly Compilation Public Papers
Nominations	Congressional Record Congressional Serial Set Senate Journal Weekly Compilation Public Papers
Press Releases	Department of State Bulletin Weekly Compilation Public Papers
Proclamations	Department of State Bulletin Congressional Record Federal Register Title 3, Code of Federal Regulations Statutes at Large Weekly Compilation Public Papers

Public Laws	Slip Laws
	Statutes at Large
	United States Code
Reorganization Plans	Congressional Serial Set
	Congressional Record
	Federal Register
	Title 3, Code of Federal Regulations
	Statutes at Large
	Title 5, United States Code
	Weekly Compilation
	Public Papers
Treaties and Agreements	Congressional Serial Set
	Department of State Bulletin
	TIAS
	UST
	Bevans

REFERENCES

1. According to a Department of State ruling, Grover Cleveland is counted twice, as the Twenty-second and the Twenty-fourth president, because his two terms were not consecutive.

2. *Inside O.M.B.*, a biweekly report on the Office of Management and Budget, is available commercially from P.O. Box 7167, Ben Franklin Station, Washington, DC 20044.

3. Laurence F. Schmeckebier and Roy B. Eastin, *Government Publications and Their Use*, 2nd rev. ed. (Washington: Brookings, 1969), p. 341.

4. See the committee print *Summary of Executive Orders in Times of War and National Emergency* (Washington: Government Printing Office, 1974).

5. President Gerald Ford's pardon of Richard Nixon was issued as Proc. 4311, September 8, 1974 (39 FR 32601; 3 CFR, 1971-75 Comp., p. 385).

6. For earlier official and privately published compilations of presidential materials, see Schmeckebier and Eastin, pp. 330-47.

7. *The Role of the Senate in Treaty Ratification*, a committee print prepared for the use of the Senate Foreign Relations Committee (Washington: Government Printing Office, 1977), p. 1.

8. Ibid., p. 3.

9. Margaret A. Leary, "International Executive Agreements: A Guide to the Legal Issues and Research Sources," *Law Library Journal* 72: 1 (Winter 1979).

10. *The Role of the Senate in Treaty Ratification*, p. 27. See also *International Agreements: An Analysis of Executive Regulations and Practices*, a committee print prepared for the use of the Senate Foreign Relations Committee, March 1977.

11. Earlier international law digests included those compiled by Cadwalader, Wharton, Moore, and Hackworth.

12. Michael L. Tate, "Studying the American Indian through Government Documents and the National Archives," *Government Publications Review* 5: 289 (1978).

13. See also Michael L. Tate, "Red Power: Government Publications and the Rising Indian Activism of the 1970s," *Government Publications Review* 8A: 499-518 (1981).

14. Miles O. Price, et al., *Effective Legal Research, Fourth Edition* (Boston: Little, Brown and Company, 1979), pp. 97-98.

15. Capitol Services, Predicasts, IHS, and BRS are all sister companies of a conglomerate called Indian Head Company, located in New York City.

9

Selected Categories of Executive Branch and Independent Agency Publications

INTRODUCTION

In Chapter 8 we discussed some of the exemplary publications that reflect presidential activities. But the president, as administrative head of the executive branch of government, must delegate to the departments and their many subordinate agencies his mandate under the Constitution to insure "that the laws be faithfully executed." To accomplish this task, a president must rely upon his cabinet, and that group of officers must rely upon the much maligned "bureaucracy" to carry out the policies of the administration.

The cabinet is an oddity. Although it has existed since George Washington's administration, it is not mentioned by name in the Constitution. The only reference to this body is in the Twenty-fifth Amendment, which states that a vice-president "and a majority of either the principal officers of the executive departments or of such other body as Congress may by law provide" may declare a president unable to discharge the powers and duties of his office. Thus the cabinet is a creation of custom and tradition; a cabinet officer is nominated by the chief executive, approved by the Senate, and serves at the pleasure of the president.

There is a saying that whereas administrations come and go, the bureaucracy endures forever. While this is an implied comment upon the limitations of presidential power over the departments and agencies that the chief executive titularly heads, it also misleadingly suggests a static quality. In fact, the bureaucracy endures while suffering many sea changes. Reorganization of existing agencies is an ongoing process. New agencies and, indeed, departments themselves are created, enjoy their place in the federal sun, and die—sometimes with a bang, often with barely a whimper. As we have noted elsewhere in this text, government reorganization affects the issuance of public documents, sometimes in drastic and dramatic ways. Mergers and dissolutions that occur signify a change in the lines of issuing authority. Bursts of economy may signal a publication's demise. A change in purpose carries with it a concommitant change in the content, periodicity, or even design of a document. And of course the classification notation of the Superintendent of Documents, based as it is on the principle of provenance, is affected by reorganization.

As a result of minor reorganization, which is noted in the *Federal Register*, and major reorganization, which is submitted to the Congress in the form of a reorganization plan (see Chapter 8), the enumeration of public documents is a hazardous business. Moreover, efforts to reduce the cost of government, changes in public policy, commercial encroachment on government publishing, the vagaries of things for which accountability is difficult to fix—all these factors and more render a discussion of "important" series and their titles fraught with danger. While no one expects that the *United States Government Manual* or the *Statistical Abstract of the United States* will cease to be, over two thousand federal publications were eliminated within a period of one year following President Reagan's notorious "war on waste" ukase published in the April 24, 1981 issue of the *Weekly Compilation of Presidential Documents*.[1]

Accordingly, the government materials discussed in this chapter are organized by selected categories, groupings of publications and collections which serve an important reference or research function. Because virtually every document is of potential value to some user, this type of broad coverage will inevitably omit specific titles or series of interest. Users' needs cannot be circumscribed by one person's experience and judgment, and the writer begs the reader's indulgence.

ADMINISTRATIVE RULINGS

Congress delegates to the departments and agencies within the executive establishment, including the independent agencies, the power to issue rules and regulations which have the force of law. In this respect, administrative rulings can be considered as "delegated legislation," sometimes called "sublegislation." The major instruments of promulgation are the *Federal Register* and the *Code of Federal Regulations*.

FEDERAL REGISTER

Presidential documents that appear in the *Federal Register* and in Title 3 of the *Code of Federal Regulations* were the proper concern of our discussions in Chapter 8. But the vast bulk of materials found in the FR and in the other titles of the CFR consist of department and agency pronouncements having general applicability and legal effect.

CONTENTS

The Federal Register Act of 1935 (44 U.S.C. Ch. 15) provides that, in addition to presidential documents, the kinds of materials to be printed include "documents or classes of documents that may be required so to be published by Act of Congress." Moreover, notices of hearings or miscellaneous agency announcements, including those of proposed rules, are to be published and the public given timely notice to respond.[2] The documents so ordered are arranged in the *Federal Register* under the following headings:

1) *Presidential Documents* (Chapter 8).

2) *Rules and Regulations*; this section contains regulatory documents having general applicability and legal effect. When published, they are keyed to and codified in the CFR. Temporary rules having a time-expiration date or those of limited applicability are also published, but do not carry over into the CFR.

3) *Proposed Rules*; this section consists of changes or amendments to already existing regulations, or new rules that an agency is considering. Their publication permits interested parties to comment on the proposals through hearings or by submitting written statements to the agency.

4) *Notices*; this section contains information other than rules or proposed rules that are applicable to the public. It includes changes in agency organization too small to be submitted as a presidential reorganization plan; announcements of hearings, investigations, and committee meetings; delegations of authority; opinions which are advisory and non-binding; and miscellaneous announcements.

OTHER FR FEATURES

Beginning with the April 2, 1979 issue, the FR adopted some format changes. At the beginning of the issue the table of contents is followed by the List of CFR Parts Affected in This Issue, a numerical guide to the parts of the CFR affected in the issue. At the back of the issue, a new part called "Reader Aids" was introduced. This part includes phone numbers for information and assistance; a Cumulative List of CFR Parts Affected during the current month; and a series of "reminders" such as rules going into effect in today's issue, a list (but not the text) of public laws which cumulates periodically, and, on Wednesdays, a list of documents relating to federal grant programs, information on next week's deadlines for comments on proposed rules, next week's meetings, and next week's public hearings.

With the issue of February 22, 1982, two useful features, "Dial-a-Reg" and "Highlights," were discontinued because of reduced personnel resources at the Office of the Federal Register. The latter, which appeared on the cover, was replaced by "Selected Subjects" beginning with the issue of May 17, 1982 on an experimental basis. "Selected Subjects" was compiled from subject terms supplied by agencies for some of their rule and proposed rule documents and selectively supplements the table of contents.

Classed in GS 4.107 and available to depository libraries in paper copy (item 573-C) or on microfiche (item 573-D), the FR has an index that cumulates monthly into an annual issue. In 1977 the Office of the Federal Register announced a *Thesaurus of Indexing Terms* designed to improve the subject terms and cross-reference structure of the *Federal Register Index*. The announcement appeared in the February 17, 1981 issue of the *Federal Register*, pp. 12618-43.

CODE OF FEDERAL REGULATIONS

44 U.S.C. 1510 calls for "the preparation and publication ... of complete codification of the documents of each agency," and this is accomplished in the *Code of Federal Regulations*. Just as the *Statutes at Large* are codified in the *United States Code*, so the daily issues of the FR are codified in the CFR; the

former represents statutory law while the latter expresses legislation implemented by agencies as rules and regulations.

The CFR is divided into fifty titles, some of which parallel the titles of the U.S.C. Each volume of the CFR, unless no amendments were promulgated in the FR,[3] is revised at least once each calendar year and issued on a quarterly basis as follows:

Titles 1-16   as of January 1
Titles 17-27   as of April 1
Titles 28-41   as of July 1
Titles 42-50   as of October 1

The specificity of administrative law is reflected in the imperious structure of the CFR. *Titles* represent broad subject areas (e.g., Title 10, *Energy*; Title 14, *Aeronautics and Space*). Some titles have *Subtitles* designated by capital letters (A, B, C, etc.). *Chapters* are numbered in Roman capitals (I, II, III, etc.) and are usually assigned to a single issuing agency; they are sometimes divided into *Subchapters*, in capital letters, to group related parts. Each chapter is divided into *Parts*, numbered in Arabic throughout each title. A part consists of a unified body of regulations applying to a single function of the issuing agency or devoted to specific subject matter under the control of the agency. Parts are normally assigned to chapters as follows: Chapter I (Parts 1 to 199); Chapter II (Parts 200 to 299); Chapter III (Parts 300 to 399); etc. Sometimes *Subparts*, which are assigned capital letters, are used to group related sections within a part.

Sections comprise the basic unit of the CFR. Each section number includes the number of the part set off by a decimal point preceded by the symbol "§." Internal divisions of a section may include *Paragraphs*, and these may be further divided alphanumerically. The whole constitutes a hierarchy which permits an extraordinarily detailed explication of rules governing institutional conduct.

While citation to the *Federal Register* where the regulation was first published is by volume and page with date, citation to the CFR is by title, section, and year of revision. Thus 36 FR 24927 (December 24, 1971) is codified in 9 CFR§91.10 (year). Classed in GS 4.108, the CFR is available to depository institutions in paper copy (item 572-B) or on microfiche (item 572-C).

RESEARCH PROCEDURE

To update the CFR, some or all of the following steps may be taken.

1) To locate the title and part one is concerned with, consult an unnumbered volume called the *CFR Index*. Revised annually as of January 1, it provides subject access to the CFR volumes. Beginning with the July 1979 edition, the *CFR Index* has been improved to offer more direct subject entries and greater cross-references.[4]

2) Because of the quarterly publishing schedule of titles, references in the *CFR Index* will include material in the basic CFR volumes as well as amendatory material promulgated in the daily FR through January 1 but not yet incorporated into the printed CFR volumes. Therefore users should consult a separate pamphlet entitled *LSA — List of CFR Sections Affected*. Issued monthly in cumulative form, the December, March, June, and September *LSA — Lists*

provide an annual cumulation for the CFR titles listed on the cover, and these issues must be saved. Organized by titles and appropriate subdivisions, the *LSA – List* references the page numbers of the FR where amendatory information has been published.

3) To complete the updating of the most current (today's) issue of the *Federal Register*, consult:
   a) "CFR Parts Affected during [Month]." Located in the back of each daily FR, this cumulative table also provides references from the CFR titles and subdivisions to *Federal Register* page numbers.
   b) "CFR Parts Affected in This Issue." Located in the front of each daily FR, this table completes the updating information and is similarly arranged.

Figure 25 provides a typical *LSA – List* and illustrations of "CFR Parts Affected during [Month]" and "CFR Parts Affected in This Issue" in the same day's *Federal Register*.

Figure 25
Tables Updating the Code of Federal Regulations

82   LSA—LIST OF CFR SECTIONS AFFECTED

CHANGES APRIL 1 THROUGH NOVEMBER 30, 1981

Title 25, Chapter I—Continued

	Page
103a Added	47774
103b Added	47775
105 Removed	26475
115 Added	36136
115.5 (c) corrected	38074
120 Revised	47537
173 Removed	26476
242 Removed	26476
251.5 *See* EO 12328	50357
252.31 *See* EO 12328	50357
256.11—256.21 (Subpart B) Revised	33242
258.18 Added	40511
259.1 (e) revised	37045

Chapter IV—Navajo and Hopi Indian Relocation Commission

	Page
700.17 (a) introductory text amended	27915
Redesignated as 700.331	27921
700.301—700.321 (Subpart L) Added	46801
700.331—700.343 (Subpart M) Added	27921
700.331 Redesignated from 700.-17	27921
700.451—700.479 (Subpart N) Added	2791f

Title 25—*Proposed Rules:*

	Page
1—277 (Ch. I)	24458, 53870
43e	50565
161	2220f
258	55542
700	27967

	Page
V, and VI headings, (6), (7) (i), (ii) introductory text, and (8) revised	34570
(c)(3) example (7), (5), (d) (4) example (7), (e)(3) example (8), (g)(2) tables VII through IX, (9), (10), and (11) added	34570
Correctly designated	39589
(d)(1)(ii)(A) and (f)(6)(iv) corrected	39589
1.507-2 (c)(1)(iv)(A) amended	37889
1.509(a)-3 (a)(1) heading, (2) heading, and (4) heading added; (a)(1), (4), (c)(1)(i) and (iii)(*a*), (c)(3), 6, (d)(2) and (3) (iii), and (e)(4)(i)(*f*) amended; (a)(3) revised	37889
1.509(a)-4 (k)(2) amended	37890
1.509(a)-5 (a)(1), (b)(1) and (c) amended	37890
1.671-4 Revised	57481
1.819-2 Determination	20162
1.956-2 (b)(1)(ix) revised	57675
1.1033(g)-1 (b)(1) and (2)(i) (A), and (b)(2)(iii) heading corrected	23235
1.1244(a)-1 (b) revised	29467
1.1244(b)-1 Revised	29467
1.1244(c)-1 Revised	29468
1.1244(c)-2 Revised	29470
1.1244(d)-3 Revised	29472
1.1244(d)-4 Revised	29473
1.1244(e)-1 (a) revised	29473
(a)(2)(vi) corrected	31881
1.1441-4 (d)(1) revised	27636
(d)(1) corrected	31409

(Figure 25 continues on page 208)

Figure 25 (cont'd)

Federal Register

Vol. 47, No. 32

Wednesday, February 17, 1982

CFR PARTS AFFECTED DURING FEBRUARY

At the end of each month, the Office of the Federal Register publishes separately a list of CFR Sections Affected (LSA), which lists parts and sections affected by documents published since the revision date of each title.

3 CFR

Administrative Orders:
Presidential Determinations:
No. 82–4 of
  January 28, 1982............6417
No. 82–5 of
  February 2, 1982............ 6419
Executive Orders:
February 26, 1852
  (Revoked in part
  by PLO 6120)................5423
March 15, 1872
  (Revoked
  by PLO 6125)................5425
July 14, 1884
  (Revoked in part
  by PLO 6118)................5422
December 14, 1886
  (Revoked in part
  by PLO 6131)................6646
February 10, 1908
  (Revoked by
  PLO 6131)......................6646

11562 (Revoked by
  EO 12345)....................5189
12242 (Revoked by
  12346).........................5993
July 2, 1910
  (Revoked in part
  by PLO 6140
  and PLO 6141)....6853, 6854
July 9, 1910
  (Revoked by
  PLO 6146)......................6856
December 28, 1910
  (Revoked by
  PLO 6140)......................6853
July 26, 1911
  (Revoked in part
  by PLO 6128)................6849
March 22, 1912
  (Revoked in part
  by PLO 6141)................6854
April 21, 1914
  (Revoked by
  PLO 6140)......................6853

Federal Register / Vol. 47, No. 32 / Wednesday, February 17, 1982

CFR PARTS AFFECTED IN THIS ISSUE

A cumulative list of the parts affected this month can be found in the Reader Aids section at the end of this issue.

3 CFR
Executive Orders:
July 2, 1910
  (Revoked in part
  by PLO 6140
  and PLO 6141).....6853, 6854
July 9, 1910
  (Revoked by
  PLO 6146)......................6856
December 28, 1910
  (Revoked by
  PLO 6140)......................6853
July 26, 1911
  (Revoked in part
  by PLO 6128)................6849
March 22, 1912
  (Revoked in part
  by PLO 6141)................6854
April 21, 1914
  (Revoked by
  PLO 6140)......................6853
August 3, 1914
  (See PLO 6140).............6853
July 19, 1915
  (Revoked in part
  by PLO 6141)...........6854

34 CFR
624....................................... 6826
625....................................... 6826
626....................................... 6826
627....................................... 6826

39 CFR
111....................................... 6826

40 CFR
52 (4 documents)............. 6827–
                6829
123....................................... 6831
180....................................... 6832
205....................................... 7186
256 (2 documents)............ 6833,
                6834
405....................................... 6835
406....................................... 6835
407....................................... 6835
422....................................... 6835
424....................................... 6835
426....................................... 6835
429....................................... 6835
432....................................... 6835
Proposed Rules:
32.. 7194

1201................................... 6879
1241................................... 6879
1248................................... 6879
1249................................... 6881
Proposed Rules:
1051................................... 6904

50 CFR
621...................................... 6881
Proposed Rules:
23.. 7190

CFR FINDING AIDS

The unnumbered *CFR Index* volume, in addition to its subject index, also includes tabular guides and other aids. Table I is a Parallel Table of Statutory Authorities and Agency Rules. Table II contains Acts Requiring Publication in the Federal Register. Also included are a list of CFR Titles, Chapters, and Parts, an alphabetical list of CFR Subtitles and Chapters, and lists of current and superseded CFR volumes.

Moreover, all CFR volumes have a "Finding Aids" section following the regulatory material. This section includes a Table of CFR Titles and Chapters, an Alphabetical List of Agencies Appearing in the CFR, and a List of CFR Sections Affected, which is divided into yearly units. Separate volumes of the latter have been compiled for past years. For example, *List of CFR Sections Affected, 1964-1972, Volume I* (Titles 1-27) and *Volume II* (Titles 26-50) include all CFR sections which have been expressly affected by documents published in the *Federal Register* during these years. Prior to 1964, a separate volume, *List of CFR Sections Affected, 1949-1963*, should be consulted.

USERS GUIDE

The Federal Register: What It Is and How to Use It (GS 4.6/2:F31/year; item 569-B) is subtitled *A Guide for the User of the Federal Register—Code of Federal Regulations System*. The 1980 edition of this manual contains historical background information, an explanation of the rulemaking process, the organization of the FR and CFR, samples of pages in the FR and CFR, indexes and finding aids, a useful section on public participation in the rulemaking process, and various other kinds of directory and reference information.

MICROFORM EDITIONS OF THE FR AND CFR

There are several commercial and governmental editions of the FR and CFR available in a microformat. These have been issued on fiche and film and cover various years. Some are retrospective projects, others are current, and a few combine both features.

Microform editions of the *Federal Register* include those which have been or are currently available from the GPO (item 573-D), National Archives and Records Service, University Microfilms International (Ann Arbor, Michigan), Information Handling Services (Englewood, Colorado), Princeton Microfilm Corporation (Princeton, New Jersey), Brookhaven Press (Washington, DC), Readex Microprint Corporation (New York, NY), Congressional Information Service (Bethesda, Maryland), and William S. Hein & Co., Inc. (Buffalo, New York). Moreover, the Administrative Committee of the Federal Register authorized the GPO to provide a microfiche edition of the *Federal Register* for sale beginning October 1, 1982, in addition to the paper edition.

Microform editions of the *Code of Federal Regulations* include those which have been or are currently available from the GPO (item 572-C), Readex Microprint Corporation, Trans-Media Publishing Co., Inc. (Dobbs Ferry, New York), William S. Hein, Congressional Information Service, and Information Handling Services. Trans-Media's microfilmed CFR is accompanied by *Guides to the Use of the Code of Federal Regulations*, compiled by Erwin C. and Robert E.

Surrency, which functions as a "reel guide" to the film. Information Handling Services (IHS) produced an *Index to the Code of Federal Regulations, 1938-1979* to accompany its fiche file and a 1980 annual supplement. However, this printed *Index* was continued in 1981 by Congressional Information Service. Because these commercial aids often represent an improvement over the official government edition but are also quite expensive, the buyer should consult reviews or employ other means of determining their value to the collection.[5]

PAGE/DATE GUIDE TO THE FR

Beginning in 1970 the *Federal Register Index* included at the end of each monthly and cumulative issue a useful parallel table referencing the inclusive page numbers to the date of the daily issue. The Detroit Public Library compiled a guide which lists month, volume, year, and pagination of the *Federal Register* from 1936 to 1969. The guide is used in conjunction with the library's microfilm collection of the FR. Because users frequently know the page number but not the date, the list facilitates the search for the correct reel of film. For the convenience of other libraries, this page/date guide was published in *Documents to the People* (January 1980), pp. 44-46.

FR ABSTRACTS

As noted in Chapter 8, Capitol Services, Inc. (Washington, DC) publishes the *Federal Register Report*, a daily service providing abstracts from the FR in topical areas pre-selected by the subscriber, and *Federal Register Abstracts, Master Edition*, a daily summary of the entire FR contents organized by topics.

SHEPARD'S CFR CITATIONS

Shepard's Code of Federal Regulations Citations shows citations to the CFR as cited by the U.S. Supreme Court, the lower federal courts, state courts in cases reported in units of the *National Reporter System*, in *Annotations* of *United States Supreme Court Reports, Lawyers' Edition* and American Law Reports, and in the *American Bar Association Journal*. Each citation includes the year to indicate currency, and letter abbreviations indicate holdings by the courts as to constitutionality or validity.

ONLINE RETRIEVAL SERVICES

The CSI Federal Register Data Base (FEDREG), online through DIALOG and ORBIT, provides a complete account of regulatory activity, on a weekly basis, as published in the *Federal Register*. REG-ULATE, produced by Legi-Slate, Inc. (Washington, DC), covers FR and CFR materials and is online through I. P. Sharp Associates (Toronto, Canada). Both the FR and CFR are also online for users of the LEXIS and WESTLAW databases (see Chapter 10).

SPECIFICITY AND READABILITY

The ferocious specificity of administrative regulations requires a clarity and precision of language not always found in the pages of the FR and CFR. Indeed, bureaucrats have been obliged to attend writing seminars to help them compose clear and concise directives. The attention to small detail in promulgating rules comes as a surprise to the student who first encounters the prose of these publications. For example, the space on vessels exporting livestock requires that "as many as four horses, or as many as seven horses weighing not more than 500 pounds each, may be shipped in pens not less than 10 by 8 feet in size. Mares in foal and stallions, however, shall be shipped only in separate stalls, which shall be not less than 8 feet deep by 3 feet wide and for mares due to foal en route shall be not less than 8 feet deep by 5 feet wide and readily accessible." And space requirements for cattle, sheep, goats, and swine are just as explicit. Only calves, lambs, kids and pigs "may be stowed at the discretion of the inspector."[6]

The *Federal Register* for 1981 totaled 63,553 pages, a 25 percent reduction over the 1980 FR. This decrease was widely hailed by administration officials as proof that Washington is serious about cutting red tape and reducing paperwork. Yet complaints of the tortuous, obfuscating prose found in the FR and CFR still abound. The creation of the *Federal Register* and the *Code of Federal Regulations* was an act of noble intent. It eliminated caprice and bibliographic chaos; it did away with "hip pocket" administrative law. How ironic, then, that having created the bibliographic machinery for this purpose, one has difficulty understanding the regulations promulgated.

SELECTED REGULATORY AGENCIES

At one time, scholars identified certain independent agencies that wield vast regulatory power; these became known as the "Big Seven." Created by Congress in the late nineteenth and early twentieth centuries, they exercise a degree of autonomy independent of the executive and the Congress.

Name	Year Established
Interstate Commerce Commission (ICC)	1887
Federal Trade Commission (FTC)	1915
Federal Power Commission (FPC)	1920
Federal Communications Commission (FCC)	1934
Securities and Exchange Commission (SEC)	1934
National Labor Relations Board (NLRB)	1935
Civil Aeronautics Board (CAB)	1938

The Federal Power Commission was abolished in the legislation that created the Department of Energy (91 *Stat.* 565), and the Civil Aeronautics Board is scheduled for abolition in 1985 as part of the deregulation of the airline industry. The remaining bodies still possess large regulatory authority. To the above list must be added the Federal Reserve Board (Fed), which was established by the

Federal Reserve Act of 1913 (38 *Stat.* 251) to set monetary policy and which today may well be the most influential of the independent establishments. In recent decades, however, other regulatory entities have been created, and these have been granted large powers to promulgate regulations affecting a number of institutional and personal activities. An updated list would certainly include, as exemplary, the following bodies, some of which operate within a cabinet department, others that are designated as "independent" bodies.

Name	Year Established
Equal Employment Opportunity Commission (EEOC)	1964
National Highway Traffic Safety Administration (NHTSA)	1970
Occupational Safety and Health Administration (OSHA)	1970
Postal Rate Commission (PRC)	1970
Environmental Protection Agency (EPA)	1970
Consumer Product Safety Commission (CPSC)	1972
Federal Election Commission (FEC)	1974
Nuclear Regulatory Commission (NUREG)	1975

Although the regulations promulgated by these entities are subject to congressional review, the decisions of the numerous agencies within the executive branch and those designated as independent have the full force and effect of law.[7] Moreover, as issuing entities they publish a number of series — reports, periodicals, bibliographies and lists, handbooks and manuals — which are available to depository libraries or for sale. Many of them participate in the NTIS database. And their purposes and programs are described in the *United States Government Manual*, a basic reference source for all libraries.

UNITED STATES GOVERNMENT MANUAL

The December 1934 issue of the *Monthly Catalog* announced that a "new loose-leaf service to be known as the United States Government Manual ... will provide factual information describing the creation and authority, organization and activity concerning all the executive units of the Federal Government, authenticated by the heads of the Departments. Organization charts will also be included."[8] Thus the *Manual*, the official handbook of the federal government, was launched.

Classed in GS 4.109 (item 577), the *Manual* provides descriptions of the programs and activities of the legislative, judicial, and executive entities, including the independent establishments and various boards, committees, commissions, and "quasi-official" agencies like the American National Red Cross. Some new feature is introduced and another dropped in virtually every edition. *Supplements* have been issued which contain changes in personnel and organization since the revision date of the annual edition. Organization charts for larger entities are published. An appendix provides brief sketches of agencies abolished, transferred, or terminated after March 4, 1933. The *Manual* is indexed by name, subject, and agency. Although the *Manual* is no longer issued in looseleaf form, its annual appearance provides users with basic information on the federal establishment.

COMMERCIAL DIRECTORIES

Information on personnel and policies of administrative and regulatory agencies is found in various commercial publications, and this information is often superior to that found in the *United States Government Manual*.

The *Federal Regulatory Directory* (Washington: Congressional Quarterly, Inc.) provides information needed by those who must deal with and want information from the several regulatory agencies. The 1981-82 edition discusses the growth of regulation and current issues such as trends toward deregulation, reform of agency procedures, cost/benefit analysis of agency actions, and methods used to select regulators. Following those discussions are extensive profiles of twelve of the largest, most important agencies—background, powers and authority, biographies of commissioners or board members, etc. Ninety-three other important regulatory agencies are also covered, with summaries of responsibilities, lists of telephone contacts, information sources, and regional offices. Two indexes cross-reference the material by agency/subject and personnel.

A companion volume, Congressional Quarterly's *Washington Information Directory*, is an annual that provides directory information for more than 5,000 key personnel in federal agencies (including Congress) and private associations. Many small units of government not found in the *United States Government Manual* are listed and briefly described in the *Washington Information Directory*, making it a most valuable resource for libraries.

The *Federal Yellow Book* (Washington: The Washington Monitor, Inc.), a companion to the *Congressional Yellow Book* (Chapter 7), is a looseleaf service that provides directory information for some 27,000 federal employees by organization, with names, titles, addresses, locations, and phone numbers. The *Yellow Book* has an agency name index similar to that found in the *United States Government Manual*. A valuable feature of this publication is its bimonthly updating service.

The *Federal Executive Directory* (Washington: Carroll Publishing Company) is reissued in paperbound format every two months. About 25,000 listings are accessed by an alphabetical index to federal executive names and a key word index to agency names. Another related Carroll Publishing Company product is *Federal Organization Service*, which includes organization charts, reissued every three months, of all cabinet-level departments, independent agencies, the Congress, and the military services.

For an overall view of federal government directories, consult Donna Rae Larson, *Guide to U.S. Government Directories, 1970-1980* (Phoenix, AZ: Oryx Press, 1981). This is an annotated bibliography of 842 directories issued by government agencies; the main entry section is arranged by SuDocs class notation, which is accessed by a detailed subject index. Entry information includes availability, coverage of contents, arrangement, and indexing.

LOOSELEAF SERVICES

The size and complexity of administrative regulations are rendered more manageable by the commercial publications of looseleaf services. Prominent publishers include Commerce Clearing House, Prentice-Hall, and the Bureau of National Affairs. The basic approach is by subject or topic (e.g., taxation, labor relations, products liability, securities), and coverage includes the administrative promulgations of the agency or agencies involved in the regulatory activity. A typical service includes all relevant materials on a given topic: texts of statutes, court decisions, and administrative rulings. Editorial comment, indexes, and rapid supplementation tie the "package" together and save the researcher valuable time.

SUMMARY

Many regard regulatory activity as a burden; complaints of enforcement of trivial rules amounting to harassment are frequent. The cost to prepare and print a relatively small number of OSHA pamphlets informing farmers that floors covered with manure tend to be slippery came to $466,700.[9] The popular pizza and its ingredients on labels and menus "take up more than 40 pages of federal documents, including some 310 separate regulations."[10] But according to a former senior economist at the Occupational Safety and Health Administration, to a surprising degree regulation is the "mother of invention." While it is true that regulation increases costs to industry, it also spawns far-reaching benefits: jobs, productivity gains, energy savings, new markets, and profits.[11] Whatever the merits of the controversy, the agencies that promulgate administrative law have, in the words of former Supreme Court Justice Robert H. Jackson, become a "veritable fourth branch of the Government."[12]

SOURCES OF STATISTICAL INFORMATION

The statistical system of the federal government is a decentralized one. A number of agencies gather various kinds of data and report these data for the use of the private sector and government itself. So vast is this enterprise that an enumeration of all statistical compendia would comprise a separate volume. This section will attempt to summarize the important sources of statistical information on a selective and exemplary basis.

GENERAL GUIDES

STATISTICAL ABSTRACT OF THE UNITED STATES

Published annually since 1878, the *Statistical Abstract* (C 3.134; item 150) is the basic summary of statistics on the social, political, and economic organization of the United States. Data are selected from many statistical series, both governmental and private. The tabular data in the *Statistical Abstract* may be used by themselves to answer questions or serve as a guide to more detailed information. The latter function is accomplished by the introductory text to each section, the "source notes" which refer the user to the issuing entity where more comprehensive information may be found, and by appendixes that contain a "Guide to Sources of Statistics" and "Guide to State Statistical Abstracts." Each edition adds, drops, or refines features of the *Abstract*, but the contents, divided into sections, typically cover over thirty broad areas, from population, vital statistics, education, and the labor force, to energy, science, transportation, and comparative international data. With its scope and valuable source notes, the *Statistical Abstract* is one of those government publications that may safely be called indispensable.[13]

HISTORICAL STATISTICS OF THE UNITED STATES

Historical Statistics of the United States, Colonial Times to [year] (C 3.134/2; item 151) is revised once every several years and contains over 12,500 time series, largely annual, on American social, economic, political, and geographic development from 1610 to the current edition.[14] Well over 1,000 pages, this massive compilation includes source notes for additional information, definitions of terms, a descriptive text, and a detailed subject index. An appendix in the annual *Statistical Abstract* serves as an index to tables in the *Abstract* that are continued in *Historical Statistics*.

POCKET DATA BOOK, USA

The *Pocket Data Book, USA* (C 3.134/3; item 150-A) consists of condensed data taken from the *Statistical Abstract*. Designed for quick and easy reference, it contains graphic and tabular data on population, vital statistics, law enforcement, education, health, businesses, housing, energy, and other topics of interest.[15]

STATE AND METROPOLITAN AREA DATA BOOK

The 1979 edition of the *State and Metropolitan Area Data Book* (C 3.134/5; item 150) was the first in a new series to be published biennially. It presents data for the United States as a whole, each state, and each Standard Metropolitan Statistical Area (SMSA). Data items for the latter are grouped into population-size categories. Population, housing, governments, manufactures, retail trade, wholesale trade, selected services, mineral industries, and agriculture data are represented, as well as statistics from many other government and private agencies. Also featured are descriptive text, explanatory notes, source citations, and appendixes.

COUNTY AND CITY DATA BOOK

The *County and City Data Book* (C 3.134/2; item 151) presents statistics for each county in the United States, almost 300 SMSAs, and over 900 incorporated cities having 25,000 inhabitants or more. In addition, information for census divisions and regions, states, and standard federal administrative regions is provided. Based largely on the decennial and quinquennial censuses, revisions of this volume are not up to date.

CONGRESSIONAL DISTRICT DATA BOOK

The *Congressional District Data Book* (C 3.134/2; item 151) presents population and housing data from the decennial census along with voting information from recent presidential and congressional elections. One valuable feature of the *Congressional District Data Book* is a series of maps for each state showing district boundaries. Like the *County and City Data Book*, this volume tends to suffer a time lag. The information in the current basic volume is supplemented by a Congressional District Data (CDD) series (C 3.134/4; item 140-B-1).

THE HISTORICAL ATLAS OF UNITED STATES CONGRESSIONAL DISTRICTS: 1789-1983

The Historical Atlas (Riverside, NJ: Macmillan Professional and Library Services), compiled by Kenneth C. Martis, provides a complete set of congressional district boundary maps for each of the ninty-seven Congresses, with the names of over 10,000 elected representatives and their districts. Other features include the history, development, and theory of geographical representation in Congress; inset maps for urban districts; session dates, number of seats, boundary changes, and dates of admission and secession of states for each Congress; detailed historical information on redistricting laws; and indexes. Begun as a WPA project in 1936, this valuable source was abandoned at the beginning of World War II and was completed by Martis almost a half a century after it was started.

STATISTICS SOURCES

Statistics Sources (Detroit, MI: Gale Research Company) is revised periodically and is subtitled *A Subject Guide to Data on Industrial, Business, Social, Educational, Financial, and Other Topics for the United States and Internationally*. In addition to covering international sources like the United Nations and its specialized agencies, *Statistics Sources* includes federal information—periodicals, the publications of major censuses, the *Statistical Abstract* and its "Supplements" noted above, and a section on machine-readable data sources.[16]

INDEX TO STATISTICAL SOURCES

The single best index to federal statistical publications is *American Statistics Index* (Chapter 6). Published by Congressional Information Service, Inc. (Bethesda, MD), ASI indexes and abstracts virtually all statistical sources issued by federal government entities, including over 800 statistical periodicals. The monthly issues cumulate into annual index and abstract volumes. The index volumes consist of several separate indexes by subjects and names, categories (economic, demographic, and geographic breakdowns), titles, and agency report numbers. The abstracts provide full bibliographic information, a description of the publication's purpose and subject matter, and an outline of specific contents such as tables and articles referencing specific page ranges. The *ASI Microfiche*

Library and *CIS Periodicals on Microfiche* provide the full text of publications indexed in the ASI volumes. Moreover, ASI is online through ORBIT and DIALOG.

STATISTICAL PRODUCTS OF SELECTED AGENCIES

As the contents of any issue of *American Statistics Index* demonstrate, there are numerous agencies that generate statistics related to their own programs. In addition, there are several large agencies that have as their primary function the collection and dissemination of data for their own publishing programs and those of other federal entities. These are called "general purpose statistical agencies" and number among them the Bureau of the Census and the Bureau of Labor Statistics. The following represents a selection of the more important products and services within this general purpose category.

BUREAU OF THE CENSUS

Of all the vast statistical generating federal machinery, that of the Census Bureau is best known. Census publications are the core of a library's collection of statistical data. The information that is obtained from the products and services of the Census Bureau is used in a variety of ways by government and the private sector. As the principal general purpose statistical agency of the federal government, the Bureau's primary function is to collect, process, compile, and disseminate statistical data for the use of other government agencies, groups in the private sector, and the general public. The Bureau publishes more statistics than other agencies do, covers a wider range of subjects, and serves a greater variety of needs. Moreover, Article I, Section 2 of the Constitution, construed by the one-person, one-vote principle established by the U.S. Supreme Court, requires congressional redistricting based upon population shifts recorded in the decennial census.[17]

The first census was taken in 1790 and was repeated each succeeding decade. In 1902 the Bureau of the Census was established as a permanent office (32 *Stat.* 51). By laws codified in Title 13 of the *United States Code* and in virtue of Article I, Section 2 of the Constitution, the Bureau is enjoined to take a census of the population every ten years. Furthermore, as a result of legislation passed by Congress in 1976, the Census Bureau is authorized to conduct a mid-decade census beginning in 1985 and every ten years thereafter. In approving this legislation, Congress intentionally did not establish the scope and content of the undertaking; rather, the law allows the Secretary of Commerce to conduct a mid-decade statistical program "in such form and content as he may determine," taking into account the needs of the data user community. However, the law specifically prohibits the use of mid-decade census results for apportioning the House of Representatives or delineating congressional districts.[18]

Although the attention of the media focuses upon the decennial census of population and housing, there are other lesser-known censuses taken on a five-year schedule. These quinquennial censuses include agriculture, governments, and the "economic censuses," which comprise retail trade, wholesale trade, service industries, construction industries, manufactures, mineral industries, and transportation, and in 1977 included Outlying Areas, Enterprise Statistics,

Minority-Owned Business Enterprises, and Women-Owned Businesses series. In addition, the Bureau conducts various U.S. and foreign censuses and surveys in its international research and foreign trade programs. Figure 26 summarizes Bureau programs and products as shown in the May 1979 issue of *Factfinder for the Nation.*

Because users need information far more frequently than on a decennial or quinquennial schedule, the Bureau's intercensal activities are continual. Current reports issued annually, quarterly, monthly; special censuses, for example, those requested by local governments; and other surveys and studies update and supplement the major five- and ten-year counts.

In the 1970s, reorganization obliged the Superintendent of Documents to reclassify census publications. This reclassification was unfortunate because the created entity requiring a new class stem was itself abolished subsequently, the Bureau was returned to its former place within the Commerce Department hierarchy, and Bureau documents reverted to their original classification.[19] Currently, Census Bureau series are classed in "C3," and virtually every printed census report and study is available to depository libraries in paper copy or on microfiche.

Basic Bibliographic Sources

The *Bureau of the Census Catalog* (C 3.163/3; item 138) is published annually and provides information about selected products which became available to the public during the reported year. Organized in chapters by subjects (agriculture, business, population, foreign trade, etc.), the *Catalog* provides bibliographic data, abstracts, and ordering information for printed reports, computer tapes, microfiche, and maps. Access to the contents of the *Catalog* is through a geographic and a subject index.

Formerly the *Catalog* was issued quarterly with monthly supplements. Beginning January 1981, a new periodical, *Monthly Product Announcement* (C 3.163/7; item 138), was published which lists all Bureau products that became available during the previous month. Organized by publications and data files, entries in MPA include title, series designation, number of pages, and price.

Data User News (C 3.238; item 148-C), a monthly newsletter issued by the Bureau, keeps users informed about current censuses and surveys; products and programs, including computer tape files and other unpublished data sources; seminars and conferences the Bureau conducts periodically; contact sources for specific Bureau activities and products; and statistical products available from other federal agencies.

Factfinder for the Nation (C 3.252; item 131-F) is a set of topical brochures published irregularly describing the range of census materials available on a given subject. Titles in this numbered series include *Data for Small Communities* (No. 22), *Construction Statistics* (No. 9), *Reference Sources* (No. 5), and *Housing Starts* (No. 6). Individual titles are revised from time to time.

(Text continues on page 225)

Figure 26
Census Bureau Programs and Products

Statistical program	Censuses			Surveys, estimates, and projections			
	Examples of data	Publication areas	Frequency	Series	Examples of data	Publication areas	Frequency
POPULATION	Age, sex, race, ethnicity, marital status, household relationship, education, place of birth, year of immigration, language, residence and activity 5 years ago, disability, children ever born, marital history, employment status, hours worked in previous week, transportation to work, job activity, industry and occupation, income	U.S., regions, divisions, States, SMSA's, counties, places, urbanized areas, minor civil divisions (MCD's), census tracts, blocks	Years ending in "0"	Population Characteristics, P-20	School enrollment, fertility, mobility	U.S.	Annual
				Population Estimates and Projections, P-25	Population	U.S.	Monthly
					Age, sex, race	U.S.	Annual
					Population, income	Counties, specified places	Annual
				Special Studies, P-23	Youth, aging, female family heads	U.S.	Irregular
				Federal-State Cooperative Program for Population Estimates, P-26	Births, deaths, net migration, population estimates	Counties, metropolitan areas	Annual
				Farm Population, P-27	Age, race, employment characteristics	U.S.	Annual
				Special Censuses, P-28	Age, sex, race	Counties, places	Contract
				Consumer Income, P-60	Money income, low-income households	U.S.	Annual
				Collected for other Federal agencies	Labor force characteristics, health, crime, criminal justice systems and correctional institutions, longitudinal studies of socioeconomic changes, voting, education, income, government tax effort	U.S., States, large cities, governmental units	Periodic

Figure 26 (cont'd)

Statistical program	Censuses			Surveys, estimates, and projections			
	Examples of data	Publication areas	Frequency	Series	Examples of data	Publication areas	Frequency
HOUSING	Rooms, plumbing facilities, tenure, value, contract rent, telephone, vacancy status, heating equipment, water sources, fuels, automobiles, shelter costs for homeowners	Same as above	Years ending in "0"	Components of Inventory Change	New construction, conversions, mergers, demolitions, recent movers' characteristics	U.S., regions, 15 SMSA's	Years ending in "0"
				Residential Finance	Financing of non-farm homes; characteristics of mortgages, properties, owners	U.S., regions, inside and outside SMSA's	Years ending in "0"
				Housing Vacancy Survey, H-111	Vacancy rates, characteristics of vacant units	U.S., regions, inside and outside SMSA's	Quarterly, annual
				Market Absorption of Apartments, H-130	Absorption rates by size, rent, facilities	U.S.	Quarterly, annual
				Annual Housing Survey, H-150	Characteristics of housing (general, financial, quality), recent movers	U.S., regions, inside and outside SMSA's, urban and rural	Annual
				Annual Housing Survey, H-170	As above	60 selected SMSA's, with central cities and suburbs	Annual
AGRICULTURE	Acreage, land use and value, equipment, production, sales, expenses, debts, operator characteristics, agricultural services	U.S., regions, divisions, States, counties	1974, 1978, then years ending in "2" and "7"	Farm Population P-27	Age, race, employment characteristics	U.S.	Annual
	Irrigation, drainage, horticulture, farm finance	States	10 years	Cotton Ginnings, A-10	Ginnings	States	Seasonal
				Cotton Ginnings, A-20	Ginnings	Counties	7 per yr.
				Cotton Ginnings	Ginnings	U.S.	Annual
CONSTRUCTION INDUSTRIES	Employees, payrolls, receipts, expenditures, assets, depreciation, project location and ownership	U.S., regions, divisions, States	Years ending in "2" and "7"	Housing Starts, C-20	Ownership, type of construction, permits, mobile home shipments, apartment building characteristics	U.S., regions, inside and outside SMSA's	Monthly
				New Residential Construction, C-21	Estimated number of units	20 SMSA's	Quarterly

Figure 26 (cont'd)

Category	Publication	Content	Geographic coverage	Frequency
CONSTRUCTION INDUSTRIES (Con.)	Housing Completions, C-22	No. of units	U.S., regions, metropolitan/ nonmetropolitan	Monthly
	New One-Family Homes Sold and For Sale, C-25	Sales	U.S.	Monthly
		Financing	U.S.	Quarterly
	Characteristics of New Housing, C-25	Physical and financial characteristics	U.S., regions, inside and outside SMSA's	Annual
	Price Index of New One-Family Houses Sold, C-27	Changes in sales, prices by physical characteristics	U.S.	Quarterly
			Regions	Annual
	Value of New Construction Put in Place, C-30	Private and public buildings, utilities, nonbuilding construction, residential alterations	U.S.	Monthly
	Housing Authorized by Building Permits and Public Contracts, C-40	Excludes hotels, motels, institutions	U.S., regions, divisions, SMSA's, places	Monthly, annual
	Housing Units Authorized for Demolition in Permit-Issuing Places, C-45	Demolition, new construction	U.S., regions, divisions, SMSA's, selected cities	Annual
	Residential Alterations and Repairs, C-50	Expenditures	U.S.	Quarterly
		Expenditures by type of construction, other characteristics	U.S.	Annual
RETAIL TRADE		Kind of business, sales, payroll, organization, employment, size, specialized data	U.S., States, SMSA's, counties, places, selected MCD's, CBD's, MRC's	Year ending in "2" and "7"
	Monthly Retail Trade, BR	Estimates of sales and receivables	U.S., regions, divisions; selected States, large SMSA's, and cities	Monthly
		Summary	Same as above	Annual
	Monthly Department Store Sales in Selected Areas, BD	Comparative sales by month and year	200 areas	Monthly
	Advance Monthly Retail Sales, BR-11	Trend analysis	U.S., selected SMSA's, and cities	Monthly

Figure 26 (cont'd)

Statistical program	Censuses			Surveys, estimates, and projections			
	Examples of data	Publication areas	Frequency	Series	Examples of data	Publication areas	Frequency
WHOLESALE TRADE	Kind of business, sales, payroll, employment, organization, size, expenses, inventories, specialized data	U.S., States, SMSA's, counties, selected places	Years ending in "2" and "7"	Monthly Wholesale Trade, BW	Sales, inventories	U.S., divisions	Monthly
				Canned Food: Stock, Pack, Shipments, B1	Comparative data	U.S.	5 times a year
				Green Coffee: Inventories, Imports, Roastings, BG-41	Data for roasters, importers, and dealers	U.S.	Quarterly
SERVICE INDUSTRIES	Receipts or revenue, payroll, expenses, employment, organization, specialized data	U.S., States, SMSA's, counties, cities	Years ending in "2" and "7"	Monthly Selected Service Receipts, BS	Comparative receipts	U.S.	Monthly
TRANSPORTATION	The Census of Transportation consists of four surveys			National Travel Survey	Volume, characteristics of travel and travelers, destinations, accommodations	U.S., regions, selected States and foreign areas	Years ending in "2" and "7"
				Truck Inventory and Use Survey	Characteristics, use, fleet size, area of operation, products, mileage	U.S., divisions, States	
				Commodity Transportation Survey	Manufacturers' intercity shipments	States	
				Motor Carrier Survey	Public carriers not subject to Federal regulation	U.S., States	
				Annual Housing Survey, H-150	Transportation to work, travel time, distance	U.S., regions, selected SMSA's	Annual
MANUFACTURES	Employment, hours, payroll, inventories, assets, expenditures, costs, contract work, product shipments, selected characteristics	U.S., regions, divisions, States, SMSA's, counties, cities	Years ending in "2" and "7"	Annual Survey of Manufactures	Same as census, except product class shipments	U.S., States, SMSA's, large industrial counties, selected cities	Annual
				Current Industrial Reports (a series of more than 100 separate reports, by subject)	Detailed commodity data, pollution abatement, plant capacity, research and development	U.S., some for States, SMSA's	Annual, quarterly, monthly
					Monthly shipments, inventories and orders	U.S.	Monthly

Figure 26 (cont'd)

Statistical program	Sources	Series	Examples of data	Publication areas	Frequency
MINERAL INDUSTRIES			Employment, hours, payroll, expenses, capital expenditures, energy consumption, assets, organization, selected characteristics	U.S., regions, States	Years ending in "2" and "7"
		Annual Survey of Oil and Gas	Field exploration, development, production	U.S., on and off shore	Annual
GOVERNMENTS			Organization, taxable property values, assessment-sales ratios, tax rates, employment, labor-management relations, payrolls, revenues, expenditures	U.S., States, counties, places, MCD's, school and special districts	Years ending in "2" and "7"
	Popularly elected officials			Same as above	
		Government Employment, GE	Comparative employment and payroll	U.S., States, counties, places, special districts	Annual
		Government Finance, GF	Tax collections, finances	Same as above	Annual
		Finances of Selected Public Employee Retirement Systems, GR	Assets, receipts, benefits, withdrawal payments	100 major State and local systems	Quarterly
		Quarterly Summary of State and Local Tax Revenue, GT	Collection by type of tax and level of government	States; selected SMSA's, counties, local areas	Quarterly
		State and Local Government Special Studies, GSS	Labor-management relations, criminal justice expenditures, property values	Varies	Periodic

Surveys or reports

Statistical program	Sources	Series	Examples of data	Publication areas	Frequency
FOREIGN TRADE	Customs declarations, lading documents	Summary, detailed, and annual reports on imports and exports	Imports, exports, bunker fuels, vessel entrances and clearances, means of transportation, imported cotton manufactures, trade with Puerto Rico and U.S. possessions	U.S., world areas	Monthly and annual
GENERAL ECONOMIC	Various economic censuses	Minority-Owned Business Enterprises, MB	Basic economic data for Black, Spanish-origin, Asian American, American Indian, other minorities	U.S., divisions, States, SMSA's, counties and cities with 100 or more minority firms	Years ending in "2" and "7"
		Women-Owned Businesses, WB	Basic economic data	U.S., divisions, States, counties, SMSA's, cities	
		Enterprise Statistics, ES	Establishment-company relationships, centralized management and support services	U.S., selected areas	
	Annual surveys and administrative records	County Business Patterns, CBP	Employment, size of establishment, payrolls	U.S., selected areas	Annual

Figure 26 (cont'd)

Statistical program	Sources	Surveys or reports			
		Series	Examples of data	Publication areas	Frequency
INTERNATIONAL RESEARCH	Foreign censuses, surveys, estimates and projections.	Research Documents, RD World Population, WP Country Demographic Profiles, DP Family Planning Profiles, FP	Estimates and projections	Foreign countries	Periodic
		International Population Statistics Reports, P-90; International Population Reports, P-91	Population and labor force estimates, analysis, and bibliography	Foreign countries	Periodic
		International Population Reports, P-95	Population, labor force, wages, statistical systems, economic subjects		
DEMOGRAPHIC AND ECONOMIC ANALYSIS	Various U.S. and foreign censuses and surveys	Social Indicators	Health, education, housing, population, income, crime, etc.	U.S.	Periodic
		Agreed Basic Statistics	Population estimates and projections	Foreign countries	Periodic
		Foreign Economic Reports	Input-output and gross value data, analysis of economic subjects		
GEOGRAPHIC	U.S. demographic and economic censuses	Maps, GE-50	Socioeconomic characteristics (race, income, education, etc.)	Counties	Periodic
		Maps, GE-70	Urban/rural population distribution	U.S.	Periodic
			Older Americans, heating fuel	Counties	
		Urban Atlas, GE-80	Socioeconomic characteristics	Selected SMSA's by census tract	Periodic
		Congressional District Atlas	Boundaries and indexes, maps	Congressional districts	Each Congress

The *Bureau of the Census Catalog of Publications, 1790-1972* is a massive volume which provides a comprehensive historical bibliography of sources for Census Bureau statistics covering these years. This volume combines the previously issued *Catalog of United States Census Publications, 1790-1945*, prepared by Henry J. Dubester, Chief, Census Library Project, Library of Congress, with the *Bureau of the Census Catalog of Publications, 1946-1972*, which is a compilation of data published in the annual issues of the *Bureau of the Census Catalogs* from 1946 to 1972.

Format and Availability

In addition to the conventional printed reports, census data are increasingly available in microform, computer tape, and data maps. While printed information is available from GPO, data files and special tabulations are available by contacting the Data User Services Division, Customer Services (Publications), Bureau of the Census, Washington, DC 20233. A useful reference source, the *Directory of Data Files* (C 3.262; item 148-F) is issued in looseleaf form and contains abstracts describing summary statistics, microdata, and geographic reference data as well as software. Available to depository institutions, the *Directory* may be purchased from Customer Services at the above address, and subscription to the basic manual includes periodic updates announcing new files. Customer Services also makes available deposit accounts for the convenience of data users; these accounts permit the ordering of data files, technical documentation, microfiche, paper prints from microfiche, photocopies of unpublished tables, and unpublished maps without sending a check each time an order is placed.

Many Census Bureau series are available to depository libraries in printed form, but some items (for example, the Women-Owned Businesses series) are available on microfiche only. Moreover, the Bureau is said to maintain some 120 census depository libraries "chosen on the basis of population in the case of a city library, or enrollment in the case of a college or university library, as well as on the basis of distance from the nearest Government Depository Library." A census depository library listing can be obtained from the Bureau's Customer Services. Other sources of availability of census materials include the Bureau's State Data Center Program, the National Clearinghouse for Census Data Services, Census Bureau Regional Information Services, and Department of Commerce District Offices.[20]

Earlier population census schedules from 1790 through 1910 are available to the public on microfilm at the National Archives and its regional centers. Most of the 1890 schedules, however, were destroyed by fire in 1921. Researchers looking for specific names in the 1790 census should consult the publication *Heads of Families at the First Census of the United States Taken in the Year 1790*. In the intradecennial years, particularly in the nineteenth century, a number of state and territorial censuses were taken. These are described in Henry J. Dubester's *State Censuses: An Annotated Bibliography of Censuses Taken after the year 1790, by States and Territories of the United States*. An appendix in that volume provides information on the location of existing records.

Personal Data Search

The Bureau maintains a staff of employees at Pittsburg, Kansas, whose function is to search the census files from 1900 through 1980 and provide at a nominal cost personal data from these records to individuals who lack other documents of birth or citizenship. These transcripts are used for a variety of purposes — to qualify for old-age assistance, to get jobs, to obtain naturalization papers, to get passports, to establish a claim to an inheritance, to get an insurance policy, or to trace ancestry. Applications may be mailed directly to the Personal Census Services Branch, Pittsburg, Kansas 66762.

Census Publications in Microform

Retrospective editions of census materials in a microformat have been published by the government and by private companies. They include the following:

The National Archives (Washington, DC) has the first eleven censuses, 1790-1890, on 35mm positive microfilm. In 1974 the Archives opened its 1900 census records to individuals, and in 1982 announced the lifting of all restrictions on access to the 1910 records. The latter are available on microfilm (with Soundex or Miracode indexes) from the National Archives Trust Fund, Washington, DC. Research Publications, Inc. (Woodbridge, Connecticut) sells decennial census publications, 1790-1970, on 35mm positive microfilm. Congressional Information Service, Inc. (Bethesda, MD) offers a collection of census reports and serials (exclusive of decennial materials) covering the period 1820-1967. The collection is divided into two parts. Part 1 covers the period 1820-1945 and is based on Dubester's *Catalog of United States Census Publications, 1790-1945*. Part 2 covers the years 1946-1967 and is based on the *Bureau of the Census Catalog of Publications, 1946-1972*. Both parts are divided into sections representing specific censuses (agriculture, foreign trade, transportation, etc.) and may be purchased by individual sections. Part 1 contains about 2,500 reports on 5,924 fiche, and Part 2 contains approximately 400 reports, for which there are 4,226 fiche and 181 reels of microfilm for Section III (foreign trade) only. Moreover, Congressional Information Service sells a comprehensive microfiche file of the 1970 decennial census, available as a single collection or in three separate parts: population, housing, or population and housing.

The 1980 Census

On June 5, 1982, a wooded park in De Soto, Missouri was officially dedicated as the population center of the United States. The population center is the imaginary point where a flat, rigid map of the nation would balance if identical weights were placed on it representing the location of each person counted in the 1980 census. The selection of the park on the edge of De Soto marks the first time the population center has been located west of the Mississippi.

The census of population is the oldest of the censuses taken, and it has been enumerated every ten years since 1790. The first census of housing was taken in 1940, although counts of "dwelling houses" were obtained in earlier censuses of population. Beginning in 1940, a housing census has been taken every ten years in conjunction with the population count. Today, published reports covering both results usually refer to the combined census of population and housing.

The 1980 census of population and housing, an official count of the total number of people in the United States as of April 1, 1980, was largely conducted by questionnaires mailed to over 90 percent of households throughout the nation. In a few areas, primarily those with thinly settled population, "enumerators" went from door to door to obtain the information directly from the households. Two questionnaires were used in 1980: a "short form" containing questions asked of all households, and a "long form" containing additional questions that approximately one out of every six households received.

A vast amount of detailed information was generated thereby.[21] Tabulations of the 1980 data were made available in the variety of formats noted above. The data presented in printed reports were similar in kind and quantity to the data contained in reports from the 1970 census. Arranged in tables, population and housing characteristics are given for specified geographic areas, such as the number of rented housing units in a census tract, the number of persons sixty-five years of age or older in a city, or the total population of a county. In many series there is one report for each state plus a U.S. summary report; in others, one report for each SMSA; in still others, reports are by topic rather than by area.

The publications of the 1980 census are released under the following categories: *1980 Census of Population and Housing, 1980 Census of Population*, and *1980 Census of Housing*. A number of the population census reports contain some housing data, and, conversely, a number of the housing census reports contain some population data.

For the *1980 Census of Population and Housing* there are *Preliminary Reports* presenting population and housing unit counts compiled in the census district offices. These are followed by *Advance Reports*, provisional population counts classified by race and Spanish origin and final housing unit counts prior to their publication in final form. The *Advance Reports* figures supersede the preliminary counts. *Final Reports* in this category present population and housing unit totals and sample-estimate data for blocks, census tracts, governmental units, SMSAs, provisional estimates of social, economic, and housing characteristics, and congressional districts of the Ninety-eighth Congress.

For the *1980 Census of Population* there are *Final Reports* presenting final population counts and statistics on characteristics of the population: number of inhabitants, household relationships, social and economic statistics, detailed characteristics, and a series of subject reports for racial and ethnic groups, type of residence, fertility, migration, employment, income, etc. Supplementary reports deal with specific populations subjects such as nonpermanent residents by state and county, race of the populations by state, etc.

For the *1980 Census of Housing* there are *Final Reports* presenting final housing unit counts and statistics on housing characteristics. Like the *Final Reports* of the *1980 Census of Population*, housing data cover the United States, each of the fifty states, the District of Columbia, Puerto Rico, and the outlying areas of Guam, Virgin Islands, American Samoa, and the Trust Territory of the Pacific Islands. Included are general and detailed housing characteristics, metropolitan statistics on microfiche, subject reports, components of inventory change, residential finance, and a supplementary report on selected housing characteristics by states and counties.

In addition to the above reports, issued in print or on microfiche, results of the 1980 census are also provided on computer tape for the United States and

Puerto Rico. *Summary Tape Files* (STFs) present extensive cross-tabulations that provide greater subject and geographic detail than the printed or microfiche reports. There are five STFs, and the amount of geographic and subject detail presented varies. STFs 1 and 2 contain complete-count data; STFs 3, 4, and 5 contain sample-estimate data. For example, STF 1 provides 321 cells of complete-count population and housing data, while STF 2 contains 2,292 cells. The term *cell* is used by the Bureau to refer to the number of subject statistics provided for each geographical area, and the number of cells is indicative of the complexity of the subject content of the file. These data include the United States, regions, divisions, states, SMSAs, urbanized areas, SCSAs, congressional districts, counties, county subdivisions, places, census tracts, enumeration districts in unblocked areas, and blocks and block groups in blocked areas.

Other computer tape files include state-by-state tabulations for legislative reapportionment and redistricting; an extract of STF 1 for those who need a master list of geographic codes and areas; GBF/DIME (geographic base file/dual independent map encoding) files, computerized versions of the Metropolitan Map Series (*infra*), Public Use Sample (PUS) files of microdata containing most population and housing characteristics as shown on a sample of individual census records; and others. PUS files are purged of names, addresses, and other information that would tend to identify individuals in accordance with the confidentiality provision set forth in 13 U.S.C. 9.

It is important to remember that computer tape files contain essentially the *same information* as that found in the printed reports or on microfiche—but in much greater detail. In general, computer tapes are of value to those users who need to manipulate, aggregate, or otherwise extensively process census data. Some of the computer tape products are available on microfiche; for example, the STF microfiche are issued a state at a time, followed by the national-level fiche. These include data from the STF 1 file set and tabulations for legislative redistricting.

Census maps are necessary for virtually all users of small-area census data to locate specific geographic areas and for analytic purposes. Metropolitan Map Series maps cover the urbanized portion of SMSAs. Each map sheet shows the names of streets and other significant features, boundaries and names or numbers of places, minor civil and census county divisions, congressional districts, census tracts, enumeration districts, and blocks. GBF/DIME files, noted above, are computerized representations of the Metropolitan Map Series with block-by-block address ranges, ZIP codes, and X-Y coordinate values at intersections. County maps cover those portions of counties not included in the Metropolitan Map Series and all of those counties outside of SMSAs. County maps are usually reproductions of maps obtained from individual state highway departments with census geography superimposed. Place maps cover all 1980 census-incorporated and census-designated places not included on the Metropolitan Map Series. Usually based on maps supplied by local agencies, place maps identify streets and show boundaries for places, minor civil divisions, congressional districts, enumeration districts, and, when appropriate, census tracts and blocks. Tract outline maps show the boundaries and numbers or names of census tracts, counties, and all places with a population of 10,000 or more for all SMSAs. County subdivision maps of states show the location and names of counties and minor civil divisions or census county divisions; there is generally one map sheet for each state. The Metropolitan Map Series, tract outline, and county subdivision maps are issued with specific census publications but may also be purchased separately. However, county and place maps are not published but are available on special order for the cost of reproduction.

Three kinds of materials from the 1980 census are available on microfiche: data from selected summary tape files, maps, and printed publications. Selected data files such as block groups, enumeration districts, election precincts, and ZIP code areas are available on computer output microfiche (COM) arranged in tabular form with header and stub entries identifying each data item. The microfiche of selected STFs present data hierarchically for the basic summary levels—states, counties, county subdivisions, places, census tracts, and block groups or enumeration districts. Since no printed data are available for the latter two levels, small area data users will find this microfiche of value. As noted, maps are critical to the use of census data for small areas. Tracts, blocks, enumeration districts, and other small statistical areas can be identified only through maps designed for that purpose. For ease of storage and user convenience, maps are available on microfiche from the Bureau. Microfiche of maps defining blocks are included as part of the microfiche of block statistics reports and are grouped and sold in conjunction with the microfiche of summary tape data. Those maps not produced on microfiche oblige users to refer to printed maps issued by GPO for the definition of blocks, block groups, tracts, and larger units in areas covered by block statistics. The microfiche of published reports are sold through the Superintendent of Documents, while the microfiche of summary tape data and unpublished maps are sold through the Bureau's Customer Services.[22]

Originally, GPO had hoped to offer depository libraries a choice of microfiche or paper format for the distribution of most of the 1980 census publications issued in paper by the Bureau. The Depository Library Council in 1981 approved a resolution requesting that the Public Printer "communicate to the Census Bureau the importance to the library community and to the public at large, of having the text and statistical tables of the 1980 *Census Tracts, Block Statistics*, and *Detailed Characteristics* available in paper copy." When these concerns were communicated to the Bureau, the director responded by citing "severe budgetary pressures" facing the Bureau. Stating that the "census tract reports will be paper as originally planned," the director did not "see a likelihood of paper for other reports for which only microfiche is planned."[23] In July 1982, GPO announced that detailed population characteristics (PC 80-1-D) and metropolitan housing characteristics (HC 80-2) will be distributed in either paper copy or on microfiche to depository libraries. However, block statistics information (PHC 80-1) was distributed to depository institutions on *Shipping Lists* 154-M, 155-M, 156-M, and 157-M and included forty-eight reports on microfiche.

State Data Center Program

The State Data Center Program was initiated by the Bureau in 1978 to improve access to the many statistical products available from the agency. The Bureau furnishes products, training in data access and use, technical assistance, and consultation to the states, which, in turn, disseminate the products and provide assistance in their use within the state. The organization of each State Data Center (SDC) varies from state to state but generally includes a major state executive or planning agency, a major state university, and the state library.

Similarly, the structure of the individual state programs varies, but in all cases consists of a primary agency and several affiliates. These serve as the principal service, delivery, and coordinating units. A listing of SDC lead agencies may be obtained from the Bureau's Customer Services. In addition, *Data User News* carries listings of Center lead agencies and affiliates periodically.

Data Processing Centers

A number of Summary Tape Processing Centers in the private and public sector process Census Bureau machine-readable data for users by creating their own computer software package and by establishing their own cost structure for services. Obtaining data from one of these organizations may be no more expensive than buying the products from the Bureau. Moreover, Processing Centers, which are user-oriented, may provide information more specifically related to one's needs.

Centers are not franchised, established, or supported by the Bureau. They have developed through local initiatives and respond to needs recognized by their organizers. They are located in state agencies, special laboratories, market research organizations, and universities. Cooperative ventures are common, wherein organization members of a data user group will employ their collective purchasing power to acquire machine-readable copies of Bureau surveys and censuses, write a file to meet the needs of members, and make it available at a reduced cost. In the higher education enterprise, notable programs are well established at Princeton University, the University of Florida Libraries, and at other university centers; and they have been serving census data users both within and without the academic community capably.

Moreover, private industry cooperates with the Bureau to disseminate its products and services. For example, the National Planning Data Corporation of Ithaca, New York rescued a 1980 census program that the Bureau was forced to cancel because of budgetary problems. The firm paid the Bureau $250,000 to tabulate 1980 census data for the nation's five-digit ZIP code areas. The Corporation distributed the ZIP code data through a consortium of data users that included retailers, direct mailing organizations, private data firms, an insurance company, a publisher, and a university; and these institutions aided the Corporation in funding the project.

Intercensal Publishing Patterns

The several decennial and quinquennial censuses are supplemented and updated by a variety of annual surveys, current reports, and other studies. They are available from the Bureau's Customer Services or GPO as noted in *Monthly Product Announcement* and the annual *Bureau of the Census Catalog* in the several formats described above. Depository libraries, too, participate in this process through item selection.

A few examples of intercensal publishing illustrate the way in which the Census Bureau accomplishes its mission between major censuses. The series noted below are issued on a periodic or irregular basis, offered to depository libraries under various items, and sold through the Superintendent of Documents.

Current Population Reports (C 3.186) are continuing, up-to-date statistics on population counts, characteristics, and other special studies. Separate series include Population Characteristics (P-20), Special Studies (P-23), Population

Estimates and Projections (P-25), Federal-State Cooperative Program for Population Estimates (P-26), Farm Population (P-27), and Special Censuses (P-28). The latter are taken at the request of city or other local governments.

Current Housing Reports (C 3.215) provide data on various housing characteristics. Separate series include Housing Vacancies (H-111), Housing Characteristics (H-121), and Market Absorption of Apartments (H-130). The *Annual Housing Survey* (AHS) consists of a sample national survey of housing units and a metropolitan area survey of housing units every four years. The latter survey covers sixty SMSAs, of which fifteen are surveyed each year on a rotating basis. The AHS is conducted by the Census Bureau for the Department of Housing and Urban Development (HUD).

Current Business Reports cover data found in the quinquennial economic censuses. The reports present estimates of sales, inventories, and other economic measures for selected business categories and geographic areas. Titles in this series include *Advance Monthly Retail Sales* (C 3.138/4), *Monthly Retail Trade* (C 3.138/3-3), and *Annual Retail Trade* (C 3.138/3-2), all available under item 147-B; and *Monthly Selected Services Receipts*, sold by the Bureau's Customer Services.

County Business Patterns (C 3.204) presents annual information on employment, number and employment size of establishments, and payrolls by two-, three-, and four-digit levels of the Standard Industrial Classification (SIC) for states and counties. The series includes a separate report for the United States, each state, and the District of Columbia, and is sold by the Superintendent of Documents in paper and issued to depository libraries in that format (items 133-A-1 to 133-A-53). In addition, the data by county and by industry are available on computer tape from the Bureau's Customer Services.

Summary

The foregoing is but a small indication of the indefatigable activities of the Census Bureau as they are reflected in the production and distribution of data in printed form, microfiche, computer tape, and maps. And although these publications are listed in the *Monthly Catalog* and *Serials Supplement* to a degree, the most appropriate method of keeping abreast of Census Bureau materials and services is through perusal of current awareness sources like *Data User News, Monthly Product Announcement* and through the accessing capabilities of *American Statistics Index*.

BUREAU OF LABOR STATISTICS

Another large general-purpose statistical agency is the Bureau of Labor Statistics (BLS) of the Labor Department. BLS generates a multitude of data on such crucial aspects of the economy as wholesale prices, consumer prices, unemployment, work stoppages, occupations, productivity and costs, union wages and benefits, etc. These figures appear in press releases and, later, in monthly, quarterly, or annual publications, most of which are available to depository libraries or by sales subscription. And when figures are released on a specific indicator, these data are accorded swift and solemn treatment by the news media. Some examples of BLS publications will indicate their importance and sociopolitical volatility.

Employment and Earnings (L 2.41/2; item 768-B) provides monthly data on employment, hours, earnings, and labor turnover for the nation as a whole, for individual states, and for more than 200 local areas. The headline news is the *rate* of unemployment, a percentage showing that portion of the labor force actively seeking work but unable to find it. The present formula for measuring unemployment is but one of several measures devised by BLS statisticians, designated U-1 through U-7, and these series are regularly published in tabular form. As one measures from U-1 to U-7, the rate of unemployment grows progressively higher. The official rate is a middle ground, called U-5, and is defined as "total unemployed as a percent of the civilian labor force." It includes anyone who is not employed but who made specific efforts to find employment sometime during the preceding four weeks.[24]

CPI Detailed Report (L 2.38/3; item 768-F), a monthly, measures the price change of a constant market basket of goods and services over a period of time. The data are used to measure retail price changes affecting the purchasing power of the dollar, which is to say the rate of inflation or deflation. During periods of rising prices, it is an index of inflation and is used to measure the success or failure of government economic policy. Like employment figures, the Consumer Price Index (CPI) is the object of media attention. The CPI began during World War I (then called the "cost-of-living" index, a term still used by the media) as a way of determining a fair wage scale for the shipbuilding industry, and it has undergone several major revisions in methodology since then. Each revision has been called an "improvement" by the BLS. Despite these improvements, the determination of the index population and the categories of goods measured remains controversial and is the subject of many scholarly analyses. Much is at stake in the construction of the CPI. Millions of workers are covered by collective bargaining contracts which provide for increases in wage rates based on increases in the CPI. Various federal statutes mandate adjustments in wages and benefits as the CPI rises or falls. And the CPI affects the official definition of poverty, which becomes the basis of eligibility in numerous health and welfare programs at the federal, state, and local government level.

Producer Prices and Price Indexes (L 2.61; item 771-B), a companion periodical to the *CPI Detailed Report*, was formerly called the *Wholesale Price Index* and shows monthly price movements at the primary market level, including statistical tables of summary indexes for groups of products and for most commodities. Fluctuations in producer prices foreshadow CPI rates and are closely watched and analyzed by government, business, and the press.

The *Monthly Labor Review* (L 2.6; item 770) covers most BLS series and carries articles on employment, the labor force, wages, prices, productivity, unit labor costs, collective bargaining, workers satisfaction, social indicators, and labor developments abroad. Indexed in many indexing and abstracting services, it is perhaps the most respected government periodical extant.

The *Occupational Outlook Quarterly* (L 2.70/4; item 770-A) contains articles on new occupations, training opportunities, salary trends, career counseling programs, and the like. It updates occupational information between editions of the well-known *Occupational Outlook Handbook* (L 2.3; item 768-A-1), a biennial publication in the numbered BLS Bulletins series. This series includes important recurring studies such as *Area Wage Survey, Major Collective Bargaining Agreements, Wage Chronology,* and *Analysis of Work Stoppages.*

Current Wage Developments (L 2.44; item 768-D) is a monthly account of wage and benefit changes resulting from collective bargaining settlements and unilateral management decisions. It includes the appropriate statistical tables and special reports on wage trends.

Data from the *CPI Detailed Report, Monthly Labor Review, Producer Prices and Price Indexes, Employment and Earnings*, and related information are online through DIALOG. And *American Statistics Index*, which provides the most comprehensive database for federal statistics, is online through ORBIT and DIALOG.

OTHER STATISTICAL COMPENDIA

For virtually every government activity there are statistical compilations that vary in periodicity from daily to yearly and beyond. The *Daily Treasury Statement* (T 1.5; item 923-A-2) provides information on the cash and debt operations of the United States Treasury. *Crime in the United States* (J 1.14/7; item 722) is the much used (and abused) annual compilation of Uniform Crime Reports submitted to and analyzed by the FBI. *Economic Indicators* (Y 4.Ec7:Ec7; item 997) furnishes monthly data on leading indicators such as prices, wages, production, business activity, credit, money, and federal finance. The *Survey of Current Business* (C 59.11; item 228) provides monthly information on trends in industry, the business outlook, and other statistical measures relevant to the business world. *Business Conditions Digest* (C 59.9; item 131-A) covers 500 economic indicators and is online through ADP Network Services, Inc., and Chase Econometrics/Interactive Data. The *Digest of Educational Statistics* (ED 1.113; item 460-A-10) is an annual coverage of enrollment, number of teachers, finances, and educational achievement for all levels of education. The list is seemingly endless.

Fortunately, the general sources of information like the *Statistical Abstract of the United States* and the indexing resources available through ASI permit the user to manage this vast statistical outpouring. The larger problem, however, is that of interpretation. The statistics found in federal government publications come from a variety of sources. Statistics produced by trade associations, commercial enterprises, and corporations reflect an attempt to persuade the user in support of policies favorable to the organization's competitive position. Statistics obtained by government from non-federal sources procured through contracts and grants—especially those labeled "research"—are seldom subject to review because the granting agency lacks the talent and personnel to evaluate the qualifications of bidders and academicians skilled at writing proposals. And statistics generated by government agencies tend to reflect a self-serving motivation to survive or to build an empire.

Although there is outright fabrication of data in any number of government publications, not all information found between the covers of a government document or in machine-readable form is fatally flawed. However, we are never sure that the statistics we must use achieve a comfortable degree of reliability. Therefore, it is important to read carefully the footnotes, source notes, and explanatory material that generally accompany the tables and charts. In any analysis of statistical data, the aphorism attributed to Disraeli should be kept in mind: "There are three kinds of lies: lies, damned lies, and statistics."[25]

GOVERNMENT PERIODICALS

Government periodicals, defined for this section as publications with semiannual or more frequent issuance, are an underrated and underutilized category of federal documentation. They provide current information of reference and research value, indicate public policy, contain articles, reviews, and many other useful features, and serve as indexing and abstracting sources. Despite these characteristics, the indexing of federal periodicals has been haphazard until recent times, and even today the bibliographic apparatus for document retrieval and information retrieval of government periodicals is largely unsatisfactory.

Although government periodicals are listed in the *Serials Supplement* and in *Price List 36* (Chapter 3), those sources account for a relatively small percentage of total federal periodical publishing. Indeed, it is safe to say that there are no reliable figures on the total number of periodicals issued by the entities of the federal establishment. One egregious example of this failure of accountability will suffice.

In 1972 Senator J. William Fulbright ordered an investigation of the number of periodicals published by the Department of Defense (DoD) and the military services. Units of DoD and the armed services reported that as of FY 1972 a total of 1,402 periodicals—not including newspapers—were being published at an annual cost of almost $13 million. This figure was startling even to the veteran senator, who had become resigned to dealing with DoD appropriations of magnitudes approaching the renowned googol. Fulbright ordered the list of the 1,402 Pentagon magazines to be read into the *Congressional Record*. Unfortunately, it is not a very useful list for librarians since it appeared in the CR neither in alphabetical nor logical order.[26]

Fulbright's revelation prompted a crackdown by then Secretary of Defense Melvin Laird, who expressed a desire to see "the Pentagon's proliferating publishing program brought under control," and by FY 1977 the Pentagon was able to announce that "the number of ... magazines has been cut in half."[27] But inflation has kept the cost of publishing high. Figures on periodical production alone are elusive, but a 1982 OMB report to the Senate Appropriations Committee on Administrative Expenses pegged total spending on periodicals and pamphlets by DoD at about $30 million for FY 1982.[28]

Exacerbating the problem of determining total federal periodical publishing is the lack of adequate indexing of periodicals. While the *Document Catalog* (Chapter 6) and the earlier *Monthly Catalog* selectively indexed the contents of some government periodicals, current *Monthly Catalog* practice involves bibliographic notation only. The 1981 *Serials Supplement*, for example, lists 2,124 titles defined as "publications issued three or more times per year and a select group of annual publications and monographic series titles." Current issues of *Price List 36* include subscription services as well as dated periodicals. While a number of government periodicals are themselves indexing or abstracting services (e.g., *Index Medicus, Energy Research Abstracts, Monthly Checklist of State Publications*), these sources largely cover non-federal government materials. The systematic indexing of certain government periodicals is a phenomenon of the 1970s, with the appearance of two useful resource tools, *Index to U.S. Government Periodicals* and *American Statistics Index*.

INDEX TO U.S. GOVERNMENT PERIODICALS

The *Index to U.S. Government Periodicals* (IUSGP), published by Infordata International Inc., a Chicago-based commercial firm, is subtitled *A Computer-Generated Guide to ... Selected Titles by Author and Subject*. IUSGP indexes close to 200 federal periodicals which, in the opinion of the publisher, offer substantive articles of lasting research and reference value. IUSGP appears in three paperbound quarterlies and an annual hardbound cumulation. A retrospective project involving hardbound annual cumulations is ongoing, and, as of 1981, volumes are available going back to 1970.

Although the articles are not abstracted, the subject indexing is quite good; it is based on a thesaurus developed to meet the indexing requirements which arise from the variety of subject matter. Coverage is eclectic and ranges from highly technical journals such as the *Journal of the National Cancer Institute* to nontechnical magazines for a special audience such as *Airman*. Although the number of federal periodicals indexed is but a fraction of total periodical publishing by the United States government, many periodicals in IUSGP are neither available to depository libraries nor for sale by the Superintendent of Documents. And the text of the periodicals indexed is available from Microfilming Corporation of America (Glen Rock, New Jersey).

AMERICAN STATISTICS INDEX

The merits of ASI have been discussed in Chapter 6 and elsewhere in this text and need no further elaboration. The over 800 statistical periodicals indexed and abstracted include many that are not available for sale or to depository institutions. The sophisticated indexing of the contents of periodicals is illustrated in Figure 11 *supra*. Moreover, through the *ASI Microfiche Library* and *CIS Periodicals on Microfiche* the text of federal journals indexed is available.

OTHER INDEXING SOURCES

When one considers that ASI was first published as an annual in 1973 and the first issue of IUSGP covered the period January-March 1974, one becomes aware of the fortuitous state of the art prior to this period. Harleston and Stoffle, in a 1975 article, described the indexing and abstracting activities of fifty-four indexing services; of the some 800 periodical titles listed, ASI and IUSGP considerably outdistanced other indexing services.[29] In a 1978 analysis of federal periodical indexing, McClure found that, after ASI and IUSGP, a marked decline in indexing occurred. Indeed, McClure discovered that of the 1,500 journals covered in *Social Science Citation Index*, only 5 were government periodicals.[30]

Selective indexing of government periodicals in services other than ASI and IUSGP is found in a number of places, but it represents a scatter-shot pattern. Old standbys like *Public Affairs Information Service Bulletin* (PAIS) are still useful, but in PAIS titles vary from year to year. Science and technology periodicals appear in *Biological Abstracts, Chemical Abstracts*, and – to a lesser, disappointing extent – *Science Citation Index*.[31] One would expect to find *American Education* covered in *Education Index* and CIJE, the *Pesticides Monitoring Journal* indexed in *Biological Abstracts* or *Chemical Abstracts*, and the *Social Security Bulletin* covered in *Business Periodicals Index* or PAIS. Search strategy would suggest first going to IUSGP or ASI (for statistical journals) and then using guides like *Ulrich's International Periodical Directory* or *Chicorel's Index to Abstracting and Indexing Services* or by knowledge and intuition directly consulting an appropriate specialized index.

While IUSGP and ASI represent a singular advance in the indexing and abstracting of periodicals, bibliographic coverage of this major category of government publishing is far from adequate. Given the number of periodicals issued by government entities and the lack of agency accountability, it is unlikely that federal periodicals can ever be brought under comprehensive, systematic, and reliable control.

GEOGRAPHIC SOURCES

The task of providing an introduction to the geographic products and services of the federal government is formidable. A 1973 report of the Federal Mapping Task Force (FMTF) found numerous problems in the production and distribution of cartographic activities within the federal establishment. Most work, the Task Force found, is accomplished in house at many facilities throughout the country. Agencies creating computer-assisted automated systems have made little effort to develop compatible techniques. Millions of maps and charts are distributed by different agencies; customers do not know where to turn for correct ordering information. Within the federal establishment there are agencies that sell maps and related cartographic materials but do not produce them, agencies that produce maps but do not issue or sell them, and agencies that both produce and sell their cartographic products. This diffusion of effort inevitably produces duplication of activity and a lag in services.[32]

In 1981 a panel that reviewed the 1973 FMTF report reached a dismaying conclusion: "The present situation with respect to the proliferation of surveying, mapping, and related activities among the 39 federal agencies involved is not much different than it was in fiscal year 1972, the year used as the base for the 1973 Federal Mapping Task Force ... report." While the panel did find some advances and improvements in technology, coordination between agencies, concern about users' needs, and private sector cooperation, "there has been no definitive action on the key recommendation made in 1973 — *that there be a single civilian agency for these activities*" (original italics).[33] The following is an attempt to review the current status of publishing and distribution activities with regard to federal mapping, charting, geodesy, surveying, and gazetteer endeavors.

LIBRARY LITERATURE

The literature about mapping is rather extensive, and the best information is either problem-oriented or state-of-the-art surveys. Mary Larsgaard, *Map Librarianship: An Introduction* (Littleton, CO: Libraries Unlimited, 1978) includes government maps within an overall survey of map librarianship and is considered "must reading for anybody contemplating running a map library."[34] Jane Grant-Mackay Low, "The Acquisition of Maps and Charts Published by the United States Government," *University of Illinois Graduate School of Library Science Occasional Papers No. 125* (November 1976) covers, for federal maps and charts, current selection tools, map evaluation, agencies distributing maps, the map depository program, and a detailed account of federal departments and agencies which publish these materials. Charles A. Seavey, "Collection

Development for Government Map Collections," *Government Publications Review* 8A: 17-29 (1981) reviews problems of and suggests a methodology for collection development. Laurence F. Schmeckebier and Roy B. Eastin, *Government Publications and Their Use*, 2nd rev. ed. (Washington: Brookings, 1969), devote Chapter 16 (pp. 406-440) of their book to federal mapping activities. In general, the librarian in this field "has to keep up with the professional literature of map libraries, geography, geology and related disciplines." Other current awareness sources include "the Special Libraries Association (SLA), Geography and Map Division, *Bulletin*; the Western Association of Map Libraries (WAML) *Information Bulletin*; and the acquisitions lists of the various major map collections." These "are just the bare beginnings of required reading. Each [government map] collection developer should formulate a list of journals regularly checked for cartographic news in a given area or subject of interest." Moreover, "attendance at meetings of ALA, SLA, and WAML will also produce a tremendous amount of information usable in map acquisitions."[35]

SELECTED CARTOGRAPHIC AGENCIES

Earlier in this chapter we discussed Census Bureau mapping activities, its printed and microfiche maps and GBF/DIME files. In addition to maps that provide political and statistical information, there are mapping, charting, geodesy, and surveying programs that contribute to the exploration, ownership, and development of the lands, seas, and airspace, and their resources. Among the principal federal agencies engaged in these activities are the U.S. Geological Survey (USGS), National Ocean Survey (NOS), Bureau of Land Management (BLM), and Defense Mapping Agency (DMA). USGS and BLM are entities within the Department of Interior, NOS is a unit within the Commerce Department, and DMA is a component of the Department of Defense.

U.S. GEOLOGICAL SURVEY

USGS, an agency within the Department of Interior, has a unit called the National Mapping Division. It was organized in 1980 to consolidate mapping, charting, geodesy, and surveying programs and activities that were formerly the responsibility of other divisions and programs within USGS. The Division provides geographic and cartographic information, technical assistance, and conducts related research in the national interest.

In addition, USGS operates the National Cartographic Information Center (NCIC), which provides a national information service on maps, charts, aerial and space photographs, geodetic control, and other cartographic data. NCIC is able to inform the customer about the sale and distribution of maps produced by other federal agencies and provide instructions on placing orders. Moreover, the Center publishes various brochures which have useful information. Many of these informational pamphlets are free and often are received by depository libraries in the Geological Survey's General Publications series (I 19.2; item 621). In addition, the Center publishes an irregular *Newsletter* (I 19.71; item 624-E).

Sales items are available from GPO by mail or in GPO bookstores. A number of depository series are available from USGS through the general depository library program. It should be noted that series like the Professional Papers (I 19.16; item 624) and Bulletins (I 19.3; item 620) include individual publications that contain maps in the pocket of the document. *The National Atlas of the United States* (I 19.2:N 21a; item 621) was received by depository libraries in the General Publications series. A handsome, hardbound, 431-page volume, *The National Atlas* describes America in a cartographic format using multicolored reference and special subject maps and an extensive gazetteer.

The Open-File Reports series (I 19.76; item 624-H), long desired by depository libraries, was in the past available only in limited numbers. However, in October 1980 the USGS began placing almost all current Open-File Reports on microfiche, thus making them readily available as a depository item. These valuable reports, which include hydrogeologic investigations, seismicity studies, and the like, usually contain maps, manuscripts, basic data, field notes, and other research information.

Basic sources of USGS information include a monthly catalog called *New Publications of the Geological Survey* (I 19.14/4; item 622), which furnishes a list of materials available with ordering information; and *A Guide to Obtaining Information from the USGS* (I 19.4/2; item 620-A), which is issued as Geological Survey Circular 777 and is revised periodically.

Certain USGS reports, including most of the Water Resources Investigations (WRI) and many compilations of data, can be purchased in paper copy or on microfiche only from NTIS; these reports are listed in *New Publications of the Geological Survey*. Reports in the WRI series not released through NTIS are available for reference at the Hydrologic Information Unit, USGS, Reston, Virginia. Because USGS products and services are available from many sources, *A Guide to Obtaining Information from the USGS* is an important document to keep in a convenient location.

USGS Topographic Maps

Perhaps the best known of this agency's activities is the production of topographic maps. A topographic map "is a line-and-symbol representation of natural and selected man-made features of a part of the Earth's surface plotted to a definite scale. A distinguishing characteristic of a topographic map is the portrayal of the shape and elevation of the terrain by contour lines. The physical and cultural characteristics of the terrain, as determined by precise engineering surveys and field inspection, are recorded on the map in a convenient, readable form. Topographic maps show the location and shape of mountains, valleys, and plains; the networks of streams and rivers; and the principal works of man."[36]

Topographic maps are one of the truly great federal government series. They "have many uses as basic tools for planning and executing projects that are necessary to our way of life. They are of prime importance in planning airports, highways, dams, pipelines, transmission lines, industrial plants, and countless other types of construction. They are an essential part of ecological studies and environmental control, geologic research, studies of the quantity and quality of water, and projects for flood control, soil conservation, and reforestation." Moreover, "the growing list of map users includes many who have discovered the advantages of topographic maps in outdoor activities such as hunting, fishing, and vacationing. Reliable maps showing relief features, wooded areas and clearings, and watercourses are of inestimable value to the hiker. In fact, all of the outdoors can be better understood and appreciated with the aid of topographic maps."[37]

Although topographic maps are immensely popular in large public libraries where a heterogeneous clientele consult them for research and pleasure, a survey by Rudd and Carver showed that for academic libraries "the level of acquisition of [topographic maps] is remarkably low compared to the stated need for [them]." The major problems inhibiting robust collection development were identified "as loss of depository receipts, inadequate funding support, inflated map prices, increased production, and government restrictions." To rectify this unfortunate situation, the authors urge "that academic libraries recognize the value of this resource and that they actively support the acquisition of mapping which meets the research needs of their institutions."[38]

Regional mapping center units of NCIC sell (but only over the counter) USGS topographic maps of various states and distribute topographic map reproducibles, advance copies of topographic maps in progress, and geodetic control lists. Maps are also available for sale from the USGS, National Mapping Program, Reston, Virginia 22092. More than 2,000 map dealers throughout the United States sell topographic maps. Formerly, a list of dealers and their addresses were located on the back of each state's topographic map index. Current publishing plans are to list map dealers in a "catalog of published maps for each state, which will accompany the index." Topographic map indexes are available free by mail and over the counter from all regional offices of the USGS Distribution Branch, and over the counter from NCIC offices and from Public Inquiries Offices located in various cities throughout the United States.[39]

For many years the Geological Survey designated selected libraries as "map reference libraries" for deposit of its topographic, geologic, and hydrologic maps. Topographic quadrangle maps are deposited for one state, a group of states, or all states; but other topographic maps, such as state base maps, national parks, and the U.S. 1:250,000-scale series, are sent by full series, without geographic selectivity. USGS map reference libraries for each state are listed on the back of the *Index of Topographic Maps* for the state; their addresses are also available from NCIC and from the several Public Inquiries Offices.[40]

Since 77 percent of USGS depositories are also Title 44 depositories or belong to the same institution as a Title 44 depository, the two depository systems were consolidated in 1982. Accordingly, more citizens are now able to access USGS maps and charts under the general (Title 44) depository program or a designated recipient as well as a specialized "map reference library" that is not a Title 44 depository library.[41]

Topographic maps on microfiche are available commercially from Micrographics Laboratory (University of Northern Colorado, Greeley, Colorado 80639). These include national, geographic areas, and state quadrangles. A *National Lands Index* includes all of the designated non-military lands indicated on the national maps (scale 1:250,000) designed to accompany the microfiche set of national topographic maps. The national series is indexed by titles, subjects, states and territories, coordinates, names of cities and towns (taken from *The National Atlas of the United States*), and maps cited in the *Index*.

Topographic maps are produced with the cooperation of other agencies like DMA, NOS, the Tennessee Valley Authority (TVA), Forest Service, and Mississippi River Commission. In addition, state or local agencies on occasion participate in mapping projects.[42] But the USGS does not issue topographic series only; indeed, the "thematic mapping of the USGS includes geologic maps at large and small scales, mineral resource maps, hydrologic maps and geophysical maps."[43]

NATIONAL OCEAN SURVEY

When the National Oceanic and Atmospheric Administration (NOAA) was created by Reorganization Plan No. 4 (1970), the functions of the old Coast and Geodetic Survey were incorporated into a new unit within NOAA, the National Ocean Survey. NOS activities comprise mapping, charting, and surveying services and operations of the NOAA fleet and ship bases. NOS provides charts for safe navigation of marine and air commerce, ocean and coastal surveys and maps, geodetic surveys, and related services responsive to NOAA missions. Indeed, NOS "is the primary publisher of nautical charting for U.S. marine waters including its dependencies and Puerto Rico, the Great Lakes and certain other navigable waterways."[44] The agency's "principal products ... are nautical and aeronautical charts, which are basic tools needed to maintain the nation's sea and air transportation system."[45] As "Chartmaker to the Nation," NOS and NOAA issue large quantities of navigational charts each year; a catalog of this activity can be obtained from the National Ocean Survey, Distribution Division, Riverdale, Maryland 20840.

NOS issues several series for depository libraries under different item numbers, including United States Coast Pilots (C 55.422) on microfiche and Tide Tables (C 55.420). But the general depository program does not provide the majority of charts issued by NOS. Indeed, collection building of NOS cartographic products must be accomplished through purchase[46] or participation in the Survey's specialized chart depository arrangements. According to Sivers, "full or partial NOS depositories are available to libraries in the United States which can provide evidence of adequate storage capacity, and agree to give public access to revised charts as furnished."[47]

BUREAU OF LAND MANAGEMENT

The cadastral survey organization of the BLM is responsible for the legal boundary surveys required by the federal government. Surveys conducted by BLM include initial surveys of federal public lands to create boundaries that may be used for the management and sale of public lands; the maintenance of the Public Land Survey System, with resurveys and remonumentation of the original surveys; and boundary surveys required by BLM and other federal agencies to delineate management tracts within the public lands or between federal and non-federal lands. To accomplish these tasks, BLM has a Division of Cadastral Survey in Washington, DC, state offices responsible for the cadastral surveys within their areas, and Service Center Offices in Denver, Colorado and Portland, Oregon that are responsible primarily for the cadastral surveys required by other federal entities.[48]

For general depository libraries, the Bureau distributes a Maps and Map Folder series (I 53.11; item 629-B) which includes individual intermediate-scale maps of wilderness areas and land ownership and public management. And BLM publications received under other depository items include environmental assessment and cultural resources management reports which contain maps with the text.

DEFENSE MAPPING AGENCY

The Defense Mapping Agency was established within the Department of Defense (DoD) in 1972 to unify all DoD mapping operations and to separate the intelligence functions of DoD from its mapping activities. DMA absorbed most of the staff and functions of the former Mapping and Charting Division, Defense Intelligence Agency.

DMA is responsible for providing mapping, charting, and geodetic support to DoD. In addition, the agency has statutory responsibility for providing nautical charts and marine navigation data for the use of all vessels of the United States and of navigators generally. DMA's hydrographic, topographic, aerospace, and nautical products make the agency "one of the largest mapping organizations in the world." Moreover, though DMA produces some mapping of the United States, its primary activity "is the compilation and publication of small, medium and large scale topographic mapping, thematic mapping, nautical and aeronautical charting for world areas exclusive of the United States, its territorial waters, its dependencies and Puerto Rico."[49]

Like USGS and NOS, the Defense Mapping Agency has designated selected libraries to participate in its special map depository program. This program includes 245 participating institutions, of which 89 percent are also Title 44 depository libraries. In 1982 DMA depositories and Title 44 depositories were consolidated in order to increase the availability of DMA mapping products to the general public. The arrangements and options are similar to the centralized distribution procedures that were coordinated between GPO and USGS (*supra*).

Three types of DMA products are available to depository institutions. Aeronautical products include Operational Navigation Charts, Jet Navigation Charts, and Global Navigation Charts; maps in these series may be selected for several geographic areas (Africa, Antarctica, Europe, Pacific, etc.) and the world. Topographic products include Area Outline Maps, Mid-East Briefing Maps, World Plotting Series, Road Maps for Allied Forces, and the like; maps in these series may be selected for geographic areas and the world. Nautical charts include a general series as well as series covering international, great circle, omega plotting, loran plotting, and coastal charts; each of these series may be selected by regions.[50]

Altogether, forty-three different series of DMA maps and charts are now available to participating depository libraries; these series account for over 200 depository item categories for selection. Item selection for specific geographic areas permits libraries to meet the specialized needs of their clientele. About 2,600 maps and charts comprise a complete set, and DMA officials estimate that approximately 600 products were distributed to depository institutions during fiscal year 1983.[51]

GEOGRAPHIC NAMES

Uniformity in the spellings and applications of geographic names is essential to all levels of government, commerce, and to those sciences that deal with the Earth and geographical distribution. A federal agency whose purpose it is to establish and maintain uniform geographic name usage is the United States Board on Geographic Names. Located within the Interior Department but with a Defense Department connection, its policies and procedures govern the use of both domestic and foreign geographic names as well as underseas and extraterrestrial feature names. Although the Board was established to serve the federal government as a central authority to which all name problems, name inquiries, and new name proposals can be directed, it also plays a similar role for the general public.

The Board issues a quarterly called *Decisions on Geographic Names in the United States* (I 33.5/2; item 617-A), with the subtitle *Decision List.* The lists are designated by a numbering system in which the first two digits represent the year of publication and the next two the issue within the year. The numbered series, while not a sales item, is available free to professionals and is a depository selection. Each *List*, running some twenty-five to fifty pages, is a systematic account by state of decisions on names in the United States approved by the Board during the quarterly period.

Board policy for domestic names recognizes present-day local usage or preferences whenever possible. To implement this policy, there is close cooperation with state geographic boards, state and local governments, and the general public. Policy also recognizes that when a local name is derogatory to a particular person, race, or religion, the Board may disapprove such names and seek alternate local names for the features.

The significance of Board decisions for the cartographic community, including map librarians, is manifest. For example, "every square mile of the U.S. boasts at least one named place. This means that map librarians who wish to enhance their professional competence by penetrating cartography and geography to reach the underlying layers of history beneath the lines of latitude and longitude must grapple with 3,500,000 names on the land."[52]

There is an interesting organizational link between the Defense Mapping Agency and the Board on Geographic Names. Since 1955 the Board has been the issuing agency for an irregularly produced series of gazetteers, each volume covering a single country or group of countries. The gazetteers have been acknowledged as "the authoritative source of geographic names in the areas covered, and their spelling and application, that are official for use by our Federal Government.... They include new and changed names resulting from changes in administrative divisions or other governmental actions, and new forms or spelling resulting from orthographic changes officially adopted and implemented by those countries."[53] When the Board was the provenance, the Gazetteers series was classed in I 33.8 and was available to depository libraries under item 617. Under DMA control, the policies have changed little if at all. Producing and distributing Gazetteers became part of the Agency's overall mission of supporting foreign-area scientific studies. The volumes are still based on the work of linguists, geographers, and cartographers. Wherever possible the endeavor is carried out with the cooperation of the concerned country. And the names used in the gazetteers are approved by the Board on Geographic Names. Gazetteers are now classed in D 5.319 and are available to depository libraries under item 617, the same controlling number that served the former provenance.[54]

GEOGRAPHIC NAMES INFORMATION SYSTEM

The success of a national program to establish uniform geographic-name usage depends a great deal on effective management of name information. Large amounts of interrelated data involving official names and their applications to specific features, places, and areas must be collected, processed, stored, retrieved, and disseminated to a variety of users. One method of managing this kind of information is by use of a system developed around automatic data processing.

The Geological Survey employs an automated Geographic Names Information System (GNIS). The System is capable of providing basic information on about 3 million names used in the United States. Designed for use by all levels of government, industry, educational institutions, and the general public, GNIS contains names identified as official by the Board on Geographic Names.

GNIS furnishes data to those who use the information for reference purposes and those who use the file as a base or subset for other specialized files. Initial compilation consisted of systematic collection of name data from large-scale maps and charts published by the Geological Survey and National Ocean Survey. The names files for states are available to users in three ways: direct access by an outside computer terminal; open-file products such as magnetic tape, punch cards, computer printouts, and microfiche; and printed products such as alphabetical and topical lists. Information on these products and services is available from either NCIC or the Branch of Geographic Names, USGS, National Center, Reston, Virginia 22092.

NATIONAL GAZETTEER

The USGS, under the authority of the Board on Geographic Names, has embarked upon an ambitious publishing program under the rubric "National Gazetteer of the United States." Produced on a state-by-state basis, the National Gazetteer series includes, for each state, new names, formal name changes, and corrections. The volumes are being issued as chapters of USGS *Professional Paper 1200* (I 19.16; item 624). Entries identify official name, feature class, county in which feature is located, geographic coordinates, Board on Geographic Names decision date, elevation of place or feature, and USGS map or maps on which the feature may be found.

SUMMARY

In 1977 a monograph entitled *Types of Maps Published by Government Agencies* (I 19.2: M32/10/977; item 621) identified twenty-nine publishing and distributing entities. The 1981 National Research Council study identified no fewer than thirty-nine agencies involved in surveying, mapping, and related activities. The proliferation of a national cartographic program through many agencies has reduced the effectiveness and efficiency of the enterprise.

The 1973 Federal Mapping Task Force report noted that consolidation of DoD mapping into the Defense Mapping Agency resulted in a major improvement in that entity's capabilities. The 1981 NRC report avers that similar benefits would derive from the establishment of a single agency for civilian mapping, charting, geodesy, and surveying "and would add the multipurpose cadastre to this list."[55] If this structure were adopted, the present bibliographic complexity would be alleviated.

Depository distribution has been greatly improved by the cooperative arrangements negotiated with USGS and DMA discussed above. In April 1981 "the JCP invited five map-producing agencies, the GPO, and the Library of Congress to a meeting to discuss cooperative distribution and indexing of maps."[56] Out of this initial contact the beginnings of a centralized distribution system for cartographic materials were effected with the Geological Survey and the Defense Mapping Agency. Other mapping entities, such as NOS, are logical candidates for cooperation in depository distribution. Of the 126 NOS special depository libraries, for example, 100 are also Title 44 general depository institutions.[57] Moreover, a unified map distribution program is a salutary development especially since the Library of Congress "now recognizes GPO as final authority for its map cataloging."[58]

Despite these advances in public access, costly duplication of effort remains and more coordination is desirable. Only the creation of a single cartographic entity will remedy the larger problems of production and distribution.

AUDIOVISUAL INFORMATION

Federal departments and independent agencies spend over $80 million annually on audiovisual (AV) products and services. The Department of Defense alone accounts for over one-half of this total.[59] A sizeable number of audiovisual personnel are employed in units of the Congress, GPO, Library of Congress, CIA, the major departments, some twenty-six independent agencies, and eight boards, committees, and commissions.[60] Yet with all this activity, bibliographic control of audiovisual materials is neither systematic nor comprehensive.

In the brief summary that follows, an attempt will be made to indicate some of the basic sources of AV materials produced by or for government agencies, and their sales, loans, and rental services.

GENERAL GUIDES

Although the PRF, *Monthly Catalog*, and *Subject Bibliography* series provide some access to catalogs and directories that list certain AV information, they do not occupy a prominent bibliographic position in this area. *Subject Bibliography 073*, for example, rarely exceeds four pages in length and lists but a handful of titles and series. These include the *Catalog of Copyright Entries, Cumulative Series, Motion Pictures* and several catalogs issued by agencies that list films, slide sets, audio and video tapes, recordings, and other AV materials available for distribution.[61] But these sources certainly do not account for all federally produced or sponsored audiovisual sources of information.

NATIONAL AUDIOVISUAL CENTER

Some improvement of access was achieved when, in 1968, the National Audiovisual Center was authorized by Bureau of the Budget *Bulletin No. 69-7*, and was established by General Services Administration *Bulletin FPMR B-21*,

December 9, 1969. A division of the National Archives and Records Service of the GSA, the National Audiovisual Center (NAC) "rents and sells government-produced films, slides and filmstrips to the public on [a] wide range of subjects; provides reference service for locating films not available through [the Center]. Publishes comprehensive and subject catalogs of audiovisual materials produced by the U.S. government, and an annual overview of federal audiovisual activity."[62] The Center maintains a reference service to help the public learn what federal AV materials are distributed through NAC, other federal agencies, or non-governmental services. In this respect, the function of the Center is analogous to the clearinghouse function of the National Cartographic Information Center for mapping and charting products and services.

The Center also issues printed materials "as a means of keeping the public informed of selected titles that are available for sale and/or rent.... The information for these publications is stored on a computer data file. Indexes and other search tools are prepared from this file to aid the reference staff in their searching for specific subject area titles. This material, as well as on-site preview facilities, is available to the public by appointment."

Because NAC has developed a sophisticated retrieval system to conduct online searches in response to customer needs, "the data could be made available on computer tapes, microfilm, or publications of selected titles appropriate to [user] requests." NAC's "ultimate goal is to provide on-line searching via time-sharing networks."[63]

NAC PUBLICATIONS

The following publications, issued under the provenance and SuDocs classification of the National Archives and Records Service, provide information on NAC products and services.

A Reference List of Audiovisual Materials Produced by the United States Government (GS 4.2: Au2/yr.; item 569) consists of a basic volume and periodic supplements. The basic volume lists over 6,000 AV materials selected from over 10,000 programs produced by 175 federal agencies. Major subject concentrations in the Center's collection include medicine, dentistry, education, science, social studies, industrial/technical training, safety, and the environmental sciences. The 1978 edition of the *Reference List* marked the first time that this important tool was made available to depository libraries. The 1980 *Supplement* contained about 600 titles added to the Center's collection of more than 13,000 titles. The basic list and supplements have an alphabetical list of titles and a subject section. Individual entries in the title section provide bibliographic data: date, availability, organization producing the material, NAC title number (to use when ordering), and a description of contents. Rental and purchase policies and a price list are additional features of the *Reference List*.

A List of Audiovisual Materials Produced by the United States Government for [subject] (GS 4.17/5-2; item 569-C-1) is a series of individual pamphlets on selected subjects. Lists have been prepared for Special Education, Career Education, Engineering, Dentistry, Safety, and Library and Information Science. A typical subject list is organized by broad topics with a title index. Entries are annotated and provide bibliographic information, including price. Films which may be rented are so indicated, and ordering procedures are given on the inside back cover.

Quarterly Update (GS 4.17/5-3; item 569-C-1) is a listing of recent additions and other changes within NAC's collection. Its purpose is to provide a convenient supplement to the other catalogs, brochures, and information lists published by the Center.

Medical Catalog of Selected Audiovisual Materials Produced by the United States Government (GS 4.17/6:year; item 569-C-1) is a specialized list of AV materials in medicine and related areas.

Directory of U.S. Government Audiovisual Personnel (GS 4.24:year; item 567-B) lists federal government agencies and their audiovisual personnel, defined as those involved in radio, television, motion pictures, still photography, sound recordings, and exhibits. The *Directory* does not attempt to provide an "exhaustive listing of all persons involved in Federal audiovisual activities, but it is an effort to list each agency's key audiovisual personnel."[64] The organization of the *Directory* follows the format of the *United States Government Manual*: personnel are listed by name, title, phone number, and mailing address. The *Directory* is accessed by a name and organization index. This would be a useful source if it were updated more frequently.

NAC PURCHASE, RENTAL, AND LOAN POLICIES

All the AV materials listed in the various catalogs and announcements mentioned above are available through sales, rental, or loan referral programs, and current information is provided in the catalogs. AV formats available for purchase from the Center (Washington, DC 20409) include motion pictures, videotapes, slide sets, audiotapes, and multimedia kits. For 16mm films, some of the more popular titles are available for rent, and rental fees for a three-day period are indicated. NAC does not loan materials free, but some materials are available to the public from commercial distributors and from regional federal agency offices. NAC will refer the user to the closest free loan source whenever this information is known.

NATIONAL MEDICAL AUDIOVISUAL CENTER

Although NAC issues a *Medical Catalog*, noted above, the National Medical Audiovisual Center (NMAC), a component of the National Library of Medicine, Department of Health and Human Services (HHS), acquires and distributes AV materials for the health science instructional professions. The Center issues a *National Medical Audiovisual Center Catalog: Films for the Health Sciences* (HE 20.3608/4:year; item 508-H-5). The 1981 edition of the *Catalog* lists over 700 16mm motion pictures available on short-term loan from NMAC for use in health professions education. Many of the titles listed are also available in ¾-inch videocassette format.

The NMAC *Catalog* is arranged in two sections: Name/Title and Subject. The Name/Title section provides full bibliographic information for each title, including an abstract. Titles are listed alphabetically by the first significant word. In the Subject section, films are listed under subject terms selected from *Medical Subject Headings* (MeSH), the medical thesaurus of the National Library of Medicine.

Order forms for films are located at the end of the Subject section. Films may be borrowed for a nominal service charge. NMAC film and video productions, as well as slide/tape packages, may be purchased from the National Audiovisual Center. It should be noted that the films listed in the NMAC *Catalog* are available for health sciences professional educational use only.

References to those films that have undergone peer evaluation under the auspices of the Association of American Medical Colleges are included not only in the NMAC *Catalog* but also in the National Library of Medicine's online database AVLINE (*Audio-Visuals* on LINE). AVLINE contains citations to some 10,000 audiovisual packages produced and distributed by academic, commercial, and governmental organizations. As part of the National Library of Medicine's MEDLARS system, AVLINE can be searched from over 1,500 institutions that belong to the MEDLARS network.

OTHER AGENCY AV SOURCES

The existence of a central clearinghouse like the NAC is virtually indispensable in attempting to keep up with the amount of AV materials available for purchase, rental, or loan. But there are several agencies that publish lists and catalogs of their audiovisual products. Many, but not all, of these bibliographic sources are available to depository libraries.[65]

Like census data, mapping, and charting, the public and private sectors share in federal audiovisual production and distribution activities. The following example is not uncommon. A 1981 Department of Labor press release announced that the Occupational Safety and Health Administration (OSHA) issued three 16mm documentary films on job safety and health. While a limited number of copies of each film were made available for loan from OSHA regional and area offices, the purchasing and rental arrangements were handled by Association Films, Inc., a New Jersey-based commercial firm.[66] And while the catalogs of the National Audiovisual Center and the National Medical Audiovisual Center are available to depository libraries, there is no free deposit of the AV materials themselves.

SUMMARY

Although the NAC plays an important role in making accessible information on the audiovisual activities of federal entities, its catalogs and lists, plus those of specific agencies, do not comprise a total bibliographic picture. An effort to overcome this problem began in 1981 when GPO officials, in discussions with the Library of Congress and NAC, set forth procedures to have the Superintendent of Documents catalog approximately 600 audiovisual items a year. But much remains to be done. There is, for example, no master list of federally produced or sponsored audiovisuals. Nor is there any list, to the author's knowledge, of materials produced but not available to the general public. The number of training films alone produced by or for DoD and its components seems limitless, as anyone who has served in the armed forces will attest.

As McCauley observes, the economics of NAC publishing and distribution constitutes a major problem. "Cost of inventory, cost of distribution of audiovisual materials, and the cost of information transfer about these products have become a very pragmatic concern." And as NAC improves its information dissemination capabilities with the aid of the computer, "it will be necessary to determine what information products can be provided with appropriated funds and what information services may require a charge to the requestor." But the "need for a centralized information source about all audiovisuals federally or commercially produced" is manifest.[67]

CONCLUSION

Administrative law, statistical compilations, federal periodicals, geographic and cartographic publications, audiovisual products and services—all are issued in their several formats to fulfill in part the purpose and mission of the agencies. They represent a small but important part of executive branch publishing activity.

Every year the United States Senate Committee on Governmental Affairs issues a large chart entitled *Organization of Federal Executive Departments and Agencies.* Sold by the Superintendent of Documents and available to depository libraries, the chart provides a remarkably detailed breakdown of the federal establishment, including the independent agencies and selected commissions, with precise data on the number of federal employees by administrative unit. It is supplemented by a committee print issued in pamphlet form.[68]

The 1981 edition of *Organization of Federal Executive Departments and Agencies* shows the total number of federal civilian employees (excluding employees of the Central Intelligence Agency) to be in excess of 2,800,000. A significant function of this bureaucracy is to publish documents to instruct, regulate, provide statistics, list, direct, and guide; and even with retrenchment as a national policy of the 1980s, the production of federal documentation is awesome. As long as government publications represent a validation of and justification for the existence of agencies, the quantity and variety of information produced by and for these federal entities will remain substantial.

REFERENCES

1. *Weekly Compilation of Presidential Documents* 17: 447 (April 24, 1981).

2. 44 U.S.C. 1505, 1508.

3. When no amendments are promulgated to a volume during the scheduled period, a reprint of the cover of the volume with the new date and new color is sent to subscribers and depository libraries. This cover can be stapled to the volume and serves to direct that the unrevised issue be retained.

4. The final issue of the periodical *Federal Register Update*, pp. 5-6, contains an explanation of the changes incorporated into the *CFR Index.* Unfortunately, this excellent government serial was discontinued with the August 1979 issue, owing to lack of sufficient funds.

5. For example, see *Microform Review* 8: 279-84 (Fall 1979).

6. 9 CFR 91.10 (1972).

7. See Nancy P. Johnson, "Federal Administrative Decisions," *Legal Reference Services Quarterly* 1: 49-65 (Spring 1981).

8. "Notes of General Interest," *Monthly Catalog of United States Government Publications* (December 1934), p. 433.

9. *Congressional Record* (daily edition), June 8, 1976, p. E3173.

10. *U.S. News & World Report*, May 31, 1982, p. 55.

11. Ruth Ruttenberg, "Government Regulation Can Be the Mother of Invention," *Albany Times-Union*, August 16, 1981, p. E-2.

12. *F.T.C. v. Ruberoid Co.*, 343 U.S. 470, 487 (1952).

13. The 1980 and 1981 editions of the *Statistical Abstract* contain a pocket-sized insert called *USA Statistics in Brief*. Available separately as a reprint, *USA Statistics in Brief* contains population data for the states from the 1980 census, which became available too late for inclusion in the tables of the 1980 *Statistical Abstract*.

14. Earlier editions of *Historical Statistics* covered colonial times to 1957, and a "Bicentennial Edition" covering the period 1610 to 1970.

15. The sixth edition of *Pocket Data Book, USA* had a publication date of 1979.

16. *Statistics Sources, 7th Edition* (1982) was edited by Paul Wasserman and Jacqueline O'Brien.

17. *Wesberry v. Sanders*, 376 U.S. 1 (1964).

18. *Data User News* 15: 1 (January 1980).

19. The Social and Economics Statistics Administration was established within the Commerce Department in 1972 and abolished in 1975. However, during SESA's short life as an intermediate management entity between Census and the Secretary of Commerce, the Superintendent of Documents managed to classify a number of Bureau publications in "C 56.200," causing bibliographic turmoil within the documents librarians community.

20. U.S. Bureau of the Census, *Bureau of the Census Catalog: 1980 Annual*, Washington, DC, p. 2.

21. The 1980 census of population and housing yielded an estimated 300,000 pages of summary statistics and over 1,500 computer summary tapes containing several billion data items.

22. *Data User News* 15: 3-5 (October 1980).

23. PDH 51/52: 3 (April/June 1982); see also *Administrative Notes* 3 (July 1982).

24. See Julius Shiskin, "Employment and Unemployment: The Doughnut or the Hole," *Monthly Labor Review* 99: 3-10 (February 1976).

25. See the author's "The Uses and Misuses of Information Found in Government Publications," in *Collection Development and Public Access of Government Documents*, edited by Peter Hernon (Westport, CT: Meckler Publishing, 1982), pp. 57-71.

26. *Congressional Record* (daily edition), May 18, 1972, pp. S17984-17995.

27. Joe Morehead, "The Pentagon's Magazine Publishing Empire," *The Serials Librarian* 5: 10 (Fall 1980).

28. Office of Management and Budget, *Report to the Senate Appropriations Committee on Administrative Expenses*, Washington, DC: March 1982, p. 11. Total FY 1982 spending on periodicals and pamphlets for all departments and agencies was an estimated $138 million.

29. Rebekah Harleston and Carla J. Stoffle, "Government Periodicals: Seven Years Later," *Government Publications Review* 2: 323-43 (1975).

30. Charles R. McClure, "Indexing U.S. Government Periodicals: Analysis and Comments," *Government Publications Review* 5: 412, 418 (1978).

31. Ibid., p. 412.

32. U.S. Office of Management and Budget, *Report of the Federal Mapping Task Force on Mapping, Charting, Geodesy and Surveying* (Washington: Government Printing Office, 1973), pp. i, iii, 147-52.

33. National Research Council, *Federal Surveying and Mapping: An Organizational Review* (Washington: National Academy Press, 1981), pp. 1-2.

34. Charles A. Seavey, "Collection Development for Government Map Collections," *Government Publications Review* 8A: 28 (1981).

35. Ibid., pp. 27-28.

36. Theodore D. Steger, *Topographic Maps* (Washington: Government Printing Office, 1981), p. 3.

37. Ibid., p. 6.

38. Janet K. Rudd and Larry G. Carver, "Topographic Map Acquisition in U.S. Academic Libraries," *Library Trends* 29: 377, 388-89 (Winter 1981).

39. U.S. Geological Survey, *A Guide to Obtaining Information from the USGS, 1982* (I 19.4/2:777/4; item 620-A), pp. 15, 16.

40. *A Guide to Obtaining Information from the USGS, 1982*, p. 19.

41. A recipient designated by a Title 44 depository, for example, may be a university library that allows another campus library or an academic department to receive the maps.

42. Jane Grant-Mackay Low, "The Acquisition of Maps and Charts Published by the United States Government," *University of Illinois Graduate School of Library Science Occasional Papers No. 125* (November 1976), p. 3.

43. Robert Sivers, "Federal Map and Chart Depositories," *Government Publications Review* 2: 13-14 (1975).

44. Ibid., p. 12.

45. Low, p. 14.

46. Each chart catalog, available from the central office in Riverdale, Maryland, contains a list of authorized dealers from which NOS charts may be purchased.

47. Sivers, p. 13.

48. *Federal Surveying and Mapping: An Organizational Review*, pp. 58, 60.

49. Sivers, p. 11.

50. The DMA Hydrographic/Topographic Center, located in Brookmont, Maryland, publishes Sailing Directions, Loran Tables, and Omega Tables series, which have been available to Title 44 depository libraries for many years.

51. Attachment 1 to letter, Chairman, Joint Committee on Printing, to all depository libraries, July 26, 1982.

52. Richard Dillon, "Names on the Land," *Special Libraries* 62: 406 (October 1971).

53. John L. Andriot, *Guide to U.S. Government Publications, Vol. 2* (McLean, VA: Documents Index, 1979), p. 1007.

54. When DMA was established in 1972, the office of the Executive Secretary of the Board on Geographic Names was relocated within DMA (Bldg. 56, U.S. Naval Observatory, Washington, DC 20305). DMA's Hydrographic/Topographic Center has a Geographic Names Data Base Division, which is located at the same address. However, information and inquiries on domestic names should be addressed to Domestic Geographic Names, U.S. Geological Survey, National Center, Reston, Virginia 22092.

55. *Federal Surveying and Mapping: An Organizational Review*, p. 2.

56. Bernadine E. Abbott Hoduski, "Federal Depository Library System," *Drexel Library Quarterly* 16: 9-10 (October 1980).

57. Ibid., p. 10.

58. DttP 10: 149 (July 1982).

59. Office of Management and Budget, *Report to the Senate Appropriations Committee on Administrative Expenses*, p. 13. DoD's estimated spending on AV products for 1983 was $53 million.

60. *Directory of U.S. Government Audiovisual Personnel, 6th Edition*, 1977 (GS 4.24:977; item 567-B). This was the latest published edition as of June 1982.

61. Subject Bibliography (SB) 073, *Motion Pictures, Films, and Audiovisual Information*, November 16, 1981.

62. *Washington Information Directory, 1981-82* (Washington: Congressional Quarterly, Inc., 1981), p. 277.

63. Margery J. McCauley, "Information Policy and the National Audiovisual Center," *Government Publications Review* 8A: 216 (1981).

64. "Introduction" to the sixth edition, 1977. An earlier edition was published in 1970.

65. For example, *Forest Service Films Available on Loan for Educational Purposes* (A 13.55; item 83-A) is issued annually.

66. *United States Department of Labor News*, January 15, 1981, pp. 1-2.

67. McCauley, p. 218.

68. *Organization of Federal Executive Departments and Agencies*, January 1, 1981 (Y 4.G 74/9: Ex 3/981; item 1037-B).

10

Legal Sources of Information

INTRODUCTION

The judicial branch of the federal establishment forms a pyramid. At the bottom of the pyramid stand the United States district courts. On the next level stand the United States courts of appeals. At the pyramid's apex stands the Supreme Court, the highest tribunal in the land. District courts and courts of appeals for the eleven circuits and the District of Columbia have geographic jurisdiction. A United States Court of Appeals for the Federal Circuit, created by the Federal Courts Improvement Act of 1982 (PL 97-164, 96 *Stat.* 25), represents a merger of the Court of Customs and Patent Appeals and the appellate division of the Court of Claims. This Federal Circuit Court of Appeals is unique in that its jurisdiction is defined by subject matter rather than by geography.

In addition, special courts have been established from time to time by the Congress to deal with particular types of cases. Among these are the Tax Court, Court of Military Appeals, Bankruptcy Courts, and, in 1982, a United States Claims Court that replaces the trial division of the United States Court of Claims (96 *Stat.* 25 *supra*). Moreover, those administrative agencies with quasi-judicial powers, such as the Federal Trade Commission and National Labor Relations Board, may be included here because the review of their decisions is handled by the district courts in some instances or may be appealed directly in the courts of appeals.

State courts have general, unlimited power to decide almost every type of case, subject only to the limitations of state law. They are located in every town and county and are the tribunals with which citizens most often have contact. The federal courts, on the other hand, have power to decide only those cases in which the Constitution gives them authority. Article III, Section 1 of the Constitution states that "the judicial power of the United States, shall be vested in one supreme Court, and in such inferior Courts as the Congress may from time to time ordain and establish." Thus the only indispensable court is the Supreme Court, and the Congress has indeed from time to time established and abolished various other federal courts.

The independence of the judicial branch is assured by the Constitution, even though federal judges are appointed by the president with the advice and consent of the Senate. Under the Constitution, federal courts can be called upon to exercise only judicial powers and to perform only judicial work. The courts cannot be called upon to make laws or to enforce and execute laws. Federal judges hold their positions "during good behavior" and can be removed from office against their will only by impeachment. Independence is further insured by compensation that "shall not be diminished during their continuance in office"; that is, neither a president nor the Congress can reduce the salary of a federal magistrate.[1]

Although independence and the concommitant ideal of integrity theoretically characterize the federal judiciary, selection is largely a political process. Tradition has awarded to senators of the president's party the prerogative of naming persons for federal judgeships within their states. Judicial appointment is a powerful patronage lever for an incumbent president.

A few important decisions of the district courts may be appealed directly to the Supreme Court, but the appellate process generally rises hierarchically from district court to court of appeals and then to the Supreme Court. The courts of appeals review decisions of the district courts within their circuits and also some of the actions of the independent regulatory agencies. This structure serves a twofold purpose. First, the Supreme Court and the courts of appeals can correct errors which have been made in the decisions in the trial courts. Secondly, these appellate courts can assure uniformity of decision by reviewing cases where two or more lower courts have reached different results.

Lower court judges are required to follow the precedents established by the Supreme Court, but the system is not a monolithic unit in which, like the military chain of command, orders flow from the top. District and circuit judges have wide latitude in determining the lineaments of Supreme Court decisions. Those at the lower levels often take a different point of view toward legal disputes than do the members of the high court. And, since few of the thousands of cases adjudicated reach the Supreme Court, the magistrates of the lower federal courts are important policy-makers. The federal judiciary, like the legislative and executive branches, reflects in its judgments the shifting and variegated interests of the body politic.

REFERENCE AND RESEARCH AIDS

The scope of legal reference and bibliography is vast and at first seemingly complex. But the bibliographic apparatus adheres to a logic and an elegant symmetry not evident in other areas of government publications. The account that follows is intended merely to introduce the reader to some of the salient materials supportive of federal case law. The nature of publications in this field is such that a host of commercial materials surrounds and amplifies a relatively small number of official government documents.

BASIC RESEARCH GUIDES

Librarians working with legal materials have several useful sources of information to consult. Morris L. Cohen's *Legal Research in a Nutshell* (St. Paul, MN: West Publishing Co., 1978) affords a concise introduction to legal bibliography. J. Myron Jacobstein and Roy M. Mersky, *Fundamentals of Legal Research, Second Edition* (Mineola, NY: The Foundation Press, Inc., 1981) is more detailed than Cohen but is still an introduction to legal resources. A paperbound abridgment of *Fundamentals* by the same authors serves as an excellent text for law librarianship.[2] Miles O. Price, et al., *Effective Legal Research* (Boston: Little, Brown and Company, 1979) is very detailed and serves a reference function for American and foreign legal sources. The book is in its fourth edition.

LEGAL CITATION FORMS

Citation rules and examples and tables of abbreviations are found in Appendix A of Jacobstein and Mersky, *Fundamentals of Legal Research, Second Edition*, in Price, *Effective Legal Research, Fourth Edition*, Chapter 32 and Appendix III, and in law dictionaries and citation manuals like *A Uniform System of Citation*, published by the Harvard Law Review Association and revised periodically. It must be pointed out that there is no universally accepted source for abbreviations and citations among publishers of government documents and legal materials.

ENCYCLOPEDIAS

Two general legal encyclopedias dominate the field and provide topical coverage of the law in narrative form. They are *American Jurisprudence Second* (Am.Jur.2d) and *Corpus Juris Secundum* (C.J.S.). The former is published by the Lawyers Co-operative Publishing Company/Bancroft-Whitney Company; the latter is issued by West Publishing Company. As will become evident, these two publishers are responsible for most of the sources that will be mentioned in this chapter. Hereafter they will be referred to as Lawyers Co-op and West, respectively.

Both Am.Jur.2d and C.J.S. are multivolume works arranged alphabetically by topic, with general indexes plus an index in each volume. Footnotes in C.J.S. purport to cite all reported cases, while Am.Jur.2d cites selected decisions in its footnotes. Both are supplemented by annual pocket parts and replacement volumes. Each cites to its own sister publications.

Am.Jur.2d and C.J.S. differ in certain features. For example, Am.Jur.2d has a table of statutes absent in C.J.S. Neither encyclopedia has a table of cases. C.J.S. provides definitions of words and phrases and legal maxims interfiled alphabetically with the narrative topics and in each volume preceding the index. Am.Jur.2d provides definitions only through the general index. Generally speaking, however, their similarities outweigh their differences.

DICTIONARIES

Law dictionaries vary in size and purpose. Standard one-volume dictionaries include *Black's Law Dictionary* (West) and Ballentine, *Law Dictionary with Pronunciations* (Lawyers Co-op), both of which are revised from time to time. Law dictionaries provide precise definitions of words, phrases, and maxims, and furnish citations to authority. The multivolume *Words and Phrases* (West) covers definitions used in reported cases from earliest times to the present, "but as it is limited to those words which were involved in litigation, it is not a true dictionary."[3] However, the dictionary function of *Words and Phrases* and legal encyclopedias must not be overlooked.

DIRECTORIES

A comprehensive directory known to reference librarians is the multivolume *Martindale-Hubbell Law Directory* (Summit, NJ: Martindale-Hubbell, Inc.). Published annually, it lists virtually all lawyers admitted to the bar, providing typical directory information and a "confidential" rating; contains law digests of states and territories; provides information on United States copyright, patent, tax, and trademark law; includes uniform model acts and codes; and the like. In addition to general directories like *Martindale-Hubbell*, there are specialized directories that list only attorneys that practice law in a certain field, judicial directories which list addresses and telephone numbers of federal judges and other court personnel, directories of law professors, etc.[4]

LEGAL PERIODICAL LITERATURE

The legal profession has developed a considerable publishing industry to list, control, and access the information found in law school reviews, bar association journals, law practice periodicals, legal newspapers, and subject journals. A selection of the more prominent bibliographic sources for legal periodical literature follows.

INDEXES

Current Law Index (CLI) and *Legal Resource Index* (LRI) began publication in 1980 and are both published by Information Access Corporation, Menlo Park, California.[5] CLI covers almost 700 law and law-related periodicals as recommended by an Advisory Board of the American Association of Law Libraries. It appears in printed form monthly with quarterly cumulations and an annual cumulation. Articles are accessed by author and subject. Book reviews are entered under the author and title of the book. A table of cases lists all substantive cases cited in the articles.

LRI is issued monthly as a cumulated Computer-Output-Microfilm (COM) product. Each month LRI cumulates totally so that no supplements need be checked. A ROM-4 COM terminal is provided for viewing with each LRI subscription. Like CLI, the index provides access by subject, author, and table of cases filed in three separate sections. LRI indexes all the periodicals covered in CLI and, in addition, includes a few legal newspapers (e.g., *The National Law Journal*), some general periodicals indexed in *Magazine Index*, a few general newspapers (e.g., *The Wall Street Journal*), some academic periodicals, legal monographs, and selected federal government publications.

Each month, subscribers receive a cumulation in one reel of 16mm COM. Information Access Corporation plans to continue cumulating LRI for five years when, in December 1984, subscribers will receive an annual printed volume containing all 1980 indexing. Thereafter, one month of 1980 indexing will be dropped from the COM tape as one month of 1980 indexing is added, thus insuring that five years of indexing will always be available on COM. In addition to the COM feature of LRI, the database is available online through DIALOG.

The H. W. Wilson Company's *Index to Legal Periodicals* covers almost 450 periodicals published in the United States, Canada, Great Britain, Ireland, Australia, and New Zealand. Also included are a selection of yearbooks, proceedings of annual institutes, and annual reviews on a particular topic or in a given field. The *Index* is issued monthly with quarterly, annual, and triennial cumulations. Organized by interfiled subjects and authors, it features a Table of Cases Commented Upon, a Table of Statutes Commented Upon, and a Book Review Index.

CHECKLISTS

Checklists permit libraries an opportunity to review the completeness of their holdings. Current examples of this activity are Eugene M. Wypyski (ed.), *Legal Periodicals in English* (Dobbs Ferry, NY: Glanville Publishers, Inc.) and *Checklist of Legal Periodicals* (Buffalo, NY: William S. Hein & Co.). The former offers a comprehensive bibliography of legal periodicals published in the English language worldwide. The latter is limited to those titles that have been or are now included in the *Index to Legal Periodicals.*

CURRENT CONTENTS

Legal Contents (Northbrook, IL: Management Contents, Inc.), formerly called *Contents of Current Legal Periodicals*, is published biweekly and provides table of contents information for selected legal periodicals. Each issue reproduces the table of contents of the most recent issues of major law reviews and journals, and each issue features a Table of Cases, a Subject Index, and a Directory of Legal Periodicals that appear in the issues of *Legal Contents.*

SHEPARD'S CITATIONS

Shepard's Law Review Citations is arranged by volume and page of over 100 legal periodicals with reference to federal and state courts and other law review articles which have cited an article that appears in the periodical. *Shepard's Federal Law Citations in Selected Law Reviews* reverses the process. In this unit of Shepard's the cited matter includes the United States Constitution, *United States Code*, federal court rules, and the decisions of federal courts, while the citing sources are articles appearing in some twenty prominent law school reviews.

DIGESTS

A digest, simply defined, "is an index to reported cases, providing brief, unconnected statements of court holdings on points of law, which are arranged by subject and subdivided by jurisdiction and courts."[6] The West Publishing Company's *American Digest System* is the most comprehensive of case law digests in this country. It consists of the *Century Edition* and the several *Decennial Digests* and purports to cover "all standard law reports from appellate courts rendering written decisions from 1658 to date. It also digests selective opinions from certain courts of first instance, including those of the federal district courts and some lower state courts."[7]

The pattern of publishing the *American Digest System* is as follows:

Name	Years Covered
Century Digest	1658-1896
First Decennial	1897-1906
Second Decennial	1907-1916
Third Decennial	1916-1926
Fourth Decennial	1926-1936
Fifth Decennial	1936-1946
Sixth Decennial	1946-1956
Seventh Decennial	1956-1966
Eighth Decennial	1966-1976
Ninth Decennial, Part I	1976-1981

The *Ninth Decennial, Part I* covers a five-year period because of the rapid growth in the volume of reported cases digested. This unit features new and expanded digest topics. The decennial units are updated by a *General Digest* numbered series. For example, the *Ninth Decennial, Part I* supersedes the first thirty-three bound volumes of the *General Digest, 5th Series.* When the *Ninth Decennial* is completed in 1986, a *General Digest, 6th Series* will begin.

Digests are abstracts of points of law set forth in the written opinion of a court case. Using West's topic-key number system, they reference the units of the *National Reporter System*, bringing together all cases on a similar point of law. They feature case tables and a *Descriptive-Word Index*, which is a huge alphabetical interfiling of topics and specific catchwords and phrases descriptive of the facts and points of law of the abstracts contained in that digest. For our purposes there are specialized digests for federal case law.

FEDERAL DIGESTS (WEST)

The *Federal Digest* is the permanent index to federal case law from earliest times to 1938. *Modern Federal Practice Digest* includes cases from 1939 through 1960. *Federal Practice Digest 2d* contains digests of opinions from 1961 to date. Individual volumes are updated by annual cumulative pocket supplements and pamphlet supplements issued during the year. The *Descriptive-Word Index* of *Modern Federal Practice Digest* also covers the *Federal Digest.*

United States Supreme Court Digest contains abstracts of all cases decided by the U.S. Supreme Court, thus duplicating the Supreme Court cases in the *American Digest System*. Other West digests include those for bankruptcy, military justice, claims, etc.

DIGEST OF UNITED STATES SUPREME COURT REPORTS, LAWYERS' EDITION

This digest, published by Lawyers Co-op, is a twenty-volume digest to all U.S. Supreme Court decisions, has its own distinctive classification scheme, and provides cross-references to the sister publications of Lawyers Co-operative Publishing Company.

ANNOTATED LAW REPORTS

American Law Reports (A.L.R.) comprise a selective number of appellate court decisions. This series, published by Lawyers Co-op, consists of decisions that, in the opinion of the editors, are of general interest to the legal profession. A.L.R. is important "not for the decisions it reports [which can be found in official reporters or in units of West's *National Reporter System*] but for the editorial service that follows each reported decision, or what the publishers call *Annotations*. These are encyclopedic essays or memoranda on the significant legal topics from each case selected for publication in the American Law Reports."[8]

Stated another way, cases chosen for *Annotations* are those that either lend themselves "to an exhaustive treatment of an important subdivision of the law of a major topic" or those that treat "limited areas of the law which are not covered at all or are covered insufficiently in other law books."[9] Written by experts in the field, *Annotations* present an organized commentary on previously reported like decisions, and in this sense function as a case finding tool, analogous to the West digests.

The *American Law Reports* are published in the following series:

Series	Cited As	Years Covered
First	A.L.R.	1919-1948
Second	A.L.R.2d	1948-1965
Third	A.L.R.3d	1965-1980
Fourth	A.L.R.4th	1980 to date
Federal	A.L.R.Fed.	1969 to date

A.L.R.Fed. includes only leading decisions of the federal courts followed by an annotation as described above.

The A.L.R. series are supplemented as follows:

Series	Supplementation
First	A.L.R. Blue Book of Supplemental Decisions
Second	A.L.R.2d Later Case Service
Third	annual cumulative pocket supplement
Fourth	annual cumulative pocket supplement
Federal	annual cumulative pocket supplement

These updating sources provide citations to subsequent decisions on the same topic of law as the annotations. Moreover, any A.L.R. annotation may subsequently be *supplemented* or *superseded*. A *supplementing annotation* is one in which the later cases in point are gathered and a new annotation is written. However, one should read the new annotation in connection with the earlier one. A *superseding annotation* is one that is completely rewritten, so that the earlier annotation is no longer required to be read. To determine if an annotation has been supplemented or superseded, consult either the *A.L.R. Blue Book of Supplemental Decisions* or the "Annotation History Table" located in the back of both the bound volume and the pocket supplement of the *ALR 3d-4th Quick Index*. The latter table is more convenient than the *A.L.R. Blue Book* and shows annotations in A.L.R., A.L.R.2d, and A.L.R.3d which have been supplemented or superseded in A.L.R.2d, A.L.R.3d, or A.L.R.Federal. The pocket supplement updates the coverage of this *Quick Index* and its tables and is issued periodically.

Subject access to the A.L.R. series is provided by one-volume indexes called *Quick Index*; they are arranged alphabetically to the annotations in the A.L.R. volume, and have tables of cases and cumulative pocket supplements. The *ALR 3d-4th Quick Index* combines the "descriptive-fact-word, legal-concept approach with the schematic arrangement typical of a digest. All major and many minor topics contain a simplified sectional breakdown for ease in locating particular concepts. The annotation references are presented in the form of annotation title ... thus saving much time lost in looking up ambiguous phrases."[10]

The important feature of the A.L.R. series is the editorial annotation. Once an A.L.R. annotation is located, either through the appropriate *Quick Index* or as cited in a journal article, a unit of Shepard's, an encyclopedia, etc., it will summarize in essay form previous court decisions on the topic. Then one can consult the various supplementation books listed above to locate cases in point and supplementing or superseding annotations subsequent in time to the basic annotation.

LOOSELEAF SERVICES

We noted in Chapter 7 the value of a looseleaf service like CCH's *Congressional Index*. There are numerous looseleaf services prepared for the legal community on specific topics, from accounting to taxation. The major publishers of these services are Commerce Clearing House (Chicago), Prentice-Hall (Englewood Cliffs, New Jersey), and the Bureau of National Affairs (Washington, DC).

The advantages of looseleaf reporting services include immediate access to subscribers; a "package" format that consists of the full text or digests of federal and state statutes, court decisions, rulings, administrative regulations, Attorney General opinions, and other relevant documentation; editorial explanations and annotations; and up-to-date indexing by subject, case tables, and other finding aids.

Moreover, looseleaf services cut across jurisdictional boundaries and present similar laws or court decisions on a subject among the several states and the federal government. For example, CCH has a Legislative Reporting Service which informs subscribers of the nature and progress of both federal and state bills tailored to the users' specialized requirements. Thus subscribers interested in following all laws affecting motor vehicles receive copies of bills, reports of actions, and finally law texts from all state legislatures or the Congress on this specific subject. The online version of this system is called *Electronic Legislative Search System* (ELSS) and has been described in Chapter 7.

SHEPARD'S CITATIONS

Because the law is a dynamic process, the lawyer must know what acts or cases are valid and may properly be cited as authority. Citators or citation books provide current information on valid authority, and the most complete set of books and services for determining valid authority is known as *Shepard's Citations* (Colorado Springs, CO: Shepard's/McGraw-Hill). Indeed, the word

"Sheparddizing" is used in legal parlance to describe the procedure used in determining the applicability of cases, statutes, and other documents as authority. In addition, the citator process enables one to develop research leads to periodical articles, Attorney General opinions, A.L.R. annotations, and a host of other primary or secondary law sources.

In Shepard's terminology, the word *citation* precisely signifies a reference in a later authority to an earlier authority. The earlier authority is known as the "cited" case, statute, etc., and the later authorities are referred to as the "citing" case, statute, etc. Librarians who have any familiarity with *Science Citation Index* or *Social Science Citation Index* should not find the Shepardizing process too inscrutable. Through the appropriate Shepard's units, one can determine whether a decision has been reversed by a higher court, a statute repealed, a regulation held unconstitutional, a treaty amended, etc. The attorney who fails to Shepardize a case correctly runs the risk of embarrassment if not incompetence.[11] Hence the old saw "Not to Shepardize is to jeopardize" reflects an abiding truth.

In addition to the "history" of a case (whether affirmed, dismissed, modified, or reversed on appeal), Shepard's provides "treatment" of a case in subsequent decisions (whether criticized, distinguished, followed, dissenting opinion, etc.). These are indicated by abbreviations which are explained in the introductory pages of each unit of *Shepard's Citations*.

For every set of court reports there is a set of *Shepard's Citations*. This set comprises states, regions, federal, and special units covering administrative law, criminal justice, patents and trademarks, municipal ordinances, legal periodicals, court rules, labor law, etc. Currency is maintained by cumulative paper supplements to the bound volumes and for some units interim advance sheets. Moreover, subscribers can use Shepard's *Federal Law Daily Citation Update Service*, a computerized listing of the latest citing references to Supreme Court and lower federal court cases, the U.S. Constitution, the *United States Code*, and federal court rules. This information can be obtained by telephone or by writing to Shepard's Citation Service, Colorado Springs, Colorado 80901.

Shepard's Citations are online through LEXIS (Mead Data Central) and WESTLAW (West Publishing Company). A brochure, *How to Use Shepard's Citations* (Colorado Springs, CO: Shepard's/McGraw-Hill), provides greater detail with many illustrations of the various Shepard's units.[12]

POPULAR NAME LISTING

We noted in Chapter 7 that *Shepard's Acts and Cases by Popular Names, Federal and State* (which is *not* a citator unit but functions as an index) provides a list of acts by their popular names with citations to their location in the *Statutes at Large* and *United States Code*. This publication provides similar information for cases, where citations to the reporters that carry the text of the decisions are given (e.g., 361 F2d 250). *Shepard's Acts and Cases* is updated by pamphlet supplementation.

OTHER SOURCES OF THE LAW

The bibliographic structure of American law also encompasses court rules and procedures, opinions of the Attorneys General, treatises and texts, restatements of the law, uniform laws, model codes, form books, etc. For these and other topics, the reader is advised to consult one of the basic texts noted at the beginning of this chapter.

THE FEDERAL COURT SYSTEM

The magisterial bibliographic apparatus created and maintained by commercial publishers like West and Lawyers Co-op is necessary in large measure because of the doctrine of *stare decisis*, "which states that when a court has formulated a principle of law as applicable to a given set of facts, it will follow that principle and apply it in future cases where the facts are substantially the same."[13] From this construct, it follows that an attorney must have access to the latest cases in order to advise his client correctly. Commercial publishing of case law is geared to prompt reporting, not only of the opinions and decisions of courts but also of the indexes and other finding aids. The process is crucial to effective legal deliberation.

Decisions relied upon as precedent are usually those of appellate courts. Consequently, availability of published decisions increases in ascending order of the federal court hierarchy. Whereas only selected decisions of district courts are readily available, virtually all written and *per curiam* (literally "by the court") decisions of the appellate courts and the Supreme Court are reported either in their official edition or commercially.

Federal court reports can be placed within the context of West's *National Reporter System*, a network of reporters that includes the opinions of state, federal, and special courts. State reports consist of seven regional reporters covering the opinions of several adjacent states, and units that cover the courts of New York, California, and Illinois.[14] Federal courts and special courts are covered in West's *National Reporter System* units as follows.

DISTRICT AND APPELLATE COURTS

During most of the nineteenth century, decisions of the United States district courts and courts of appeals were published in a number of separate series cited by the names of their official reporters. This "nominative" reporting, which caused bibliographic confusion, was rectified by the publication of a multivolume series known as *Federal Cases* (West). *Federal Cases* (1789-1897) is arranged alphabetically by name of case and numbered consecutively. Some 18,000 lower federal court decisions are reported in this series.

For the years 1880 to the present, three units of West's *National Reporter System* are consulted.

FEDERAL REPORTER

Federal Reporter consists of two series. The first series (F.) covers 300 volumes; the second series (F2d.) began anew with Volume 1. Both series cover cases reported in the district courts, courts of appeals, and special courts like the Court of Claims, Court of Customs and Patent Appeals, Emergency Court of Appeals, and a couple of courts, like the Commerce Court, that were abolished.

FEDERAL SUPPLEMENT

The *Federal Supplement* (F.Supp.) connects with Volume 60 of the *Federal Reporter, Second Series*, and reports decisions of the Court of Claims (1932-1960), district courts since 1932, Customs Court since 1956, and Judicial Panel on Multi-District Litigation since its inception. But federal district court decisions are published only selectively. It has been noted that many "federal district court decisions can be located by consulting a looseleaf service."[15]

FEDERAL RULES DECISIONS

Federal Rules Decisions (F.R.D.) reports the opinions of the district courts involving the federal rules of civil and criminal procedure not published elsewhere.

SPECIAL COURTS

As noted at the beginning of this chapter, the Congress has created from time to time special courts to deal with particular types of cases. Appeals from the decisions of these courts may ultimately be reviewed in the Supreme Court. The official district and appellate court reports have been discontinued, but the GPO still publishes reports from some of the special courts. Special court reports available to depository libraries include *Cases Decided in the Court of Claims* (Ju 3.9; item 730), *Customs Cases Adjudged* and *Patent Cases Adjudged* (Ju 7.5; item 733) in the Court of Customs and Patent Appeals (see p. 253), *United States Customs Court Reports* (Ju 9.5; item 736), and *Reports of the Tax Court* (Ju 11.7; item 742). The latter reports are far better covered in looseleaf topical reporters such as CCH's *Tax Court Reports, Tax Court Memorandum Decisions,* and *U.S. Tax Cases,* and useful series on tax law issued by Prentice-Hall and the Bureau of National Affairs.

Commercial coverage of special courts includes the *Military Justice Reporter* and the *Bankruptcy Reporter* series, both published by West. The former reports decisions of the United States Court of Military Appeals and the Courts of Military Review for the Army, Navy, Air Force, and Coast Guard. The latter reports selected decisions from the United States Bankruptcy Courts and decisions from the district courts dealing with bankruptcy matters not reprinted in the *Federal Supplement.* In addition, West's *Bankruptcy Reporter* furnishes reprints of the bankruptcy decisions of the Supreme Court and the court of appeals. This series, however, may be affected by a 1982 Supreme Court ruling that bankruptcy judges are insufficiently protected from political pressure because they do not have life tenure. The Court gave Congress until October 1982 to correct the situation, but many members of Congress seem disposed to reverse the liberal provisions of the 1978 Bankruptcy Reform Act.

For current awareness, one can consult *West's Federal Case News,* which is not a reporter but a weekly summary of cases decided in the Supreme Court, courts of appeals, district courts, and the several special courts. Each summary provides the essential points of the case, the name of the case, the court and name of the judge deciding the case, and the filing date and docket number of the case.

CASE FINDERS

The *American Digest System*, with its key number classification scheme, provides access to the units of the *National Reporter System*. Specifically, *Modern Federal Practice Digest* and *Federal Practice Digest 2d* abstract cases found in *Federal Reporter, Federal Supplement,* and *Federal Rules Decisions.* The *United States Supreme Court Digest* covers the *Supreme Court Reporter.* West's *Bankruptcy Digest* and *Military Justice Digest* index cases in the appropriate reporters for those special courts. Because these specialized digests are keyed to the corresponding *National Reporter System* units, it is not necessary to use the *Decennial Digests* or current *General Digest* series.

SHEPARD'S CITATIONS

Shepard's Federal Citations is the appropriate unit for ascertaining the history and treatment of cases reported in the two *Federal Reporter* series, *Federal Supplement,* and *Federal Rules Decisions.*

THE SUPREME COURT

The United States Supreme Court consists of nine justices, one of whom is designated chief justice, who are appointed for life by the president with the advice and consent of the Senate. The Court's term extends from the first Monday in October until late June or, sometimes, early July. Popular opinion holds that the Supreme Court is an ultimate court of appeals for all, a bulwark of freedom to which every citizen can press his or her claim under federal law or the Constitution. In actual fact, the Supreme Court is quite limited in its jurisdiction. It hears disputes between states, disputes between a state and the federal government, cases in which a federal court or the highest court of a state has held an act of Congress unconstitutional, and a very few other categories. Moreover, it has discretionary power to decline to hear a large number of appeals. Indeed, the Court "actually hears only a minute proportion of the cases brought to federal and state courts. Even within the federal court system, the Court hears fewer than 1 percent of the cases handled by the district courts."[16] Yet the cases that it does hear are those of great importance and interest, and the decisions of this tribunal are legally and politically of momentous consequence.

The following series contain the full text decisions of the Supreme Court, with appropriate finding aids and other access tools.

UNITED STATES REPORTS (Official Edition)

The official GPO edition of Supreme Court reports is issued in three stages; in order of appearance they are as follows:

1) *Slip opinions* (Ju 6.8/b; item 740-A) are printed individually when rendered by the high court. Information includes docket number, date of argument, date of decision, and where feasible, a syllabus (headnote) prepared by the Reporter of Decisions for the convenience of the reader.

2) *Official Reports of the Supreme Court: Preliminary Print* (Ju 6.8/a; item 740-B) are issued in paperbound form and cover a two- or three-week period. They contain an index and cumulative table of cases reported. The pagination of the preliminary prints is the same as that which will appear in the bound volumes.

3) *United States Reports* (Ju 6.8; item 741) are bound volumes which contain tables of cases reported, a table of statutes cited, and a topical index. Like the material included in the preliminary prints, the *United States Reports* contain written opinions, *per curiam* decisions, orders, and chamber opinions.

UNITED STATES SUPREME COURT REPORTS, LAWYERS' EDITION

Published by Lawyers Co-op, this commercial edition of Supreme Court reports is issued first in Advance Reports published biweekly. The page numbering is identical with that which will appear in the bound volumes. Advance reports contain a Current Awareness Commentary, a cumulative table of cases and statutes, and an index. Cases summaries precede the headnotes, which are classified to the *U.S. Supreme Court Digest, Lawyers' Edition.* Total Client-Service Library References provide citations to the sister publications of Lawyers Co-op.

In a separate section of the bound volumes there are *Annotations* for selected important cases and summaries of briefs of counsel. Bound volumes have pocket supplementation that includes a Citation Service, a Later Case Service, and Court Corrections.

SUPREME COURT REPORTER

This is a special unit of West's *National Reporter System,* and as such contains the typical features of West's topic and key number classification system. Headnotes referencing topic and key number are classified to the *American Digest System.* Features of the advance sheets, issued biweekly, and the bound volumes include tables of cases, statutes construed, federal rules of civil and criminal procedure, ABA standards for criminal justice, dispositions, words and phrases, key number digest, and judicial highlights (synopses of current state and federal cases of special interest).

Figures 27, 28, and 29 (see page 266) show examples of an official preliminary print, an advance report (Lawyers Co-op), and an advance sheet (West), respectively.

(Text continues on page 272)

Figure 27
United States Reports

232   OCTOBER TERM, 1980

Syllabus   449 U. S.

FEDERAL TRADE COMMISSION ET AL. *v.* STANDARD OIL COMPANY OF CALIFORNIA

CERTIORARI TO THE UNITED STATES COURT OF APPEALS FOR THE
NINTH CIRCUIT

No. 79–900.   Argued October 15, 1980—Decided December 15, 1980

The Federal Trade Commission (FTC) issued a complaint against respondent and several other major oil companies, alleging that the FTC had "reason to believe" that the companies were violating § 5 of the Federal Trade Commission Act (Act), which prohibits unfair methods of competition or unfair or deceptive acts or practices in commerce. While adjudication of the complaint before an Administrative Law Judge was still pending, respondent, having unsuccessfully sought to have the FTC withdraw the complaint, brought an action in Federal District Court, alleging that the FTC had issued its complaint without having "reason to believe" that respondent was violating the Act, and seeking an order declaring the complaint unlawful and requiring that it be withdrawn. The District Court dismissed the action. The Court of Appeals reversed, holding that the District Court could inquire whether the FTC *in fact* had made the determination that it had reason to believe that respondent was violating the Act, and that the issuance of the complaint was "final agency action" under § 10 (c) of the Administrative Procedure Act (APA).

Held: The FTC's issuance of its complaint was not "final agency action" under § 10 (c) of the APA and hence was not judicially reviewable before the conclusion of the administrative adjudication. Pp. 238–246.

   (a) The issuance of the complaint was not a definitive ruling or regulation and had no legal force or practical effect upon respondent's daily business other than the disruptions that accompany any major litigation. *Abbott Laboratories* v. *Gardner,* 387 U. S. 136, distinguished. Immediate judicial review would serve neither efficiency nor enforcement of the Act. Pp. 239–243.

   (b) Although respondent, by requesting the FTC to withdraw its complaint and awaiting the FTC's refusal to do so, may have exhausted its administrative remedy as to the averment of a "reason to believe," the FTC's refusal to withdraw the complaint does not render the complaint a "definitive" action. Such refusal does not augment the complaint's legal force or practical effect on respondent, nor does it diminish the concern for efficiency and enforcement of the Act. P. 243.

Figure 27 (cont'd)

FTC *v.* STANDARD OIL CO. OF CAL. 233

232 Opinion of the Court

(c) The expense and disruption in defending itself, even if substantial, does not constitute irreparable injury to respondent. P. 244.

(d) Respondent's challenge to the FTC's complaint will not become "insulated" from judicial review if it is not reviewed before the FTC's adjudication concludes, since under the APA a court of appeals reviewing a cease-and-desist order has the power to review alleged unlawfulness in the issuance of an agency complaint, assuming that the issuance of the complaint is not "committed to agency discretion by law." Pp. 244–245.

(e) Since issuance of the complaint averring "reason to believe" is a step toward, and will merge in, the FTC's decision on the merits, the claim of illegality in issuance of the complaint is not subject to judicial review as a "collateral" order. *Cohen* v. *Beneficial Loan Corp.,* 337 U. S. 541, distinguished. P. 246.

596 F. 2d 1381, reversed and remanded.

POWELL, J., delivered the opinion of the Court, in which BURGER, C. J., and BRENNAN, WHITE, MARSHALL, BLACKMUN, and REHNQUIST, JJ., joined. STEVENS, J., filed an opinion concurring in the judgment, *post,* p. 247. STEWART, J., took no part in the consideration or decision of the case.

Solicitor General McCree argued the cause for petitioners. With him on the briefs were *Deputy Solicitor General Wallace, Elliot Schulder, Michael N. Sohn, Howard E. Shapiro, Joanne L. Levine,* and *Mark W. Haase.*

George A. Sears argued the cause for respondent. With him on the brief were *Richard W. Odgers* and *C. Douglas Floyd.**

JUSTICE POWELL delivered the opinion of the Court.

This case presents the question whether the issuance of a complaint by the Federal Trade Commission is "final agency action" subject to judicial review before administrative adjudication concludes.

---

*Daniel J. Popeo and *Paul D. Kamenar* filed a brief for the Washington Legal Foundation as *amicus curiae* urging affirmance.

Figure 28
United States Supreme Court Reports, Lawyers' Edition

UNITED STATES, Petitioner,

v

NEW MEXICO, et al.

— US —, 71 L Ed 2d 580, 102 S Ct —

[No. 80–702]

Argued December 8, 1981. Decided March 24, 1982.

Decision: Imposition of New Mexico's gross receipts and compensating use taxes on federal contractors doing business in state, held valid.

SUMMARY

Three contractors who performed management, maintenance, and construction and repair work for the United States Department of Energy at government-owned atomic laboratories located in New Mexico worked under contracts providing, among other things, for an "advanced funding" procedure to meet contractor costs whereby the contractor was allowed to pay creditors and employees with drafts drawn on a special bank account in which United States Treasury funds were deposited, so that only federal funds were expended when the contractor met its obligations. New Mexico imposes a gross receipts and a compensating use tax on those doing business in the state, the gross receipts tax operating as a tax on the sale of goods and services, and the compensating use tax functioning as an enforcement mechanism for the gross receipts tax by imposing a levy on the use of all property that has not already been taxed. The United States brought an action in the United States District Court for the District of New Mexico, seeking a declaratory judgment that advanced funds were not taxable gross receipts to the contractors, that the receipts of vendors selling tangible property to the United States through the contractors could not be taxed by the state, and that the use of government-owned property by the contractors was not subject to the state's compensating use tax. The District Court granted the United States summary judgment, concluding that the contractors were procurement agents for the government and holding that the gross receipts tax could not constitutionally be applied to purchases by the contractors, that the compensating use tax as a correlative of the receipts tax was also invalid, and that advanced funds did not serve as compensation

Figure 28 (cont'd)

HEADNOTES

Classified to U.S. Supreme Court Digest, Lawyers' Edition

Sales and Use Taxes § 2; Taxes § 82 — state gross receipts and compensating use taxes — imposition on

federal contractors — validity

1a, 1b. For purposes of applying a state's gross receipts and compensating

---

TOTAL CLIENT-SERVICE LIBRARY® REFERENCES

68 Am Jur 2d, Sales and Use Taxes §§ 28, 199; 71 Am Jur 2d, State and Local Taxation § 231

22 Am Jur Pl & Pr Forms (Rev), Sales and Use Taxes, Form 5; 22 Am Jur Pl & Pr Forms (Rev), State and Local Taxation, Forms 151 et seq.

US L Ed Digest, Sales and Use Taxes § 2; Taxes § 82

L Ed Index to Annos, Sales Tax; Taxation

ALR Quick Index, Sales or Use Tax; Taxes

Federal Quick Index, Tax Exemption

ANNOTATION REFERENCES

State sales or use tax as violating immunity of United States. 44 L Ed 2d 719.

Immunity from state taxation of independent contractors with United States or federal agencies. 96 L Ed 270, 2 L Ed 2d 1789.

UNITED STATES v NEW MEXICO
71 L Ed 2d 580

nate against the federal government, or substantially interfere with its activities.

Courts § 128 — tax immunity for federal contractors — role of Congress

9a, 9b. If the immunity of federal contractors is to be expanded beyond its narrow constitutional limits, it is Congress that must take responsibility for the decision, by so expressly providing as respects contracts in a particular form, or contracts under particular programs; if political or economic considerations suggest that a broader immunity rule is appropriate, such complex problems are ones which Congress is best qualified to resolve.

Sales and Use Taxes § 2 — tax on federal contractor — validity

10a, 10b. A state use tax on a federal contractor may be valid only to the extent that it reaches the contractor's interest in government-owned property.

United States § 128 — purchase transaction — United States as purchaser

11. The fact that title passes directly from a vendor to the federal government cannot make the transaction a purchase by the United States, so long as the purchasing entity, in its role as a purchaser, is sufficiently distinct from the government.

Figure 29
Supreme Court Reporter

AMERICAN TOBACCO COMPANY,
et al., Petitioners,

v.

John PATTERSON, et al.

No. 80–1199.

Argued Jan. 19, 1981.

Decided April 5, 1982.

EEOC and class of black employees brought race and sex discrimination action against employer. Following remand by Court of Appeals, 586 F.2d 300, after relief in favor of plaintiffs was granted, the United States District Court for the Eastern District of Virginia, Albert V. Bryan, Jr., J., entered modified judgment and denied defendant's motion for relief from judgment, and employer appealed. The Court of Appeals, James Dickson Phillips, Circuit Judge, 634 F.2d 744, affirmed in part, vacated and remanded in part, and certiorari was granted. The Supreme Court, Justice White, held that section of Civil Rights Act of 1964 providing that it shall not be an unlawful employment practice for employer to apply different standards of compensation, or different terms, conditions or privileges of employment pursuant to a bona fide seniority or merit system, provided that such differences are not the result of an intention to discriminate and are not limited to seniority systems adopted before the effective date of the Act, since to construe it as so limited would be contrary to plain language of statute, inconsistent with Supreme Court's prior cases, and counter to national labor policy.

Vacated and remanded.

Justice Brennan filed a dissenting opinion in which Justices Marshall and Blackmun joined.

Justice Stevens filed a dissenting opinion.

---

* The syllabus constitutes no part of the opinion of the Court but has been prepared by the Reporter of Decisions for the convenience of

1. Statutes ☞188

In all cases involving statutory construction, court's starting point must be the language employed by Congress, and court assumes that the legislative purpose is expressed by ordinary meaning of the words used; absent a clearly expressed legislative intent to contrary, that language must ordinarily be regarded as conclusive.

2. Statutes ☞181(2)

Statutes should be interpreted to avoid untenable distinctions and unreasonable results whenever possible.

3. Civil Rights ☞9.12

Section of Civil Rights Act of 1964 providing that it shall not be an unlawful employment practice for employer to apply different standards of compensation, or different terms, conditions or privileges of employment pursuant to a bona fide seniority or merit system, provided that such differences are not the result of an intention to discriminate and are not limited to seniority systems adopted before the effective date of the Act, since to construe it as so limited would be contrary to plain language of statute, inconsistent with Supreme Court's prior cases, and counter to national labor policy. Civil Rights Act of 1964, § 703(h) as amended 42 U.S.C.A. § 2000e–2(h).

Syllabus *

Section 703(h) of the Civil Rights Act of 1964 (Act) provides that "it shall not be an unlawful employment practice for an employer to apply different standards of compensation, or different terms, conditions, or privileges of employment pursuant to a bona fide seniority or merit system, . . . provided that such differences are not the result of an intention to discriminate because of race, color, religion, sex, or national origin." Actions were brought in Federal District Court by black employees of petitioner employer and by the Equal

the reader. See *United States v. Detroit Lumber Co.*, 200 U.S. 321, 337, 26 S.Ct. 282, 287, 50 L.Ed. 499.

Figure 29 (cont'd)

Cite as 102 S.Ct. 1534 (1982)

Employment Opportunity Commission, charging that certain lines of progression for job advancement established by the employer in agreement with petitioner labor union after the effective date of the Act constituted a racially discriminatory seniority system in violation of Title VII of the Act. The actions were consolidated for trial and injunctive relief was initially granted, but ultimately the Court of Appeals, without deciding whether the lines of progression were part of a seniority system, held that even if they were, § 703(h) does not apply to seniority systems adopted after the effective date of the Act.

Held: Section 703(h) is not limited to seniority systems adopted before the effective date of the Act. To construe it as so limited is contrary to § 703(h)'s plain language, inconsistent with this Court's prior cases, and counter to the national labor policy. And there is nothing in the legislative history to indicate that § 703(h) does not protect post-Act adoption of a bona fide seniority ,system or that Congress intended to distinguish between adoption and application of such a system. Pp. 1537–1542.

634 F.2d 744 (4th Cir.), vacated and remanded.

Henry T. Wickham, Richmond, Va., for petitioners American Tobacco Co., et al.

Ronald Rosenberg, Washington, D. C., for petitioner Unions.

Henry L. Marsh, III, Richmond, Va., for respondents John Patterson, et al.

David A. Strauss, Washington, D. C., for respondent E.E.O.C., pro hac vice, by special leave of Court.

Justice WHITE delivered the opinion of the Court.

Under *Griggs v. Duke Power Co.*, 401 U.S. 424, 91 S.Ct. 849, 28 L.Ed.2d 158 (1971), a prima facie violation of Title VII of the Civil Rights Act of 1964, 78 Stat. 253, as amended, 42 U.S.C. § 2000e *et seq.*, "may

be established by policies or practices that are neutral on their face and in intent but that nonetheless discriminate in effect against a particular group." *Teamsters v. United States*, 431 U.S. 324, 349, 97 S.Ct. 1843, 1861, 52 L.Ed.2d 396 (1977). A seniority system "would seem to fall under the *Griggs* rationale" if it were not for § 703(h) of the Civil Rights Act. *Ibid.* That section provides in pertinent part:

"Notwithstanding any other provision of this subchapter, it shall not be an unlawful employment practice for an employer to apply different standards of compensation, or different terms, conditions, or privileges of employment pursuant to a bona fide seniority or merit system, ... provided that such differences are not the result of an intention to discriminate because of race, color, religion, sex, or national origin, nor shall it be an unlawful employment practice for an employer to give and to act upon the results of any professionally developed ability test provided that such test, its administration or action upon the results is not designed, intended or used to discriminate because race, color, religion, sex, or national origin...."

Under § 703(h), the fact that a seniority system has a discriminatory impact is not alone sufficient to invalidate the system; actual intent to discriminate must be proved. The Court of Appeals in this case, however, held that § 703(h) does not apply to seniority systems adopted after the effective date of the Civil Rights Act.[1] We granted the petition for certiorari to address the validity of this construction of the section. —— U.S. ——, 101 S.Ct. 3078, 69 L.Ed.2d 951.

I

Petitioner American Tobacco Company operates two plants in Richmond, Virginia, one which manufactures cigarettes and one which manufactures pipe tobacco. Each plant is divided into a prefabrication department, which blends and prepares to-

---

1. Title VII became effective July 2, 1965, one year after its enactment.

Method of Citing

While it is "customary to cite only the official report in federal courts if the official report has been published,"[17] it is not uncommon to find in the written opinions of *United States Reports* a reference as follows:

> *Lassiter v. Department of Social Services*, 452 U.S. 18,
> 68 L.Ed.2d 640, 101 S.Ct. 2153 (1981).

The sequence is that of volume, reporter, page, and finally year. U.S. refers to the official *United States Reports*, L.Ed.2d stands for the identical case published in *United States Supreme Court Reports, Lawyers' Edition, Second Series*, and S.Ct. stands for the identical case published in West's *Supreme Court Reporter*.

The first ninety volumes of the *United States Reports* are cited using the names of their reporters. Early nominative reporting is characterized as follows:

Name of Reporter	U.S. Reports	Years Covered
Dallas	v. 1-4 U.S.	1790-1800
Cranch	v. 5-13 U.S.	1801-1815
Wheaton	v. 14-25 U.S.	1816-1827
Peters	v. 26-41 U.S.	1828-1842
Howard	v. 42-65 U.S.	1843-1860
Black	v. 66-67 U.S.	1861-1862
Wallace	v. 68-90 U.S.	1863-1874

Thus, a citation to an early report would be phrased as follows:

> *Marbury v. Madison*, 5 U.S. (1 Cranch) 137, 2 L.Ed. 60 (1803).

Because the first ninety volumes, from official reporters Dallas through Wallace, were renumbered in 1875, we can use the conversion table above to determine that, for example, Cranch's reports, in nine volumes, were renumbered volumes 5-13, and the *Marbury* decision may be read either in the official edition or in the *Lawyers' Edition* (first series).[18]

THE UNITED STATES LAW WEEK

Published by the Bureau of National Affairs (BNA), *The United States Law Week* (U.S.L.W.) is a looseleaf weekly law reporter that consists of two sections. The Supreme Court Section provides the full text of Supreme Court opinions mailed the same day as rendered, along with these features: the Court's journal of proceedings, minutes of all the Court's sessions for the week, cases docketed with subject matter summaries, a table of cases and case status report which is cumulated and mailed at three-week intervals, and a topical index cumulated at six-week intervals. U.S.L.W. also has a General Law Section that features summaries of legal developments, analyses of the week's leading cases, new court decisions, the text of selected federal statutes, and a topical index. A general index to U.S.L.W. cumulates and is issued six times a year.[19]

UNITED STATES SUPREME COURT BULLETIN

Published by Commerce Clearing House, this looseleaf service sends facsimile reprints of Supreme Court opinions to subscribers. It also features a statement of actions taken by the Court for the preceding week, Court rules, a summary of docketed cases, a table of cases, highlights of recently docketed cases and those awaiting decisions, and the usual detailed subject indexing.

SEARCH STRATEGY

Because of their recency, U.S.L.W. and CCH's *Supreme Court Bulletin* may be used for current awareness. As time goes on, the advance parts of the *Lawyers' Edition, Second Series* and West's *Supreme Court Reporter* become useful. Retrospective coverage is presented in the bound volumes of West and Lawyers Co-op.

SHEPARD'S CITATIONS

Shepard's United States Citations: Case Edition provides citations to the citing cases under the official *United States Reports*, the *Lawyers' Edition*, and the *Supreme Court Reporter*. These are organized in separate sections of a base volume and bound supplements. The sections covering the two commercial editions provide parallel references in parentheses from their citations only to the official edition. Moreover, when one Shepardizes using the commercial versions, "citations are given exclusively to cases from the federal courts. When a state court cites a U.S. Supreme Court decision, it is listed only under the U.S. citation." In addition, decisions which contain concurring or dissenting opinions are indicated by name of justice only in the official section. And under the official section, the heading "first" is used to refer to the summary which appears at the beginning of opinions in the *United States Reports*.[20]

COMPUTERIZED LEGAL INFORMATION SYSTEMS

Computer technology in legal research has become a growth industry. The professional literature on the subject expands almost at an exponential rate. Several journals in the legal field – *Computer/Law Journal, Law and Computer Technology, Computer Law Reporter* – are devoted solely to the topic. It seems that almost every issue of *Law Library Journal* carries an article on some aspect of electronic legal retrieval. Moreover, specialized journals such as *Database* and *Online* publish frequently on computerized legal systems.

The potential of computerized legal research has been evident for many years. As early as 1946, a proponent of the impact of the computer on the legal field noted that, because of its capabilities,

> the lawyer will be freed to do his distinctively legal tasks. Thus freed from the insuperable burden of plodding from library to library, refreshing his recollection upon index systems of various books, pulling them out and ploughing through them, and then making laborious notes in longhand, the lawyer can devote his time and mind to the social, political, and economic aspects of law and justice.[21]

By 1980 it was generally agreed that "computer-assisted legal research is now approaching full maturity," and one expert went so far as to say that by the year 2000 "there will be little need for any attorney to do manual case-law research."[22]

Two commercial online services, WESTLAW and LEXIS, epitomize the growth and development of computerized legal systems, and the competition between them has accelerated the maturation process. The following is a brief account of their salient characteristics. Keep in mind that these systems are dynamic and continually evolving.

WESTLAW

WESTLAW is West Publishing Company's computer-assisted legal research system. It is interactive, which means that queries may be modified as frequently as desired to broaden or narrow the scope of a search. It contains bibliographic data and full text materials that are found in printed form in the several units of the *National Reporter System* as well as other documentation.

In 1975 the WESTLAW database consisted only of headnotes for recent state and federal cases. In 1978 West included the full text of the opinions. Responding to the competitive environment, WESTLAW has expanded the types of materials and the scope of coverage dramatically. In 1982 the federal "libraries" in the WESTLAW databases included taxes, securities, antitrust and business regulations, government contracts, patent, trademark and copyright, communications, labor, Delaware corporation law, military justice, and bankruptcy. Moreover, state "libraries" provide headnotes, synopses, and full text opinions, and include Attorney General opinions for the several states.

Search strategies for case law retrieval may be accomplished by name of litigants, name of judge, specific words and phrases, case citation, jurisdiction, court hierarchy, synopsis, headnotes, key numbers, legal concepts or topics, and year. Documents retrieved and displayed are given a rank number on the basis of the frequency of occurrence of the search terms in each document.

Federal files include Supreme Court cases with full text opinions beginning in 1925, courts of appeals cases from 1938, district court cases from 1950, Court of Claims cases from 1950, and Court of Customs and Patent Appeals cases from 1938. Also included, with varying dates for beginning of full text coverage, are *Tax Court Memorandum Decisions*, IRS *Cumulative Bulletin* series, NLRB Decisions, the *Military Justice Reporter*, Bankruptcy Court cases, *Federal Rules Decisions*, the current *United States Code*, current *Code of Federal Regulations*, and *Federal Register* from April 1980. Only one file (for example, *Federal Supplement, Supreme Court Reporter*, etc.) may be searched at a time.[23]

Other features of WESTLAW include a federal case "quick" file, which provides full text coverage of "not yet published" opinions from the courts of appeals, and an automated citation service based on *Shepard's Citations*, which allows the user to determine the subsequent history of any case retrieved.

Hardware for the components of the WESTLAW system includes a central computer located at West headquarters in St. Paul, Minnesota, a video display terminal (VDT) and keyboard for office or library linked to the central computer, and a printer which allows the user to obtain copies of any information displayed on the screen.

The WESTLAW terminals are linked to the central computer through the TYMNET telecommunications service, thus making available a large information network of compatible database suppliers. Among the optional databases available are those of the DIALOG and ORBIT vendors. Accordingly, a WESTLAW search can be complemented or supplemented by any number of related subject disciplines. For example, one of the files in the WESTLAW federal securities library contains selected Securities and Exchange Commission (SEC) administrative decisions. The user can then access the DISCLOSURE II database through DIALOG for related financial information filed with the SEC.

LEXIS

LEXIS is a service of Mead Data Central (New York City). Like WESTLAW it is a full text, interactive commercial online legal retrieval system. The information available in LEXIS is organized into "libraries" which are made up of files. Files are further subdivided into documents (a specific case, a section of a statute, a subsection of a federal regulation). Documents are composed of segments, such as date of decision, text of opinion, author of dissenting opinion, etc. In 1982 the types of libraries in LEXIS largely corresponded to those found in WESTLAW. Federal law libraries in the LEXIS system include general, tax, securities, trade regulation, patent, trademark, and copyright, communications, labor, bankruptcy, energy, and public contracts. In addition, LEXIS contains state law libraries, the Delaware corporation law library, and those of the United Kingdom and France.

Search strategies for case law retrieval may be accomplished by words and phrases, case citation, court jurisdiction, name of judge, names of litigants, date of decision, etc. The most frequently used LEXIS format is keyword-in-context (KWIC), where the computer will display the language from the text of the opinion that deals with the subject of the search.

Federal files include Supreme Court decisions with full text from 1925 to the present, courts of appeals cases from 1938, district court cases from 1960, Court of Claims cases from 1960, the current *United States Code*, the current *Code of Federal Regulations*, and the *Federal Register* from July 1980. Other files include the IRS *Cumulative Bulletin*, Supreme Court briefs (the full text of all briefs submitted to the high court for cases scheduled for oral argument, beginning with the October 1979 term), legislative histories (public laws and House, Senate, and Conference reports for the 1954 *Code* and amendments thereto), the *Federal Reserve Bulletin*, and many more.

Other features of LEXIS include *Auto-Cite, Shepard's Citations*, works published by Matthew Bender & Company, and NEXIS. *Auto-Cite*, developed by Lawyers Co-op, is a computerized verification system that permits one to check the status of any cited case as authority. In addition to verifying the accuracy of a citation, it gives parallel citations to that case and cites any case that directly affects its validity as precedent. *Shepard's Citations*, found in WESTLAW also, gives parallel citations and subsequent history. Matthew Bender publishes a range of treatises on legal subjects, from accounting to worker's compensation.

NEXIS is a full text library of general and business news and information. The "libraries" in NEXIS include newspapers, magazines, wire services, newsletters, and DISCLO, abstracts and extracts of reports filed with the SEC by companies and made available through Disclosure, Inc. (Bethesda, Maryland). One of the files in the magazines library is *CQ Weekly Report* (see Chapter 7).

Moreover NEXIS offers the annual reports of selected corporations and the fifteenth edition of the *Encyclopaedia Britannica* (known as *"Britannica 3"*).

A contractual arrangement between DIALOG and Mead Data Central enables subscribers to LEXIS and NEXIS to gain access to the numerous databases available on the DIALOG system. These include *CIS/Index*, ASI, NTIS, ERIC, the *Monthly Catalog, Legal Resource Index*, and many others discussed in this text (see Appendix A). Mead Data Central users who wish to access the DIALOG system through the Mead computers must be authorized DIALOG users and must specifically contract for DIALOG services available through the Mead Data transmission network.

The addition of files and special features to both the LEXIS and WESTLAW databases, fostered by the intense competition between West and Mead Data Central, is rapid. As one law librarian succinctly noted, "For those who use LEXIS or WESTLAW on a regular basis, it is no revelation that nearly every sign-on announces the availability of new files with information never before accessible by electronic means."[24]

COMPARING WESTLAW AND LEXIS

As you can see from the above account, there is a great deal of duplication between the two online systems. Both provide full text retrieval of federal and state decisions, the *United States Code*, the FR, and the CFR. It is anticipated that both systems will remain largely alike in their library collections and the addition of special features as time goes on. As Sprowl pointed out, perhaps the "most dramatic difference between the WESTLAW and LEXIS systems is the presence of West summaries, headnotes, and key number indexing within the WESTLAW system. While some of the LEXIS libraries contain summaries and headnotes, many do not contain them, and the LEXIS cases are not indexed at present.... The presence of indexing within the WESTLAW system also provides another benefit that deserves consideration: it can help a researcher to find the proper key-number category which may then be searched manually. The WESTLAW system thus provides one with an excellent entry point into the West digest system." On the other hand, LEXIS has the *Auto-Cite* function for rapid verification lacking in WESTLAW.

Because West continues to issue its digests and full text in printed form, the "cost of typesetting and editing the decisions is covered by the publication of the cases [and digest paragraphs] in book form, so the WESTLAW service obtains computer-readable copies of the cases for very little additional cost as a by-product of computer-based typesetting. Mead Data Central does not publish the cases in book form at present, so the LEXIS system must presently bear the full cost of keying the cases into the LEXIS computer." If, however, Mead Data Central "were to team up with a publisher such as Lawyer's Cooperative, then the LEXIS system could obtain its computer-readable copies of the cases as a byproduct of the publication of the cases in book form by Lawyer's Cooperative, and West's cost advantage would disappear. Hence, future cooperation between Mead Data Central and Lawyer's Cooperative may result in the establishment of a second national publisher of U.S. opinions."[25]

OTHER ONLINE SYSTEMS

Some computer-assisted legal systems, like JURIS and FLITE, are not commercially available. JURIS is a system in the Department of Justice. A full text program, it holds two basic types of data files: federal statutory and case law, and the "work product" of the Justice Department consisting of briefs, memoranda, policy directives, procedural manuals, and other materials generated by the attorneys in Justice in their day-to-day work routines. FLITE (Federal Legal Information through Electronics) was developed by the Judge Advocate General, U.S. Air Force. Like JURIS, FLITE is a full text system, and its availability is limited to federal, state, and local government agencies.

The National Criminal Justice Reference Service (NCJRS) database covers all aspects of law enforcement and criminal justice from police organizations, courts, correctional institutions, and law-related entities. NCJRS acts as an international clearinghouse for the exchange of information on law enforcement improvement and criminal justice. Its clientele include state and local governments, criminal justice agencies, colleges, public interest groups, professional associations, and the like. NCJRS is online through DIALOG.

SUMMARY

The enthusiasm over computerized legal research should not lead one to denigrate manual searching procedures. The important difference between manual and computerized services "relates to their indexing methods." The computer "creates its own index and includes within it every significant word, phrase, and number that appears within the underlying data base. Each significant word, phrase, and number within the data base thereby becomes an index term linking the researcher directly to every document within the data base that contains the word, phrase, or number." For case law, the computer's index "has been created by the judges who wrote the case decisions.... The computer thus replaces the limited index and the restricted grouping capability of the manual research tools with a much broader index and a generalized grouping capability."

On the other hand, this very flexibility is "perhaps the most serious limitation upon the power of the computer as a research tool." The computer "does not channel a researcher's thinking in the same way that a manually prepared index does." It does "not help the researcher ... select index terms or ... group them except to the extent that they are discovered by chance." This suggests that "inexperienced researchers and those wading through unfamiliar waters should start their research with the conventional research tools such as treatises and law review articles." However, the "skilled practitioner ... may do better to begin the research task with the computer, since he or she is familiar with the language the cases contain. By remembering an insignificant detail of a case, such as an incidental reference to the name of a town, such a practitioner can frequently use the computer to locate in a few seconds a case that it might take hours to locate manually."

But indexing can be built into any computerized system, and the WESTLAW headnotes and key-number divisions and subdivisions of a topic permit users to narrow the scope of a search. Generally, however, the "manual tools excel over the computer in their ability to draw the researcher's attention to new issues and new ways of looking at a problem. The computer excels at permitting the researcher to carve out from a large case collection a subset of cases relating to a particular topic and then to search the subset for patterns of words and phrases. The computer is also an excellent tool for capturing all the cases in a given area decided by a particular judge, relating to a particular fact situation, or involving particular parties."[26]

LEGAL MATERIALS IN MICROFORM

The revolution in micropublishing has encompassed sources of the law as well as government publications generally. The rapidly growing number of legal series available in one or more of the several microformats—film, fiche, ultrafiche, COM, micro-opaques—is of great benefit to law libraries in terms of cost saving and space saving as well as other characteristics commonly associated with all microform products. What follows is a sampling of legal information in various microformats, designed to give the reader some flavor of the scope of the enterprise.

GENERAL GUIDE

A useful bibliographic source is Henry P. Tseng, *Complete Guide to Legal Materials in Microform* (Arlington, VA: University Publications of America, 1976), which lists all law and law-related microforms known to the author "whether domestic or international, English or foreign languages (such as Chinese, French, Indonesian, Japanese, Russian, and Spanish) and believed to be in print or in the process of completion as of November 2, 1975."[27] Tseng has published *Supplements* covering November 1975-November 1976 (University Publications of America, 1977), December 1976-November 1978 (AMCO International, 1979), and December 1978-January 1980 (AMCO International, 1980).

SELECTED SERIES IN MICROFORM

The following represent a few instances in the area of case law.

NATIONAL REPORTER SYSTEM

West's ultrafiche editions of the *National Reporter System* include the entire regional reporters first series, volumes 1-450 of the *Federal Reporter 2d Series*, the first 300 volumes of *Federal Supplement*, and volumes 1-150 of all the National Reporter second series "will be available by 1985." Statistics provided by West indicate that the above series, comprising over 3,000 volumes, can be stored in approximately two cubic feet compared to "the more than 400 linear feet of shelf space required to house the same number of conventionally bound Reporter volumes." While readers and reader/printers are available for sale from the company, the fiche can be used with any one of several commercially available compatible readers and reader/printers.[28]

CCH ULTRAFICHE TAX LIBRARY

Available from Commerce Clearing House are ultrafiche editions of retrospective and current CCH reporters. They include *U.S. Tax Cases* (1913 to date), *Tax Court Memorandum Decisions* (1943 to date), *Tax Court Reports* (1943 to date), IRS *Cumulative Bulletins* (1919 to date), and *Board of Tax Appeals Reports* (1924-1942). The latter is a completed set. After 1942, the series became known as *Tax Court Reports. Cumulative Bulletins* are reproduced from the official biweekly *Internal Revenue Bulletin* (T 22.23; item 957), which in its semiannual cumulations is called *Cumulative Bulletin* (T 22.25; item 960). The series is issued in seven binders using plastic 4x6-inch fiche, and each ultrafiche card can accommodate up to 1,700 book-sized pages.

UNITED STATES REPORTS

The Supreme Court reports, official edition, are available from University Microfilms (Ann Arbor, Michigan), Lawyers Microfilm, Inc. (Rogers, Arkansas), William S. Hein (Buffalo, New York), Information Handling Services (Englewood, Colorado), and Law Library Microform Consortium (Honolulu, Hawaii).

U.S. SUPREME COURT RECORDS AND BRIEFS

Records and briefs, the "appeal papers" that must be submitted to the appellate court from the lower court, are a "unique, immensely valuable and untapped source for scholars in many fields of American studies, as well as a valuable research source for practicing attorneys. The study of the briefs and records leads to an increased understanding of the issues and allows a comparative analysis of the reasoning process of the opposing parties."[29] Among the micropublishers of Supreme Court records and briefs are the Bureau of National Affairs and Congressional Information Service. BNA's *Law Reprints* includes current argued and non-argued cases in both fiche and print with an annual cumulative index. CIS in 1982 began distributing the retrospective records and briefs and a current *U.S. Supreme Court Records and Briefs Express Service*, products formerly issued by the Professional Data Services division of Capitol Services, Inc. Moreover, CIS has enhanced the value of these collections through the development of improved finding aids.

LAW LIBRARY MICROFORM CONSORTIUM

The Law Library Microform Consortium (LLMC) is a self-governing, non-profit corporation organized in 1977 by the law schools of the University of Hawaii and Wayne State University. As of 1981 the Consortium numbered almost 200 participating libraries and had delivered to its subscribers over 350,000 standard microfiche volumes amounting to over 3 million separate microfiche. The Consortium markets its microfiche products directly to participating institutions and offers its publications for sale through established commercial law book dealers on a commission basis. As of late 1981, William S. Hein & Company (Buffalo, New York) and Fred B. Rothman & Company (Littleton, Colorado) were established as authorized dealers.

In addition to a number of legislative and executive branch series, LLMC sells federal and state law reports. Federal case law series include the Supreme Court reports (official edition) noted above and selected years of *Federal Cases*, U.S. Court of Claims reports, *Reports of the Board of Tax Appeals*, and *Tax Court Reports*.

SUMMARY

While the proliferation of legal materials in microform is a boon to librarians concerned with storage and cost considerations, it is not necessarily a panacea for a library's clientele. As Schwark and Breakstone point out, user disaffection includes "eye fatigue, difficulty in browsing, lack of circulation policies, lack of ability to write on microforms, embarrassment over ineptness in using the equipment, hindrance of having use restricted to one area, bad lighting, inadequacy of hardware, bad state of repair and maintenance of equipment, poor quality of the product, lack of bibliographic access, lack of standardization, and the psychological factor that microforms are not like books."[30] However, problems of quality control and internal library management are amenable to correction, while users will have to overcome their reservations as microform distribution becomes all but ubiquitous and users' options become increasingly circumscribed.

CONCLUSION

When viewed bibliographically, it is said "that the law is a seamless web ... and as treated by the courts and other law-making bodies, the various sources of law are inter-related and rarely meaningful or usable in isolation. To understand a statute, one needs the decisions which have interpreted it; to understand a court's decision, one needs the statute which it has applied; to understand an administrative regulation, one must see the statute by which it was authorized; even to read a legal periodical or a treatise, one needs access to all of the primary sources it cites and discusses."[31] Statutory and administrative law have been treated in earlier chapters of this text. The foregoing discussion of case law sources should enable the reader to relate its bibliographic structure to that of legislative activities and executive promulgations.

REFERENCES

1. A useful account of the basic functions, organization, jurisdiction, and procedure of the federal courts is found in a House Judiciary Committee print, *The United States Courts: Their Jurisdiction and Work* (Y 4.J89/1: C83/6/year). Revised periodically, this brochure gives an illustration of the distinction among cases that may be tried in state or federal courts.

2. *Legal Research Illustrated* (Mineola, NY: The Foundation Press, Inc., 1981). Accompanying the text are an assignment workbook and "Noter Up," a periodic updating service to chapters in the text.

3. J. Myron Jacobstein and Roy M. Mersky, *Legal Research Illustrated* (Mineola, NY: The Foundation Press, Inc., 1981), p. 315.

4. Ibid., pp. 317-20. See also Miles O. Price, et al., *Effective Legal Research*, 4th ed. (Boston: Little, Brown and Company, 1979), pp. 302-304.

5. Information Access Corporation also publishes the *National Newspaper Index, The Magazine Index, The Business Index*, and *NEWSEARCH: The Daily Online Index*.

6. Jacobstein and Mersky, p. xxii.

7. Price, et al., pp. 193-94.

8. Jacobstein and Mersky, p. 97.

9. Price, et al., pp. 172-73.

10. "Foreword" to *ALR 3d-4th Quick Index* (Rochester, NY: The Lawyers Co-operative Publishing Co., 1980).

11. See Jacobstein and Mersky, p. 232, note 1.

12. *How to Use Shepard's Citations* is revised periodically and is available free from Shepard's/McGraw-Hill in Colorado Springs.

13. Jacobstein and Mersky, p. xxxii.

14. *New York Supplement* reports decisions of the New York Court of Appeals, Appellate Division of the New York Supreme Court, and other lower courts. *California Reporter* reports decisions of the California Supreme Court, District Courts of Appeal, and Superior Court, Appellate Department. *Illinois Decisions* reports cases decided by the Illinois Supreme Court and Appellate Courts.

15. Jacobstein and Mersky, p. 37.

16. Lawrence Baum, *The Supreme Court* (Washington: Congressional Quarterly Press, 1981), p. 12.

17. Price, et al., p. 483.

18. West's *Supreme Court Reporter* did not begin its series until the October term of 1882.

19. The *Journal of the Supreme Court*, issued daily, is reprinted in *The United States Law Week*.

20. Jacobstein and Mersky, pp. 236-37.

21. "Does the Law Need a Technological Revolution?," *Rocky Mountain Law Review* 18: 391 (1946).

22. James A. Sprowl, "WESTLAW vs. LEXIS: Computer-Assisted Legal Research Comes of Age," *Illinois Bar Journal* (November 1979), p. 156.

23. By the end of 1982 WESTLAW contained eleven libraries and over eighty files plus *Shepard's Citations*, the *Forensic Services Directory*, and EUROLEX (coverage of English, Scottish, and European materials).

24. "Databases: Which of the 1,000 Should You Buy?," *The National Law Journal* 4: 19 (June 21, 1982).

25. Sprowl, pp. 161, 163.

26. James A. Sprowl, "Legal Research and the Computer: Where the Two Paths Cross," *Clearinghouse Review* 15: 151-52, 154 (June 1981).

27. Tseng, *Complete Guide* (1976), p. xvii.

28. *West's Law Finder: A Research Manual for Lawyers* (St. Paul, MN: West Publishing Company, 1980), p. 66.

29. Henry P. Tseng, "Recent Advances in Legal Materials on Microform," *Legal Research Journal* 5: 8 (1981).

30. S. Schwark and B. R. Breakstone, "Microform Update: Current Trends for Law Libraries," *Law Library Journal* 71: 133 (1978).

31. Morris L. Cohen (ed.), *How to Find the Law, 7th edition* (St. Paul, MN: West Publishing Company, 1976), p. xvi.

Appendix A

Selected Online Databases for Federal Government Information

A number of databases for searching federal government materials have been discussed in various chapters throughout this text where appropriate. The following summary is intended as a convenience to the reader. Reference is to the chapter where the information was *first* discussed. In the case of some databases, like ASI and *CIS/Index*, the online services are reiterated in subsequent chapters as appropriate.

The summary represents information available as of 1982 and uses the terminology found in the authoritative *Directory of Online Databases*, published quarterly by Cuadra Associates, Inc. (Santa Monica, California). The editors of the *Directory* have divided the many types of databases into those that refer users to another source for more detailed information and those that contain complete data or the full text of the original source. These are further subdivided. *Reference* databases are "bibliographic" (containing citations to or abstracts of the printed material) and/or "referral" (containing references to or summaries of non-published information). *Source* databases are "numeric" (containing original survey data and/or statistically manipulated representations of data, usually in the form of time series), "textual-numeric" (containing a combination of textual information and numeric data), or "full text" (containing complete records such as a court decision).

The databases designated in this appendix are commercially available online (not just in computer-readable form) for use in an interactive mode. Thus FLITE and JURIS, noted in Chapter 10, and LEGIS, mentioned in Chapter 7, are not included, since at present they cannot be accessed by librarians and their clientele. Other databases covering literature generated by or for the federal government that were not discussed in the text include AGRICOLA (Department of Agriculture), PATDATA (utility patents issued by the Patent and Trademark Office), MEDLINE and TOXLINE (National Library of Medicine), AIDS (Federal Aviation Administration), SCAN (Federal Home Loan Bank Board), and other rather specialized databases.

The reader is warned that the growth and volatility of the online database industry require constant attention to changes in the contents of files, producers, vendors, corresponding printed products, timesharing firms, prices, and the like. Publishers' announcements and guides like the Cuadra Associates *Directory* must be consulted to keep abreast of the rapidly fluctuating state of the art.

In addition, mergers, dissolutions, and other vicissitudes that characterize this industry (as well as micropublishing enterprises) oblige database users to consult current sources for the latest names, acronyms, and addresses of database producers and online service organizations (vendors). This information may be located in the *Directory of Online Databases* and other reference tools.

Name of Database	Type	Producer	Online Service	Chapter in Text
ASI (American Statistics Index)	Reference (Bibliographic)	Congressional Information Service, Inc.	DIALOG; ORBIT	6
AUTO-CITE	Reference (Referral)	Lawyers Co-operative Publishing Company	LEXIS	10
AVLINE (AudioVisual oₙLINE)	Reference (Referral)	National Library of Medicine	National Library of Medicine (MEDLARS)	9
BCD (Business Conditions Digest)	Source (Numeric)	Bureau of Economic Analysis, Department of Commerce	ADP Network Services, Inc.; Chase Econometrics/Interactive Data	9
BLS Consumer Price Index / BLS Employment, Hours, and Earnings / BLS Labor Force / BLS Producer Price Index	Source (Numeric)	Bureau of Labor Statistics, Department of Labor	DIALOG	9
CIS/Index	Reference (Bibliographic)	Congressional Information Service, Inc.	DIALOG; ORBIT	6
CRECORD (Congressional Record Abstracts)	Reference (Bibliographic)	Capitol Services, Inc.	DIALOG; ORBIT	7
DISCLOSURE II	Source (Textual-Numeric)	Disclosure, Inc.	DIALOG; NEXIS	10
DOE ENERGY; DOED; EDB	Reference (Bibliographic)	Technical Information Center, Department of Energy	BRS (DOED); DIALOG (DOE ENERGY); ORBIT (EDB)	5
ELSS (Electronic Legislative Search System)	Reference (Bibliographic)	Commerce Clearing House, Inc.	General Electric Information Services Company	7

Name of Database	Type	Producer	Online Service	Chapter in Text
ERIC (Educational Resources Information Center)	Reference (Bibliographic)	National Institute of Education, Department of Education	BRS; DIALOG; ORBIT	5
FEDERAL INDEX	Reference (Bibliographic)	Capitol Services, Inc.	DIALOG; ORBIT	7
FEDEX (Federal Energy Data Index)	Reference (Bibliographic)	Energy Information Administration, Department of Energy	BRS	5
FEDREG (Federal Register Abstracts)	Reference (Bibliographic)	Capitol Services, Inc.	DIALOG; ORBIT	8
LEGI-SLATE	Reference (Referral); Source (Textual-Numeric)	Legi-Slate, Inc.	I. P. Sharp Associates; Source Telecomputing Corporation	7
LEGISLEX	Reference (Referral)	Legislex Associates	National CSS, Inc.	7
LEXIS	Source (Full Text)	Mead Data Central and others	Mead Data Central	10
LRI (Legal Resource Index)	Reference (Bibliographic)	Information Access Corporation	DIALOG	10
MONTHLY CATALOG	Reference (Bibliographic)	Superintendent of Documents, Government Printing Office	BRS; DIALOG; ORBIT	3
NCJRS (National Criminal Justice Reference Service)	Reference (Bibliographic, Referral)	Department of Justice	DIALOG	10
NEXIS	Source (Full Text)	Mead Data Central	Mead Data Central	10
NTIS (National Technical Information Service)	Reference (Bibliographic)	National Technical Information Service, Department of Commerce	BRS; DIALOG; ORBIT	5

Name of Database	Type	Producer	Online Service	Chapter in Text
OCLC (Online Computer Library Center)	Reference (Bibliographic)	Library of Congress; subscribers to OCLC	OCLC Online Computer Library Center, Inc.	3
PRF (Publications Reference File)	Reference (Bibliographic)	Superintendent of Documents, Government Printing Office	DIALOG	3
REG-ULATE	Reference (Bibliographic, Referral)	Legi-Slate, Inc.	I. P. Sharp Associates	9
VOTES	Source (Textual-Numeric)	Policy Review Associates, Inc.	ORBIT	7
WESTLAW	Reference (Bibliographic, Referral); Source (Full Text)	West Publishing Company and others	West Publishing Company	10

Appendix B

Abbreviations, Acronyms, and Citations Used in This Text

AACR	Anglo-American Cataloging Rules
ABA	American Bar Association
AEC	Atomic Energy Commission
AHS	Annual Housing Survey
A.L.R.	American Law Reports
A.L.R.Fed.	American Law Reports Federal
Am.Jur.2d	American Jurisprudence, Second Series
ASI	American Statistics Index
AV	Audiovisual
Bevans	Treaties and Other International Agreements of the United States of America, 1776-1949
BLM	Bureau of Land Management
BLS	Bureau of Labor Statistics
BNA	Bureau of National Affairs
BRS	Bibliographic Retrieval Services
CAB	Civil Aeronautics Board
CAF	Corporate Author File
CCH	Commerce Clearing House
CDD	Congressional District Data
CFR	Code of Federal Regulations
CIA	Central Intelligence Agency
CIJE	Current Index to Journals in Education
CIS	Congressional Information Service
CJS	Corpus Juris Secundum
CLI	Current Law Index

COM	Computer Output Microfilm
CONSER	Conversion of Serials
COSATI	Committee on Scientific and Technical Information
CPI	Consumer Price Index
CPSC	Consumer Product Safety Commission
CQ	Congressional Quarterly
CR	Congressional Record
CRS	Congressional Research Service
CSI	Capitol Services, Inc.
C-SPAN	Cable-Satellite Public Affairs Network
DDC	Defense Documentation Center
DDIS	Depository Distribution Information System
DIALOG	DIALOG Information Services, Inc.
DMA	Defense Mapping Agency
DocEx	Documents Expediting Project
DoD	Department of Defense
DOE	Department of Energy
DSB	Department of State Bulletin
DTIC	Defense Technical Information Center
DttP	Documents to the People
EAPA	Energy Abstracts for Policy Analysis
EAS	Executive Agreement Series
ED	Department of Education
EDB	Energy Data Base
EDRS	ERIC Document Reproduction Service
EEOC	Equal Employment Opportunity Commission
EIA	Energy Information Administration
ELSS	Electronic Legislative Search System
EO	Executive Order
EPA	Environmental Protection Agency
EPRF	Exhausted GPO Publications Reference File
ERA	Energy Research Abstracts
ERDA	Energy Research and Development Administration
ERIC	Educational Resources Information Center
F.	Federal Reporter
FACA	Federal Advisory Committee Act
FBI	Federal Bureau of Investigation

FBIS	Foreign Broadcast Information Service
FCC	Federal Communications Commission
FEA	Federal Energy Administration
FEC	Federal Election Commission
Fed	Federal Reserve Board
FMTF	Federal Mapping Task Force
FPC	Federal Power Commission
FR	Federal Register
F.R.D.	Federal Rules Decisions
F.Supp.	Federal Supplement
FTC	Federal Trade Commission
FY	Fiscal Year
GBF/DIME	Geographic Base File/Dual Independent Map Encoding
GNIS	Geographic Names Information System
GODORT	Government Documents Round Table
GPO	Government Printing Office
GPR	Government Publications Review
GRA&I	Government Reports Announcements & Index
GSA	General Services Administration
H.Con.Res.	House Concurrent Resolution
H.doc.	House Document
HHS	Department of Health and Human Services
H.J.Res.	House Joint Resolution
H.R.	House of Representatives Bill
H.Res.	House Resolution
H.rp.	House Report
HUD	Department of Housing and Urban Development
IAA	International Aerospace Abstracts
IAL	Identifier Authority List
IAPs	Information Analysis Products
ICC	Interstate Commerce Commission
IHS	Information Handling Services
INIS	International Nuclear Information System
IR	ERIC Clearinghouse on Information Resources
IRS	Internal Revenue Service
IUSGP	Index to U.S. Government Periodicals
JCP	Joint Committee on Printing

JPRS	Joint Publications Research Service
KWIC	Key Word in Context
KWOC	Key Word out of Context
LC	Library of Congress
L.Ed.	United States Supreme Court Reports, Lawyers' Edition
LLMC	Law Library Microform Consortium
LRI	Legal Resource Index
MARC	Machine-Readable Cataloging
MEDLARS	Medical Literature Analysis and Retrieval System
MeSH	Medical Subject Headings
MLC	Major Legislation of the Congress
MPA	Monthly Product Announcement
NAC	National Audiovisual Center
NACP	Name Authority Cooperative Project
NASA	National Aeronautics and Space Administration
NCIC	National Cartographic Information Center
NHTSA	National Highway Traffic Safety Administration
NIE	National Institute of Education
NLRB	National Labor Relations Board
NMAC	National Medical Audiovisual Center
NOAA	National Oceanic and Atmospheric Administration
NOS	National Ocean Survey
NRC	National Research Council
NSA	Nuclear Science Abstracts
NTIS	National Technical Information Service
NUREG	Nuclear Regulatory Commission
OCLC	Online Computer Library Center
OMB	Office of Management and Budget
ORBIT	SDC Search Service
OSHA	Occupational Safety and Health Administration
PAIS	Public Affairs Information Service Bulletin
PB	Publications Board
PDH	Public Documents Highlights
PL	Public Law
PRC	Postal Rate Commission
PRF	Publications Reference File
Proc.	Proclamation

PUS	Public Use Sample
R&D	Research and Development
RIE	Resources in Education
RPI	Research Publications, Inc.
RTOPs	NASA Research and Technology Objectives and Plans
S.	Senate Bill
SB	Subject Bibliographies
S.Con.Res.	Senate Concurrent Resolution
S.Ct.	Supreme Court Reporter
SDC	State Data Center
S.doc.	Senate Document
SEC	Securities and Exchange Commission
SESA	Social and Economic Statistics Administration
S.Exec.rp.	Senate Executive Report
SIC	Standard Industrial Classification
S.J.Res.	Senate Joint Resolution
SLA	Special Libraries Association
SMERC	San Mateo Educational Resources Center
SMSA	Standard Metropolitan Statistical Area
S.Res.	Senate Resolution
SRIM	Selected Research in Microfiche
S.rp.	Senate Report
SSIE	Smithsonian Science Information Exchange
STAR	Scientific and Technical Aerospace Reports
Stat.	United States Statutes at Large
STFs	Summary Tape Files
S.Treaty doc.	Senate Treaty Document
SuDocs	Superintendent of Documents
TAB	Technical Abstract Bulletin
TIAS	Treaties and Other International Acts Series
TIC	Technical Information Center
TIF	Treaties in Force
TS	Treaty Series
TVA	Tennessee Valley Authority
U.S.	United States Reports
U.S.C.	United States Code
U.S.C.A.	United States Code Annotated

U.S.C.C.A.N.	United States Code Congressional and Administrative News
U.S.C.S.	United States Code Service, Lawyers' Edition
USGS	U.S. Geological Survey
USHDI	United States Historical Documents Institute
U.S.L.W.	United States Law Week
UST	United States Treaties and Other International Agreements
WAML	Western Association of Map Libraries
WRI	Water Resources Investigations

Selected Title/Series Index

Subject/Name Index